Dissonant Identities

MUSIC / CULTURE

A series from Wesleyan University Press

Edited by George Lipsitz, Susan McClary, and Robert Walser

Published titles

My Music by Susan D. Crafts, Daniel Cavicchi, Charles Keil,
and the Music in Daily Life Project

*Running with the Devil: Power, Gender, and Madness in
Heavy Metal Music* by Robert Walser

Subcultural Sounds: Micromusics of the West by Mark Slobin

*Upside Your Head! Rhythm and Blues
on Central Avenue* by Johnny Otis

*Dissonant Identities: The Rock'n'Roll Scene
in Austin, Texas* by Barry Shank

BARRY SHANK

Dissonant Identities

THE ROCK'N'ROLL
SCENE IN
AUSTIN, TEXAS

WESLEYAN UNIVERSITY PRESS

Published by University Press of New England

Hanover & London

WESLEYAN UNIVERSITY PRESS
Published by University Press of New England, Hanover, NH 03755
© 1994 by Barry Shank
All rights reserved
Printed in the United States of America 5 4 3 2 1
CIP data appear at the end of the book

The lyrics from Guy Clark, "Desperados Waiting for the Train,"
© 1973 Chappel & Co., are used by permission.

For Shari

Contents

Preface

When I moved to Texas I was dead set on doing what it was I wanted to do.
I had never really fit in anywhere, and when I moved to Austin, I decided, I'm
really gonna apply myself to drama and music and have a really good time. Nobody knows me; I'll only have to be here a year. I can make a complete ass out
of myself if that's what it takes, but I'm going to do something. So I decided to
just start all over again. Just start from scratch. And I went a little bit haywire.
I wore weird clothes right off the bat. It was like, no one knows me and they
don't know that I haven't worn all this stuff all my life. And it was just great.
And I met this friend named Jeb Nichols who told me what was really good
about music. And I believed him, and he introduced me to Jonathan Richman
and Elvis Costello. And he introduced me to Raul's. And the drinking age was
eighteen. So we'd go to the clubs and we'd see all these great bands. I remember
going to Raul's and being really intimidated. People were very strange and a lot
older than me and seemingly sophisticated in a real worldly sense. These people,
the scene, I mean, I'm sure a lot of it was self-imposed, but they seemed to
have soul. Hardship, they knew hardship. They seemed so urban. From Austin.
Which is really funny. But to me it was like this real eye-opening experience—
that people could actually do something they believed in. Like to be weird or
something.   —Kim Longacre[1]

Every business has its research and development function. We have that in
spades. It's the clubs and the musicians, the songwriters. But all industries have a
production function, sales and marketing, distribution, and point of sale, where
you reach the consumer with the product. In the music industry, production
is made up of recording studios and the personnel to effect that function. This
personnel includes production managers, which are record producers, it also
includes managers and publishers. Sales and marketing in the music business is
performed by publicists, concert promoters, managers, and record labels. Distribution is handled by record companies and distributors and booking agents.
The final point of sale, which is the other end we have plenty of, includes record
stores and the nightclubs and concert venues. So it is clear what we need to
focus on, what we need to encourage. We need better studios, more professional
producers, stronger publishing companies, labels with international distribution, managers with international aspirations, booking agents with international aspirations. We need to educate bankers that music is a legitimate industry
and increase their comfort in dealing with those in that industry.
                                                            —Ernie Gammage[2]

The rock'n'roll scene in Austin, Texas, is characterized by the productive contestation between these two forces: the fierce desire to remake oneself through musical practice, and the equally powerful struggle to affirm the value of that practice in the complexly structured late-capitalist marketplace. Insofar as this book is an attempt to represent that scene, it too has been produced out of this struggle and bears its marks. Growing out of a complex set of contradictory and historically constructed factors, "the Austin music scene" indicates a constellation of divergent interests and forces, and the effort to depict it requires both an attention to empirical detail and an expansive theoretical framework. Not only does this particular story of the Austin music scene beg to be told in all of its fantastic specifity, but the details of that story give us many new ways to think about how the performance of popular music functions as a process of identity-formation. Therefore, this book carries on two quite different arguments at the same time. In so doing, it brings together two antagonistic analytical paradigms and, consequently, breaks certain familiar scholarly rules. Deliberately.

I began this project with the belief that no signifying practice capable of transforming identities operates in isolation, but always within an historically structured cultural and economic context. Therefore, I have spent considerable time detailing that contextual history. But my major fascination with the music made in Austin derives from its extravagant subjective power—its ability to change the lives of those (such as Kim Longacre) who participate in it. Consequently, I have also struggled to construct a theory of identification in musical practice that is based in the poststructuralist appropriation of Lacanian psychoanalysis. I am arguing that the performance of rock'n'roll music in the clubs of Austin creates an environment conducive to the exploration of new identities. In fact, I believe that this performance of new, sometimes temporary but nevertheless significant, identities is the defining characteristic of *scenes* in general as well as their most important cultural function.

My second argument in this book is related to the historical context of the Austin scene. I argue that a major transformation has taken place in the organization of music-making in Austin. During the mid-1980s, the production of popular music in Austin became more closely linked with the requirements and the values of the national recording industries. This resulted in a shift not only in the economic organization of the city's rock'n'roll scene, but also in the musical and cultural aesthetics of that scene and, therefore, in the subjective qualities of any identities it might produce.

The intersection of my two arguments takes place at that moment of restructuring. During this period, I was living in Austin and playing music in the clubs. Part of my intense fascination with the power of musical practice in Austin derives from this personal experience. Something happened to me while I was playing music in this town. Slowly, I became a member of the scene. Through that process, my tastes changed, my desires and interests changed, quite subjective feelings of pleasure, belonging, loyalty, along with jealousy, frustration, and envy changed, and thus, my identity changed along with them. Through living the mundane everyday life of a rock'n'roll musician in Austin, I identified with and incorporated a musical signifying pattern that then shaped and constructed my experience. I attempt to theorize that process here even as I chronicle important changes in the conditions that, even now, make it possible.

Broadly speaking, this book inhabits the genre of critical cultural studies ethnography.[3] Thus, it attempts to represent the intersection of diverse cultural forces—musico-aesthetic, economic, ideological—within an historicized depiction of lived experience. The effort to write both diachronically and synchronically, theoretically and empirically, radically complicates the already difficult problems of ethnographic representation. But the ethnography of complex (post)modern cultures—particularly of commercialized cultural practices—demands such an approach, even as this approach creates problems of its own.

Any ethnographer must recognize that the object of knowledge—whether conceived of as a culture or a practice under study—does indeed exist beyond what he or she could possibly say about it, and at the same time that the culture or practice is constituted only through similar and innumerable, decentered yet interested cultural acts.[4] Ethnographic descriptions have effects on the culture or practice being described—creating new angles from which to view the object—and ethnographers are responsible for these discursive effects. Therefore, important questions must be asked: What form should the descriptions take? Should they remain wholly academic and impersonal? On the other hand, should they explicitly avow their inescapable interests? Can an admittedly interested and involved ethnographer say something meaningful about the cultural practices in which he or she is involved? Or do the personal interests limit the validity of the ethnographer's interpretation? Finally, do such representations excessively test the patience of their readers through their necessary blurring of genres?

Following the implications and assertions of postmodern ethnography, I believe that no cultural description can be neutral. Every representation is drawn from a particular limited perspective which produces its own effects. Yet all cultural practice, not only ethnography, consists of such actions—speech acts, performances, material constructions—each of which spins new connections among already existing threads within a cultural web, changing not only the shape of the web, but the direction, the meaning, the value, of the threads. Ethnography is simply another cultural practice, a writing that originates from somewhere between literature and social science. According to its generic rules, the written text gestures toward something—a culture, a practice, other texts—with the intention of interpreting its meaningful characteristics. In order to accomplish this interpretive goal, ethnographers try to build models out of words that represent the distinctive contours of their object, even as they ascribe new surfaces to its shape. Ethnography, then, is not a reduction of practice to text, nor merely a translation between these modes, but instead bears the burden of creation.

Ethnographic creation, however, must remain a representative interpretation of the significant characteristics of the cultural object. Ethnography is the inscription of meaningful metaphors that arise when the subject (the writer) and the object (the culture) "muddle their borders." Through participation in cultural practice, ethnographers experience a subjective identification with the internal dimensions of their object. Writing an ethnography then becomes an attempt to recreate a necessary distance between this object and our writing selves, to re-establish the borders, using the materials of our craft—words and sentences, phrases and paragraphs. It therefore becomes doubly important to describe explicitly the ground upon which ethnographers stand. In several of the following chapters, I have inserted myself as an actor in the stories I tell. By announcing my interests, I hope to mark out my specific placement in the constellation of forces and to use that positioning to achieve a dialectic of distance and intimacy, subject and object, generality and particularity, description and object described, throughout the book. This, it seems to me, becomes the point of postmodern ethnography: performing Pygmalion in reverse, ethnographers transform a loving dialogue into an imitative object.[5]

In the end, however, my act of ethnography is a layered narrative that I have constructed about music-making in Austin. Therefore, this book cannot contain *the final story* of the Austin music scene. Rather, it attempts to describe, from the ground floor, the important cultural functions of this scene during a specific moment of transformation along with the historical background of that transformation. I have not written extensively about Austin's major recent recording "stars." The late Stevie Ray Vaughan, the Fabulous Thunderbirds, Joe Ely, and even

Marcia Ball, appear only in retrospect and mostly in passing. Without a doubt, the story I have told would be quite different if I were to have focused on the commercial successes that have been produced through this transformation. Instead, the contribution of these "stars" to the story told in this book comes from the time in their careers when they too were struggling quasi-professional performers making their most impassioned music in the city's nightclubs. This is where I have focused my interest: on musicians who have not reached stardom but who continue to struggle through performance, and on the fans who identify with that constitutive struggle.

This book begins with an imaginary tour of the some of the most significant sites of the Austin music scene: record stores, nightclubs, rehearsal rooms, city neighborhoods, streets, and alleyways. On a hot night in August, I lead the reader through space and time, sketching out the history of the town itself and its relations with the rest of the state. The second chapter begins a lengthy discussion of the history of music-making in Austin. I trace the cultural importance of local musical performance back to the links constructed by John Avery Lomax between an idealized vision of Texan identity—the cowboy—and an equally idealized representation of musical practice—Lomax's collection of cowboy songs.[6] I then follow the dissemination of this tradition through the development of the singing cowboy and the effects of this image on the commercial trajectory of hillbilly music. A brief discussion of the development of honky-tonk culture sets up an analysis of the revival of folksinging by university students and local, traditional, amateur musicians at Threadgill's bar. Through this vitally important rearticulation of tradition and youth, music-making in Austin became the most significant local means for the performance of identity. These performances spread throughout the next several decades and encompassed many different musical styles. From country to psychedelic rock to blues to punk, music-making in Austin attracted the desires and the ambitions of several generations of students, resulting in a sedimented tradition of musical signifying practice. Chapters 3, 4, and 5 follow this shifting history of musical styles and cultural transformation.

Chapters 6 and 7 contain a different discussion; they attempt to theorize the musical production of subjectivity and support this theorization through an extensive ethnography of musical practice. I argue that the cultural function to which local musical performance is put (that is, the construction of identity and community) results in a musical aesthetic organized around a postmodern concept of sincerity. Sincerity becomes a value that can only be signified through an evident resistance of the disciplinary constraints of the dominant culture. Yet, the articulation of this refusal through the commodifying structures of popular culture demands a certain disciplined acquiesence. Thus, the performance of identity in the practice of popular music involves a constant renegotiation of the relationships between Imaginary sincerity and a commodified Symbolic. Chapter 8 concludes the historical discussion, arguing that a radical transformation in the economic base of music-making has not only altered the conditions within which rock'n'roll is produced in Austin but has also placed constraints on the identities that can be performed.

Regardless of any momentary arresting effects produced by this objectifying ethnography, the scene in Austin maintains itself in constant flux. Most of the fans whose subjective impressions shape my argument no longer frequent the clubs; most of the nightclubs I mention have closed or changed ownership; most of the bands I discuss have broken up. But the final assertion of this book remains: a certain semiotic excess continues to be generated in the production of collective musical pleasure by each new generation of musicians and fans in each new generation of the city's clubs. And, further, such moments of mutual pleasure contain a promise that transcends any competitive drive for individual gain. Through this musicalized experience, the Austin music scene fights against the newly industrialized conditions of its own existence and re-creates a momentary postmodern community. The remainder of this book is intended to support these assertions; in so doing, this ethnographic object hopes to represent convincingly *something of life* in the rock'n'roll scene in Austin, Texas.

Sixty different musicians, fans, writers, and industry support personnel agreed to be interviewed for this study. Their names are listed in an appendix, but I want to begin these acknowledgments by thanking them collectively for their help. As Shotgun Willie once said, "You cain't make a record if you ain't got nothing to say." They gave me something to say. This book began as a dissertation for the American Civilization department at the University of Pennsylvania. There, I was fortunate to work under the direction of Janice Radway; I remain extremely grateful for her patient and assured guidance in matters both academic and personal. George Lipsitz not only carefully read and critiqued many versions of this work, he consistently encouraged me to complete this unorthodox project. I would like to thank the staff of the *Austin Chronicle*, particularly the editor and the publisher, for allowing me access to their entire run of issues. The librarians at the Barker Texas History Center extended more than professional excellence, courteously responding to desperate long-distance phone calls. John Wheat aided in the selection of illustrations from the Barker's extensive collection of posters. Jim Franklin and Kerry Awn graciously authorized the reproduction of their poster art. Pat Blashill kindly allowed the use of his photographs of Austin clublife. Greg Sowders and the staff of Jack Rosner's office at Warner Chappell music were friendly, efficient, and helpful. The following people read drafts of this work: Roger Abrahams, Peter Casagrande, Mellissa Cobb, Terry Cochran, John Gennari, David Katzman, Cheryl Lester, Kathy McTee, Robert St. George, Randall Stross, Shirley Wajda, Robert Walser, and an anonymous reader for the Press. I would like to thank them for the work they did for me, for their stimulating criticisms and their supportive comments. Finally, this book is dedicated to Shari, who understands the personal importance of history and who every day makes it real.

Dissonant Identities

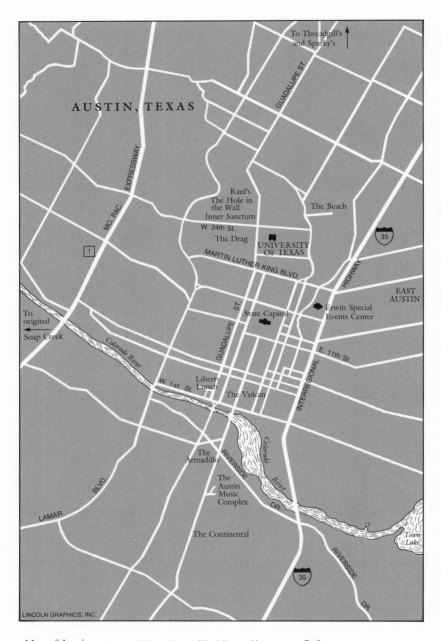

Map of Austin. Drawn with the assistance of Shari Speer and her computer, Emily.

CHAPTER ONE

The Imaginary Tourist
An Introduction to Austin's Rock'n'Roll Scene

There are nights in Austin when the air grows hotter once the sun goes down. When you no longer see the heat rising in waves from the pavement but you feel it, you walk through it, you breathe it. The heat holds your clothes against your skin. And the sweat that drips from you has nowhere to go. It is one of those nights during the summer of 1991. I am standing at the corner of 26th and Guadalupe, looking down the drag toward the university. The rusting hulk of the studios for the radio-television-film school leans over the street from the left. On the right, the marquee for the Hole in the Wall lists tonight's show of Teddy and the Tall-Tops and last night's show of some two-month-old band that only got the gig because they whined for it three days in a row while eating Reality Sandwiches, extra-real.[1] The bartender, who is also the booking agent and the cook, was impressed by their ability to consume jalapeños and grease and figured they had the makings of a real band, someday. So the Post Stompers got to play their guitars in the corner of the Hole in the Wall on a Thursday night. The cover charge is usually small at the Hole in the Wall and the beer is always cold, but we're not going in there. I want to walk up the drag one more block, to 27th Street, and show you where Raul's used to be.

Some will say that Raul's is sort of a sacred space. They mean the memory of the place, not the actual building. The building now holds a dump called the Showdown. The front of the building by the street is covered with brown shingles that splinter off into your back if you lean up against it. But no one leans up against it. No longer are there crowds waiting around outside. The Showdown's only attraction seems to be a remarkable ability to think new ways around whatever no-happy-hour rules the state legislature can invent. At 4:30 every afternoon, the bar fills up with those good ol' boys who no longer can drink while they drive home from work. So they throw back about half a dozen Shiner Bocks at fifty cents a pop while they curse the white collars in the capitol.

Of course, Raul's was a dump, too. Ten years ago, the inside walls were caked with graffiti and sweat so that when you leaned up against them on nights like this, splinters didn't pierce your skin but instead band names—like the Offenders, and the Huns, and the Re*Cords— would be imprinted backward on your shirt. Raul's began as a Mexican bar, featuring bands like Salaman and the Mexican Revolution. But one night in January 1978, Joseph Gonzalez, Jr., agreed to let the Violators play punk rock for their trendy friends at his club. Quickly, Raul's became the CBGB's and Joseph Gonzalez became the Hilly Kristal of Austin punk.[2] For a couple of years, this club was the center of the music scene.

It is not a coincidence that punk rock received its first home in Texas at a Mexican bar. In this other place, young (mostly white) people who had read about the Sex Pistols and listened to the Ramones could gather to explore the relations between a musical and theatrical performance style and the social and industrial context within which it was produced and which it directly confronted. The special significance of Raul's was confirmed on September 19, 1978, when a particularly clear confrontation between divergent cultural practices took place.

Phil Tolstead, the lead singer of the Huns, was not very different from the hundreds of other Johnny Rotten imitators leaning into microphones all over the United States and Great Britain, but that night his performance of antidisciplinary logic ran into an equally compelling performance of state power. During the Huns' set, Steve Bridgewater and several other plainclothed and uniformed officers of the Austin police department entered the club and shut down the show, arresting Tolstead and five others. The punk scene in Austin was instantly legitimized. Before this confrontation, punk was another passing trend that amused a few disaffected college students. Like the Tex-Mex music that was played other nights at Raul's, punk didn't even count as Austin music. Across the state and nationally, in newspaper articles and in record company offices, "Austin music" meant progressive country or, at most, progressive country and a rising community of young white blues musicians. After the police arrested the singer and four fans of the Huns, punk rock in Texas represented a musical style with the power to threaten the dominant cultural identity.[3]

The arrest demonstrated the breakdown of the cross-generational hegemony that had been hailed as the great achievement of the progressive country scene in Austin during the early and middle seventies. While the cosmic cowboys celebrated the healing of an earlier generational wound, punk rock opened a new gash on the smooth surface of the dominant power bloc of Texas. In terms of commodity aesthetics—that is, as a cultural product that determines its specific worth by distinguishing itself through marketplace competition with thousands of other cultural products—the Huns were not very good. But in the light of local conflicts and local meanings, the Huns were a great band whose performances brought to the surface underlying tensions in the Austin music scene—between international musical styles and local traditions, between that component of the local population interested in alternative cultures and alternative politics, and the group more interested in stability and order and maintaining a profitable way of life.

Later I will argue this more carefully, but now it is time to step back outside into the heat and walk on down the drag. Here at 24th and Guadalupe we will turn right, head down the street a block, and duck into Inner Sanctum records. During the seventies, this was the record store of record; this small, airless space was stuffed with music. From 1974 to 1978, a guy named Cowboy worked here. He knew all the progressive country musicians and really understood that sweet sound. But here also, Richard Dorsett spent hours convincing regular customers who previously had bought every Charlie Daniels record to try out the Ramones or the Dictators—bands from New York who played simple but loud music and were kind of funny looking. One night Dorsett managed to convince Louis Black that Jonathan Richman's naive sincerity was more interesting than Peter Gabriel's clever intellectualism, that direct expressions of personal commitment meant more than instrumental virtuosity. Louis has used the pages of his *Austin Chronicle* to tell everyone else that for the past nine years.[4]

During the eighties, Inner Sanctum hosted record release parties for local bands. The Standing Waves, the Big Boys, and the Dicks played in the parking lot while rock critics drank free beer and skate punks swerved through the crowd. Eventually, however, Inner Sanctum began to lose touch with its customers. Chain store competition for the student market increased at the same time that other independent stores opened that better understood the audiences for new music in Austin. Waterloo Records opened in 1982 with a complete moneyback guarantee, even for nondefective records. A rack by the front door displayed the commercial recordings of local talent. The Sound Exchange, a small chain based in Houston that sold new and used records, landed a tremendous retail location at the corner of 21st Street and Guadalupe. They hired clerks like Geoff Cordner, who knew both the new music and the musicians in the bands. The rapid transition to compact discs hurt Inner Sanctum also and, gradually, they became the third or fourth place to look for new hot tunes. Record release parties now happen at Waterloo or at Sound Exchange, where they have turned into promotional events, valued for the amount of product moved, not for the music heard or the amount of beer consumed.[5]

Back on the drag, every light pole carries posters from the last several weeks' worth of shows. Old flyers are torn down every week or so, but occasionally you can see one from a year or two ago, on an alley wall or a newspaper stand. Poster art has been important in the Austin music scene since Jim Franklin first began drawing little armadillos to promote shows at the Vulcan Gas Company in the late sixties. While flyers do not work as successful advertisements for specific shows—they do not draw people into the clubs to see bands they have never seen before—they do work as another way to display aspects of a band's image to those willing to pay attention. It can be fun to see yourself staring at yourself from one of these poles. Some bands use their flyers to carry on public conversations with critics, with booking agents, and with other bands. Others simply spread paper-thin slices of their publicity machine over utility poles near the university, near record stores, and near clubs—sticky pictures of their crafted surfaces peering from the gleaming structures that surround the stroller down the drag.[6]

There is a flyer advertising Bouffant Jellyfish, Sprawl, and Joe Rockhead for a Friday night at Liberty Lunch. These groups play an amalgam of white-boy speed-metal and learned-from-records funk-rap much like that developed by the Red Hot Chili Peppers. The poster displays the bands' names around a xeroxed picture of Malcolm X. Such bands will achieve fame by any means necessary. There is a flyer for Happy Family's show at the Texas Tavern on Saturday. Happy Family sings songs like "Cavemen in Neckties" and "Trashcan" that foreground contradictory aspects of gender construction. The flyer says that the women in the band will be wearing bikini tops for the show. There are stick figure drawings of the band members and a hand-lettered quote, "We promise." Uh-huh, sure. These flyers are free art selling art, decorating the spaces carved out from within the retail center of university life. Viewed against the store window displays that scream low prices on textbooks and orange-and-white sweatshirts, the mocking self commodified on these flyers appears different and intelligent, instead of merely sarcastic, petulant, or bitter.

This section of Guadalupe, between 24th and 21st streets, is the center of the drag. Across the street is the west mall of the university campus where official student organizations distribute materials to the heavy traffic that passes in front of the undergraduate library and the student union. Historically, the west mall has been the site of many interesting confrontations between different representatives of the university. Here, the Students for a Democratic Society used the concept of Gentle Thursdays to provoke anxiety among the fraternity and sorority groups by playing guitars on the grass in the early sixties. Here members of the theater group Art and Sausages campaigned to take over student government in the seventies. In the eighties, touring evangelists like Sister Sarah beat their breasts while they denounced their wicked pasts, sponsored by the Campus Crusade for Christ.[7] The west mall is also referred to as the free speech area. It is where the antiapartheid shanty recently stood. Free speech at the University of Texas is confined to this small rectangle flanked at one end by the administration building and cut off at the other by the drag. Fronting the west mall on Guadalupe Street are book stores, fast food restaurants, and clothing stores that function as the front line in the effort to engage the students in the local economy. From free speech to free market, the grand political illusions of American society flirtatiously invite the participation of each new generation of students.

Tonight, though, it is pretty quiet. During the day, acoustic musicians stand in the shade by these stores, playing fiddle and guitar, singing with their cases lying open on the street in front of them. At night some of these musicians go to the clubs; others go to the river to camp under a bridge. There they join other homeless who had spent the day panhandling on the drag. Only a few of the homeless actually spend the night on the street. This man sitting on the stairs by the bagel shop looks to be about twenty-five years old. I have seen him around here for six years. I used to walk by him in the mornings on my way to work, when I worked at a bookstore called the University Coop. He is always smiling, even when he sleeps. His shirt is always unbuttoned, even in the winter. His hair grows longer and then is cut, but that is the only change I ever see. He spends the night right around the corner, in an alley off 22nd Street. He has never asked me for money; I have never said a word to him. I won't talk to him tonight either.

I want to step into Sound Exchange quickly and see if they have the newest Squat Thrust tape. This store now features the most direct access to the music of the underground scene. They carry the best selection of homemade tapes by local bands and host record release parties for even the noisiest amateur productions. The Butthole Surfers have played here, the Skatenigs have played here; it can get really loud inside. And on hot nights like this, it usually is this crowded, with about thirty-five people squeezing through the aisles, looking through cds, tapes and vinyl, T-shirts, posters, and magazines—men with ponytails and women with their hair dyed black, everyone wearing T-shirts and shorts and boots. The guy behind the counter has worked here for years. He always says something to me about whatever tape or magazine I buy, but I don't know his name. There is a woman who works here sometimes, who I have lusted after for years, but I don't know her name either. She never speaks to me. Let's pick up a *Chronicle* for its club listings before we go out the door. I know who I want to show you tonight, but there's always tomorrow. Before we go to tonight's show, we have to drive around and look at some of the old places, where some important clubs used to be. While we are driving, I will tell you a few stories about the history of this town. We had better roll up the windows. Even though it is hours after dark, it is still hot enough to turn on the air conditioner.

In January 1839, Mirabeau B. Lamar, president of the Republic of Texas, commissioned a group to scout out a location for the permanent capital of Texas. A year before, he had camped by the town of Waterloo, and he instructed the commissioners to inspect that spot he remembered. They sent back an enthusiastic report focusing on the natural beauty of the surrounding area: the river and the many creeks, the hills covered with trees, and the rich plain that spread out from the hills. It did not matter that the beautiful river was not navigable and that the location was far from the republic's Anglo population centers. The site of the capital of Texas was chosen for aesthetic reasons.[8]

This beautiful land of the Republic had been taken by force from American Indians and Mexicans by migrating southerners who hoped to use it to become rich planters. Its boundaries still required violent enforcement. This tension between a love for the physical beauty of the land and the need to possess it, to make it one's own and thereby transform it into a *capital*, motivates much of the history of Austin, Texas.[9] By 1860 Austin's population had grown to 3,494. During the secession debates three distinct positions emerged. One group argued for remaining in the Union, one group argued for joining the Confederacy, the third wished that Texas would regain its independent status as a single republic. The vote in Travis County went against secession, 704 to 450—the first in a long line of elections where the opinions of voters in the Austin area differed from those in the remainder of the state.[10]

In 1871 the first railroad came to Austin and the transportation troubles that had limited the town's effectiveness as a center for the state were alleviated. Only then, in 1872, did Austin become the official capital. By 1883, when the University of Texas opened its first term with 218 students, the city was hooked up to two railroads; it had a library, an opera house, a theater, and four dance halls.[11] As the location of the state government, and the place where the state's children pursued higher education, Austin had to provide adequate intrastate transportation and appropriate cultural fare.

Here we are just north of the engineering part of the university campus, at a club that used to be the Beach. Before 1983 it was called Folkville, now it is a beer pub called the Crown and Anchor. It is cleaner and quieter than it was, but it really looks about the same as it did six years ago when bands like Zeitgeist, the Dharma Bums, Texas Instruments, the Wild Seeds, and Doctors' Mob, and their insistent psychedelicized fans turned this ex-ice cream parlor and folk club into the most exciting musical performance site in town. The tide of rock'n'roll music rose at the Beach once the effects of the Raul's punk explosion were integrated into local musical traditions. It collapsed when the drinking age was raised to twenty-one. On the nights when my band would play this club, I would grab a beer and sit outside here on the patio, watching the people come in, agonizing over the size of the crowd and whether or not we would be good enough to satisfy them. The last show I ever played in Austin was here in July 1986. We opened for Zeitgeist; the place was packed. I remember that the audience liked us that night. We were really loud. Let's get back in the car and head south; at least in the car it is air conditioned.

In 1900, with the population near 25,000, Austin still had no major industries.[12] Agricultural marketing, particularly of cotton and corn, was an important component of the local economy, linking local farmers to the railroads and thereby to mills in other parts of the state.[13] The most important public works concern was taming the Colorado River, which tended to exceed its banks at unpredictable yet frequent intervals. Dam projects for flood control and the production of electrical power were proposed from the 1890s to the 1930s with varying degrees of success. Several dams were destroyed by the floods they were built to control, and the current system of dams and lakes was not completed until World War II.[14]

The Austin Chamber of Commerce was founded in 1914. For the next thirty-five years, the Chamber pursued a policy of encouraging "a steady rate of municipal growth through the improvement and enlargement of its educational, governmental, recreational and commercial facilities."[15] The business community of Austin encouraged projects that improved local transportation, developed the recreational aspects of the area's natural resources, and worked to make Austin more attractive to conventioneers and tourists.[16] This strategy differed from those of Chambers of Commerce across the country, who tended to pursue manufacturing projects, but the approach fit in well with a service economy already oriented to the after-hours desires and the leisure needs of politicians and students. In 1950, Travis County had the lowest proportion of manufacturing employment of any county in the United States with over 100,000 people.[17] Throughout the first half of this century, Austin remained a slow-paced town, geared to the rhythms of the school year and a once-every-two-years legislative session.

Now we are crossing the Colorado River on the Congress Avenue bridge. We are a couple of miles south of campus; the pink granite of the Capitol is right behind us. On Barton Springs Road, we turn right and drive over to where the Armadillo World Headquarters reigned for over ten years. This empty twenty-story office building rises from the same ground where once stood the most heavily promoted music venue this town has ever seen. For many, the Armadillo will always be the spiritual home of Austin music. Throughout the seventies, in article after article, from *Time* magazine to the *Chicago Tribune* to *Oui* to *Mother Jones*, the Armadillo World Headquarters dominated any description of music in Texas. It was described as a "groover's paradise," a "counterculture concert hall," and a home for "queer-minded social misfits."[18] Many writers trained in Austin—at the student newspaper the *Daily Texan*, at the progressive biweekly, the *Texas Observer*, as well as at a number of "underground" or "alternative" papers like the *Rag* and the *Sun*—went on to write for national magazines or big-city dailies. Wherever they went, they wrote about the music made in the town they came from. And they always wrote about the Armadillo. Despite the fact that the basic form of the musical style known as progressive country, or redneck rock, or cosmic cowboy music, had already been hashed out in jam sessions at other clubs like the Jade Room, the New Orleans Club, the Chequered Flag, and the Vulcan Gas Company, the Armadillo became associated with the cultural significance of this musical amalgam.[19] Perhaps this is because the hall was big enough to contain the different groups that this music was supposed to have brought together. Or perhaps it was because the original partners, Mike Tolleson, Eddie Wilson, and Bobby Hedderman, were masterful publicists who, in competition with other clubs and other promoters, effectively created this unshakable association in the minds of music fans in Austin and across the country between one performance site, one rather narrow slice of Austin music, and a specific image of Texan identity.

In 1976, after six years of operating in the red, leaving a history of unpaid volunteer employees and bounced checks, the original visionaries turned the operation over to one of their janitors, Hank Alrich. The son of a silentscreen-era movie cowboy, Alrich had inherited a considerable amount of money, and he struggled for another four years to operate the Armadillo on a cash basis while paying off the hall's bankruptcy settlement. But he had to give up when the Austin real estate boom became too powerful. Hikes in the property tax made it impossible for the landlord, M. K. Hage, to continue the five-cents-a-square-foot monthly rent that he had charged since Wilson first negotiated for the building. During 1980, several firms made serious offers for the land. After the zoning for the area was changed to allow highrise construction, the Hage family sold out, and the Armadillo era ended.[20]

People say that many magical nights happened here. The concerts of Willie Nelson are particularly singled out as paradigmatic examples of the musical construction of community. Nelson was a master of sincere performance. He would look out into the audience and, while making eye contact with someone, his voice would dip behind the beat a little and his head would tilt slightly. At that instant, that audience member *knew* that Willie was singing genuinely, honestly, directly to her or him. As his band rolled through an unending medley of hits—great songs like "Crazy," "Night Life," "Family Bible," "Whisky River," "Me & Paul"— Nelson would smile and nod and sing to everyone in the room. His small town Texas roots and his Nashville training enabled him to connect with such generationally divergent individuals as the coach of the University of Texas football team, the speaker of the Texas House of Representatives, the mayor of Austin, as well as the college students and the hippies from whom he bought his dope. Because each of these fans felt connected to Willie, they felt connected together, as they performed with him the reunification of a Texan cultural bloc.[21]

The Armadillo had been torn down before I moved to town, and I have never seen Willie Nelson perform. But his legend permeates the music scene. Everyone knows the stories about Willie leaving Nashville and coming back home to Texas where his people loved him and let him be himself. They admire how he was able to grow his hair long and smoke marijuana and top the country charts all at the same time. What a hero. I did talk to his sister, Bobbie, on the phone once. That was pretty exciting.

I will not have time to show you all of the clubs that have opened and closed downtown. There have been so many. We won't even look at the parking lot that used to be Club Foot, or the joint that used to be the Chequered Flag, or the office building that used to hold the Vulcan Gas Company and, later, Duke's Royal Coach Inn. We cannot stop now to trace the circular moves of the Soap Creek Saloon from the hills west of town to a highway north of town to a location only a few blocks from here on South Congress. But on our way to the freeway, we will drive by the Austin Opera House and look at the complex of music industry related services that is growing there.

In 1977, this place was opened by Tim O'Connor and Willie Nelson as a concert hall that would compete with the Armadillo to book nationally touring acts. Its opening night show headlined both Waylon Jennings and Willie during the height of the "outlaw" craze. The building originally had been designed as a motel and convention center. It had two main ballrooms, several smaller meeting rooms, and a long hall from which branched many rooms that could be remodeled into offices or storefronts. Over the past thirteen years, this place has been transformed from a simple attempt to cash in on the Austin sound to a complex of music businesses. The increasing sophistication of the music scene in Austin can be read in the carefully thought-out commercial strategies signified by the changes in this building. More than a concert hall, this long, low, brick building is now the home for Arlyn recording studios, the local chapter of the American Federation of Musicians, the Austin Guitar School, a management company, and an independent record label. Austin Community College hopes to hold its music management classes here soon. It has become one of the centers for the industrialized production and distribution of Austin music.[22]

Now that we are finally heading north on Interstate 35, recrossing the Colorado, we can see the racial segregation of the city vividly displayed before us. This highway was built in 1950, adding a barrier of rushing cars and concrete to the line between East Austin and the rest of the town. The mostly empty postmodern architecture of downtown makes jokes about the eighties real estate boom to our left, while to the right sits the mostly Latino portion of town. That district blends into the African-American section by 6th Street or so, and this section stretches up to the airport by 38th Street. The Anglos live in the western part of town, near the hills. This segregation isn't quite so strict now as it used to be. In the wake of the civil rights movement, the Chicano movement, and various progressive political projects since then, some whites have moved into East Austin, a very few blacks have moved west, some hispanics have bought homes in the northern suburbs. South Austin, from just south of the river down into the newer subdivisions, is the home for working people of all ethnicities. But this town was built to serve the Anglo politicians and students, to be the center of knowledge and political power in the largest state in the South. And the degree of social and residential segregation still evident reflects that origin.

In the first two decades of this century, most of Austin's black population were servants for the state power brokers, living near downtown and near the university in small neighborhoods called Wheatville and Clarksville. But Austin's first black high school had been built in East Austin, on 11th Street, in 1884. Children from these neighborhoods in the west portion of town had to ride the trolley to 11th Street and Congress Avenue and then walk two miles east to go to school.[23] Some families began to move east. Lying just to the west of the cotton fields of Texas, Austin had become a labor market for agricultural workers; the Austin Chamber of Commerce operated a bureau that recruited cotton pickers in 1925.[24] During this decade, the market for cotton pickers and corn shuckers drew more African-Americans and Mexican-Americans to the capital city.

In 1928, the city council responded with a plan that included "a design for the deliberate segregation of the city." Mexican-Americans were to be removed from the region between Shoal Creek and Congress Avenue and between 6th Street and the river, either across the river into South Austin, or across East Avenue into East Austin. The laboring population of Mexican-Americans could not be allowed to interfere with Austin's main task of commercially servicing state representatives and students. According to the plan, "The property values on Congress Avenue going south from Sixth Street drop very abruptly at Fifth Street and continue to decrease as the river is approached. . . . Austin cannot afford to have its retail business district throttled by the presence of an obstruction of this nature."[25] The Chicano Catholic parish had been moved to East Austin three years before; the city plan then reinforced this eastward Mexican-American migration.

Austin's African-American population was to be moved out of their old downtown neighborhoods and into another area of East Austin, near 11th and 12th Streets. The city's two black colleges were already located east of East Avenue, as well as the "separate but equal" high school.[26] The city segregation plan intended to follow this lead, concentrating municipal facilities for blacks in this part of town. The rhetoric of the plan is straightforward. "All the facilities and conveniences [should] be provided the negroes in this district, as an incentive to draw the negro population to this area." It was argued that only in East Austin could black schools be given "adequate playground space and facilities similar to the white schools in the area."[27] Exploiting the implications of the 1896 Supreme Court decision, Plessy v. Ferguson, the city of Austin worked to move its African-American population out of the western portions of the town and across East Avenue. The city plan of 1928 residentially segregated Austin's population, reinforcing an ethnic separation that still exists.

By 1940, 75 percent of the city's black population lived in East Austin.[28] This degree of population density encouraged and reinforced the establishment of a Negro Citizens' Council, a Negro Community Center, and an extensive commercial district that encompassed the east side of 11th and 12th Streets.[29] This part of town became the home for blues music in Austin. African-Americans who were recruited to pick cotton by the Chamber of Commerce might work in the fields with Texas Alexander, and maybe they would attend parties where Ragtime Texas would play the quills. Back home in Austin, they would buy the blues recordings that labels like Paramount and ARC were marketing. A few nightclubs opened along 12th Street where traveling blues musicians would play. While never rivaling the musical activity of the blues scenes in Houston or in Dallas, the African-American community in East Austin nurtured a blues culture that would come to reinforce the developing white blues scene in the late sixties and seventies—even as one remained clearly and firmly separated from the other.[30]

We get off the freeway at Airport Boulevard and head west on 45th Street. Now we are north of the university campus, north of downtown and the Capitol. Finally it is cool enough to turn off the air conditioner and open the car windows. The wide streets in this part of town are fronted by tree-covered lots, and the individual houses are all freshly painted. This is the northern end of a residential area called Hyde Park. It was built in the 1890s as a community "exclusively for white people."[31] During the late seventies and early eighties large portions of Hyde Park were thoroughly renovated and refurbished in the gentrification movement of the time. Almost no musicians can afford to live in Hyde Park; most of the homes belong to lawyers, doctors, university professors, successful entrepreneurs, and a sprinkling of high-tech workers. Behind us, across the highway and near the airport, live quite a few of the musicians who are currently active in the scene. Many more live to our right, just north of Hyde Park, where the rents are cheaper because airplanes landing at the airport roar overhead at depressingly precise intervals. This is where many bands experience their first public performances: in backyard parties hosted by other musicians, under the roar of landing airplanes.

I am taking you to one of these houses that musicians rent. This is the home of Ed Hall, one of the most exciting underground bands in Austin. I interviewed Kevin Whitley, the drummer, on this unpainted porch one evening, while the rush hour commuter flights landed only a quarter of a mile away. Kevin invited us over tonight to catch a little bit of the band's practice. I had to promise that we would leave if we bother them. Kevin says that the musical and emotional balance within the band is rather tenuous right now. They used to all write songs together, each contributing spontaneously to the group creation. Now that method is not working as well as it used to, and they find themselves bickering over the scales, the rhythms, and the structures of new songs.[32]

All three of the members of Ed Hall live here, as well as a couple of fans and anyone else who drops by for a night and needs a place to stay. The house is a small three-bedroom affair, a single story with a slanting asbestos roof. The members of Ed Hall are ex-art students, and the walls inside the house are covered with the self-referential illustrations of contradiction and angst common to such educational experiences. In the front room is a couch covered with that dark-green ribbed material that furnishes dormitory lounges all over the country. One of the wooden legs is missing and that corner is held up by several small pieces of red brick. The table in the kitchen is covered with sheets of paper torn from a sketch pad. Most of them show only two or three lines traced across their surface by a crayon. Glancing to your left, you see a sink with very few dishes in it. The boys don't eat here that often, instead either going out or eating at their girlfriends' homes. Behind the kitchen is the rehearsal room. Kevin hollers at us to come on back.

The room is filled with amplifiers and drums and tape machines and microphones. Everywhere there are electrical cords that twist across the rug and through the air, connecting all the separate machines into one sound generator. You can barely see the rusty dreadlocks of Kevin's white-boy rasta hair behind his drums. Gary is across the room, tuning his guitar at a volume that concretizes overtones. Larry strips off his shirt before he picks up his bass, and sweat begins to coagulate in the air as we find a place to stand against the wall. Without looking at either of the other two, Larry begins to play a line on his bass that whoops and swooshes, jumping around the lower two strings of his instrument, and then sliding to the top of the neck just at the moment when the line repeats. It is a one-bar, four-beat riff that rises in pitch and increases in rhythmic complexity over that short musical period. Kevin looks up sharply and slowly rattles his ride cymbal into alertness, drawing his drumsticks from the center out to the edge of this large circle of brass. Gary just listens, standing with his head cocked to one side, until Kevin shifts in his seat and finds the pulse with his kick drum. Much of what makes Ed Hall exciting is the interplay between Kevin's kick drum and Larry's swooping bass lines. In this song, Kevin is a little ahead of the two beat as defined by the bass part and just a hair behind the four beat. This effect increases the feeling of instability in the song and makes Larry jump up and down and sideways a few times. Then Gary steps on one of the foot pedals he has wired together and stretches the strings on his guitar into a high-pitched banshee wail that descends slowly as he relaxes the strings and finds the chord that now defines the key. This single bar of music then repeats almost four hundred times, with only slight variations in the details of pitch and rhythm. The volume of the music and its unrelenting forward tension make the room seem alive, while the bodies of the musicians—the hands of Larry and Gary, and Kevin's legs and arms—move like puppets pulled by a very complex web of pulleys and wires. I like it when the music gets this loud, when it seems to invade my head and the blood in my temples pulsates with the driving motion of its purple sound. But anymore, I just cannot stand it for very long. We have to leave before they start another song. It is almost eleven o'clock and time to go the show. We wave goodbye to Kevin, nod at Larry and Gary, and head out the door.

Driving back down Guadalupe, it is quiet enough that you can almost sense what this town was like twenty years ago, before the first oil crisis pumped millions of new dollars through the Texan economy, before Jerry Jeff Walker, Michael Murphey, and Willie Nelson moved to town, before hundreds of other, unknown musicians moved here, lured by the low cost of living and the plentiful opportunities to perform—before Austin expanded beyond its city limits. You could imagine that we might be going to the Vulcan to smoke pot and listen to the Conqueroo play their swirling rhythm and blues, or to the Split Rail to drink beer and dance the two-step. We might be joining the students and the politicians and the other hangers-on who appreciate the quality of service at clubs like the Jade Room, the Id, the New Orleans Club, the Saxon Pub, or even the Eleventh Door, Charlie's Playhouse, or the Chequered Flag.[33] For decades this has been true: at this time of night, the energy of this town is wired through its nightclubs, linking power amps and speakers, transistors and tubes into a clashing counterpoint of discordant tonalities played together.

And then the boom happened. Motorola, IBM, and Texas Instruments opened plants in Austin, initiating the city's taste for high-tech industries. Between 1965 and 1975 student enrollment at the university increased by almost 50 percent from 28,868 to 42,598.[34] The Armadillo opened in 1970. In 1973, the Majewskis opened the Soap Creek to provide more opportunities for area bands. In 1975, Castle Creek, the One Knite, the Back Room, the Hole in the Wall, Mother Earth, and the Broken Spoke were all booking local musicians. Clifford Antone opened his blues joint on 6th Street that summer, and the university opened a beer hall called the Texas Tavern. In 1976, the Rome Inn and Liberty Lunch added to the offerings of Austin music.[35] And those are only the most well-known venues, those that catered to students, musicians, and journalists. The number of nightclubs per capita peaked in 1976. In that year there were 28 places to hear live music for every 100,000 people in Austin.[36] As the population was just over 300,000, that meant there were close to 84 stages from which musicians could perform. The national reputation of the progressive country scene continued to attract more musicians even as the national appetite for ever-more expensive oil pushed more money into Texas, driving up land values and turning Austin from a slow-paced town into a rapidly growing sunbelt capital. And in 1978, the year that punk invaded Raul's, per capita income in Austin exceeded the national average for the first time.[37]

Throughout this period and even up to the mid-1980s, Austin's rock'n'roll scene was supported by a honky-tonk economy that reinforced a local set of traditional cultural meanings and established a flexible yet consistent musical aesthetic. Beneath the tonalities, rhythms, and lyrics that generically distinguished the various musical styles performed in the clubs lay an emphasis on personal sincerity that, in turn, enabled the mutual blending of personalities in each band's musical expression. This belief in the importance of sincere personal expression established a communicative atmosphere that elicited a willing and pleasurable identification among Austin's young music fans. These young fans developed a tendency to group together in the city's music clubs—listening, dancing, and fantasizing along with the performances of local musicians. Once this tradition was established, the clubs of Austin began to function as a cultural synecdoche. The cultural distinctions between the relatively liberal town of Austin and the remainder of the highly conservative state of Texas were represented and intensified in the beliefs and behaviors constructed and reinforced through musical practice.

Ironically, the cultural aesthetic produced through this practice retained a powerful conservative strain. The critique of modern commercialized society developed by Austin musicians throughout the sixties and the early seventies had depended upon a romantic nostalgia for a premodern society. Encoded into the musical and lyrical expressions of these musicians was a naive anticommercialism and a longing for a populist egalitarianism of unalienated labor and spontaneous expression. As the music scene developed during this period, playing music came to be seen as a way to "not have to work," a means toward a life "relatively free of hassle." This aesthetic reached its zenith at precisely the point when the Texan economy achieved national integration and complete modernization—during the oil crises of the seventies. For a brief moment—the much-acclaimed era of the cosmic cowboy and the Armadillo World Headquarters—Austin music appeared to define the cultural meaning of being Texan. An astounding alliance developed among progressive country musicians, long-haired pot-smoking young people, radio disc jockeys, nightclub owners, football players, and even local and state politicians. However, in order to build this cultural alliance, Austin's music scene had had to emphasize some of the more regressive aspects that it had inherited from its origins in honky-tonk culture and cowboy songs. The cultural identity promulgated in Austin's progressive country scene increasingly reinforced a set of characteristics traditionally associated with white, male, Texan entrepreneurs.

The moment of cultural alliance did not last long. Efforts to market Austin's music nationally were not successful. Although musicians like Willie Nelson, Jerry Jeff Walker, and Michael Murphey did have national hits, they were all relative newcomers to the city. No locally nurtured talent built a successful recording career while retaining a home base in Austin's music scene. The national attention drawn to the Armadillo did not bring with it a stream of capital sufficient to sustain and reinforce the local conditions that had enabled its musical/cultural synthesis of progressive country. During the second half of the seventies, competition increased among live music clubs just as many of the city's most promising musicians moved away and the town's college students carried on a momentary fling with disco. Progressive country had not managed to produce a life "relatively free of hassle" for any of its constituents.

As the seventies turned into the eighties, a new generation of college students entered the city. Just as the state of Texas had become increasingly interlinked with the national economy, this new generation of students was significantly more comfortable with a mass-mediated, nationally oriented, commercialized culture. Rather than looking to the dominant Texan traditions of popular music, these young people were paying attention both to new recordings and to stories in the national news media that were representing a sound stripped of frills and a raw musical attitude. The version of punk rock that took hold in Austin's music scene was a peculiar hybrid of New York's art-scene bohemia, London's flagrant nihilism, and Austin's own outrageous individualism. Almost a self-aware simulacrum, the performance of punk rock at Raul's was always deflected through an ironic sideways glance, an oblique self-parody of its own conditions of performance. But this new music also carried with it a do-it-yourself ideology that merged quite easily with the long tradition of Texan entrepreneurialism. The result of this cultural syncretism was an increasing emphasis on improving and modernizing the economic base of music-making in Austin.

During this period of economic restructuring, the underlying aesthetic principles of Austin music held. Music-making was still centered on live performance in the clubs, and this music was still valued by the members of the scene to the extent that it represented a sincere expression of the personalities of the musicians and enabled a sincere integrative response on the part of the fans. But as long-time participants in the scene worked together with local music-business owners and the Chamber of Commerce to orient and stabilize the flow of capital through Austin's music-related businesses, they reorganized music-making in Austin. They deliberately and self-consciously built an industrial infrastructure modeled on that of the national recording industry. After this restructuring, it was still possible to explore innovative subjectivities through the mutual performance of musicalized identities in the city's clubs. However, by the beginning of the nineties, live performance in the clubs had been reconceived as a process of research and development for the production of recordings.

We are almost back down at the river again, at a club called Liberty Lunch. We can park across the street in this city government lot; they don't ticket at night. The city owns the land that Liberty Lunch stands on. It is part of a block of warehouses that one day will be a new city hall. The city manager used to threaten every year to tear down the club, but now that city coffers are empty and the Chamber of Commerce sees Austin music as a clean growth industry, Liberty Lunch appears to be one of the safer musical institutions. Its landlord is interested now in the continued success of this important club. With a capacity of about eight hundred, Liberty Lunch is one of the few places large enough to be able to book touring alternative acts. Yet it is so cheap to run that it can break even with local bands most nights. At any rate, we don't have to worry about parking here.

Liberty Lunch sits on this part of 2nd Street that always looks to me like the dark end of a tunnel, leading out of the downtown area and into an unknown world. The streetlights barely cut through the obscurity around us. We find ourselves lured toward the club not by a neon sign or a flashing marquee but by a sound that slips through the structure of the building, a vibration that runs across our skin, contracts our stomach muscles, and quickens our step. We are going to see the Reivers. I feel my body tightening a little, telling my hips to slow down, to stroll towards the door. We must not rush as we pay our five dollars and go in.

They have already begun to play. John, wearing his T-shirt inside out, stares at the neck of his Telecaster. Kim and Cindy dance and play together. And we feel rather than see Garret work his drums. I know that it looks very crowded up front, but we should be able to stand over to the right and see pretty well. This band used to pack this place. Although they no longer fill the largest clubs in town, their crowds are still decent. Just last fall they lost their recording contract; they were dropped from Capitol Records. But the band seems almost relieved. Onstage, they appear lighter, happier.

The song they are playing is from their second album, *Saturday*. It's called "Once in a While." See the kids sort of swaying back and forth, moving their weight from side to side, not yet actually dancing, but comfortable? This is the way the Reivers start. And their audience starts this way with them. This band breaks no new dance ground, but their rhythmic conservatism provides no obstruction for their ever-younger audience. In fact, the simple rhythms of the lower-pitched beats support the more intriguing upper harmonics of the guitars (emphasized by a "chorus" pedal and a bi-amped system), much as John's gruff and somewhat stiff vocals provide the backdrop for Kim's more liquid singing. "Once in a While" floats on, contrasting loud and quiet passages that gesture toward a greater engagement, a greater interest to come.

After a few more songs, they click. As they start a number called "Baby," the crowd folds in on itself and then bursts out, dancing. The men look down at their feet, studying their own unfamiliar movements while they dance their first real joy of the night. Kelly, wearing a polo shirt and khakis, looking like the recent UT computer science graduate he is, leans over and says, "I'm feelin' a familiar rhythm." Looking over to the left, we see Josh shaking his long hair up and down. This slow headbang is what Josh, with a sort of self-deprecating irony, calls "his dance." He sees us watching him and points up at John onstage before disappearing back into the crowd. In front of us is Rita, the Baylor student who said hello when we first walked up. As "Baby" starts, she shouts and begins dancing with considerable intensity, her waving elbows forcing us backward a few steps.[38]

Several women, some of whom have been dancing all along, focus their attention on Kim Longacre. There is a young girl leaning against the stage, with loosely permed light yellow hair, a slightly turned up nose, and bleached Guess jeans, who appears to mirror Kim's performance. While John sings the verses, Kim strums and sways, nodding at Cindy and laughing. During the bridge of the song, she steps forward to sing the line, "Leave me alone just for a while." Everyone in the audience sings along, as one mass echoing this chant, but Blondie-in-Guess-jeans does more than that. She literally copies every physical move that Kim makes. She mimes Kim's guitar strum, she bobs her head from side to side as though circling a microphone with the prosody of the phrase, and she hops backward at the end of the vocal line when Kim steps back and John reassumes the melody.

Kim looks at us here taking notes and steps down from the stage to say, "It's magic, you know. It feels like you could do whatever you wanted to. It feels so uninhibited. It feels like you could look over at John and he's making a weird face and you could laugh at him and he would just laugh back. It feels like I could stand on the monitor and act like a rock star, stick my tongue out at someone in the audience and not worry about being sharp or flat or finding the right chords. It's that zen thing. It's a physical thing. I like the way it makes me feel. It's heaven up there you know, when it all comes right through and it's effortless. It's just this voice coming out."[39]

Smiling, John looks over at Kim, down at us, and out at the audience. "The success of this band," he says, "is fundamentally based on providing an almost religious experience for the audience, producing that feeling and making sure the audience gets it. What I want to have happen is for them to understand. It's like there's something there that you maybe can't sit down and analyze, but they are there and they understand. It's a real cathartic thing."[40]

And so while the Reivers continue to play, the men in the audience awkwardly dance, their bodies struggling to understand, and while the women nod and sing along with their understanding, I try to stand still and scribble words in a notebook, "Leave me alone just for awhile." I just have to think about this a little bit.

CHAPTER TWO

Constructing the Musicalized
Performance of Texan Identity

Cowboy Lore

Music-making in Austin grows out of a long history, a history that struggles to center the meaning of being Texan in the voices and the sung narratives of specific historical individuals representing certain groups. The effects of this history are still felt in the popular memory of those who continue the musicalized performance of identity in Austin's nightclubs and the recording studios. As individual musicians come to terms with the institutional and discursive structures that constrain and enable their performances, they map out a relation to this history—a relation described as a continuance of a powerful tradition or, conversely, as a throwing off of this tradition's burden. In its most elaborated narratives, the popular history of music-making in Austin looks beyond the disruption of tradition at Raul's, back through the cosmic cowboys performing a reconstructed tradition at the Armadillo, back through the psychedelic fires stoked at the Vulcan, back beyond even the self-conscious revival of folksinging at Threadgill's, and traces its powerful articulation of performed song and performed identity to the folkloristic construction of the singing cowboy.

By the late 1880s, cowboy lore, ranging from dime novels to academic folk song collections, was developing into an ongoing process of mythologizing, a discursive construction of legends, tales, myths, and songs that intermingled and produced images of an idealized western male. Throughout the early part of the twentieth century, these idealized representations worked their way through academic, popular, and commercial expressions, effectively legitimating a variety of Texan cultural practices as the work of real cowboys. Texan populism, Texan democracy, Texan business, and Texan music all drew on the image of the cowboy as an independent entrepreneur, a strong masculine hero freely participating in the creation of Texan society.

John Avery Lomax contributed to this process with the first publication of *Cowboy Songs and other Frontier Ballads* in 1910.[1] He was determined to represent a more authentic cowboy than those depicted in popular culture. The "Collector's Note" for the first edition of *Cowboy Songs* insisted that, "Still much misunderstood, he is often slandered, nearly always caricatured, both by the press and by the stage. Perhaps these songs, coming direct from the cowboy's experience, giving vent to his careless and his tender emotions, will afford future generations a truer conception of what he really was than is now possessed by those who know him only through highly colored romances" (Lomax 1910, xxvii). Lomax argued that these songs, anchored in the cowboy's experience, were directly expressive of the cowboy's true character. His argument carried the authority of his own experience: Lomax was a Texan who had heard these songs himself as a child.

In his autobiography, *Adventures of a Ballad Hunter*, Lomax described his first encounter with the material that would become his life's work:

I couldn't have been more than four years old when I first heard a cowboy sing and yodel to his cattle. I was sleeping in my father's two-room house in Texas beside a branch of the old Chisholm Trail—twelve of us sometimes in two rooms. Suddenly a cowboy's singing waked me as I slept on my trundle bed. . . . These sounds come back to me faintly through the years, a foggy maze of recollections; and my heart lept even then to the cries of the cowboy trying to quiet, in the deep darkness and sifting rain, a trail herd of restless cattle.[2]

By the time of Lomax's autobiography (1947), he had already been acknowledged as one of the foremost ballad and folk song collectors in the United States and was considered to be an authority on the musical culture of the cowboy. As this passage makes clear, Lomax's professional reputation had been built on a nostalgic celebration of the work culture of a few men who lived and worked near his boyhood home. On the basis of this "foggy maze of recollections," Lomax had constructed a romantic representation of an autonomous, strong, independent, and, sometimes, violent guardian at the edge of civilization, and then spread this representation through the collections of cowboy songs that he produced during the first fifty years of the twentieth century. The edge of civilization guarded by the cowboy—the boundary between nature and culture—was marked by lines of race and gender, and the work of policing this boundary carried an implicit class ideology. The image of the Anglo-Texan cow*boy* who worked hard—transforming the natural material of cattle into the cultural material of wealth—and played hard—

singing and dancing as one in a presocial utopia—became the myth of the originary Texan. This formed the core of Texan identity that was propagated throughout both popular and academic culture during the first half of the twentieth century.

According to the literary standards shaping folklore research during the early part of the twentieth century, all ballads were by definition produced by "the homogenous folk." For George Lyman Kittredge, this phrase conveyed a "community whose intellectual interests are the same from the top of the social structure to the bottom." Cultural production for this folk occurred when they gathered

under very simple conditions of life, for the purpose of celebrating some occasion of common interest. . . . The dancing and singing in which all share are so closely related as to be practically complementary parts of a single festal act . . . a singing, dancing throng subjected as a unit to a mental and emotional stimulus which is not only favorable to the production of poetry, but is almost certain to result in such production.[3]

For Lomax, who was following these conventions of ballad scholarship, this presocietal moment of communal creation existed at the end of the nineteenth century, on the cattle trail and in the cow camps of Texas.

The assumptions of ballad scholarship contained both historical and ethnological components. If the ballad form of the cowboy songs defined them as folk poetry, the content was valued for "the light they [shed] on the conditions of pioneer life, and more particularly because of the information they contain[ed] concerning that unique and romantic figure in modern civilization, the American cowboy" (Lomax 1910, xxv). In addition to their literary merit, these ballads were valued as documents of past ways of life where important cultural traditions were anchored in the material daily practices of nonelites. The dancing, singing throng provided the locus for the origins of cultural values, and the study of cowboy ballads was one means of recovering these values. Within the Herderian tradition that American ballad scholarship inherited, these originary values, to a greater or lesser extent, established the inherent legitimacy of a people and a nation. According to the tradition of ballad scholarship, cowboy ballads displayed cultural values that were directly linked to a premodern world where men worked together, transforming the natural world for mutual profit.[4]

In the third edition of *Cowboy Songs*, Lomax emphasized specific aspects of the cowboy heritage:

We cannot trace all the influences, but we do know that the aftermath of the Civil War sent to Texas many a young Virginia aristocrat; many sons of Alabama, Mississippi, and Georgia Planters; many a coon hunter from Kentucky;

roving and restless blades from all over the South (and everywhere else). From such a group, given a taste for killing in the Civil War, in which Southern feeling and sentiments predominated, came the Texas cowboy and the cowboy songs.

These may have been rough, raw, wild individuals but, according to the academic rules of song collecting, the blood in their veins and the spirit in their songs indicated southern descendants from the purest Anglo-Saxon patricians. Despite the obvious influence of the Mexican vaquero tradition from which the cowboy's work (and the guitar) derived, and Lomax's own acknowledgment that "it was not unusual to find a Negro" on the trail, his song collection was valued to the extent that it demonstrated the continuing dominance of an Anglo-Saxon cultural tradition.[5]

Lomax's representation of cowboy culture inserted the Anglo-Saxon patrician into a condition of rugged freedom, "hundreds of miles from places where the conventions of society were observed. . . . These men lived on terms of practical equality. Except in the case of the boss, there was little difference in the amount paid each for his services. Society, then, was here reduced to its lowest terms. The work of the men, their daily experiences, their thoughts, their interests, were all in common" (Lomax 1910, xxvi). Here in this imagined world of masculine equality and freedom, the social contract was renegotiated daily. Social power came from the cowboy's ability instantly to enact his desires, from a willingness to provoke confrontation, and from the physical agility to defeat an opponent face to face. On the trail, where everyone's interests and even their thoughts were supposedly in common, these aggressive behaviors worked together for the good of the community.

The ballads collected by Lomax contain representations of some of the originary values of Texan presociety. "Sam Bass" is a typical cowboy ballad. According to Lomax (and, again, following the necessary conventions), "it sprang from the people. No one has ever claimed to be its author. Its sources are as mysterious and unknown as the Texas grasses that grow above his grave." Nevertheless, "during cattle-trail days, in Texas, 1868–1892, every singing cowboy carried Sam Bass in his repertoire."[6] As published in Lomax's first collection, it tells the story of a young man from Indiana who moved to Texas to become a cowboy. According to the song, Bass wanted to live the life of impulse and freedom that the West promised. In other words, within the narrative of the ballad, an idea of the cowboy already existed in Indiana, and this idea, whether it would have come from Joseph McCoy's historic sketches or from a Ned Buntline melodrama, drew Sam Bass to Texas, the place where one could be a cowboy.[7]

Bass is a Robin Hood figure, "a kinder-hearted fellow you seldom ever see." After a drive north, Bass and his crew go on a "spree," robbing trains on their way back to Texas. When they get back to Denton, he shares his wealth with all his friends. Sam's ability to act on his desires is celebrated in the ballad; he robs trains, spends money freely, and drinks good whiskey. But the ballad does not give us the journalistic details of his crimes, details common to native American balladry. We don't know where the robberies occurred, and there is some confusion over how many there were. We do learn about Sam's companions, that they were bold and daring and tough enough to whip the Texas Rangers. One stanza tells us how Arkansas, a gang member, was shot by a ranger named Thomas Floyd, who is "a deadbeat on the sly." One stanza is devoted to the scene of Sam's death. But three of the eleven stanzas detail the actions, the motives, and the expected future for Jim Murphy, the man who betrayed Sam to the authorities. Jim Murphy and Sam Bass form a binary opposition of cowboy morality. In this narrative, Murphy's act is a crime that must be punished. "Perhaps he's got to heaven, there's none of us can say/But if I'm right in my surmise he's gone the other way."[8]

"Sam Bass" ranks masculine qualities according to the opposition between Bass and Murphy. Bravery, agility, generosity, forthrightness, toughness, and impulsiveness are the positive virtues associated with Bass; being a deadbeat and disloyalty are the negative behaviors of Murphy. In the world of the cowboy song, Bass and his gang are a premodern roving band of hunters devoted to mutual self-survival. But their communality is threatened by Murphy. His actions indicate disagreement and conflict. Even worse, he admits outside authority into the presocial democracy of the cattle trail. Ultimately, this is Murphy's crime.[9]

Lomax intended to correct the popular caricature of the rough and tumble cowboy by including songs that express "careless and tender emotions" (Lomax 1910, xxvii). Far from careless, however, much of the tenderness found in *Cowboy Songs* is encoded in a strict sentimentality. "The Gal I Left Behind Me," first appeared in the 1916 edition of Lomax's collection.[10] It describes a cowboy who "struck the trail in seventy-nine," yet who was constantly reminded of his sweetheart. No matter what danger the cowboy rode through—a storm, a stampede, an Indian attack—he thought only of her. The dangers are, of course, described with numerous details, while his thoughts of her consist solely of the refrain, "that sweet little gal, that true little gal, the gal I left behind me" (Lomax 1916, 344).

Contrast that typical rigidity with the convincing expressions of respect, affection, and even love reserved for other cowboys. Cowboy ballads celebrated those men who most heartily embodied the image of the western hero. With a passion that cannot be found in their strictly disciplined declarations of heterosexual love, these ballads describe the actions and often the corpses of the cowboy hero. "Utah Carroll" provides a convincing example. Lomax first published it in the 1910 edition and it appeared essentially unchanged in the 1916 publication. But by 1938, "Utah Carroll" had acquired a heightened dramatic narrative. The story was essentially the same in the later version, only more polished, with more elaborate detail.[11]

The ballad begins with the narrator stating what makes him "sad and still, and why my brow is darkened like clouds upon the hill." Utah Carroll is dead, and the ballad will tell us just how he died, how brave and strong he was, and how glorious was his death. The narrator was Utah's "pardner." "We rode the range together and rode it side by side; I loved him as a brother; I wept when Utah died." Carroll dies saving the boss's daughter from a stampede she carelessly caused. As she was riding her pony in front of the cattle herd, a corner of her red blanket slips out from beneath her saddle, throwing the animals into a rage. When Lenore, the daughter, sees the stampeding cattle she falls from her pony, carrying the red blanket with her to the ground. Their passions further inflamed, the herd rushes toward her, sure to crush her under their hooves. At this moment, Utah spurs his own horse into a race with the cattle. He gets to her before the herd and reaches down to sweep her up onto his saddle. But the weight of the two of them together is too much for the cinches. They snap, and Utah and Lenore are thrown back onto the ground together with the red blanket. Then comes the moment of Utah's ultimate sacrifice. "Utah picked up the blanket. 'Lie still,' again he said,/Then he raced across the prairie and waved the blanket o'er his head." His fellow cowboys can only watch in awe. "He has saved the boss's daughter, though we know he's bound to die." Utah succeeds in turning the cattle away from Lenore, then turns and pulls his gun. "He was bound to die a-fighting, as all brave cowboys do." Although he shoots the lead steer, the herd does crush Utah. The lesson of Utah's sacrifice is emphasized in the next stanza. Lenore goes unmentioned. "Every boy upon the cow ranch knew how bravely Utah died, / And they passed his grave in sorrow and they spoke his name with pride; / For he died as a cowboy, never bending, never a fear, / When the cattle were upon him and the rush of death was near." In the last stanza we learn that Utah was buried with "that very red blanket that brought him to his end" (Lomax 1938, 125–28).

One of the key moments in this narrative is when the red blanket shows underneath the saddle. Just beneath a layer of cowboy utility, indeed under Lenore's seat, lies a hidden passion. Lenore shows her inadequacy first by displaying this passion and then by falling to the ground at the obvious result, when the animals go out of control. The next key moment is when the cinches fail. The tools of cowboy presociety are strained beyond their limits when forced to carry the weight of both men and women. Finally, Utah snatches up the blanket, retrieving the emblem of passion from the unworthy, and, running across the prairie, he waves it over his head only in the moment of his death. Verging on parody, this ballad sings of masculine virtue enacted and admired. When the homosocial utopia of the cattle trail is disrupted by the presence of Lenore, Utah's sacrifice redeems the community, and all the boys in the camp learn the lesson. The narrator loved Utah Carroll. He can only think of him in his grave with the red blanket wrapped around him. This love is a self-love, the love of an image of who the cowboy should be. Through the song, the love of the narrator is transformed into the love of the singer and then identified with the love of the listener. All of these desires, misrecognized in the mirror of popular song, reproduce the passionate attachment to the idealized western male.

Lomax intended his collection to be "frankly . . . popular" (Lomax 1910, xxix). Although it was funded as an academic enterprise, he hoped there would be a larger audience for his work. By the 1919 publication of his second volume of cowboy songs, *Songs of the Cattle Trail and Cow Camp*, popularity had become his main concern. In this second book, Lomax admittedly included songs collected from newspapers and even "Western verse" written and published by contemporary authors. The level of overt romanticizing in the introduction was much higher. The commercial value of cowboy song collections had been demonstrated, and was enhanced by the elements of romantic nostalgia that Lomax emphasized in his new introduction. "Herein, again, through these quondom songs we may come to appreciate something of the spirit of the big West . . . may sense, at least in some small measure, the service, the glamour, the romance of that knight-errant of the plains—the American cowboy."[12] As the nation grew increasingly complex, urbanized, and industrialized, this mythical identity, rooted in a presocial utopia, grew more attractive. The academic work of folk song collectors like Lomax contributed not only to the development of a canon of song but also to the commercial production of popular cowboy lore. This industrially disseminated culture would soon come to promulgate these cultural values, the beliefs and desires rooted in the mythic presociety of the Texan cowboy, throughout the southwest, and eventually across the country.

The effects of Lomax's canon formation can be directly observed in the career of an early professional singing cowboy. RCA-Victor copyrighted the phrase "The Original Singing Cowboy" for its recordings of Jules Verne Allen released in the late twenties and early thirties. Allen had acted in cowboy movies in Hollywood and played cowboy roles on radio dramas in Dallas and San Antonio. He had also grown up working as a cowboy on ranches throughout Texas. In 1933, Allen published a book version of his popular San Antonio radio shows. *Cowboy Lore* includes definitions of cowboy terms, jokes, stories from Allen's youth in the cattle trade, and a detailed and illustrated explanation of cattle brands. Half of the book is taken up with cowboy songs—in Allen's words, "taken down from my voice, just as I sing them." Allen claims the same authority by which Lomax authenticated his collection twenty-three years previously, that of lived experience, "in the main most of [the songs] are presented here just as I learned them on the range."[13] The collection includes thirty-six songs. All but three of them were previously published in Lomax's collection. Of those three, one was written for Allen's recording career; the other two are the noncowboy songs, "Barbra Allen" and "Buffalo Gals."[14] Whether Allen learned the other thirty-three songs on the range or not, the versions published in his book were nearly identical to those in Lomax's collection. The commercial representation promulgated by Allen over the radio did not significantly differ from the academic representation disseminated by Lomax in journals or at the meetings of learned societies.

Whether Allen learned his songs directly from the Lomax collection is not so important as the demonstration that, by 1933, the traditional cowboy song canon had been formed. Cowboy songs existed before the work of John Lomax. They had even been collected and published before. However, once this canon was established, the conventions that defined "cowboy songs"—necessarily imbued with conscious and unconscious political and social assumptions—began to limit the types of experiences and expressions that fit the qualifier "cowboy." Lomax's canon codified "a set of practices normally governed by overtly or tacitly accepted rules . . . which seek to inculcate certain values and norms of behavior." Just as Eric Hobsbawm claims for all invented traditions, these songs were used to establish "the membership of groups, real or artificial communities," the legitimation of "institutions, status or relations of authority," and "the inculcation of beliefs, value systems, and conventions of behavior."[15] After the moment of canonization, a song had to display a certain set of characteristics to achieve the status of a cowboy song. The tradition of cowboy songs then carried social and political meanings that worked to legitimate specific musical events as the authentic expressions of a dominant social group. When a Jules Verne Allen, who did spend his youth in cow camps and on cattle trails, published identical arrangements of the same songs that appear in Lomax's collection, he was clearly borrowing the authority of this invented tradition in order to authenticate his own status in much the same fashion as Lomax himself borrowed the authority of an academic tradition to legitimate his status as a serious scholar. By this point, a discourse of cowboy authenticity was already constructing the cultural practices and, indeed, the lived experience of some Texans.

The Popular Dissemination of the Cowboy Singer

Whether or not cowboy songs were ever functionally integrated into the life of the cattle trade, by the end of the 1920s the cowboy singer was a professional entertainer participating in a commercial medium. The industrial dissemination of the cowboy image wouldn't reach its full speed until the late 1930s, but the commercial viability of cowboy-related cultural products began to accelerate throughout the twenties. During this decade, J. Frank Dobie, an English professor, Texas historian, and folklorist, was publishing articles and books on cowboy lore for ever-increasing audiences. Cowboy singers were performing on record and on the radio. Powerful radio stations began broadcasting barn dance programs, distributing a specific representation of rural culture into the homes of both rural and newly urbanized listeners. In January 1923, WBAP out of Fort Worth, Texas, broadcasted the first national barn dance. Carl Sprague recorded "When the Work's All Done This Fall" (included in Lomax's 1910 edition of *Cowboy Songs*) for Victor in 1925. Sprague insisted that he learned all his songs while he was sitting around campfires with "real cowboys." But it was his recording that sold over 900,000 copies.[16] Oscar Fox was a classically trained composer who directed the choral society at the University of Texas. As early as 1924, while Lomax was also working at UT, Fox copyrighted arrangements of several songs from Lomax's collection. In 1925 the Carl Fischer company of New York published Fox's arrangement of "Home on the Range." The song became a best-seller in 1933 after it was used in the Broadway play "Green Grow the Lilacs," and Franklin Roosevelt declared it to be one of his favorites. The copyright became the object of lawsuits when numerous people claimed to have written "Home on the Range."[17] It was becoming increasingly difficult to blend theories of communal composition with capitalist notions of cultural property. Nevertheless, the claim of authenticity—that a song came directly from a "real" cowboy and therefore was related to the presocial origins of Texan society and the idealized western male—would add to a song's appeal, its popularity, and its profit potential.

As part of his work with the choral society at the university, Oscar Fox produced programs of cowboy songs taken from Lomax's collection. On July 1, 1927, Fox presented a lecture-concert that included versions of "Home on the Range," "Sam Bass," "Cowboy's Lament," and other ballads. The singer was a young law student with dramatic aspirations named Woodward Maurice Ritter, later known as Tex.[18] Ritter never claimed authentic cowboy status for himself, but his interest in cowboy culture was piqued by his contact with Lomax, Dobie, and Fox at the University of Texas. By 1928, he was a singing cowboy on KPRC in Houston, and then in 1930 Ritter moved to New York to pursue an acting career.[19] There he almost immediately landed a part in the Theater Guild's production of Lynn Rigg's "Green Grow the Lilacs."

"Green Grow the Lilacs" was called a folk-play by the New York critics. It was alternately hailed and reviled for representing too clearly the rituals, the lifeways, and the emotions of "the folks of the cornfields and the prairies."[20] Ritter won an actual acting role in the production, but he also joined in with the dozen singers who were hired solely to perform "authentic songs of the plains" between the scenes of the play. This "ensemble of cowboys and Oklahoman maidens . . . were vivid and pliant, earthy and folksy, alive and urgent," and were recruited from the Madison Square Garden rodeo.[21] Many obliging critics and reviewers touted their cowboy authenticity in articles that described their abilities to perform rodeo tricks. Arthur Chapman made the point in the *New York Herald-Tribune* that, "it is doubtful if the New York public realizes how far the Theater Guild has gone in quest of reality. A first-class rodeo could be organized right out of the cast now performing at the Guild."[22] During the Boston previews, Franklin Jordan wrote for the *Transcript* that, "Most of these cowboy actors are followers of rodeos and almost without exception have taken one or more honors in various events during the year." Nevertheless, "Though they have been in Wild West shows and in the movies, their first speaking part onstage brought out a streak of shyness."[23]

Margaret Larkin performed the lead cowgirl singing role during the Boston run. In her own book of cowboy songs she repeated a distinction she learned from this performing troupe. "Cowboys usually enjoy teaching their songs to an unpretentious tenderfoot, but they are likely to criticize Drug Store, Moving Picture, and Radio cowboy singers on the ground that they are unable to ride a bucking horse. I have heard some of the best known cowboy singers condemned as follows, 'What does he know about cowboy songs? He never was nothing but a honky-tonk singer. He don't know a maverick from a branding iron.'"[24] Despite the fact that he was a radio cowboy singer, Tex Ritter had been academically trained in cowboy lore, received from Dobie, Fox, and Lomax, and this training enabled his performance in this staged display of authentic cowboy life that was wholly convincing to the most sophisticated east coast theater critics. Ritter went from Broadway to singing on the popular WHN radio barn dance in New York. His performances on this radio station caught the ear of movie producers looking to cash in on the craze of Hollywood singing cowboys and, in 1936, Ritter moved to California.[25]

During the thirties, Hollywood had become fascinated with singing cowboys. In 1930 Ken Maynard starred in the movie "Songs of the Saddle" and began his successful career of combining the narratives of his own cowboy songs with the plots of cowboy movies. Gene Autry had a small part in Maynard's "In Old Santa Fe," but soon moved on to starring roles of his own. Autry's first feature was "Tumbling Tumbleweeds" in 1935 and, by this point, the cinematic link between Texas, cowboys, and song was complete.[26] When Tex Ritter moved to Hollywood in 1936, his training, his accent, and his documented Texan roots marked him as a more authentic alternative to Gene Autry and Ken Maynard.[27] Ritter's first big cowboy hit was "Jingle, Jangle, Jingle," written by Cindy Walker. But among his early successful recordings was a version of "Goodbye Ol' Paint," which he first sang with Oscar Fox in 1927.[28] Ritter's use of songs from the Lomax collection contributed to his reputation as a real cowboy and a real Texan. Even on the large screen, in opulent movie palaces, the real Texan was the real cowboy, and the real cowboy sang real cowboy songs, however they were learned.

Obviously, some Texans were included and some were excluded by this discourse as it spread throughout the popular culture of movies, radio, and records. Hispanics and Native Americans were the targets of much of the easy violence of the cowboy. The dominant rationale for the separation from Mexico and the founding of the Republic of Texas was to enable the Anglo cotton farmers to continue the practice of racial slavery. Women were by definition excluded from the homosocial utopia of the cattle trail.[29] And just as obviously, the category of cowboy songs in no way exhausts the plethora of musics produced in Texas in the early decades of the twentieth century. The Deep Ellum section of Dallas was the home for a thriving blues community, centered on the performances of Blind Lemon Jefferson and Huddie Ledbetter. Hispanic communities in San Antonio, El Paso, and smaller towns throughout the Rio Grande valley boasted large dance bands that blended traditional Latin tonalities and rhythms with jazz instrumentation, creating orquesta and norteno music. Small towns in central Texas featured polka bands and traditional Central European song and dance styles.[30]

However, the image of the authentic cowboy inherited from Lomax's initial formation continued to describe the dominant cultural power in terms of an idealized Anglo-Saxon male rooted in a presocial masculine utopia: autonomous, strong, independent, acquisitive, free from the constraints of society, generous, impulsive, quick to anger and willing to use violence to settle disputes, distrustful of women but capable of a rigidly constrained sentimentality. The more closely a Texan male approximated the cowboy model, the more authority accrued to his cultural practice. The more aspects of the authentic cowboy he could identify with, introject into the construction of his own ego, and project with his performances, the more closely he could approach the cultural power of the dominant group in Texan society.

Cowboy songs themselves were an amalgamation of a variety of musical practices, developed by many different groups of people. But in the process of canonization, because of the conditions under which such canonization occurred, certain attributes of these songs were deemed to be definitive. They had to be the communal creations of males of Anglo-Saxon descent engaged in a particular occupation. The canon simultaneously defined the cultural practice and the people who engaged in the cultural practice by describing the songs as the direct expression of a way of life. Rather than dispelling the romantic myth of the cowboy that had already become popular, cowboy songs contributed to its strength. But at the same time, linking the definition of the cowboy to an ongoing cultural practice of popular music opened the door to a process of redefinition that continues today.

Obviously, popular music is not the only field in which such negotiation takes place. But it is an important one. Because of its simultaneous aesthetic and social textures, along with its peculiarly motile relationship with the rising culture industries, Texan music provided the cultural site where the cowboy, the idealized western male, was first reduced from the specifics of Lomax's son of the South to the abstract set of characteristics I have enumerated. Through the cultural practice of popular music, new groups negotiated their way into this discourse, becoming authentic Texans through their demonstrated ability to perform authentic Texan music. The varieties of Texan music continued to intermingle, borrowing from and mutually influencing one another. Each new identification was a transformation, a translation that retained something of the original structure but that introduced change as well. The field of authentic Texan music began to include more than cowboy songs even as each newly won authenticity was anchored by reference to the newly transformed cowboy image.

From Jimmie Rodgers to Honky-Tonks: The Modernization of a Cultural Practice

In 1929, Jimmie Rodgers, the most popular hillbilly singer in the country, moved to Kerrville, Texas, forty-five miles west of Austin. Suffering from tuberculosis, Rodgers was drawn to the sanatoriums in the small hill-country town. Rodgers was born in Mississippi and had lived in a number of places throughout the South. But as still happens in central Texas when a successful musician moves to town, he was warmly welcomed and instantly referred to as a local hero. There is one publicity still of Rodgers in a cowboy outfit, taken right after he moved to Texas. But he never performed in this outfit, and he only recorded two songs with cowboy themes. The importance of Jimmie Rodgers to the development of the Austin music scene is more transitional than iconic. Jimmie Rodgers was the first star of commercial hillbilly music. He translated the image of the singing cowboy's idealized male into the successful professional musician. Rodgers's recording career mapped the core of the traditional southern masculine hero onto a modern commercialized landscape. Jimmie Rodgers lived out the narrative of the independent entrepreneur who, through hard work and determination, transformed nature for a generously shared profit, and he did it in the new medium of the record business.[31] No longer did the southern hero have to sing of his work at the cow camp, no longer did cowboy songs have to echo the rhythm of the strolling pony, no longer were these songs the anonymous production of an impersonal folk. Instead, a singer could live the myth of the independent cowboy by turning his own natural resource—his voice, his personality, his very self—into a highly desirable commodity. By writing and singing songs that communicated a very personal style, a son of the South could, in effect, transform personal nature for mutual profit, through the magic of radio and records.

Even as Rodgers and his record company were turning his talent into a marketable commodity, his success was dependent upon an audience who now bought its music, either directly—on records—or indirectly—by listening to specific radio programs. This broad change, the development of the culture of consumption, enabled the transformation of the cowboy singer reflecting a life of independent autonomy into a professional entertainer achieving a life of independent autonomy through the marketing of cultural products. What remained constant were the masculine virtues displayed in the songs and the images of the stars. Rodgers inspired probably thousands of young Texans to try their hand, not at cattle raising, nor at oil well drilling, but at singing, writing, and selling songs.

Ernest Tubb was one of the many so inspired. As a youth, Tubb enjoyed the songs and stories of Jules Verne Allen, listening to Allen's program on WFAA out of Dallas. But it wasn't until he heard a Jimmie Rodgers song that he decided to become a professional musician.[32] Tubb searched out Mrs. Jimmie Rodgers in San Antonio in 1935 after finding her name in the phone book. She encouraged him to continue singing because she thought that he sounded sincere and believable, that audiences could tell how he felt. Mrs. Rodgers felt that this was the key to Jimmie's success. He sang sincerely, so the audience could identify with real feelings; their feelings could become identified with Rodgers's through his performance of genuine expression. After six more years of struggle, Ernest Tubb had his big hit, "Walking the Floor," which sold over 400,000 copies in 1941. The success of the song won him a movie contract. In Hollywood, western director Charles Starrett tried to get Tubb to sing "one of those old cowboy songs like Jules Verne Allen used to sing. I told them, I used to sing 'em, but those kind of songs are dead. Why bring me out here in the first place, if it wasn't to sing 'Walking the Floor Over You'?"[33] Indeed, by the time that this young man who had learned cowboy songs by listening to Jules Verne Allen on the radio and who learned all of Jimmie Rodgers's songs from his records had his own hit, the commercial performance of masculine independence, strength, and spontaneity required that every singer have an individual style and an individual sound.

Tubb changed the image of hillbilly music. He insisted that the company for which he recorded, Decca, market his records under the category of "country" music. By 1949, the important trade magazine *Billboard* had renamed its hillbilly charts, following Decca's lead.[34] Through his focus on the power of this image and this marketing label, Tubb emphasized the connections between the musical projection of Texan identity and commercial recording success. Another important change accompanied this modification of image. Tubb did not sing in the high tenor range common to Anglo-Saxon male folksinging. His relaxed tonality and lower range were more suited to the recording and broadcasting technologies of his day. Paradoxically, this contributed to the authenticity of feeling communicated in his singing; in the media where it was more frequently heard, Tubb's voice sounded more "real," more like the voices heard everyday by his fans.

Apparently, Ernest Tubb's songs directly reflected his life and therefore directly communicated to his audience. However, Tubb's sincerity was wholly a performance style. Thirty-five years after the first success of "Walking the Floor" he could still sing that song with the same emotive signs of genuine feeling.[35] The fact that the song still sounded convincing to his audience speaks to the endurance of this genre of sincere performance and the cultural power of the signs associated with it.

This genre of "sincere" country and western performance was most clearly and importantly displayed at a specific cultural site known as the honky-tonk.[36] During the 1920s, the oil fields of the Permian Basin began pumping dollars into rural Southern Baptist communities. The Depression exacerbated the differences between those still dependent on a farm economy and those successful individuals whose land held oil. The honky-tonk was one of the important social institutions for negotiating the conflicts between poor rural families with strict religious backgrounds and a rising generation of newly wealthy and newly urbanized Texans. Such conflicting cultural values often could battle within a single person, when one who was raised in one world came of age into another.

Every social and economic system excludes elements of humanity from its productive processes. But these excluded elements cannot remain permanently repressed. Cultures develop traditions of expression and celebration that display excluded elements, usually transformed, exaggerated, or intensified.[37] Traditionally, celebrations of release require sensory stimulation at multiple levels simultaneously. Music, dancing, contrasting visual levels of light and darkness, food and drink, all contribute to an intoxication of the senses that allows for the recognition and pleasurable acknowledgment of repressed areas of the human. In the disciplined homosocial work world of the cattle trail, this release came in the frontier towns, where the cowboys "tripped the fantastic toe to wretched music" with "beings fully degraded as the most vile."[38] With the regularity of the seasons, these workers made their way up the trail to a special place where, flush for a moment, they could display exaggerated forms of the skills they used in their work, invert value systems otherwise necessary for survival, and satisfy appetites elsewhere denied. With the end of the cattle trails, the cowboy carnival moved into other arenas. The traditions of the county fair and the rodeo filled the need for an exaggerated display of skills and a celebration of the harvest, and many of these fairs and rodeos held dances in the evenings. But such dances tended to remain fairly calm, more a place for stable family entertainment. The site where values were inverted, where the culturally repressed returned, and where the tensions and conflicts of a changing social world were fought over became the honky-tonk.[39]

Generally located on or near the city limits, on the margins between country and town where law enforcement was less consistent, honky-tonks began as a place to buy bootlegged whiskey during Prohibition. They were a favorite hang-out for men who worked in the oil fields. People who lived in the city would drive just out of the jurisdiction of the local police and drink and dance to the band or to records on the juke box. People who lived in the country would drive to the edge of the city for the regular display of music and lights and movement and liquor. Honky-tonks were magical places where promises were made and new possibilities of life could be imagined in the free recombination of repressed elements of the human. While carnivals, frontier towns, and rodeos were tied to the seasons, available only at certain times of the year, the honky-tonk was continually present. In the same way that the cultural practice of folksinging became a commercial medium for popular entertainment, the cultural practice of carnival was transformed into the commercially oriented honky-tonk.

The liminal arena had moved to the edge of town where it could be entered any night the cowboy desired. As Bill Malone argues, the music responded to this context of intensified physical release by emphasizing its rhythms. Focusing on its role as dance music, highlighting its African-American influences, honky-tonk drums and bass, accompanied by firmly struck electric guitars, laid down a beat loud enough to be heard over conversation and drinking noises, steady enough for the most lame-footed cowboy to dance to.[40] And so country and western music, as it now began to be called, took a dominant role in the dialectical modernization of Texan life. Here the commercialized country and western star could perform the role of the traditional masculine hero in an increasingly rigidified, ritualized, and controlled—because marketed—version of the carnival.

In the honky-tonks, as in all carnival traditions, the rituals, images, and symbols of corporeality, sexuality, and sexual relations formed a ripe field for the negotiation of cultural tensions. The turmoil derived from modernizing a rural culture that had rooted its values in a premodern homosocial utopia was displayed, heightened, critiqued, and lived in the previously hidden arena of sexuality. As systemic capitalism grew ever more successful in producing a subject whose desires could be instantly aroused by the latest styles, the genre of cheating and drinking songs became quite popular.

In 1951 Hank Thompson recorded "The Wild Side of Life."[41] The text is set to the same traditional tune and sung in the same tempo Roy Acuff used to glorify the Bible in "Great Speckled Bird." But Thompson adds the steady beat and the singing steel guitars of the honky-tonk style to Acuff's sparse accompaniment. Thompson sings from the discursively constructed position of masculine virtue identified with a performance style that reinforces its authority, but the song's lyrics describe a world of instantly remolded desires, shaped anew each night in the honky-tonk. The song contains generic signs of sincere expression as the narrator, singing directly to the angel, puts his private feelings into song because she wouldn't read his letter if he wrote to her.

Implicitly, the singer met his angel in the honky-tonk, where the modernization of culture is played out. A conservative critique of modern capitalism is aimed at this "gay night life" where "the wine and liquor flow." There, in the fluid, modernizing world of the honky-tonk, the angel waits to be "anybody's baby." Her desires are not her own, instead they can be stimulated by any passing object. The narrator of "Wild Side of Life" was the truest love she'll ever know, a sincere, stable model of premodern masculine virtue. He once loved her, and she is still an angel. But even though the honky-tonk itself causes her infidelity, she willingly goes back there every night. The desires produced within an intoxicating modernity cannot easily be left behind. He "might have known [she'd] never make a wife." From the conservative perspective articulated by country and western music, social forces are not capable of producing such subjective, private feelings. Therefore, only God could have made her that way.

Months after the release of Thompson's hit, in perhaps the finest answer song ever recorded, Kitty Wells sang, "It Wasn't God Who Made Honky-tonk Angels."[42] Using again the same melody and the honky-tonk style, Wells snaps up the tempo and sings with a barely restrained vibrato. She insists that, "Too many times married men think they're still single. That has caused many a good girl to go wrong." In this song, the sociosexual hierarchy is inverted and all broken hearts are "because there always was a man to blame." Honky-tonk angels are not the creation of the supreme being, but instead are forged by the duplicitous actions of men. Kitty Wells's performance provides a challenge to the discursive construction of masculine virtue and authority, giving voice to women's sense of frustration both at the shifting desires of the men around them, and at bearing the blame, in the male version of the story, for the cultural disruption.

In the honky-tonk—a magical modern marketplace of pleasure and possibility—social, economic, and cultural tensions are deflected into the realm of sexual relations. There they are lived, felt, and experienced. The language of honky-tonk romance, which includes a musical style, a performance style, and an encoded moral history, structures these tensions into generic expressions of good love gone bad that necessarily carry a nostalgic air, a look backward to better times.

In the modernized marketplace, signs do not have stable meanings, and desires are instantly created and instantly disappear. This unstable context informs the paradox of the honky-tonk. The processes of modernization, which disrupt older cultural practices and replace them with signs and commodities, enable the constant presence of the carnival arena. Only within the commercially enforced boundaries separating honky-tonk reality from the rest of the world does it becomes possible to display, in an intensified sexualized form, the most troubling aspects of contemporary life. For the generation of white Texans reaching maturity immediately after World War II, these aspects reflected the effects of powerful economic forces, the solidification of a class structure, the rising wealth of some and the lingering poverty of others, the increasing use of culture to signify distinction, the development of the cultural marketplace, and the commodification of cultural practice. Other Texans and other generations would deal with different sets of conflicts. But the Austin music scene was built on this foundation of a commercialized cultural tradition of popular music, centered in the liminal arenas of honky-tonks, and performed with an assumed air of Anglo-Saxon masculine moral authority inherited from the mythical presocial origins of the state of Texas through the discourse of cowboy lore.

CHAPTER THREE

Desperados Waiting for a Train
The Development of Progressive Country Music

Throughout the summer and the fall of 1933, the Texas state legislature busied itself debating the proper method of licensing drinking establishments. The twenty-first amendment had returned to each state the authority to regulate the sale of alcoholic beverages. But the liquor issue was not a simple matter in Texas. The large state, torn between its vast but sparsely populated rural spaces and its growing urban centers, encompassing extensive German and Latin cultures to whom the reformist motives of the Anglos made little sense, had depended upon a system of county control before federal prohibition had been enforced. The gubernatorial election of 1911 had been fought over the prohibition issue. After the single federal standard was repealed, no immediate consensus could be formed to replace it. While county control seemed again to be the obvious compromise, the old reformist bloc hoped to retain a prohibition on liquor, allowing for only the sale of beer and wine in the state.[1]

However, sentiment in the capital city ran toward total legalization. On October 3, 1933, The *Austin American* published an anonymous article calling for a twofold system of liquor licensing. Its argument took the form of an analogy between tastes in liquor and tastes in music. Just as there were clearly two types of music, and two distinct groups of people who appreciated each, there were two types of alcoholic beverages, and two distinct populations of drinkers. "High-brow people" preferred "high-brow music" and cocktails; others could rest content with beer and wine and the rough sounds of less than polished entertainment. Since it would be clearly inappropriate to mix these two groups of people in the same establishment, the obvious solution was to create two types of licenses. The more expensive liquor license would allow for the proper atmosphere in downtown hotels, while the cheaper beer and wine license could be purchased by any saloon in the county. The *American* reasoned that while each citizen of Texas had the right to his personal taste in alcohol and in music, a clear homology existed between the two. Beer and hillbilly music marked the pleasures of the low-brow.[2]

An oft-repeated legend (in fact almost always acknowledged as a legend when repeated) insists that Kenneth Threadgill bought the first beer and wine license issued in Travis County in 1933.[3] The building that housed Threadgill's Bar had been an old gasoline station located near the northernmost edge of the town. The legend also says that, during Prohibition, customers at the filling station often bought a gallon of hooch with their gasoline. What is known for sure is that Kenneth Threadgill bought the place in the middle thirties and furnished the front room of the station with a few old round tables, about twenty or thirty chairs, and two old coolers stashed behind a countertop. By 1946, he was selling soda pop and beer out of those coolers while some of his friends played guitar or fiddle and sang hillbilly songs.[4] Threadgill had taught himself to yodel after he heard Jimmie Rodgers perform in 1928, developing "a pretty large repertory of Jimmie Rodgers' songs" as well as a few phrases and verses of even older, more traditional, material. By the middle nineteen-fifties, Shorty Ziegler, Cotton Collins, and a few other local singers and musicians were congregating first on Friday nights and later on Wednesdays to sing a few of their favorite songs and drink a few of their favorite beers. While Mr. Threadgill tended bar, the musicians would perform for fun and one or two free rounds; his few steady customers would pay for their drinks, listen to the musicians, and occasionally join in the singing.[5]

Most of Threadgill's customers during this period were local working men—mechanics, day laborers, and "cedar choppers." But by 1959, a group of graduate students from the university had discovered the pleasures of the low-brow. Bill Malone was writing a dissertation on the history of the country music business. Stan Alexander was an English graduate student who loved traditional folk songs and ballads. Willie Benson was devoting equal attention to the study of psychology and bluegrass guitar, while Ed Mellon was playing the mandolin and idolizing Bill Monroe. These four young men had been meeting regularly in Mellon's apartment, listening to and trying to copy the recordings of traditional and bluegrass material that they had discovered in the Austin public library. Once Willie Benson heard about Threadgill's, he dragged the quartet out to the bar, where they played "at least once a week, and sometimes more, for three or four years."[6]

The enthusiasm that these graduate students shared for older music endeared them immediately to the regular performers and customers of the old honky-tonk. For the first two years that the group of graduate students performed at Threadgill's, the music they played was exclusively the music of the older generation—oldtime country and bluegrass. Benson would back up Mr. Threadgill while he yodeled his Jimmie Rodgers songs. Shorty Ziegler would announce the keys for each song so that the younger musicians could play along. "We're going to do this one in A. A as in Aig," Shorty would holler and then emphasize the rhythm with his "sock" style of guitar playing. Malone and Alexander would sing duets like "Gathering Flowers from the Hillside," and every now and then the four younger musicians would cut loose on one of their bluegrass numbers. Since almost everyone who came to Threadgill's on Wednesday nights could sing at least a little, there was not much distinction between performer and audience. Only during the virtuoso performances of the bluegrass ensemble and the yodeling of Mr. Threadgill was a clear difference in musical ability displayed.[7]

At first, the graduate students brought only a few close friends with them and the audience, small as it was, remained basically the same people who had drunk and sung at Threadgill's for over ten years. But gradually, the reputation of this little bar spread. In 1960, the university added a "folksinger" to the faculty of its English department. Soon after Roger Abrahams arrived that fall, he was introduced to Malone and Alexander and to Threadgill's. Abrahams also became the faculty sponsor of a folksinging club that met at the Chuckwagon in the student union. On the college campuses of the east coast, folksinging had become a popular pastime, as students attempted to recreate the conditions of premodern, precommercialized cultural practice. Because of the sense of active participation that came from amateur group singing, the folk songs themselves seemed to be more meaningful than popular songs on the radio. During the folk song revival Oscar Brand wrote, "For many, folk music has become an antidote to the conformity induced by our mass culture."[8]

In Austin, folksinging quickly became a way of marking one's difference from the student body represented by fraternities, sororities, and football players. Students from small towns throughout Texas who felt that their lives differed from the conservative meanings traditionally available were attracted to the folksinging club. John Clay, Powell St. John, Lanny Wiggins, Janis Joplin, Tary Owens, and others latched onto the singing of traditional folk songs as a way of actively demonstrating their difference—their "beatnik" or "proto-hippie" status. The reconstruction of a traditional, noncommercial musical practice carried an aura of authenticity. That is, participation in these performances indicated an interest in musical pleasure for its own sake, freed from any direct articulation with the commercialized and, according to the ideology of authenticity, debased world of everyday life in Texas. According to a letter John Clay wrote in 1972, "Looking back on the situation, it seems there was a generation gap affecting the early Sixties scene, but not like the one they talk about today. People like Janis and me and the others I mentioned were rejecting the standards of our own generation."[9]

The actual group of undergraduate folksingers was small but, by all accounts, intense and active. Several of them lived together in a run-down apartment complex near campus called the Ghetto. Once a week, they would congregate in the Chuckwagon area of the union to take turns passing around instruments and singing. By the time Tary Owens arrived in the fall of 1961, the Folk Sing was an important weekly gathering of members from a variety of alienated groups on campus. Writers and illustrators for the satirical campus humor magazine, *The Ranger*, were regular participants. Individuals coordinating local civil rights demonstrations recruited new members at the sing-along. Even a group of cave explorers, the spelunkers, was attracted to this practice.[10]

But it was the committed core group—Clay, Owens, and the trio of St. John, Wiggins, and Joplin—who directed each week's singing and who led the excursion out to Threadgill's. According to Owens, "We heard that Mr. Threadgill had a bar out there and that musicians were welcome." By reputation, the Wednesday night gatherings at Threadgill's were dominated by bluegrass music. As the most accomplished performer of this genre among the undergraduates, Lanny Wiggins was the first of this group to venture out to Threadgill's. But he was quickly followed by the other members of his band, the Waller Creek Boys (Powell St. John and Janis Joplin), and then Clay and Owens. Eventually, these younger student musicians became part of the regular performers at Threadgill's, joining Bill Neely, Cotton Collins, Shorty Ziegler, and the graduate students.

By the fall of 1962, the gatherings at Threadgill's had become, in Bill Malone's words, a "raucous" occasion. That year, Malone began teaching in San Marcos; consequently, the frequency of his attendance at Threadgill's diminished. But he noted that "the clientele changed dramatically" once Wiggins, St. John, Joplin, and Owens arrived. And so did the repertoire. The younger musicians brought with them a grow-ing entourage of fellow students as well as the taste for and desire to perform blues and jugband music. Where the bluegrass performers had played strictly acoustically, the crowd brought by the undergraduates necessitated the use of a microphone and a small, old amplifier to render the singer audible. Yet, Threadgill wholeheartedly welcomed his new customers, and they, in turn, gave him the respect and attention tradi-tionally tendered a patriarchal figure. When he came out from behind the bar to sing, the room grew quiet. For this younger audience, Kenneth Threadgill embodied the position of moral authority that had been tra-ditionally constructed through popular musical practice in Texas. When Mr. Threadgill yodeled his versions of Jimmy Rodgers's "T for Texas" or "Waitin' for a Train," he was performing his identification with a com-plex tradition. Through his singing, Threadgill evoked both the origi-nary myth of the Texan presocial utopia and the entrepreneur who could transform his personal resources for mutual profit. In turn, when the younger musicians sang their own versions of the traditional material, they were projecting their specific identifications with this set of in-herited positions, reinterpreting them for a new generation. The atmo-sphere in the bar remained one of mutual respect, as the eighteen- and nineteen-year-old musicians listened to and learned honky-tonk coun-try songs like "Wild Side of Life," "Your Cheating Heart," and "Waltz Across Texas," while the older musicians admired the musical and vocal talents of the youngsters.[11]

Ironically, this practice of performing traditional folksongs as well as commercial country hits with "real folk" on the outskirts of town became a way for these nontraditional students to separate themselves from their undergraduate peers. Thus, by the winter of 1962–1963, musical taste and musical practice were established in Austin as the most significant indicators of cultural difference among the generally white, middle-class students at the University of Texas. The hip sang "Jimmy Brown the Schoolboy" and "Six Pack to Go" under the tutelage of older white working men near the edge of the city limits, while the mainstream twisted to Chubby Checker records at parties near campus.[12]

The high degree of conservatism prevalent among the majority of students at Texas resulted in a harsh counterattack on the most threaten-ing representative of the folksinging group. Janis Joplin had a clear, high voice equally capable of imitating Jean Ritchie, Rose Maddox, or Bessie Smith. She also liked to drink, wear jeans, go barefoot, and flaunt her disregard for the straitjacket of femininity prescribed by traditional gen-der roles. It was the latter transgression that most offended the fraternity members on campus. After tolerating her presence for only a single semester, they blatantly acknowledged the power of her threat, naming her "the ugliest male on campus." In January 1963, Joplin left Austin and hitchhiked to San Francisco with another estranged, ugly male, Chet Helms. In her biography of Joplin, Myra Friedman emphasized the emotional impact of this moment, suggesting that Joplin's journey west was a result of this rejection. But friends of hers in Austin, people like John Clay and Tary Owens, favored a different interpretation. They insisted that the mock election only confirmed what Joplin had believed all along, that Texas was simply too square, too backward, for her to tolerate. Seeing themselves as beatniks, Joplin and Helms headed for the beatnik capital, initiating an Austin-San Francisco exchange of musicians and the culturally hip that would continue for decades.[13]

Meanwhile, the on-campus folksinging club continued to attract both the musical and the disaffected of each year's newly arriving students. Ed Guinn was the son of the third African-American to graduate from the University of Texas medical school. He had idolized his high school band director, and he came to UT to major in music. In his first semester, the fall of 1962, he joined the symphony and the jazz band but found himself barred from the Longhorn Band, the marching musical accompaniment to the most visible symbol of the university's power—its still all-white football team. "I had come as a starry-eyed youth, never dreaming that there would be a color barrier," Guinn told me. "I thought that was something that stopped at back-of-the-bus stuff. You know, that once you left working-class society that that wouldn't be a problem anymore." Believing that he was coming to the intellectual center of the state, Guinn was shocked by this display of intolerance.[14]

By the spring semester of his first year at Texas, Guinn had become a regular participant in the Folk Sing. Soon the diverse rebel groups brought together by folksinging took up Guinn's campaign to join the Longhorn band. That this clearly talented musician could not even obtain an audition for the marching band outraged and engaged the local student-led civil rights movement. They began a letter-writing campaign and gradually increased the pressure on the administration as the school year went by.

In early September 1963, Ed Guinn was given the opportunity to audition for the band. But by this point, he was no longer quite so interested. He was far more involved with the folksinging group than with any of the more official musical organizations. After Guinn passed "their silly audition," he went home and called his father, telling him that he no longer wanted to march. But when he woke up the next morning, the front page of the September 23 *Daily Texan* blared the headline, "Longhorn Band Accepts Negro." The article included a quote from the chair of the Board of Regents, W. W. Heath. Heath insisted that the "Longhorn Band has been integrated for a long time." Ed Guinn was simply the first qualified Negro who had auditioned. As Guinn told me nearly thirty years after the fact, "They decided it was time they had a Negro, and I was the one. But I'll never forget that the first song they had me play in the band was 'Dixie.'" Within two months, Ed Guinn had quit the Longhorn Band, and he soon dropped out of school. Just as Joplin had flaunted her difference from the university mainstream, so Guinn rejected its judgment in order to concentrate full time on playing his own music.[15]

The fall of 1963 brought another young dissident to campus. Jeff Shero had attended Texas A&M and Sam Houston State for a semester each, leaving both schools after organizing civil rights demonstrations for the Student Nonviolent Coordinating Committee. Over the summer, Shero had attended the second convention of the Students for a Democratic Society at Pine Hill, New York. Once he arrived at UT, Shero organized a local chapter of SDS and coordinated protests against the segregated toilets on campus, finding great support among the folksingers. He found that the "alienated and rebel groups were all in alliance in those days, the integrationist groups, the motorcycle riders, the folksingers and the cave explorers." All who differed from the mainstream of approved student behavior had been thrown together in a necessary strategy of survival. He told me that "Folksinging was the music of the time. In the civil rights movement, we'd march and sing. It was fun. And at the university, Thursday was folksinging nights. And in the context of a university dominated by fraternities and sororities, the kind of people who would come to folksinging were the rebel group. But we were so isolated. When you lay out this insurgent group, and this is including everybody, we were about 200 in a sea of 20,000." Not all two hundred would participate in any one event at any one time, but each of these overlapping practices was a way of signifying difference, each contributed to the construction of the radical group of students at the University of Texas.[16]

However, this confluence of difference did not guarantee any specific politics. Despite the fact that folksinging was the music of the civil rights movement and that, during the 1962–63 school year, most of the student members of the folksinging club were also regular customers at Threadgill's, the north-side honky-tonk had never admitted an African-American. "In fact, in the early days, there was some of what we would now call racist material on the walls in Threadgill's," Tary Owens told me. "Early on, there was even an incident where they were going to [formally] ban black people." Ed Guinn was talked out of trying to sing at Threadgill's by John Clay. Clay insisted that Guinn's presence would just be too disruptive. "I had considerable respect for John," Guinn said. "I felt no need to blow up their bucolic scene. They were all my friends, anyway. I was already playing with all of them." However strong the ties between folksinging and the civil rights movement at UT, the most committed participants in both practices did not believe that integrating Threadgill's would be worthwhile. Although Austin's folksingers had incorporated a beatnik willingness to cross racial barriers with their taste for folk music, their belief in the importance of integration conflicted with their respect for this living symbol of the connections between generations—Kenneth Threadgill. Although the associated radical student groups had adopted folksinging as a way of marking their political difference from the Texan mainstream, they could not simply avoid or ignore the conservative elements in this traditional practice. Not even the authenticity of noncommercialized musical performance could guarantee a progressive political stance. It would remain up to the less traditional, commercially oriented folk clubs to present African-American folksingers for their growing young white audience.[17]

The 11th Door was the first explicitly commercial venue for folksinging in town. Owned by Bill Simonson, the club offered the most regular performing opportunities for Mance Lipscomb and Lightnin' Hopkins, as well as Jerry Jeff Walker, Doc Watson, and other touring representatives of the folk revival. In addition to their downtown performances, many of these musicians would drive north to join in the hoots at Threadgill's, lured by the bar's reputation as a haven for the authentic. Joan Baez and the Jim Kweskin Jug Band were among the out-of-town singers who visited the honky-tonk. Such appearances added to the growing fame of Threadgill's, and soon the tiny room was overflowing with an audience of students who had come to listen to, rather than to play, folk music.[18]

Gradually, a quasi-professional group coalesced out of the musicians who were hanging out at Threadgill's. The band, called the Hootenanny Hoots, consisted of Tary Owens, Powell St. John, Lanny Wiggins, Bill Neely, Shorty Ziegler, and Kenneth Threadgill. They were paid "two dollars a night and all the beer we could drink."[19] Other former members of the UT folksinging club were turning professional as well. Ed Guinn had teamed up with a precocious white high school student named Bob Brown. During the 1964–65 school year, these two were spending many nights at the Library, a nightclub where a rock'n'roll band led by John (Toad) Andrews regularly performed. Guinn had never paid much attention to rock or pop music, and the songs that he and Brown were writing on acoustic instruments fit more closely into the folk revival genre. But whenever they went to the Library, "there were lots of girls and lots of action. It was listening to Toad that got us into rock'n'roll. It was what we wanted to do," Guinn told me. In addition, "Toad was playing a lot of clubs, but he was basically making a living playing at fraternity and sorority parties." The excitement of a scene— lots of girls and lots of action—combined with the possibility of earn- ing a living through *playing* music, captured the desires of these young musicians. Guinn and Brown identified with the imaginative possibili- ties signified by Andrews's success, and in the summer of 1965, they decided to buy electric instruments. Along with Powell St. John, Guinn and Brown formed St. John the Conqueroo, one of Austin's first cult rock'n'roll bands.[20]

In 1966, Rod Kennedy opened the Chequered Flag, and there were suddenly two clubs in town where acoustic musicians could be paid for playing their own material. The highest-paying jobs for rock'n'roll musi- cians were the fraternity parties, but these organizations insisted that the bands perform the popular hits of the day. The Conqueroo found themselves in the middle of this split. They aspired to the loud excite- ment and the musical opportunities offered by electric instruments and rock'n'roll, but they had also come out of the folk tradition carrying a distinct anti-mainstream, anti-student-body, and an anti-commercial- music attitude. It is important to emphasize this last point. The Con- queroo rejected commercial music, not the commercialized structure of musical production. The performance of commercial music catered to the tastes of the dominant mainstream of Texan culture. Although Guinn and Brown were eager to make a living from their music, they were not willing to play "Do the Freddie" for the tri-Delta sisters. Un- able to find regular paying gigs downtown, Ed Guinn went over to the east side where he talked Ira Littlefield into letting the Conqueroo play their "crippled hippie folk music with rhythm and blues presumptions" two nights a week at his I.L. Club.[21]

Playing on the east side of Austin, the Conqueroo drove away most of the I.L. Club's regular audience, but they brought with them an audi- ence of their own—girlfriends and fellow dropouts, the first hippies in Austin. According to Guinn, "It worked. The place got pretty crowded, and Ira was making money—as much money as you can make on fifty cents for a quart of beer. It was a slightly difficult marriage of the cultures, with the white guys busy protecting their girlfriends from the black guys, but basically it worked." However, it was a volatile mixture to contain in this period in central Texas. It exploded one night when the band's sound engineer used the word "niggardly" to describe a friend's plan to fix his car. A "barroom brawl" broke out, a gun went off, the police were called, and the Conqueroo's regular east-side gig came to an end. But for much of 1966, this racially mixed band entertained a racially mixed audience with original songs that were written deliberately to flout the conventions of commercial pop music. And, among the young white fans of the band, a bond between a particular taste in music and a particular attitude toward contemporary political and social relations had been again reinforced.[22]

Another ex-member of the folksinging club was perfecting her Bessie Smith imitation during regular shows at the 11th Door that spring. Janis Joplin was again living with her parents in Port Arthur and performing at professional folk clubs in Houston and Beaumont as well as in Austin. Although several of her old friends felt that she had become too polished, in fact, "commercial," others respected her new professionalism, recognizing her efforts to become "one of the great ones." The distinction was crucial.[23]

In the early days of the Folk Sing, the anticommercial stance of the members expressed an anti-mass-culture position. Folksinging had been a means of acknowledging and constructing difference in a heavily conformist cultural milieu. It was a cultural practice that marked out a space within which mainstream culture could be resisted and individual and group identity could be actively produced. However, as the urban folk revival grew and became absorbed into the recording industry, the musical parameters of folk music began to indicate an aesthetically defined genre of popular music. Topical lyrics, smoothly strummed acoustic stringed instruments, occasional but infrequent instrumental interludes (or leads), and closely harmonized sincere vocals indicated a folk, as opposed to rock'n'roll or pop, song. Eventually, this genre of "folk music" produced commercially successful singers whose talent was wholeheartedly admired by Austin's folksingers, and whose success—both artistic and financial, subsumed into the term "professional"—the local musicians desired to emulate. Jimmie Rodgers had been admired in central Texas for his success, for his ability to create and display financial independence through transforming his voice and his presence into an exchangeable commodity. Similarly, the "stars" of the urban folk revival were admired for their ability to perform their independence from mass culture. By enthusiastically identifying with these performers, fans signified their own independence. Therefore, the professional success of Janis Joplin could only tarnish her local reputation if she seemed to be compromising the identity she performed for commercial—that is, mainstream or mass-culture—tastes.

In the meantime, the New Orleans Club had broadened its booking policy beyond dixieland to include local rock'n'roll bands like the Wigs and the 13th Floor Elevators. The Wigs were a commercially oriented band. They featured a young Austin native, Rusty Wier, on drums and played a variety of Rolling Stones and Beatles material. The Elevators stood in opposition to the Wigs, playing their own compositions yet still managing to fill the club. Their ability to draw large crowds of college students was to a large extent derived from the fact that their local single "You're Gonna Miss Me" was receiving top-ten airplay on radio stations throughout central and south central Texas. Yet despite the fact that the Elevators appeared to be commercially successful, receiving AM airplay, they still attracted Austin's hip crowd, those actively distinguishing themselves from the Texas mainstream.[24]

When "You're Gonna Miss Me" was filling the airwaves of central Texas, Tary Owens was producing field recordings of rural east Texan folksingers and storytellers, but the one band he would consistently go to see was the Elevators. According to Owens, "The audience [at Elevators' shows] was mostly students. But there was also a large underground contingent of people—proto-hippies, I don't know what you want to call them—but there were a lot of people that were becoming more and more weird, student drop-outs, artists, writers, there were quite a few of that. And the Jade Room and the New Orleans Club, when the Elevators played there, it was quite a deal."[25]

The Elevators quickly became another of Austin's cult rock'n'roll bands. Their music helped define the genre of psychedelic punk. Harmonically, they used standard blues progressions with at least one and sometimes more than one unexpected chord included in order to force the melody of the song out of its common path away from and back to the tonic. Rather than exploring melodic variation within a standard pop or blues chord change, the vocal line in sixties punk tended not to stray too far from the tonic of the chords. By inserting a drastic chord change—say, by moving to a major triad built on the flatted fifth of the song's key—the Elevators forced their standard melody through an unexpected transition, contributing to a feel of "weirdness" in the song. This was precisely the feel that such a songwriting strategy achieved. An unrelentingly simple yet purposive beat drove the song through this unexpected harmonic transition, emphasizing the feeling in the song of being forced through weirdness. In an analogous move, the Elevators paid twisted tribute to the folk scene in Austin by including an electric jug in their instrumentation. The jug produced a "weird" sound in obbligatos that intertwined through many of their recorded arrangements. Over all of these odd sounds screamed the voice of Roky Erickson, promising difference with the torn shards of his vocal chords.

Onstage, Erickson would enthusiastically endorse the pleasures of drug use, particularly psychedelics. The band wrote songs about tripping, and their record liner notes spoke of being on a quest. Peyote had only recently been outlawed in Texas. For a while Austin's proto-hippies had been able to drive to San Antonio and buy whole peyote plants from Hudson's Wholesale Cactus—"five for a dollar." The promised new awareness, hinted at by the weird music and physically reinforced by psychotropic drugs, maintained the necessary ideological distance between Austin's hip and the ongoing mainstream Texan culture. The hip could mingle with the square in the New Orleans Club while the 13th Floor Elevators performed, smug in their secret knowledge that they shared an understanding with the band of the meaning of the event that no fraternity member could grasp.[26]

This rock'n'roll in Austin was marked by a contradiction at its very heart. It had grown out of the articulation of two opposing practices— folksinging as the marker of youthful distance from mass culture and the honky-tonk commodification of an antimodernist critique. Throughout the early sixties, young people from all regions of Texas had flocked to Austin as a center of cultural possibility, where they could live a bohemian, beatnik, proto-hippie life and mark their own difference from the Texan cultural mainstream through such practices as folksinging, liberal politics, and drug use. However, at the very moment when they were singing the pleasures of immediate, uncommodified, collective difference, they were also dependent upon the recognition and economic support of a system that produced a commodity from their performance.

Austin's hip population could not commercially support all these artists and musicians. Bands found themselves competing with each other for limited resources. Within the structure of the honky-tonk economy, rock'n'roll musicians in Austin could not afford to play only for the converted, the hip. The successful performance of difference required the economic participation of the very mainstream from which the musicians were struggling to distinguish themselves. Because popular musical performance in Austin developed within the context of folksinging's critique of mass culture, professional rock'n'roll musicians found themselves performing a critique of their own practice.

The Elevators soon headed out to San Francisco, where Chet Helms offered them bookings at the Avalon Ballroom. This marked one path to commercial yet nonmainstream success. Rock'n'roll musicians who were unwilling to open their performances to the Texan mainstream could learn their musical skills in the clubs of Austin and then pursue their professional ambitions in the San Francisco Bay area. Boz Scaggs, Toad Andrews, Powell St. John, and Janis Joplin, among others, made just this trip, moving west in search of a hip community large enough to provide economic support for the professional musical expression of cultural difference.

However, for those rock'n'roll musicians who stayed in Austin in the spring of 1967, there were two choices. They could play popular radio hits at private parties and venues like the New Orleans Club, or they could play their own songs for free at outdoor gatherings and occasionally for a slight fee indoors at the Doris Miller Auditorium. Rusty Wier's new band, the Lavender Hill Express, took the first path. The fact that this band could pay its members a regular wage enabled it to attract some of the more technically skilled musicians who had recently moved to the city, like Gary P. Nunn and John Inmon. The Conqueroo chose the second alternative. And consequently, the Conqueroo's continued inability to find steady paying gigs led its soundman, Sandy Lockett, to pool his resources with those of two friends, Gary Scanlon and Huston White, to start the Vulcan Gas Co. Opening in October 1967, the Vulcan soon became, in Ed Guinn's words, a "home for the freaks, where they didn't have to feel like freaks, they could feel at home, and not be hassled by the fraternity and sorority student element." [27]

This home for the freaks made no attempt to obtain a liquor license. Rather than set itself up as another rock'n'roll club, the Vulcan tried to establish itself as an alternative "community center," holding silent film festivals and bake sales in addition to hosting music performances. For a short while, the Vulcan provided a space for rock'n'roll performance that was distanced from the honky-tonk economy. But the absence of even a beer and wine license did not mean the absence of intoxicants. With the Vulcan serving as the alternative community center, all the markers of antimainstream cultural distinction were in full evidence. Marijuana was sold openly from a van parked in front of the hall. Undisciplined youthful sexuality was flagrantly displayed, and the harshly strict codes of appropriate appearance for each gender in Texas were continually violated. Several employees, including the artist Jim Franklin, simply lived in the hall, making it literally their home. [28]

This radical display of difference ensured that the regular business

Turning a commercial liability into a cultural asset: one of Jim Franklin's early flyers for the Vulcan Gas Company.   Courtesy Texas Poster Art Collection, The Center for American History, The University of Texas at Austin.

community would avoid entering into economic relations with the Vulcan. The *Austin American-Statesman* banned all advertising from the home of the freaks. No radio station would announce upcoming shows. Thus the Vulcan came to depend on lavishly illustrated posters and handbills distributed throughout the university area to attract an audience. This visual art was drawn by Gilbert Shelton, Jim Franklin, and other local artists who later became identified with underground comics. Turning a commercial disadvantage into a cultural advantage, the Vulcan initiated a tradition of posting eye-catching flyers along the drag, a tradition that soon developed its own set of aesthetic criteria, offering a pictorial means of expressing difference.[29]

The Vulcan survived for little more than two years, continually requiring new investments and never really breaking even. Toward the end of its tenure as the home of Austin's hip, the most popular band at the Vulcan was Shiva's Head Band. Fronted by Spencer Perskins, Shiva's merged the attitudes of the hip community with commercial success. While Perskins was in college at North Texas State, he had joined the folk club started there by one of the school's English professors, Stan Alexander. Alexander missed the musical communication he had enjoyed at Threadgill's; the folk club at North Texas was an attempt to reconstitute that experience. Many individuals who sang folk songs in Alexander's club moved to Austin in the late sixties and early seventies, but Perskins was the first to merge the attitudes and the style of folk music associated with the Texan folk club—an antimainstream stance and a concentration on lyrics and vocal harmonies—with extended "druggy" improvisational passages. Musically, Shiva's blended the instruments common to a Texan folk club, like a fiddle, a harmonica, and a jug, with electric guitars in arrangements that crafted extended climaxes. Like the Elevators, Shiva's Head Band had managed to gain local radio airplay for an independently released single, "Take Me to the Mountains." This airplay attracted larger audiences than could be drawn by the word-of-mouth method available to unrecorded bands like the Conqueroo. And, in addition to the Vulcan, Shiva's played many free shows and could be counted on to contribute to any benefit that the local hip community might organize.[30]

As their popularity grew, Shiva's Head Band attracted the attention of Capitol Records, a major national company. By 1970, major recording labels had seen the rise of the Liverpool sound and the San Francisco scene. MGM had attempted to market bands from Boston by signing Ultimate Spinach and the Beacon St. Union and by promoting their music as the "Bosstown Sound." Following the herd mentality common to the recording industry, Capitol hoped that the popularity of Shiva's Head Band and the existence of the Vulcan Gas Co. indicated a lively scene in Austin that they could exploit and turn to profit. With that intention, their contract offer to Shiva's included a certain amount of money for Perskins to use in Austin for artist development. This arrangement allowed Shiva's Headband (as Capitol printed their name) a perfect expression of their community orientation. Not only had the band won a major recording contract, but they would be able to help other Vulcan regulars record their music through their operations as Armadillo Productions. Unfortunately, weeks after the deal was finalized, the Vulcan was forced to close its doors for good. Now there was no hip community center, no obvious place to center Armadillo Productions and look for new talent.[31]

When Shiva's Headband signed with Capitol, Perskins hired an old college friend to manage his band and help administer the production company. Eddie Wilson began booking Shiva's Headband into honky-tonks like the Cactus Club just south of the Colorado River. According to Wilson, "It was a smoky little joint that had discovered what hippie music could do for beer sales." While the Vulcan had existed, rock'n'roll performance in Austin had been freed from its dependence on the honky-tonk economy. Operating without a liquor license, the Vulcan was not presenting music in order to sell beer, nor was it dependent on beer sales to support its music. Although this freedom undoubtedly contributed to its early demise, the Vulcan presented rock'n'roll solely for the musicalized pleasure of its fans. Fans and musicians were able to perform together a pleasurable critique of modern society without the mediation produced by the traditional articulation of commodified musical practice and alcohol by the drink. Once the Vulcan closed, that linkage was reestablished. Honky-tonks like the Cactus Club would hire bands that played "hippie music" only because their fans would buy more beer than other patrons. Very few of the bands associated with the hip community in Austin could make that claim. Under these conditions, the artist development clause in Shiva's Headband's contract and their implicit promise to their community would be quite difficult to fulfill.[32]

These were the factors that led to the founding of the Armadillo World Headquarters. One June night, while Shiva's was packing the Cactus Club, Eddie Wilson stepped outside in an attempt to avoid the long lines for the bathroom. Staring across a vacant lot, he saw an old armory that "had 'rock hall' written all over it." Initially envisioning simply a larger version of the Vulcan Gas Co, Eddie Wilson arranged for Armadillo Productions to rent the empty 30,000-square-foot building from its owner, M. K. Hage, for five cents a square foot. As the manager of Shiva's Headband, Wilson thought that this move would solve most of the big problems the band faced. The hall would provide a focal point for Austin's hip community, ensuring that Armadillo Productions would have the first look at any local bands with recording potential. It would also provide a venue large enough to hold the ever-growing audiences for Shiva's Headband, giving them the opportunity to make

Constructing a cultural icon: Jim Franklin's poster for the Grand Opening of the Armadillo World Headquarters.   Courtesy Texas Poster Art Collection, The Center for American History, The University of Texas at Austin.

more money from each performance. And it would free the band and its production company from dependence on the traditional honky-tonk economy. Consequently, Wilson invested the remainder of the band's advance from Capitol into the first and last month's rent, a sound system, some lights, and a few scraps of carpet. Here, Austin's hip community could celebrate its freedom from the compromising interactions with the straight world. The hall would pay for itself through road shows, and the production contract with the record company would ensure that talented musicians need no longer leave central Texas in order to make a living from their craft.[33]

Wilson wasted no time. The first show at the Armadillo World Headquarters featured Tracy Nelson and Mother Earth, the band that Powell St. John and Toad Andrews had started in California, for $1.50 admission on the night of July 7, 1970. Technically illegal, the first show acted more as a taste of what the Armadillo would come to offer. The club had no liquor license, no air conditioning, an inadequate sound system, and an unorganized staff. But it promised a gathering space for what really was a still-growing population of alienated young Texans, a space devoted to the construction of their alternative identities through the performance of rock'n'roll music. Wilson hoped to use that promise to attract a consistent audience. He hired Jim Franklin, the artist most closely associated with the hip community's use of armadillo imagery, to illustrate the club's advertisements, to paint murals on its walls, and to be the master of ceremonies at the club. Mike Tolleson was hired on the basis of his resume, which boasted work experience at the London Arts Laboratory and a familiarity with the Beatles' version of utopian commercialism—Apple, Inc. Other staff members were paid in brown rice, sleeping space at Wilson's house, and all the pot they could smoke. The Armadillo was going to be the headquarters of a new kind of Texan with a new way of living.[34]

On August 7, the date from which the club's anniversaries were marked, Shiva's Headband performed for the official opening. Immediately, the Armadillo leadership was confronted with the need to act as an economic agent. According to Mike Tolleson,

The place opened, we put together the first show . . . had a great party and then everybody went home, and we were left with a big pile of trash, bills to pay and rent comin' up. And we said, "Wait a minute. What are we gonna do tomorrow night, what are we gonna do next Saturday night, who are we gonna book, who's gonna sell tickets, how we gonna let people know what's happening?" None of these systems were in place because none of us had ever done this before.

The club continued to flounder economically for a year, with the managers promising to pay the musicians after the next show made money, borrowing money from drug dealers when the next show did not make money, and barely keeping the doors open. Shiva's Headband's records were not selling in the national market, so no new recording industry income was entering Armadillo Productions. Occasional successes, like the packed houses the two nights that Freddie King recorded a live album, would momentarily raise hopes again as some back bills were paid off. But gradually the Armadillo World Headquarters was forced to modify its initial plan and become more concerned with linking the performance of rock'n'roll music with strategies for commercial success and economic survival.[35]

"Frankly, I don't believe in free music," Eddie Wilson said in 1974. "The only free music is when I'm picking for myself on my porch. When it gets any more complicated than that, suddenly it's not free music anymore." In this pithy statement, Wilson acknowledged the distance that youthful musical performance in Austin had traveled over the preceding ten years. When members of the folksinging club were no longer simply "picking" for themselves and each other on their porches, in the student union, and even during the early days at Threadgill's—once they began to turn "professional"—the conditions of musical performance became more complicated and the necessary economic mediation began to have a partially determining effect on the styles and meanings of music performed in Austin.

Using $25,000 borrowed from a volunteer employee with a trust fund, the Armadillo World Headquarters remodeled in 1971 and 1972, expanding its capacity. It opened a kitchen and a beer garden and obtained a beer and wine license. By expanding its economic base to include alcohol and food sales, the club experienced its first steady cash flow. It also developed a payroll of thirty-five people who expected to be paid in dollars and cents rather than brown rice and pot seeds. But even as this articulation of musical performance with diverse economic practices increased the potential for profitable evenings, the managers of the Armadillo noticed that Shiva's, and the bands like them that emphasized the musical difference associated with psychedelics, were not filling the cavernous space. If the Armadillo World Headquarters were to continue to provide a space for the musical performance of a peculiar Texan identity, commercial considerations would require that this identity become no longer quite so different.[36]

Along with the plans to diversify and expand the economic base of musical performance at the Armadillo, Eddie Wilson and Mike Tolleson were experimenting with their booking policies, attempting to diversify and expand their audiences. In addition to local rock'n'roll performers, the club began to feature touring acts as diverse as Earl Scruggs and Ravi Shankar. They found that there were audiences in Austin who would support this variety, who were pleased by this opportunity to hear and see performers who had previously ignored central Texas. As this effort continued, the identification of the Armadillo World Headquarters with the center of Austin's community of alienated youth began to weaken. Although the club was too big for bands like Shiva's Headband to fill by themselves, when they were billed with a contrasting act like the Austin Ballet Theater, the two different audiences would be enough to ensure a full house and a profitable evening. Thus, in defiance of a forty-year-long tradition of separating the musical pleasures of the different classes in Texas, the Armadillo became "the only place in town where you drink beer and listen to Beethoven."[37]

Although some tension was inevitable when these two antagonistic groups would meet on the dance floor at the Armadillo, the management began actively looking for performers who could appeal to both segments of their audience—the alienated estranged youth and the dominant mainstream of Texan culture. According to Mike Tolleson, "We knew that different acts drew different types of people and we experimented with blending different acts to draw bigger crowds. From this experience, we were sure that certain artists from the country field would appeal to the rock'n'roll kids." From the viewpoint I have been constructing regarding the cultural functions of music-making in Austin, we can see that the uses of the building itself began to edge closer to those of a traditional honky-tonk and away from a "home for the freaks." The Armadillo would no longer insist on being an alternative community center. Instead, this overgrown honky-tonk began to provide a consistently available commodified carnival, driven economically by liquor sales yet functioning simultaneously as a modernized marketplace of diverse musical offerings and a forum for a sexualized critique of modernity. As that transition occurred, the managers of the Armadillo began seeking a musician who could perform the traditional Texan role of the center of moral authority for an audience incapable of agreeing about where that center lay.[38]

While they searched for a performer who could dissolve these two factions into one cohesive audience, a local radio station tried to expand its market share by combining the same groups. Rusty Bell was a disc jockey at a top-forty station in town who approached the dominant local country station, KOKE, with an idea for a new experimental format. Bell had worked in small radio markets all over the country, but he had been struck by the intensity with which Austin radio listeners identified themselves as Texans. He developed a musical format that he hoped would simultaneously appeal to the younger market favored by pop and rock stations and identify itself with singularly Texan musical styles. This format was called "progressive country."

Jan Reid grew up in Wichita Falls and wrote extensively about Austin music during the seventies. Reid asserted that, "The secret to the success of KOKE . . . was that Bell proposed a very liberal definition of country music. What mattered was not the identity or hair length or philosophy of the singers, but the kind of instruments that accompanied them. If anything remotely country could be discerned in a recording, it qualified." Following this argument, the success of the format depended on the specific sounds that had been traditionally identified as the sounds of country music—the timbre of fiddles and steel guitars, a steady, uncomplicated shuffle or two-step rhythm, and, at the most, a particular style of closely harmonized vocals. Rather than directly articulating an explicit set of beliefs, feelings, or ideas, the expression of Texan identity was accomplished by means of this set of musical signifiers. The lyrical content, the origin or reputation of the singers, and any other contribution to the meaning of each song were free to vary from traditional to nontraditional concerns. KOKE could play the Rolling Stones singing "Dead Flowers," follow it with Little Feat's "Willin'," and close the set with anyone from the Flying Burrito Brothers to Janis Joplin to Willie Nelson. Because of the cultural meanings encoded in this loose set of musical sounds, it all became progressive country, and it all signified Texas.[39]

The disc jockey most closely associated with this format was Joe Gracey. In 1978, Gracey looked back proudly on his years at KOKE.

I think by 1972 people were growing weary of maintaining the various cultural and political stances they had maintained during the late sixties. You just can't maintain suspicion and hate and cynicism without getting sort of ugly yourself. Country music is relatively mild-mannered; it's pretty, you can dance nonaggressive dances to it. It is music created to have fun with. There is nothing ominous about it. People were ready for something new, fun. There was the added fact that country music is essentially indigenous to Texas and people here were rediscovering their . . . roots. . . . Just like the Chicanos, just like the blacks [sic], we realized that we were about to lose our roots, and everybody said, "Just wait a damn minute. I'm from Texas, I love Texas, it's a great place to live. I love the way we eat, I love the way we dress, I love our habits and our customs, and I love the way I talk. I love everything about this state—and why wouldn't I? It's a great place!"[40]

Ironically, the very popular musical tradition that alienated young people had used to mark their distinction from the mainstream of Texan culture was being transformed into a means of dissolving those antagonisms. Where young folksingers had learned old country songs like "The Wild Side of Life" and "Walkin' the Floor" in order to indicate their active distaste for mass culture and the mainstream of Austin's college students, radio stations and music hall promoters were beginning to use the same tradition to link the diverse musical tastes of the alienated and the mainstream into a heightened consciousness of a specific meaning of being Texan. The strength of the conservative aspects to this articulation can be seen in Gracey's clearly delineated "we"—not the "Chicanos," not the "blacks," but those Texans who eat certain foods, wear certain clothes, and talk in a special way. Class lines could be crossed in Texas; the boom and bust economies of cotton growing, cattle ranching, and oil drilling combined with the historical legacies of political populism to ensure the permeability of these cultures. However, the racial and ethnic distinctions could not be so easily erased; in fact, the effort to blend audiences from different economic classes forced the progressive country movement to emphasize the traditional racial and gender characteristics associated with the mythical identity of the Anglo-Texan cowboy. The antimodernist nostalgia of honky-tonk country and western performance became the focal point for a constellation of conservative cultural signifiers, communicated through a set of specific musical sounds called "progressive country."

As the managers of the Armadillo continued their search for musicians who could perform this rearticulation of traditional Texan identity for a younger audience, they began hearing about a country singer who had recently left Nashville and who was rumored to enjoy smoking marijuana. Willie Nelson moved to Austin near the end of 1971, living "right down the street" from the Armadillo on Riverside Drive. Willie Nelson's first performance at the Armadillo took place on August 12, 1972, and his band played the hall between twelve and fifteen times over the next three years. Through his own powerful singing style and the thoroughly professional musicianship of his band, the performances of Willie Nelson became the cultural center of a reconstructed community of Anglo-Texans.[41]

Jan Reid lived through and wrote about this realliance of young white Texans with the state's cultural traditions, the commercial reconstruction of traditional community that was so effectively performed by Nelson, his band, and his audience. Here is his 1974 description of the Nelson performance style.

The guitar-and-song performance became the great American ritual well before Willie Nelson made his debut, but he was a master of the art. . . . He stood considerably less than six feet tall, his torso was beginning to belly out a little with age, and he cocked his hip and dipped his shoulder as he played his guitar and seemed forever in want of a comfortable stance. But he was always seeking eye contact with the people in front of him, nodding and grinning once it was established. Women flushed with pleasure when the skin around Nelson's eyes wrinkled in their behalf, but his look was just as direct and genuine when it fell on another male. He involved the audience with himself, his music, and they felt better for it. His songs might be sad, but he had the look of a happy man, a rare animal indeed, in these times. . . . History was etched in the lines of his aging face, and he was their link to their Texan past.[42]

Nelson's shows at the Armadillo contained and resolved through musical performance all the contradictions that were conjured up by the concept of progressive country music. His band featured the singing pedal steel guitar and the thump-thump rhythm section that signified country music. Yet his appearance and his outspoken fondness for nontraditional intoxicants appealed to younger fans who had previously thought of country music as entertainment for rural squares. This constellation of contradictory cultural signifiers was transformed into a synthetic resolution by means of Nelson's ability to perform "sincerity" for every group in his audience. Through his ability seemingly to make personal contact with every individual who watched him perform,

Nelson could embody the traditionally masculine center of moral authority respoken for a new audience of country and western music fans in a reconstructed post-hippie honky-tonk community. The new Anglo-Texan cowboy had long hair and smoked marijuana, but he was still recognizably the same good old boy who was admired for his ability to meld his own sincere desires with those of the group and then transform those desires into profit.

But Willie Nelson was not the only successful songwriter to move to Austin in the early seventies. Michael Murphey was a professional songwriter with a recording contract from A&M. In the spring of 1972, he moved to Austin and began looking for skilled musicians to join his backup band. Murphey had been another member of Stan Alexander's folksinging club at North Texas State. After he graduated, he moved from Denton to Los Angeles, where he had a successful career writing songs for Screen Gems. But when he tired of producing hits on demand for Don Kirschner's publishing company, he decided to move back home to Texas to develop his own act. By this point, Austin was where the young musicians were in Texas, so it was to Austin that he moved.[43]

The local musicians hired by Murphey had been playing the commercial rock clubs in Austin for several years. These were the professional players who had worked with Rusty Wier and other local singers in bands like the Wigs and the Lavender Hill Express, catering to mainstream musical tastes in the clubs and at private parties. In a study he conducted on the development of the solo singer/songwriter style in Austin, Hugh Sparks traced the musical characteristics of "progressive country" music to this group of musicians. Sparks located the germination of the music that would dominate Austin throughout the seventies in the efforts made by these musicians to resolve the conflicts between the economic pressures to play a certain style of popular music and their own desires to perform a music they found personally interesting and challenging. Sparks describes their struggle to develop a commercial musical practice that could signify difference and therefore be used in the construction and communication of personal and group identity. "To cover up some of their uneasiness at being associated with a style resembling, in the minds of many, straight country, regardless of its actual roots in jazz, rock and folk, members of the Interchangeable Band seemed most of the time to have their tongues firmly implanted in their collective cheeks," says Sparks, who performed with this group. While the pedal steel guitar whined, these musicians would grin impishly, turn the rhythm around into a driving rock beat, and mime the rapid inhalation of marijuana smoke. They playfully and ironically combined many of the same cultural signs associated with the performances of Willie Nelson's band, yet the core of their music—the rhythm section—was far more rock oriented than Nelson's cold country beat. These rock musicians had created a performance style that contained a certain detachment from the music they played. Initially developed in the context of performing other people's hit songs for fraternity parties and mainstream audiences in nightclubs, their ironic performance style was easily transferred to the revision of country music developing in Austin. Eventually, these musicians became known as the Austin Interchangeable Band, so called because of their ability "to perform with any artist in styles ranging from rock to jazz to progressive country to bluegrass with no notice, no rehearsal and often in a state of questionable sobriety."[44]

But more than a musical style was codified by the behaviors and beliefs of these musicians. An entire set of political and personal feelings and ideologies grew out of their placement in the contradictory conditions of popular music performance in Austin, a set that would dominate the attitudes of local musicians for over a decade to come. According to Sparks, "There was a tendency for many Austin area musicians (sidemen and songwriters alike) not to take their work or themselves too seriously and to avoid working with those who did. Rather than being solely concerned with artistic or financial matters, their primary focus seemed to be on personal pleasure and the pursuit of happiness." An anticommercial ideology grew out of the need to reconcile the frustrations these musicians felt when forced to base musical decisions on economic factors, blending neatly with the anticommercial ethos inherited by local hippies from their origins in the folksinging movement.[45]

These were the musicians who backed up Michael Murphey during local performances of his ironic swipe at Austin's progressive country scene, "(I Just Want to be a) Cosmic Cowboy." Murphey and his band felt that the rearticulation of white Texan youth with the dominant cultural traditions was not necessarily a "progressive" development. They experienced the return to country music as another in a line of commercially motivated adjustments to the tastes of their audience, and Murphey felt that the scene in general and particularly the adoption of the cowboy as the model for masculine morality was dangerous. Often Murphey would lecture to his audiences about the negative aspects of gruff, aggressive, and violent masculine behavior. And he continually insisted that he wrote "Cosmic Cowboy" as a parodic jab at Austin's unthinking trend followers who saw no contradiction in combining the cowboy tradition with the pacifist hippie ethos.

Of course Murphey himself was a professional competitive musician, struggling both to benefit and distance himself from the progressive country movement. His professionalism grated against the anticommercial ideology of Austin musicians. Murphey's habits of consulting a rhyming dictionary and taking notes on people's conversations struck his back-up band as evidence of too great a concern with professional success. Insofar as the members of the Austin Interchangeable Band were more focused on immediate personal pleasure than artistic or financial success, they began drifting away from Murphey's employ.[46]

Many of these same musicians ended up working with yet another immigrant singer and songwriter, Jerry Jeff Walker. Walker had been a folksinger associated with the Greenwich Village folk scene in the sixties, but by the time that he moved to Austin in 1971, his career was at a standstill. He was known simply as the author of a very popular song about a tap-dancer and his dog, "Mr. Bojangles." Self-destructive behavior, ranging throughout the typical humiliations of alcoholics, was part of Walker's public persona. But that attitude of to-hell-with-tomorrow-let's-have-a-drink made Walker a more congenial boss for the pleasure seekers in the Austin Interchangeable Band. These musicians first worked with Walker on his "comeback" album for MCA and quickly solidified into a more consistent and coherent group, the Lost Gonzo Band.

The most fruitful collaboration between Walker and the Gonzos was the second record they made together, *Viva Terlingua*. A blend of irony, detachment, and rough sincerity characterizes this recording, along with a combination of a respect for cultural and musical traditions and a weary resignation about the legacies they imply. Walker's alcohol-inspired looseness provided the perfect recording context wherein the members of the Lost Gonzo Band could relax their heavily disciplined defenses against trying too hard. The tracks were recorded live in an empty honky-tonk in a tiny hill-country town called Luckenback. Although the recording was for the major label MCA, every effort was made to limit outside influences. This was to be a recording that reflected the musicianship, desires, and ideologies of the singers and players of Austin. No other record in the history of Austin music has so successfully represented the experiences and attitudes performed in the city's honky-tonks. Simultaneously sloppy yet musically coherent, raucous and silly yet painfully sincere, combining precisely the surface references to Texan musical and cultural traditions that signified progressive country with a sometimes humorous, sometimes somber recognition of their absurdities, the performances on *Viva Terlingua* represented the changes in musical practice that had occurred in Austin over the previous fifteen years. As Jerry Jeff Walker's voice cracked and swayed in and out of tune, the guitars, fiddles, drums, harmonicas, piano, and background voices all projected together a musically defined community that could never be completely harmonious, yet that could continue to find a source of renewal through redefining its traditions. As Walker sang of the pleasures of "Sangria Wine" in one song and the perplexities of being "thirty-four and drinking beer in a honky-tonk, kickin' hippies' ass and raising hell" in another, the band surged and lurched through hastily thrown together arrangements that conveyed spontaneity and impulsiveness in a musical form that Austinites could easily decode.

Probably the most effective of all the songs heard on this record remains their version of Guy Clark's "Desperados Waiting for a Train." The performance begins with an erratically strummed acoustic guitar as twin fiddles harmonize on the first line from the old song "Red River Valley." Walker sings the verses with the deep half-voice of a hungover forty-year-old. "Yeah, I'd play the Red River Valley and sit in his kitchen and cry. Run fingers through seventy years of living and wonder if every well we drilled gone dry. We was friends, me and this old man, like desperados waiting for a train." In this one verse, the song lyrically sets the scene of a passing of knowledge and emotion between two men, one much older than the other, as the younger is introduced into the male aspects of honky-tonk culture. The two live near a west Texas oil field and communicate with each other through the signs, images, and sounds of commercial popular culture. The representations of Texan masculinity in Hollywood movies and country and western music become elements in this sentimental song about an evolving friendship. The old man, a "driller of oil wells," teaches the singer to drive, introduces him to life at the local honky-tonk, and gives him "money for the girls." While the singer remains young, their lives seem like "some old western movie." But the younger man slowly watches his "hero" turn into someone with "brown tobacco stains all down his chin . . . dressed up like them old men." The story of the relationship between these men stands for the relationship between the generations of male Anglo-Texans rearticulated through song. As the song's narrator watches the old man grow older and is forced to recognize how hard this life has been and with how little the old man is left, the two of them close their eyes and conjure an idealized memory of their past while they "play another verse of that old song."[47]

Melodically, the song follows traditional ballad style for its first four lines, with the final notes of each line dropping slightly. But a fifth line leads each verse into the chorus, and Walker increases the tension of that line by holding the higher note just a moment longer, suspending its resolution with the tonic center of the song. These lines are the most emotionally resonant of each verse. "We was friends, me and this old man." Or, "And I was just a kid, they all called me sidekick." And, of course, "Our lives was like some old western movie." Each of these lines leads into the chorus of Walker singing, "Like desperados waiting for a train," over steady and sober piano chords, with strummed acoustic guitars and high-pitched fiddles softly whining in the background. Just as the song ends lyrically with an affirmation of the important communicative power of Texan musical traditions across generations, the musical accompaniment of the song indicates the survival of traditional meanings even though specific elements might change. The aural textures of the song convey the historic development of progressive country music as they shift from the traditional hillbilly arrangement of fiddles and acoustic guitar, through the honky-tonk assertion of the western beat as bass, drums, and piano enter, then finally ending the song by turning that beat around into a rock shuffle while Walker repeats the chorus and an electric guitar rock lead dominates the fadeout. Listened to as a whole, the version of "Desperados" recorded by Walker and the Gonzos concisely, sensitively, and sympathetically performs the narrative of the alienation of Anglo-Texan youth from its traditions, followed by the consequent rearticulation of these generations through the power of popular culture and the particularly evocative communicative capacity of popular musical practice.

According to Archie Green, "cowboys have always read dime novels about their exploits, told idealized tales to each other, and sketched themselves on scratch pads in lines larger than life." As the cosmic cowboys of the progressive country movement in Texas, musicians in Austin were forced to come to terms with their already constructed positions within the ongoing development of local popular music performance. Like desperados waiting for a train, progressive country musicians were certain that they were onto a sure thing, a musical style that would effortlessly become popular. They also believed that this popularity would ensure that each of them, simply by pursuing his own pleasures and following his own desires for sincere expression, would find life growing increasingly comfortable. No compromises with commercial motivations would any longer be needed. The performance of a revived and revved-up honky-tonk critique of modernity, underlined by an ironic detachment from its necessary commercial base, would guarantee success for Austin's musicians.[48]

But by the spring of 1974, representatives of the national recording industry were casting doubts on this vision of a musically created anticommercial utopia. Jerry Wexler was a vice president for Atlantic Records; he was responsible for Willie Nelson's signing with the label and produced Nelson's first crossover rock success, *Shotgun Willie*. *Rolling Stone* quoted Wexler's puzzlement regarding the music scene in Austin. "I keep hearing about this great Austin scene but whenever I ask who I should sign, nobody seems to know. Is it a mirage down there?" The recording industry could not understand a music scene that was not organized around the production of nationally oriented, commercially viable recordings. Therefore, the writer of the article concluded, "the jury's still out on Austin music. It has not made any impact on the charts and those charts will determine Austin's national impact."[49]

In the same article, Jim Franklin tried to explain the local attitude. "This has always been an anticommercial scene. That's why most of the people who moved here did so. Most of the musicians are content to play the same clubs and just get by and smoke their dope and drink their beer. How do you take an atmosphere that's suspicious of capitalism and heavily anticommercial and market it?" Popular music-making in Austin grew out of a traditional practice of antimodernist critique. University students began to sing old traditional and commercial songs as a means of distinguishing themselves from their mass culture consuming fellows. By so doing, they linked themselves to a practice that carried, already inscribed into its meanings, a particular set of racial and gender codings along with a contradictory relationship to the changing economic base of musical performance. Honky-tonk culture critiqued the commodification of modern life even while the honky-tonk itself instantiated the commodification of its own practice. During the sixties and early seventies, as the state of Texas grew inexorably more urban and progressively more integrated into the national economy, the romantic nostalgia of antimodernism that lay at the heart of Austin music transformed into the romantic nostalgia of anticommercialism, accompanied by an insistence on the value of Anglo-Texan identity. While music-making in Austin remained linked to the honky-tonk economy and a critique based on romantic nostalgia, Austin music would continue to be difficult for the national recording industry to exploit commercially.[50]

CHAPTER FOUR

The Collapse of the Progressive Country Alliance

Although the recording industry had difficulty packaging progressive country for a national audience in 1974, local performers, radio disc jockeys, and nightclub owners were offering almost no other music for popular consumption. For the next two years, music-making in Austin became wholly identified with this contradictory genre. The year 1975 has been called the "peak year of the progressive country period," with 70 percent of the entertainment acts during one weekend performing "some kind of country or country-based genre."[1] In February 1976, the *Austin Sun*, an independent weekly, published its first reader's poll indicating the most popular musicians performing in Austin during 1975. Not surprisingly, readers voted Willie Nelson the best male vocalist, and Marcia Ball the best female vocalist. They declared Asleep at the Wheel the best country band, while Balcones Fault took the rock division. According to the *Sun*'s editors, they received more than 125 ballots a day, considerably more than they had anticipated. Along with Nelson, progressive country singers Jerry Jeff Walker, Steve Fromholz, Willis Alan Ramsey, and Townes Van Zandt appeared in the male top ten. Marcia Ball's band, the Misery Brothers, were a country act, and she was joined in the female top ten by country singers Lisa Hattersly of Greezy Wheels, the Reynolds Sisters, Chris O'Connel (of Asleep at the Wheel), and Cassel Webb (of B. W. Stevenson's band).

Nevertheless, the poll was not completely dominated by progressive country acts. The editors wrote that, "Many ballots revealed an appreciation of a variety of music, with selections of more obscure artists and write-in votes coupled with mainstream choices. The first five finishers for Band of the Year, could be categorized as playing hard rock, eclectic rock, country, blues and jazz, in that order."[2] The tight grip that progressive country had held on the musical tastes of Austin clubgoers was beginning to loosen.

Paul Ray, leader of the blues band the Cobras, noted the variety of styles in a letter to the editor in the following issue of the *Sun*. He referred to the poll as "a veritable rented warehouse of useful information on the musical proclivities of Austin clubhoppers." He went on to say,

The most interesting aspect of the results is the diversity of musical taste best exemplified in the "Band of the Year" vote. . . . [T]he top six vote-getters purvey a wide range of musical idioms. . . . The three year deluge of progressive country music that inundated Austin has somewhat subsided, or at least, it has been diluted. There is evidence that the "Armadillo Seal of Approval" is not a prerequisite to local success.[3]

The dissatisfaction and sense of frustration displayed in this letter had been building up among groups of Austin's musicians and clubgoers for some time. One year previously, Jeff Nightbyrd had published a thoughtful critique of the progressive country movement. Acknowledging that it successfully articulated an identity for its fans, Nightbyrd pointed out some of the more unfortunate elements in this reconstruction of traditional Texan manhood. He argued that, "Cosmic Cowboys didn't become a phenomena because of Michael Murphey, Armadillo World Headquarters or businessmen wanting to make Austin Nashville II, it worked because people wanted to feel they had some identity. And what better identity in Texas than cowboys," he continued, "even if it's a bit nostalgic and everyone really rode Schwinn bicycles when they were kids." According to Nightbyrd, the success of this identity was at least partially due to the fact that,

Any young dude can come in from Amarillo, grow moderately long hair under his cowboy hat, smoke a little grass, maybe wear a little simulated Indian jewelry, and be a cosmo cowboy. It doesn't take much. Particularly it doesn't require any changes in attitude like being a hippie in the sixties did. You don't have to know anything about the war, give a damn about race, tussle with psychedelics, or worry about male chauvinism. No internal restructuring is required. . . . You don't have to be a peaceful guy, or a hip guy, gentle or persuasive. Cosmo cowboydom allows you to be just what you always were . . . it's a relief. . . . Where hip consciousness created an unrealistic utopian vision of brotherhood, the cosmo cowboys fall back on the old mythology.[4]

It was easy for young men from west Texas to purchase and display the signs of this identity because these signs were meaningful within familiar contexts. This old mythology—the reconstruction of the idealized western male, impulsive and violent, independent and autonomous—was not strained by historical changes in the specific tastes of masculine desires. Wearing long hair and jewelry and smoking marijuana could easily fit into the catalogue of available pleasures. Nightbyrd's reading of this commercialized identity focused not on the fact that it was purchased and, therefore, inauthentic, but on a political resonance generated by the historical context within which this identity had developed. For this ex-SDS organizer, the easy identity projected by the progressive country music scene did not transform its fans or its musicians; it did not construct an imagined solution to the contradictions of commercialized modernity. Instead, Nightbyrd asserted, the successful marketing of the "cosmo cowboy" indicated the wearing of an old and comfortable mythology, an acceptance of the traditional discourses of Anglo-Texan identity.[5]

That winter, Nicholas Spitzer published a discussion of a Waylon Jennings record, "Bob Wills is Still the King," in which he described a public performance of the cosmic cowboy identity. According to Spitzer, the Opry House audience for this live recording "hoots and hollers on cue in a manner that . . . I would describe as self-conscious. That is, they are themselves performing in the fashion presumed to be truly Texan." For Spitzer, this group performance was an ironic and playful participation in a commercially promulgated musical tradition. He argued that the signs of traditional Anglo-Texan identity displayed in the performance of "Bob Wills is Still the King" were "primarily surface cultural traits" used to construct "fantasies of a simple self-reliant life in the face of a modern, complex, often unrewarding society." For Spitzer, these fantasies remained quite distinct from the everyday life of this audience. He insisted that there was no relation between the conservative images and rhetoric traditionally associated with country and western music and the pleasure experienced and given voice by its fans. Instead, the fantasies enabled by this performance were the result of a "matrix of acculturation and self-conscious romanticism that have long been the paradoxical mainstay of country and western music." For Spitzer the self-conscious celebration of Anglo-Texan identity was a surface characteristic that enabled the fan "to show his new affinities without sacrificing his deeper values." He based this conclusion on the fact that young fans he observed at this and other Waylon Jennings shows continued to live together outside of marriage, continued to smoke marijuana, and refused to attend church services. In Spitzer's analysis, these were the important cultural characteristics; they continued to signify a meaningful split between the progressive aspects of youth culture and the "surface traits" of the country and western "fashion." Spitzer insisted on the authenticity of these "lifestyle" signifiers in contrast to the inauthenticity of the signifiers associated with the music. Therefore, participation in this commercialized musical practice carried no political or social implications. In contrast to Nightbyrd's concerns, Spitzer found the appeal to traditional Anglo-Texan identity to be a benign and rather insignificant result of popular musical practice.[6]

The arguments of both Spitzer and Nightbyrd turn on a contrast between surface and depth in their readings of the cosmic cowboy identity. Both acknowledge that they are attending to surface characteristics, to the signifiers of identity available for purchase in the marketplace. For Spitzer, this commercialization limits the cultural importance of the practice. Spitzer's analysis of "romantic regionalism" distinguished the self-consciously Texan aspects of the cosmic cowboy, perpetrated by the forces of fashion, from what he saw as deeper social transformations indicated by cohabitation, drug use, and an absence of church affiliation. The surface cultural traits put on during the performance of "Bob Wills is Still the King" could be taken off as soon as the audience left the Opry House. Nightbyrd, on the other hand, was concerned about what happened while the costume was being worn. He did not assume that a deeper, more authentic identity lay beneath the hat, the boots, and the moustache. Instead, he worried about the comfort and ease with which they were worn by "the semi-hip guy from Lubbock or Big Springs."[7]

These two positions prefigured a debate on the effects of commercial culture and postmodernism that would soon come to prominence in academic analyses of popular culture. Spitzer's insistence that Waylon Jennings's audience was maintaining a playful, ironic, and distanced participation in one of many optional cultural games points toward the vision of postmodernism espoused by Francois Lyotard and Jean Baudrillard. This interpretation states that with the collapse of overarching metanarratives of knowledge and legitimation, all cultural practices are self-contained and self-legitimating, with no necessary connection to any other discrete cultural or political practice. Nightbyrd, however, maintains the relevance of history and cultural connections in his analysis of the cosmic cowboy identity. In so doing, he outlines the version of postmodernism associated with Fredric Jameson and George Lipsitz, which recognizes that commercial culture is an important site for political struggle. It is interesting that, although neither Spitzer nor Nightbyrd was explicitly discussing postmodernism, their concerns with the effects of commercialized cultural practice and the construction of identity led them into precisely the two positions that would dominate academic discussions of postmodernism in the eighties.[8]

This concern with the relationships between musical practice and identity permeated commentary on Austin music in the middle seventies. For some Austinites in 1976, the entire phenomenon of progressive country music itself—the music and its associated images—was believed to be "concocted by the media."[9] Bob Brown, guitarist and singer for the Austin rhythm and blues band Conqueroo, dismissed the entire movement. "Yee haw! Country music is whooping and hollering and pouring beer on your head."[10] Some fans of progressive country insisted that the apparent inauthenticity of the musical culture was not related to a failure of the original synthesis, but was a result of the distortion that follows from the packaging and promotion efforts that constitute mass-marketing strategies. They felt that the pure spirit of progressive country had been corrupted by commercial considerations. According to Jan Reid, the honest pastoral vision of progressive country music had been transformed into a virulent record company sales gimmick. For Reid, "Progressive country was a songwriter's poetry of homecoming, celebration of nature, intelligent soul searching." Michael Murphey, Steve Fromholz, Willie, Jerry Jeff, and the rest had created lyrical and musical paeans to a simpler life. "Sown deep in Texas tradition, sentimentally attached to the rural lifestyle, country and western was the handiest means of expressing that pastoral fantasy."[11] But 1976 had been the year that RCA-Nashville marketed a collection of songs by Willie Nelson, Waylon Jennings, Tompal Glaser, and Jessi Colter called *Wanted! The Outlaws*. The unexpected commercial success of this record (it sold over a million copies) stimulated the record industry to produce more "outlaw" product.

For Reid and other Austin critics, such popular success in itself was not harmful. In fact, many Austin musicians and writers anticipated that national popularity for their music would mark the final success of their romantic antimodern ideology. What these commentators objected to was the cultural effects of the commercially disseminated "outlaw" image played out in the attitudes and behaviors of fans in attendance at Willie Nelson picnics, Waylon Jennings concerts, and David Allen Coe performances. At a Willie Nelson concert in the Austin area, only two years after the "rise of redneck rock," Reid decided that the entire meaning of progressive country music had changed. He found the musicians to be the same, the songs to be the same, many of the individuals in the crowd to be the same, yet the feeling he received from the experience was wholly different. A nasty macho attitude—drunk, sloppy, mean, and proud—dominated the behaviors of the audience and disgusted critics like Reid. But these critics insisted that the negative characteristics had not followed from the progressive country reliance upon the traditional cowboy identity; instead, they were the result of media manipulation.

"How did the good guys of country music come to wear black hats?" Reid asked. "Outlaw country music is not just some misguided notion of the crowd. It's a sales promotion hawked by the recording industry with Madison Avenue zeal."[12]

Reid and other local critics who had championed progressive country distinguished between the "authentic" local performances of the music and the "artificial" marketing tool of the outlaw image. They insisted on a distinction between "the music itself"—for Reid, the honest pastoral poetry that envisaged a hassle-free life—and the images associated with the music through the marketing efforts of outsiders. These cultural signifiers could not be phenomena of the same order, and the pleasures they produced for their audiences could not be equivalent. One cultural construction indicated the positive elements in the musical performance of Texan identity; the other betrayed this identity through packaging that emphasized its negative components. "So we have an art form that extols violent behavior. Scrapes with the law are prestigious affairs. The sullen resentments of poor Southern whites are represented as positive values."[13] Produced in office suites far from the performances of community that unified the "real" progressive country audience, the outlaw image recreated the same caricature of the country music audience that urban record executives had always promoted. The image used by outsiders to market the music had counteracted the positive cultural contribution of the music itself.[14] It was particularly disturbing to Reid to see this inauthenticity played out in the attitudes of some audience members and reflected back to the stage.

On the streets, and in the clubs and rehearsal rooms of Austin, the outlaw marketing strategy only confirmed and exacerbated already existing tensions among differing groups of musicians. There still existed musicians in Austin who did not play country music and who resented the Armadillo's dominance of the local scene. The national fascination with the cosmic cowboy phenomenon, and the music's amazing success at forging an "affective alliance" among conservatives and Austin's hip community, left many of these Austin musicians feeling isolated and alienated from their immediate audience.[15]

Alex Napier was a bassist who played with the (with few exceptions, white) blues and southern rock musicians in town. He had performed with Angela Strehli and W. C. Clark in Southern Feeling and would soon join Paul Ray in the Cobras. This group of musicians had been completely overshadowed by the glaring media spotlight shining on progressive country. In response, they moved to the blues scene on the east side of town. In the clubs on East 11th and 12th Streets, they found an audience that had appreciated live blues performances for decades. During the late fifties and early sixties, Albert Collins, Freddie King, and B. B. King performed almost monthly at places like the I.L. Club and Charlie's Playhouse. Johnny Holmes hired blues musicians from the surrounding area for his club, the Victory Grill. There L. P. Pearson, T. D. Bell, and Erbie Bowser formed the core of a house band that set the standard for blues performance in East Austin.[16] And in the sixties, Ira Littlefield, the owner of the I.L. Club had booked Conqueroo, a west side rhythm and blues band featuring both black and white musicians, so a (somewhat tenuous) precedent for racial mixing had been set.[17] When the migration of white blues performers to East Austin occurred in the early seventies, they found an already existing community of African-American musicians, fans, and clubowners. In these clubs, an exchange of musical ideas took place, creating the foundation on which was constructed the Antone's blues scene.[18]

Alex Napier sold the the Soap Creek Saloon, an old honky-tonk west of town on Bee Caves Road, to George and Carlyne Majewski in late 1972.[19] The Soap Creek Saloon was intended to challenge the Armadillo's dominance of the music scene in Austin and to provide greater opportunities for Austin's local musicians. According to Carlyne Majer (Majewski),

The reason I opened up Soap Creek Saloon . . . was because I really felt like there was a disservice to the local music community in terms of the lack of ability for them to play. Prior to the Armadillo, there was a rich heritage of live music. I would tell you that the Armadillo World Headquarters was a national touring act club. And that although sometimes it used local band openers, it was for national touring acts. It was not that they did not want to be a part of this music, the local music scene, or that they weren't. It was that their facility was so large that it demanded national touring acts. There were some places in East Austin, but there were no significant clubs for regional and local talent, to be billed and not to be used as an opener but to have a primary focus in that type of music as opposed to the type of music that was national touring with record company backup.[20]

"Type of music" has two meanings here. It means the generic distinction between progressive country and other musical styles, and it also refers to the regional identification of local musicians. The Soap Creek was not against country music. Alvin Crow and the Pleasant Valley Boys played there regularly. During the years when Marcia Ball was a progressive country singer, she was performing at the Soap Creek. Greezy Wheels, the Lost Gonzo Band, and even Jerry Jeff Walker and Willie Nelson hailed from the Soap Creek stages. But all of these musicians were considered to be local acts, and it was this orientation that was the more significant. The meaning of music-making in Austin had to be

The re-placement of local tradition: one of Kerry (Awn) Fitzgerald's calendars for the Soap Creek.   Courtesy Texas Poster Art Collection, The Center for American History, The University of Texas at Austin.

protected. Local control, local performers, and local audiences were required to produce the context within which this meaning would remain stable. Under these conditions, the performances of local Austin musicians, regardless of whether they played country or blues, continued to project a romantic antimodernism, a critique of work, and the Soap Creek became the most important site for this honky-tonk critique.

The Soap Creek attracted a group of regular fans that Majer estimated at "maybe 5,000 strong. You know, that came back once or twice a week year in and year out. . . . Everybody knew each other and it was the counter culture."[21] This "counter culture," the aging core of the sixties hip community, formed the material base of fans, a core audience whose disposable income supported the musical performance of this antimodern identity. No longer university students, these were the same "social hangers-on" that formed the initial progressive country audience, still concerned with local music, local identity, displaying a romantic anticommercial nostalgia and yearning for a life "relatively free of hassle."[22]

Michael Ventura, a writer for the *Austin Sun*, spent many nights at the Soap Creek. In a 1977 article about Marcia Ball, he described the attitudes of the postuniversity crowd and the atmosphere in Austin honky-tonks.

Especially here in Austin, a honky-tonk city, where sometimes our collective desperation is like a knife-edge on the night. Where we drink, dance, take the drugs, laugh, cry, want, fuck, think, mock, gossip . . . [sic]* where the dark adolescent drive to consume one's own innocence has become a way of life and lasted into what's becoming the middle-age of some of us. To cruise past 30 unable to rid ourselves of adolescent drives and dreams is our peculiar fate. What's our social life but night-by-night last-ditch attempts to dowse our loneliness, and consume what's left of our innocence? It perhaps speaks well of us that we can't. Look in our eyes during the happy flashes when the dancing's good, or when we're drunkenly sincere, or the singer is just right, and you see innocence untouched, you look into the eyes of children. What an atmosphere for our singers to support their songs![23]

A relative newcomer to these honky-tonks was a young Louis Black.

And then so I came here in '74 and we were here for about four or five months. The first night we were here, I remember this, we went, we got an *Austin Sun*, and Doug Sahm was playing in the old Soap Creek out in the hills. Which at that point, you know, now going down to Bee Caves you're still in Austin, but at that point, it was like driving out of town. And, you know, you think you're lost and you drive down this dirt road and then all of a sudden there's this honky-tonk and you walk inside and there's Doug Sahm, who can be, on a regular basis, God, and was that night. And I knew I was in the right place.[24]

*Where an ellipsis occurs in the quoted source, I have indicated it in this manner.

Just as Willie Nelson could embody and project the meaning of the Armadillo, Doug Sahm became the "spiritual godfather" of the Soap Creek regulars, epitomizing the combination of counterculture roots, musical diversity, and honky-tonk orientation that the Majewskis intended to offer.[25] Sahm had grown up in San Antonio, professionally performing an astounding variety of musical styles from the age of twelve. In 1965 a local promoter, Huey Meaux, renamed Sahm's band the Sir Douglas Quintet and marketed their song "She's About a Mover" to the nation, riding the long coattails of the Beatles. For the next ten years, Sahm roamed between central Texas and San Francisco, searching for a "hassle-free life," working with basically the same band, and gradually returning to the eclectic blend of country, conjunto, swing, blues, and rhythm and blues that he had grown up performing. By 1975, Sahm's music and his personal style had become identified with the local meaning of music-making in Austin. And the Soap Creek Saloon had been constructed as a specific performance site out of a threefold struggle with the local dominance of progressive country music, with the Armadillo as the headquarters for that dominance, and with the constraints of what was by now a nationally and commercially disseminated identity that had been stripped of its local anticommercial resonance.

By the winter of 1975–1976, Austin's blues scene was offering a contrasting set of musical pleasures. Paul Ray had gone to the west coast in 1974, in order to scout out recording opportunities. He found that, "Progressive country was all the rage in Austin and L.A.; since rhythm and blues was not, Denny [Freeman], Alex, and I were back in Austin, broke and in need of work."[26] The Cobras formed that summer, playing the La Cucaracha Nightclub (in the building that used to be Charlie's Playhouse) on a weekly basis. Throughout 1975, the white blues scene consolidated, as musicians recombined into early forms of bands that survived into the eighties, and two new clubs opened across the border on the west side, providing even more opportunities for the blues crowd to play. The One Knite was located on Red River, and Antone's opened at its first location on East 6th Street—both just west of the freeway. These two clubs and the Soap Creek were the main west-side performance sites for not only the Cobras, but also the recently formed Fabulous Thunderbirds and the Nightcrawlers (with Stevie Vaughan on lead guitar and Keith Ferguson on bass).

Jimmie Vaughan had moved to Austin in 1969. He had been in rock bands in Dallas with both Paul Ray and his younger brother, Stevie. But he moved to Austin because, "I couldn't play blues in Dallas. . . . It just wasn't working in Dallas, and I knew some musicians here on the East Side, at the old I.L. Club. So I thought I'd move here and try to start playing with them. I wanted to play, play what I liked." And besides, "It was just about the only town in Texas where you could have long hair without getting the shit beat out of you." Along with harpist and singer Kim Wilson, Vaughan formed the Fabulous Thunderbirds in the fall of 1974. Soon they were garnering regular bookings at the One Knite, the Soap Creek, and Antone's. Stevie Vaughan's last show with the Nightcrawlers was New Year's Eve, 1974, and within six months he was gracing Austin stages as the featured guitarist in Paul Ray and the Cobras. The story of the central Texas white blues scene— the Cobras, the Fabulous Thunderbirds, Stevie Ray Vaughan, and the rest—requires more room than I can give it, but it is important to note that this moment of the blues scene consolidation (the second half of 1975) corresponded with the first street and club-level cracks in the progressive country, cosmic cowboy local hegemony and it was marked by the movement of the white blues musicians across the highway, back into downtown Austin.[27]

Despite what was going on in Texas, the national appeal of Austin's version of country music, whatever its label, was at its height. In the fall of 1975, Willie Nelson had released his best-selling album so far with *Red Headed Stranger*. Asleep at the Wheel's and Jerry Jeff Walker's most recent records joined Willie's in the top twenty on *Billboard*'s country charts, and within months the compilation album *Wanted! The Outlaws* would become country music's first documented platinum long player. Curiously, in the midst of this national success for the musical genre most closely associated with it, the Armadillo World Headquarters was experiencing its deepest financial crisis.[28]

By the summer of 1976, the Armadillo was $140,000 in debt. It had never been managed well. The principals had leaped into the nightclub business propelled by the availability of a small amount of record-company-provided capital and a vague urge to promote Austin as a music capital. They had lost money consistently since their first show. Legitimate difficulties that derived from the size of the hall were exacerbated by poor accounting practices and an inability to match the grandeur of their self-aggrandizing vision with the limitations of their situation. By 1976, the Armadillo was no longer the headquarters for the musical celebration of Texan identity. Competition had dramatically increased: there were more clubs in which to hear local music. Willie Nelson, the only local performer who could be counted on to sell out the hall, had shifted his local performances to the Texas Opry House.

The Soap Creek, the Ritz, and a host of smaller clubs presented local musicians, could operate with less overhead, and so risked less each time they opened. These smaller venues could afford to experiment with less mainstream musicians, thereby offering performance opportunities to a greater percentage of those musicians flooding the city in the wake of the cosmic cowboy phenomenon. In a final attempt to raise sufficient capital to retire their debts and set Armadillo Productions on a new track, with a firm financial footing, Wilson, Hedderman, and Tolleson came up with the idea of the Armadillo Special Interest Group.[29]

The chief function of the ASIG was to exploit the sixth birthday of the club, transforming it into an opportunity for massive fundraising. The strategy was in line with the grandiose Armadillo ideology. Wilson had already been discussing plans for a $50,000,000 a year software and entertainment industry that he would situate on the six acres where the Armadillo sat. It was conceived of as a "miniature Universal City." These plans were intended to spark the interest of local politicians, drawing their attention to the financial contribution that a healthy music industry could make to the local economy. The ASIG intended to promote this idea to Austin power brokers, while at the same time pushing the legend of the Armadillo's special significance in the cultural life of Texas to those musicians and fans who saw it as a temple of the counterculture. Following standard fundraising techniques, the ASIG solicited already sympathetic individuals and then added their names to a list used to attract other contributors. Contributions were structured in the form of $100 tickets to the Armadillo World Headquarters 6th Birthday Party on August 7, 1976. They hoped to sell one thousand tickets, and then use that lump sum of $100,000 to attract other investors. As of May 21, 1976, the ASIG had confirmed the contributions of ninety-one individuals or groups. Among the ticket purchasers were Ann Richards, then the County Commissioner; Jeff Friedman, the mayor of Austin; a representative of Texas State Bank, and several lawyers. By far, the bulk of the contributors were individuals with whom the Armadillo regularly did business—musicians, managers, A&R representatives from record companies, and the owners of other music-related businesses.[30]

Eventually, the hype resulted in 191 tickets sold and 26 tickets traded out for reductions in past debts. The total income (including reductions in accounts payable) was over $22,000; the amount spent on the party exceeded $13,000. The net financial gain, representing over three months of work, was slightly more than $9,000.[31] As a fundraising effort, the birthday party had been a failure. Within two months, Mike

Tolleson, Bobby Hedderman, and Eddie Wilson left Armadillo Productions, Inc., turning over the operations and the accumulated debts to their chief creditor, Hank Alrich.

By November, the *Sun* was publishing rumors of bankruptcy proceedings for the Armadillo among articles detailing a "local depression in the live music business." Alrich reduced the payroll from 143 employees to fewer than 70 and vowed to operate the club on a cash basis. In an effort to limit talent costs and to recement relationships with local musicians, Alrich announced a new booking policy that would reflect a three-to-one ratio of local to touring acts. However, these measures were not sufficient to hold off the hall's other creditors. During 1976, the hall had grossed $1,219,000 yet missed breaking even by $40,000. By January, 1977, the Armadillo's debt had increased to $152,000. Alrich further cut the staff to 36 workers, and most of them were not being paid. Prompted by a suit for overdue payments for radio ads, Armadillo Productions Incorporated filed for Chapter 11 bankruptcy.[32]

What were the factors that led to the fiscal collapse of this cosmic cowboy cathedral? I have already mentioned the increase in competition from the growing number of nightclubs and from the increased recognition given to the diversity of musical talent in Austin. But changes in the local audience exacerbated the effects of these aesthetic and commercial developments. The rise of redneck rock had been materially sustained by a continued increase in undergraduate enrollment at the university. Made more prosperous by the local effects of the oil embargo of 1973, the students attending the University of Texas during the seventies brought with them more disposable income than they had in any previous decade. Average attendance at the Armadillo probably peaked in 1974, when "suddenly the place was full most of the time." At that moment, the entertainment tastes of these students, the pleasures they chose to purchase, coalesced with the entertainment tastes of local politicians and business people around the performance of country music.[33]

The affective alliance produced through the shared pleasures of progressive country music was a contingent construction, strongest when all the components were operating in tandem. The most gifted performers had to be singing the most articulate and well played songs in a building that symbolized the coming together of traditional Texan interests with the sensibilities of the baby-boom generation. When the generationally diverse but mutually flush individuals who embodied that affective alliance were dancing next to each other weekly, or even more often, in the physical space consecrated to that cause, the celebration of the cosmic cowboy community could appear self-replicating, natural, the result of authentic, unmediated cultural practice. But, of course, none of it was unmediated. And the mediations slowly turned in other directions.

Michael Murphey, Jerry Jeff Walker, and, especially, Willie Nelson, were professional entertainers, with recording industry-oriented career demands and national aspirations. The Armadillo was a nightclub in sudden competition with several new nightclubs for the market of live music fans. The social hangers-on, the core audience for Austin music, searching for the meaning of life in a beer bottle and a song, were driven away by the influx of instantly semihip students. And the students were looking for a good time, that pleasure which comes from the creation of an instant identity that marks their student years as different, that contributes to the construction of the self as individual. While Austin critics were blaming the industrial marketing of progressive country music for its failure to extend the authentic cultural meaning of the movement, transformations internal to the system that produced this music were contributing to its decline.

In 1976, the university students, recently neglected by the ideologues struggling over the meaning of Austin music, were no longer consistently packing the live music clubs, and their allowances were no longer paying the bills, neither at the Armadillo nor at the other live music clubs that had sprung up in recent years. As Ramsey Wiggins put it, "the live music business, once a jewel in our city's crown, seems to have come on hard times, indeed." For all the talk about a lack of depth to the college student identification with the antimodern, cosmic cowboy community, the waning of their support was a serious blow to the honky-tonk economy, especially affecting those clubs that required a large audience to cover their overhead. The most recent manifestation of the student search for meaningful pleasure, the transformation of musical taste and, even more important, entertainment practices, that most directly threatened the economic foundations of live music in Austin, was the rise of disco.[34]

Disco, as a sensibility, never achieved a firm foothold on the west side of Austin. It owed too much, too directly, to African-American traditions, tastes, and pleasures, to become truly popular at a street level, able to produce locally effective meanings. Disco's ability to forge its own affective alliance was predicated upon an urban audience, with extensive contact across racial barriers, and it utilized a frank public display of eroticism foreign to the recently rural, Baptist backgrounds of most white music fans in Austin. But the college years are a time for trying out new pleasures, new identities, new meanings, and, even in Austin, disco briefly held sway.[35]

Ramsey Wiggins was the publicity manager at the Armadillo World Headquarters for three years. In 1976, he explained the appeal of disco in Austin as "part of the environment for a new social phenomenon arising from urban anomie: the prepackaged party." Wiggins categorized disco as background music as opposed to "the real thing, the opportunity to hear a famous song played and sung by the person who made it famous." He was astonished that anyone could prefer dancing to records over the face-to-face interactions with musicians that characterized a honky-tonk. But Wiggins did understand one aspect of the shift in taste. Honky-tonks tended to have a "funky, run-down ambience" whereas discos offered a "modern, safe attractive environment." He concluded that, "What we are witnessing is an increasing rejection by club-goers of the funky discomfort and passive, listeners' role offered by the performance-oriented club, in favor of the stylish comfort of the disco with its greater opportunities for dancing and social interaction."[36]

As progressive country had become more professional, it had grown away from the traditions of honky-tonk performance. Rather than forming a mutual musical celebration of collective local identity, the performances of Austin singer-songwriters had become more akin to a concert, where the audience attended to and applauded the pastoral poetry of the performers. The group participation necessary for the musicalized production of collective identity—inherited from the carnivalesque tradition of the honky-tonk and effectively syncretized with the practice of the folk song revival—was being eliminated from the experience of listening to Austin's musicians. Yet these performances were still situated in the "funky run-down ambience" common to honky-tonks. Under these conditions, progressive country could no longer form the musical center of an antimodern critique. As Wiggins pointed out, when students faced the choice between the physical activity of dancing in a clean setting and the quiet disciplined attention required by Austin's singers in a honky-tonk, they chose the modern experience.

The two most successful discos in Austin at this time were the Cabaret and the Greenhouse. Ted Simerson managed the Greenhouse and described a different set of advantages his club held over live music halls. "It's hard to beat or duplicate a real good sound system . . . there's no way you can have a live band and have the variety we have. If you have Willie Nelson on stage, it's fantastic, but he only plays one kind of music." Both Wiggins and Simerson were describing the lasting changes that the commercial form of disco entertainment would contribute to the ongoing Austin live music scene. If live music nightclubs in Austin were to continue to attract the entertainment dollars of students and the rising professional-managerial class (the extension of the government bureaucracy to which they had traditionally catered), they had to recognize the importance of dancing and active participation by the audience, they had to improve their sound quality, and they had to offer variety. And in order to compete effectively, they needed to offer something else, something more than the discos could provide.[37]

The prepackaged parties that discos sold were largely dependent on the quality of the sensual stimulation that could be guaranteed. Simon Frith has written that, "Disco had changed . . . the meaning of a good night out, and . . . this has to be understood in the context of 1970s' sexual mores." Discos made explicit the relationships between musical and physical pleasures. "The dance floor is the most public setting for music as sexual expression and has been an important arena for youth culture since the dance crazes of the beginning of the century when Afro-American rhythms began to structure white middle-class leisure, to set new norms for physical display, contact, and movement." But the experience of dancing in a disco was more than foreplay. "The disco experience is an overwhelming experience of now-ness . . . an experience in which the dancer is, simultaneously, completely self-centered and quite selfless, completely sexualized and, in gender terms, quite sexless." This on-the-dance-floor decentering of the self required an overstimulation of the senses that recent innovations in sound reproduction and lighting technologies could recreate each night. The dancer's body had to feel the sound to such a degree that cognition was erased, and all that remained were moments of movement organized by the rhythm of the music.[38]

For two years, the discos of Austin effectively packaged this experience for local students. But, even at its height, the dancing in the mainstream discos was relatively restrained and efforts were made to limit the influence of African-American cultures. During the fall of 1976, the most requested song in Austin discos was Wild Cherry's "Play that Funky Music, White Boy," a number that mocked the tensions surrounding Anglo-American incorporation of African-American musical forms. In some Austin discos, racist admissions policies prevented black and white mixing on the dance floor, ostensibly because "minorities don't slug their drinks back fast enough." The White Rabbit, a disco that opened in the winter of 1976–1977, denied admission to one African-American woman "because she was wearing a turban."[39]

But lasting changes in the expectations of the audience, and in the method of delivering live music, did take place. In addition to demonstrating the importance of physical audience participation and quality sound, discos diminished the demand for cover bands—groups of musicians who replicated the recordings of other artists. The success of discos showed that people would pay money to dance to recordings. More expensive and less dependable than high-powered stereo systems and extensive libraries of recorded music, live musicians were no longer a necessary item in a prepackaged party. Furthermore, the best disco performances were wholly studio creations. The production teams of Gamble and Huff and Bernard Edwards and Nile Rodgers, were creating sonic textures in the studio that could not be reproduced in live performance for many years to come (when new technologies of tape synchronization, more sophisticated synthesizers, and digital samplers became considerably less expensive). Live music clubs simply could not compete with discos in the presentation of already known music for the purposes of dancing.[40]

While the disco phenomenon did encourage active audience participation, this activity was distanced from the production of the music. The high level of musical expertise and the increasing amount of technological mediation between the moment of musical production and that of consumption widened the gap between the performance of the music and its reception. Instead of producing an interplay between dancer and performer, disco constructed an audience free to pay attention only to itself. In Austin, a town where musical performance represented a romantic antimodern ideology and was judged in terms of sincerity, authenticity, spontaneity, and immediacy, disco music could not function as the center of a cultural practice capable of integrating elements from the everyday life of its audience. But, in the meantime, it reinforced the local focus in live music clubs on performers who were more than human jukeboxes. Slowly, gradually, the musical influence of disco would make its way into the live music scene in Austin, but its most immediate impact was to reemphasize original music performed by musicians capable of producing something more than recorded music could offer.

Clifford Antone had already assimilated many of the business lessons discos had to teach. Antone had a clear idea of the specific type of music he wanted to provide, and he presented his acts in a comfortable setting, conducive both to listening and to dancing. "We were a little more modern and a little more together than most clubs in those times," he says. Antone's opened with Clifton Chenier playing for five straight nights in July 1975, instantly staking his claim to being the place in Austin to hear nonmainstream blues and blues-related music. Antone's did not feature musicians playing other peoples' music. And those musicians he hired could be had relatively cheaply. Within his first year of operation, Clifford Antone brought Muddy Waters, Jimmy Reed, Willie Dixon, Bobby Bland, Sunnyland Slim, John Lee Hooker, Big Walter Horton, Albert King, Buddy Guy, Junior Wells, Koko Taylor, Clifton Chenier, and other significant blues performers to the west side of Austin for the first time. In between these road shows he would feature the local blues musicians who had been playing on the east side or in south Austin at tiny honky-tonks like Alexander's Place. The touring acts were able to draw a larger crowd, mostly because they attracted fans from across the race and age barriers in Austin, significantly expanding the number of people willing to pay money to listen to the blues. According to one fan, "It was real funny, cause like in Antone's there would be almost all white people unless a road show would come. And then all the 45-year-old black people would suddenly appear." The local white blues musicians were not able to draw these fans into a downtown club.[41]

Neither did they attract an audience of students. Clifford Antone remembers the club's first year as "the peak of progressive country in Austin, which I wasn't into at all. We were outcasts. The T-Birds and the Cobras together couldn't draw 100 people on a Saturday night." Omar and the Howlers were a white blues band from Arkansas who moved to Austin in the summer of 1976. Here, they were forced to bill them-selves as a "country and blues, rhythm and western band." In the fall of 1976, the One Knite closed, reducing the number of west-side blues venues by one third. Clearly, blues in Austin was not able to attract the student audience. It remained a music of dedicated fans and musicians, increasingly performed by and for a select circle of the knowing.[42]

As Austin's national reputation continued to shine (ironically height-ened by the disavowed Outlaw image), the capital city attracted musi-cians from other sections of Texas and throughout the South. On May 24, 1976, the Joe Ely Band from Lubbock, Texas, played at the Split Rail, a traditional honky-tonk in South Austin. The Split Rail had never competed for the student audience. Bill Bass had opened the bar in 1962, and, from 1966 on, the Split Rail provided Kenneth Threadgill and the Hootenanny Hoots with their most consistent gigs. In 1969, Marcia Ball's Freda and the Firedogs had pioneered progressive country at the Split Rail. The lower cover prices that discos charged in the mid-seventies had no effect on this honky-tonk's business. Jim Parrish (who had taken over the bar in 1975) kept the club open without charging admission, and relied upon more standard country-styled musicians to pull in a beer-drinking crowd. When musicians associated with progressive country played at the Split Rail, they performed their more traditional numbers, emphasizing the country components in their music. But when the Joe Ely Band played there in 1976, they performed songs written by Ely and by Butch Hancock, one of his friends from an old group called the Flatlanders. The crowd "overflowed into the parking lot, where the band sounded like it was coming from a jukebox the size of a Trailways." By the end of the year, Ely had recorded an album for the Nashville branch of MCA, and all of the ex-Flatlanders—Jimmie Dale Gilmore, Butch Hancock, and Joe Ely—had made Austin the center of their operations.[43]

This infusion of musicians from Lubbock renewed another traditional strain of country music in Austin. While the progressive country musicians most closely associated with the city (Murphey, Fromholz, Bridger, Walker) had emphasized the lyrical aspects to their compositions, writing within acoustic "folk" music conventions that emphasized listening over dancing, these musicians from west Texas carried a hard-core, hard-drinking, and hard-driving honky-tonk sensibility that blended easily with the orientation and the attitudes of the blues musicians in town. The band's tenacious performing style strengthened the link between the rhythm and blues of performers like Doug Sahm and Delbert McClinton and the "gut" country of Alvin Crow and Marcia Ball. Stylistically, Ely's music was not very different from the outlaw music of Waylon Jennings (also from Lubbock), but his performances at the Split Rail enacted and confirmed a local orientation that blended with the efforts of other Austin musicians. In effect, the "Lubbock Mafia" provided a crucial musical discursive node within the live music scene in Austin. They reinforced the reorganization of the scene around local performance conventions and musical genres insofar as their music was specifically contrasted with the nationally marketed and stylisticly similar outlaw music. And the core audience for this harder-edged blend of country, blues, and rock'n'roll was the Soap Creek "counterculture" regulars, the "social hangers-on," the alienated, disheveled and self-reflective organic intellectuals who were, in Ventura's words, "unable to rid ourselves of adolescent drives and dreams." This slightly older hip community found their hopes sung back to them and their demons danced out of them by this locally focused blend of rhythm and blues and honky-tonk country music in Austin.[44]

By February 1977, Hank Alrich had successfully steered Armadillo Productions through its bankruptcy hearings. An arrangement was established that would allow for new accounting procedures by which all services and goods purchased, including artists fees and advertising costs, would be paid upon delivery in cash, and back debts would be paid to the court out of the net cash flow at the end of the coming year. For their New Year's Eve celebration in 1976, the Armadillo hired three local bands: Too Smooth, Paul Ray and the Cobras, and the Wommack Brothers. Over nine hundred people attended, paying five dollars each for the entertainment, free champagne, and 1977 calendars. Total talent costs were kept under two thousand dollars, and, allowing for staff costs and supplies, Armadillo Productions cleared over two thousand dollars that night, exclusive of bar profits. Alrich and the rest of the staff had to have been thrilled by this indication of the success of their new plans.[45]

At the Soap Creek, the Majewski's were continuing a booking policy of rotating local acts and bringing in regional musicians who contrasted with the progressive country genre. For the acts who came in from out of town, the Soap Creek would offer a guarantee, but local musicians would play for the door (the total of the cover charges paid to enter the club by each member of the audience). On most nights, the Soap Creek incurred no talent costs. The audience would pay a three-or four-dollar cover, and they could hear four sets by the T-Birds or Marcia Ball's band, or Paul Ray and the Cobras, or Doug Sahm. According to Carlyne Majer, these bands made their living from their regular gigs at the Soap Creek.

It was an opportunity for a dozen or more bands to be able to pay their rent, pay their bills, and continue their career because they were capable of making a lot of money. The first Soap Creek had a capacity of 600 and we could do a turn around (well, remember we added a wing to that club in '75, we added a wing that held another 200, 300 people) because turnover was what we were all about. Most bands preferred not to play with any opening act because they could save that $250. These bands would come in and play three or four sets. When the liquor laws changed and we went to two o'clock, the turnover was great. People would stop into the club, the doors were cheap, three to four dollars cover. So it meant that people would come out for a half hour, or spend two hours or three hours and then leave. Which left us a lot of turnover in terms of the door. People would come real late for the last two hours and people would come early and go home.

Some bands could make a living within the honky-tonk economy described by Majer. But it was also an opportunity for some bands to go broke. Again, in Majer's words, "The irony is you play for a percentage of the gate and whatever you're worth you make." In the context of the honky-tonk economy, the traditional material mediation for musical performance in Austin, musicians were "worth" the number of people they could draw to a club. In these terms, the worth of Austin musicians became an airy, almost magical affair, overdetermined by the complex relations of marketplace competition. When dealing with club owners, trying to book gigs, the performing musician was directly confronted with her or his position in the overlapping set of cultural systems that operate to produce her or his difference, meaning, and value. Any anti-commercial ideology would necessarily be strained by this confrontation.[46]

The ballot for the *Texas Sun* (as it was now called) 2nd Annual Readers Poll was published in the issue dated January 28, 1977. It included both a greater number of categories and specific nominations within each category. The editors nominated bands in only a single category each in order "to avoid splitting votes." Therefore, country bands were differentiated from rock bands in this ballot, resulting in an interesting fissure cracking through the progressive country edifice. The Joe Ely Band was classified as country while the Lost Gonzo Band played rock; Butch Hancock, Marcia Ball, Alvin Crow, and Greezy Wheels were all included in the country category, with Doug Sahm joining the Uranium Savages and Balcones Fault in rock. The Blues/Soul group included Paul Ray and the Cobras, Jimmie Vaughan and the Thunderbirds, and seven other bands. New categories included Best Dee Jay and Best New Band. The band of the year was the only write-in category.[47]

When the results of the voting were published two months later, Paul Ray and the Cobras were declared the most popular band in Austin. But the balloting was very close, and the results showed both a consolidation and a fragmentation of the Austin live music audience. Significantly fewer ballots were cast than had been the year before. Each genre had one (or two) key acts that were successfully promoted to the smaller Austin scene as the best for that style. Yet in the overall category, no consensus could be found. The Cobras received 9.5 percent of the total ballots. Tied for second were Alvin Crow (country), Balcones Fault (rock), and the Point (jazz), each with 7.5 percent of the votes. Not surprisingly, two of these last three groups won the generic category in which they were nominated (Alvin Crow finished second in the country division, behind Asleep at the Wheel). Progressive country continued to exert some influence as Willie Nelson and Marcia Ball repeated their victories as best male and female singers, and deejays from KOKE swept the top three slots in their category. But, in its current form, the Austin scene no longer was unified by a single musical taste. And it no longer embodied (in the tastes, pleasures, and desires of its participants) a collective representation of the nostalgic antimodernist myth that united cowboys and hippies in a consensus on the meaning of being Texan.[48]

That May, Marcia Ball signed a recording contract with Capitol Records. One of the more self-reflective singers in town, with consistent local support, Ball analyzed her relationship with the Austin audience in an interview with Michael Ventura.

Austin creates the scene. That is the magic of Austin. It makes its own scene. Austin people have to have a place to go, where they can see everybody they know. So I was a part of it, and I feel proud that I was. I feel more like an instrument—an instrument of the Austin tendency to group the way they do. It's not who's here playing music, it's that the people here appreciate it enough to make it a big deal. What draws attention is that there are clubs and clubs and clubs, and people filling them up every night.

This vital music scene was created by the "Austin tendency to group the way they do," which in turn grew out of the historical importance of the honky-tonk as a site for negotiating the tensions produced in a newly urbanized and industrialized culture. By the mid-seventies, the middle-class, Anglo population of Austin—itinerants of privilege, alienated from their origins, living in a town established on an aesthetic whim—had developed a tradition of grouping in clubs, listening and dancing to the only artistic form that made any sense out of their feelings of dislocation, anxiety, and possibility, and musically constructing a new connection with their origins.[49]

Marcia Ball was unique in being able to land a national major-label recording contract in 1977 without leaving Austin. Only the Joe Ely Band had been signed the year before. These two performers were probably the last Austin-based musicians contracted by the recording industry as progressive country acts. Other musicians with national recording ambitions were leaving Austin for the west coast, just as bands had done throughout the sixties.

That summer, Doug Sahm headed west to play on Rick Danko's solo record. He wrote an open letter to his fans that the *Sun* published in August, explaining his two reasons for moving: the increased opportunities on the west coast, "This thing with Danko could go anywhere"; but more importantly, "let's face it, fellow Austinites, the scene is rapidly decaying from the lovely, stoned, slow town it once was to a sometimes circus of egos that has made it not the fun it used to be." The city of Austin was indeed growing beyond its "lovely, stoned, slow" state, but it was the transformations in the scene itself—that traditional arena of antimodern protest—which Sahm most bitterly protests. Now a "circus of egos," the professional tensions within the music scene in Austin were a product of the increased competition for a shrinking nightclub audience (now reduced to its core constituents) and the beginnings of a reorientation of local music businesses toward the national recording industries. No longer able to subsist on earnings from live performances, local musicians had to choose between either accepting part-time jobs or focusing their attention on non-Austin audiences (including both extensive touring and soliciting the attention of major label representatives). Despite the assertions of Carlyne Majer, no Austin acts were able to support themselves solely through Soap Creek gigs. In fact, it had been Majer herself who negotiated Marcia Ball's contract with Capitol, representing her as a progressive country act, packaged for Capitol's Nashville division.[50]

In December 1977, the local press was again reporting financial troubles at the Armadillo. There had been no net positive cash flow during the year, and, therefore, no progress had been made on debt reductions. The staff had been reduced to twenty-four people—the bare minimum required to run shows at the large hall. Many of these people were not receiving checks, had given up their homes, and were sleeping in the front office. The belief that the Armadillo was the essential element in the Austin music scene was still strong among these unpaid laborers. One employee was quoted at the time, "I can't imagine what Austin would be like without an Armadillo. I feel like the Austin music scene will die, if Armadillo goes." Alrich was forced to give up his booking policy that focused on local bands because, "what we found was that nobody local can draw on this scale." Unlike the smaller clubs, the Armadillo could not survive without the participation of a large student audience. With the collapse of the progressive country alliance, there was no easily exploitable link between the local music scene and the students. Alrich saw this as bad for both the clubowners and the musicians.

There's really not an Austin sound or any great professionalism among the musicians. They're not thriving locally. You can't find a band who is making it in Austin. All of them are having to hustle out of town, because there are a tremendous number of pickers who have to take whatever the club owners will fork over, whether they're good musicians or bad.

It appeared to Alrich that, in the winter of 1977–1978, the Austin music scene had fragmented to such an extent that discriminating between good and bad local performers was no longer a simple task. The club owners competing with Alrich had contributed to this condition by hiring diverse musicians and by paying them only the accumulation of minimal cover charges. Musicians were forced to leave Austin because they could no longer subsist on live performance earnings only and because they could not win recording contracts while performing only in central Texas. In the absence of a dominant musical aesthetic, a central headquarters and effective gatekeeping by club owners, the quality of music in Austin had declined. The good musicians were forced to leave town, to go to where they could earn more money. According to Hank Alrich, bad music had driven out the good, through the inflationary pressure of too many musicians and too many clubs.[51]

In order to halt this outward flow of musical capital, Bobby Bridger argued for the development and implementation of an industrial strategy.

I've seen so many people come through here in the eight years I've been here who say, "Well, it's time to go to L.A.—we've got our shit together"—and they take off to L.A. and that's the last you hear of them. . . . And I've been screaming for years, "Hey, let's stay here and do it here." Make a different place here. Make ourselves a counter-culture music thing. Let's just do that. Just don't make us one like all those other places. Austin's a power spot. That's the way I see it. I'm not the first person to ever say it, but I'm certainly on the list of people. It's an energy spot and it catches all of us sooner or later. . . . Cause this is really the place to be right now. From all indications, it's the place to be for a long time, too.[52]

Articulating essentially the same argument that Eddie Wilson had been making for six years, Bridger was calling for a local system of industrial gatekeeping that would be sensitive to local meanings and local traditions, yet that would still be able to make qualitative discriminations and reward the select few who had proven their abilities in local live performances. Instead of having to move to L.A. or to New York to compete for a recording contract, musicians should be able to remain close to their pastoral muse, in this "power spot." The hope was that by developing and implementing a locally controlled industrial strategy, the necessary commodification of Austin music could avoid inauthenticity. No outside interests would interfere in the cycle of production and consumption. This concept of an industrial production purified of outside interests continues to be the dream of those involved in the music business in Austin: the desire to "make ourselves a counter culture music thing" that could fulfill all the functions of a music industry while maintaining strict local control over its effects.[53]

At its peak, the progressive country movement had established a cultural hierarchy of musical tastes and performers that effectively maintained an "Austin sound." At the top were Willie Nelson, Jerry Jeff Walker, Michael Murphey, and a few other artists who were consistently able to perform a powerful musical articulation of a traditional central Texan masculine identity. These musical performances created and maintained a contingent affective alliance that linked university students with musicians, business people, politicians, administrators, and even law enforcement officers. The base of the hierarchy was this audience of students who were momentarily hailed by this identity and who found pleasure in the self-conscious performance of the dominant Texan culture. For some, this commercially encountered identity took hold, providing a relatively stable position from which to encounter the world. For others, progressive country remained an enterprise organized into a circulation of commodities, where the "worth" of a particular musical performance was overdetermined by a complex of interacting cultural factors. As the experience of dressing like (Anglo)Texans, drinking like (Anglo)Texans, and dancing like (Anglo)Texans to the kind of music (Anglo)Texans like lost its appeal for the students—when performing the culture of the (Anglo)Texan no longer produced the necessarily momentary pleasures of an illusory completion—the students turned away and began to look elsewhere for reflections of themselves.

When the progressive country alliance ceased to be effective, the Austin music scene was divorced from the interests, needs, and desires of the college students. Musicians who had trained themselves within this framework found that they were playing increasingly for each other and for their aging core audience. Younger musicians attending the university were not attracted to this scene; they were put off by the perceived insularity, the relatively high level of musicianship that the genre had developed, and an increasing dissatisfaction with the vacuity of anti-modernism. According to Steve Chaney, a younger musician who had moved to Austin in the middle of the decade,

I think that that whole cosmic cowboy thing was tuned to the older musicians and it was such a big thing I think in some ways it sort of intimidated some of the younger musicians from doing stuff. There really wasn't much happening with younger people playing original music in Austin in the midseventies. There were older guys and the blues scene was burgeoning at the time, the southern rock/blues thing. That was a pretty tight little society too. Jesus, you had to know your minor ninth suspended chords just to feel like you had a place.[54]

Looking back at this time, Jeff Nightbyrd recalled, "The cosmic cowboy was a marketing device built in part around somebody who was very genuine, Willie Nelson, who was just a gifted conveyor, a gifted storyteller and song writer." But by 1977, "No alienated eighteen-year-olds at the University of Texas thought, oh, I'll be a Cosmic Cowboy. They were starting to do hard rock and metal and loud turn-up-the-amps-and-blast-our-senses stuff."[55]

Indeed.

CHAPTER FIVE

Punk Rock at Raul's
The Performance of Contradiction

Offered the choice between two self-reflective spectacles of alienation—
the disco and the local live music scene—many college students in
Austin turned their musical attentions elsewhere. In New York, London, and Los Angeles, young musicians, art students, and clothing
designers were elaborating a new musical aesthetic and a new theory of
performance that would radically change the tastes of Austin's rock'n'roll
fans, and would revitalize the city's live music scene. The musical roots
of American punk rock lay in the midwestern and west coast garage rock
of the midsixties. In the wake of the British Invasion (that period of
the midsixties where record companies in the United States promoted
any band with a mop-top and a British accent), thousands of white suburban American (usually male) teenagers formed combos that produced
a crude copy of the records created by English art students imitating
African-American musicians. Bands like the Shadows of Knight, We the
People, the Unrelated Segments, and the Chocolate Watchband created
a twisted testimonial to the (often misogynist) power of three chords
and a grunt. In 1972, a New York rock critic and historian named Lenny
Kaye compiled and annotated a collection of several of the more popular recordings of these bands for Elektra Records. The release of *Nuggets*
established the generic conventions of sixties punk rock: limited but
unrelenting rhythms, a reduced range with a strained vocal tonality,
minimal instrumental embellishment, and a constricted, whiny, "snotty"
attitude expressed both in the lyrics of the songs and in the styles of the
singers. American punk rock of the sixties took the chords, the beats,
and the lyrical images that blues musicians had developed into an expressive form of great emotional breadth and discarded all but the most
immediate signifiers of frustrated male sexuality. This was a music that

any boy could play six months after he found a guitar under the Christmas tree, a music that expressed "the relentless middle-finger drive and determination offered only by rock and roll at its finest."[1]

By the time this record was released, Lenny Kaye had already played rudimentary rhythm guitar during a poetry reading given by Patti Smith at St. Marks Church in New York. Within three years, the Patti Smith Group became the center of a New York music scene that combined the emotional orientation and the musical simplicity of sixties punk rock with a textual self-consciousness and an artistic ambition nurtured by contact with New York's literary, theatrical, and artistic circles. The misogynist thrust of this proto-punk music was subverted by Patti Smith's extended program of self-construction, a self-presentation which deconstructed rock'n'roll's gendered expectations. Performing atonal but physically expressive guitar solos, Patti Smith foregrounded and made explicit the phallic implications of lead guitar playing. In her lyrics and in her published poetry, she created a series of subject positions that demanded identifications across traditional gender lines. And in the publicity photographs taken of her by Robert Mapplethorpe, she presented herself as a more intelligent, more artistic, and (since somehow still feminine) more dangerous Keith Richards. Patti Smith cut into and opened up the surface of punk rock, creating a space for feminine intervention and performance, a space that would be exploited effectively by women in the English punk movement.[2]

Playing to the same minimalist sensibility that had supported the Velvet Underground and the New York Dolls, the seventies punk rock musicians in New York created a rock'n'roll essentialism, an antimusical formalism centered upon the idea that rock'n'roll defines an attitude.

What makes a rock'n'roll band great is not so much *what* they play as *how* they play it. . . . The talent comes in taking those six chords and putting them together better and more effectively than anybody else. . . . What makes rock'n'roll the all-powerful energizer that it is is the recognition by the performer of what's good and what's bad. It all boils down to essentials and . . . can be explained in three chords, two verses, and one chorus. Anything more is unnecessary icing.

The band that most elegantly embodied this rock'n'roll minimalism was the Ramones. Conceived in strict opposition to the technically demanding hyphen-rocks then popular on mainstream FM radio (art-rock, country-rock, jazz-rock), the music of the Ramones represented a "cartoon vision of rock and roll . . . bound to enchant anyone who fell in love with rock and roll for all the right reasons." They were described as "the most cleanly conceptualized New York rock show there is to see," and "rock'n'roll formalists, convinced that good R&R derives its maximum effects from solid shapes, from right angles and jagged edges." The Ramones first album was released in the spring of 1976, and the concept of a rock'n'roll aesthetic—the reduction of a previously expansive genre to its most bare elements, a reformulation of rock'n'roll conventions that organized a very basic structure around an ephemeral "attitude"—dominated conversations in the rock press, in nightclubs, and in the suburban bedrooms of rock'n'roll fans across the country.[3]

During the summer of 1976, the Ramones and the Patti Smith Group toured England. There they performed before a growing English punk rock movement that shared a similar minimalist musical aesthetic, but that articulated this minimalism with a set of political and cultural positions critical of the distancing effects of mass culture and concerned with encouraging the participation of the masses in the transformation of spectacle into situation. Malcolm McLaren's work with the New York Dolls in 1974 had convinced him that technical virtuosity was not a requirement for rock'n'roll music. Rather than auditioning expert musicians as he searched for a new band to manage, he began looking for individuals who could convincingly perform the contradictions that Situationists found in mass culture. According to Simon Frith, "McLaren's ambition was to turn spectacle—the passively experienced structure of reality that we, as consumers, live with—into situation, the structure blown up, its rules made clear, the possibilities for action and desire exposed." By the fall of 1975, McLaren's new band, the Sex Pistols, were playing at colleges across England (not in clubs or pubs and not in theaters like the Odeons), attempting to attract an educated audience who would observe the spectacle of the Sex Pistols, see the rules of rock'n'roll revealed, and seize the possibilities for action thereby created.[4]

The first fans of the Sex Pistols were art students. The Bromley Contingent was a group of committed Pistols fans who soon formed punk bands of their own. They met at a Pistols performance at the Ravenstone College of Art. Bernard Rhodes was a friend of McLaren's. He soon found a group of art students forming a band and, by directing them toward Situationist slogans and other strands of Marxist cultural theory, helped to create the Clash. When the Pistols played at a college in Manchester, Pete Shelley and Howard DeVoto were in the audience and, within two months, the Buzzcocks were rehearsing. Such flattery by imitation followed the Sex Pistols throughout their early performances.[5]

Soon this flurry of activity caught the attention of both young British academics and the British culture industries. Even as these two groups fought over the meaning of punk rock, such meaning escaped them and played across the surfaces of lives transformed by fandom. Increasing numbers of punk rock fans bought the records, wore the clothes, read the analyses, and developed a self-conscious awareness of the impossibility of their positions. The English punk rock rhetoric of revolution, destruction, and anarchy was articulated by means of specific pleasures of consumption requiring the full industrial operations that ostensibly were the objects of critique. This contradiction at the core of punk practice allowed for a wide diversity of interpretation, an openness toward divergent (in fact, contradictory) identifications, a complex of meanings, all of which have remained the progressive legacy of this movement.[6]

Punk smashed down the keepers' gates and encouraged participation in the production as well as the consumption of its products. Not only were fans like the Bromley Contingent motivated to start their own musical groups, but independent entrepreneurs were inspired to create new fan magazines, new design firms, new recording companies that could package, distribute, advertise, and sell this self-contradictory semiotic complex. Just as the first punk fans had recombined already existing elements of the culture into a collage signifying freedom, these punk entrepreneurs could recombine elements of the culture industries into a new distribution system. This is the aspect of punk celebrated in Dick Hebdige's classic work, *Subculture: The Meaning of Style*.

By repositioning and recontextualizing commodities, by subverting their conventional uses and inventing new ones, the subcultural stylist . . . opens up the world of objects to new and covertly oppositional readings. The communication of a significant *difference*, then (and the parallel communication of a group *identity*) is the "point" behind the style of all spectacular subcultures.[7]

When records by the Sex Pistols, Generation X, the Damned, and the Stranglers made the English top ten, this was considered to be a victory for punk rock as a movement and, by implication, for Situationist theory. The machinery of mass culture could be used to distribute representations of anti-mass-culture experiences. While this appeared on the surface to be a radical *détournement*, from a different perspective it showed the supple subtlety of capitalist cultural practice. Punk rock in England made explicit, at the level of youth culture and rock'n'roll music, the contradictions inherent in the mass reproduction of cultural signs of distinction and difference. And it showed that even the most difficult tastes could be broadly disseminated.[8]

In the United States, the commodities along with the more outrageous examples of the rhetoric of English punk rock received far better distribution than did the more thoughtful analyses. The anti-mass-culture message of punk rock was most directly marketed to those subjects of distinction-through-obscure-consumption: devoted rock'n' roll fans and record collectors. These were the individuals in the States who took rock'n'roll music seriously, and who paid rapt attention to every stylistic tremor that reverberated from the British Isles. For these fans, the smart anger of English punk rock lent an artistic aura to the dumb populism of the Ramones and extended the polymorphous sexuality of Patti Smith beyond the blurring of gender lines, suggesting the possibility of interactive relationships within the previously solitary pleasures of commodity fetishism. This new object of desire, then, blended with the rising aesthetic of rock'n'roll formalism to reinforce and make overt an already widespread American process of self-production through proper consumption. The notion that we are what we consume and that such habits of consumption align us with some groups and distinguish us from others did not require extensive theoretical argument in order to be accepted by American rock'n'roll fans. They had always distinguished themselves by the music they enjoyed. Thus, dislocated shards of critical theory began to be both articulated with and spoken as rock'n'roll common sense.

Throughout 1976 and 1977, American rock'n'roll fans devoured the latest fanzines and music papers from New York and London. *New York Rocker*, *New Musical Express*, *Sniffin' Glue*, *Punk*, *Sounds*, *Trouser Press*, (and later, *Slash* and *Flipside* from Los Angeles) provided lessons on the meaning of punk and how to buy it. At one point, *Trouser Press* established a "Rockline" that its readers could call three times a week for the latest-breaking "New Wave News." Ads for record companies, clothing designers, and other magazines provided the operating revenue for these journals of hip. The editorial content had only one goal, the promulgation of proper consumption. This was an incredibly important task. As Tom Carson put it,

Difficult as it is to say now, it's probably true that what's going on will be of large importance for the future of rock'n'roll, which is another way of saying the future of rebellion in this country. . . . Anyone involved, even in the most peripheral way—anyone who buys a record—shares some responsibility for the way things eventually turn out. . . . It's time to cut out the faking and the sloppy thinking and the inside jokes. . . . Let's have punk commandoes go out to make raids on the country side, and a half-a-dozen good new bands with wit, verve, and cool enough to spread the word. I mean, let's scrape the crap off the wall and get this fucking show on the road, man.[9]

But the forces of mass culture were a formidable adversary. In the March 1977 issue of *New York Rocker*, Alan Betrock critiqued the tight integration among the recording industry and the businesses associated with it. He attacked the "record company ads and favors [that] keep most of the rock press alive." According to Betrock, economic dependency on record company largesse was limiting the critical capacity of the rock press. "The vested and controlling interests are only concerned with fostering the incestuous nature of the business and the product, and of controlling what's sold, how it's sold, and where it's sold." After sounding a call to action, Betrock somewhat hopefully concludes that, "the whole structure of the mass media as we now know it may be permanently altered." [10]

These quotes illustrate what Frith has referred to as "a people's version of consumerism, the idea that record buyers had a right to maximum market choice, that record buying should involve customer expression rather than producer manipulation." Displaying an unspoken intuition that the production of subject positions was constrained and enabled by the available discourses, and the recognition that identification with the images and products of mass culture entailed a commitment that implied a degree of risk, rock'n'roll fans in the United States began to demand from their musicians a certain independence from the recording industry. Again in Frith's words,

> Independence in this context seemed to refer primarily to the question of artistic control: the punks . . . assumed an opposition between art and business, with honesty on one side and bureaucracy on the other. . . . Their music was progressive because it involved the direct expression of the people-as-artists. . . . Punk messages could be distorted by the process of commercial production, but only if this process was in the wrong hands. . . .

These assumptions became the core beliefs of the alternative recording industry that developed in the United States throughout the 1980s. But in 1977, such independence meant relative isolation from the networks that distributed cultural information and products across the geographic mass of North America. The rock'n'roll fan who did not live in New York or Los Angeles was forced to obtain all of his or her information at the closest small independent record store. [11]

These stores carried the magazines discussed above along with imported British singles and a selection of the growing number of independent American releases. JEM Records, the New Jersey company that pioneered nationwide distribution of imported rock'n'roll records during the seventies, serviced these independent record stores. JEM began its operations when a market developed for British art-rock records for which American companies had not picked up their options. It catered to the independent specialty stores that had developed a clientele who believed in the rock-musician-as-artist ideology. With representatives in

London, JEM could import experimental, punk, and new wave singles as soon as they were released. Within a few years, other record importers (among them Greenworld and Important) would develop additional distribution channels that would become critically important ingredients in the development of the alternative recording industry, linking the independent record stores of North America into overlapping commercial networks that processed both product and information. In record stores like Wax Trax in Chicago, Rhino Records in Los Angeles, Oarfolkjokeopus in Minneapolis, Rather Ripped in Berkeley, and Caper's Corners in Kansas City, fans bought records, argued with the clerks about what were the most important releases (and "importance" was the operative term), and posted signs asking for like-minded musicians to form bands with. The store that formed the center for all of this activity in Austin was Inner Sanctum Records.

Throughout 1977, as disco entranced the majority of students at the University of Texas, and as the local live music scene fought over the possible frameworks in which to perform nostalgia, rock'n'roll fans would wander into Inner Sanctum and argue about punk rock with Neil Ruttenberg and Richard Dorsett. Inner Sanctum Records was where Austin's punk fans first met each other, first listened to the new recordings being released, first tried to integrate elements of this new discourse into their lives. Louis Black was a graduate student in the history and criticism division of the Radio, Television, and Film department at the university.

When I came back here in '76–'77 I was listening to progressive country, and then gradually, because of Richard Dorsett who was working at Inner Sanctum, I began listening more and more to punk. Yeah, and I was actually real resistant at first. Richard and I got to be—I broke up with my girlfriend almost as soon as I got here—and I was horrible and miserable and Richard would come over and go, well, you know, the Dictators are playing at the Armadillo, you wanna come? And I'd go sure, and I'd come and I remember the Dictators cause they just blew me away. And then he made me listen to Jonathan Richman and he made me listen to the Talking Heads, and Elvis Costello. Almost all that stuff, the first time I heard it, it was because he told me it was great. And it took me a while, it was like resistance, and then I think it was Jonathan Richman when I finally, you know, I suddenly understood. I suddenly had this revelation, you know, you go through these revelations, when you realize that music didn't have to be that mature.[12]

Among those fans hanging out at Inner Sanctum, buying records, reading *New York Rocker*, and starting to talk about forming bands, was a large contingent of students from the Radio, Television, and Film and the Communications departments. Most of these individuals—Tom Huckabee, Sally Norvell, Phil Tolstead, Dave Cardwell, Randy Franklin,

Dan Puckett, Brian Hansen, Joel Richardson, Jeff Whittington, Neil Ruttenberg, and others—had come to Austin from other parts of Texas and had chosen to attend UT's production-oriented communications school because they wanted to make movies or work in journalism. They were entranced by punk rock, this art form that seemed so open. Tom Huckabee was an aspiring filmmaker who soon was drumming for two of the most important Raul's-era bands, the Huns and the Re*Cords. For him, "Punk rock was appealing because it demanded no skill. We were all dilettante artists and so an art which made no specific skill demands, which we could immediately pick up and begin performing, was very appealing. And the performance aspect was the most important. Punk rock was not music to us, it was performance art." [13]

Many of these communication students and "dilettante artists" were sensitive to the spectacle produced in punk performance. They saw the gap between the technical skills displayed by local professional musicians involved in progressive country music and the need for an expressive art form that could articulate some of the immediate local needs, desires, and frustrations of younger people in Austin. Soon they would exploit this lack in local cultural production, and, by expanding the gap rather than closing it and by importing a new set of aesthetic criteria, change the way music was made in Austin.

Several of these students were writing about punk music and its possible implications for the student newspaper, the *Daily Texan*. Jeff Whittington, in particular, was transcribing the national and international debates into locally comprehensible statements for the readers of this paper. Looking back, Louis Black remarked on the importance of his writings.

When you were saying, who was I reading, I was reading Jeff Whittington. More than anybody else, I was reading Jeff Whittington. And what I liked about Jeff Whittington was that Jeff was going to rave about the Ramones and he was going to rave about Television but he was also going to rave about the Carpenters. . . . Jeff Whittington was a cult figure. I mean, yeah, everybody would read him. You waited till Monday to see what Jeff Whittington had to say. [14]

Whittington was able to describe the rock'n'roll formalism that had been worked out by New York punk bands and critics in terms that students at the University of Texas, in a context of reception dominated by alienation from the famous local music scene, could understand and work with. In opposition to the reifications presented in both progressive country and white blues, punk rock's "roots are pure exhilaration, pure noise, pure energy, pure fun. Nothing fancy about it, not much soloing, no 'poetry' for lyrics. And it doesn't much matter if the day's musical conventions aren't taken too seriously." Whittington argued that "serious" rock fans "miss the point in assuming that rock and roll is something that can be captured in a sequence of chords." Rock and roll is defined by what it communicates, "rock and roll feelings—feelings of energy, of urgency, of involvement." These feelings challenge people, demanding a response, requiring a demonstratively active participation from the audience. For Whittington, punk represented a purification of rock'n'roll, a return to the basic function of direct communication of shared feelings and a renewal of the contract between performer and audience that demanded an interactive exchange of immediate expressions, determined only by the interdependent coexisting moments of consumption and production. His advocacy of a return to rock'n'roll basics reinvoked the mode of musical production and reception that had dominated Austin music during most of the previous fifteen years.[15]

Louis Black was also writing for the *Texan*, as were Neil Ruttenberg, Richard Dorsett, and others of the Inner Sanctum crowd. Their articles contained shortened versions of the debates they had been carrying on with each other about music and culture, debates that had been sparked by reading the national and international punk press and listening to punk music. In a review of Jonathan Richman, Black and Dorsett wrote that

Criticism demands at least the appearance of objectivity, but when talking about any art/entertainment form, it is usually only the appearance. Movies, music, paintings, dance, etc., must touch us in personal ways; in a sense, isn't that their purpose? To become obsessed with formal elegance and to announce and articulate certain aesthetic rules that the object in question must completely fulfill in order to be worthwhile is foolish. There are formal considerations in any genre, but it is the way one interacts with what is taking place that is finally most important.

In the months when the first local punk bands were forming, the Inner Sanctum crowd was articulating a position on how punk could mean in Texas, educating both musicians and fans on proper consumption, the conventions of punk performance, and reception aesthetics. This was punk redefined for Austin: a renewed emphasis on local participation and a guarantee of personal interaction between performer and audience.[16]

Another early group of punk fans was made up of young local musicians who felt excluded from the remnants of the progressive country scene. Included in this group were Kathy Valentine, Carla Olson, Eddie Munoz, and Jesse Sublett. In early 1977, Sublett and Munoz met Marilyn Dean and Kathy Valentine who, in Sublett's words, were "two young tough rock'n'roll chicks who smoked cigarettes and wore black leather and looked like Keith Richards." They were looking for women with whom to form an "all-girl punk band." Valentine had spent some time in London and had brought back with her a sense of excitement, involvement, and possibility derived from punk rock. By the end of the year, Valentine and Dean had hooked up with Carla Olson and formed a band called the Violators. They had difficulty locating a bass player, so Jesse Sublett would rehearse with them. By January 1978, Sublett had booked a gig for the Violators at a Mexican bar on Guadalupe Street.[17]

The *Sun* had been paying very little attention to any aspects of punk until the Sex Pistols announced that their tour of the States included two nights in Texas. Then the *Sun* ran a story intended to answer the question, "What is punk? Is it an entirely new lifestyle of decadence reflecting the anarchy and rebellion of disaffected British youth, or just loud, fast music played amateurishly by scrawny 19-year-olds indistinguishable from their audience?" Clearly favoring the second interpretation, Sally Jones described a night she spent at a Boomtown Rats show in London where the punk fans were really "nice, bourgeois 19 year-olds—not dead-end kids, but a bunch of harmless 'rebels without a cause,'" and the musicians were "generally middle-class boys cashing in on the Establishment money which promotes their concerts." According to Jones, sociological analyses of punk "have entirely misjudged the weight and seriousness of the revolution." Texans will have nothing to fear from this circus, Jones reassured the *Sun*'s readers, for all it creates is a "fake anarchy, a fashionable affectation."[18]

On January 8, 1978, the Sex Pistols played at a renovated bowling alley in San Antonio called Randy's Rodeo. The day before the show, they wandered around Austin, going to movies, slipping into clubs to drink a beer and smash a bottle, staring at the students, and making fun of local musicians. McLaren took advantage of every gathering crowd to spread his standard Sex Pistols promotional rhetoric, in an effort to construct an educated audience in Texas similar to that the Pistols entertained in England.[19]

Every member of Austin's fledgling punk scene drove down Interstate 35 to San Antonio that night, even those who had conflicting engagements. Louis Black was invited to a wedding party that evening, but he went to the show afterward.

Cowboy was going to get married the same night as the Sex Pistols. So first we went to the old Soap Creek up in the hills where he was getting married. And we saw Alvin Crow and there was a buffet and a whole bunch of us, you know, Ruttenberg and Richard Dorsett. And we all ate and listened to Alvin

Crow for an hour. Then we got in our cars and we drove an hour and a half south, walked into Randy's Rodeo, and in the back, there's these leisure-suited people who were, like, obviously friends of the owner who had to come see what this was. The place was packed. And then the Sex Pistols come out on stage and I had never seen anything like this. I mean, it was like—it wasn't as religious for me as it was for other people. When you look back at it, the number of bands that formed out of that night, you know, in the moment when Sid took his bass and smashed it into the audience and Johnny Rotten goes, "Oh, Sid's dropped his bass." Every moment of this, you watched it. There was very little music. They didn't do a whole lot of songs. It was more like screaming and yelling and spitting and the audience spitting back. It was just, you knew music was never going to be the same. I remember walking in. I don't remember a whole lot of concerts. I've seen hundreds, but you remember the Sex Pistols, even though it wasn't even what I would have wanted, which was like a rousing version of "Anarchy in the U.K." or something like that. It wasn't a galvanizing musical moment. If anything, it was antimusical. But it was galvanizing at the same time.[20]

Three days later, Jeff Whittington's review of the concert appeared in the *Daily Texan*. In it, Jeff tried to puzzle out the reality of the experience. The band and the crowd had behaved strangely, creating a feeling of emotional intensity. "A fairly constant rain of beer cans, paper, clothing, and food landed onstage while the band played." But much of this behavior seemed like the audience was doing what it was supposed to do, as though the rock'n'roll audience in central Texas was acting self-consciously like punks. "The apparent volatility of the audience reflected the popular stereotype of violence at punk-rock concerts in England—a stereotype which has little basis in reality." But this performance of punk artifice was disturbingly convincing. "There was something schizoid about the event—at times it seemed that cans and firecrackers were being thrown in a twisted spirit of fun, at other times genuine malice seemed to be the motive. . . . All through the show it was difficult to be sure which emotions, on the part of the group and of the audience, were real and which were feigned—what was pretense and what was in earnest." Whittington's reaction was precisely that desired by McLaren. The distinction between spectacle and reality had been deconstructed to the extent that the most knowledgeable local critic could not discern any difference between them.[21]

Whittington's story did not mention the event that dominated local television news coverage, the moment when Sid Vicious swung his bass into the audience in an ineffective attack on a heckler. He was much more intrigued and troubled by his own inability to read this concert, the fact that he was unable to establish a coherent interpretation and create a single stable meaning by which to explain the Sex Pistols in Texas. His only conclusion was that a performance medium so saturated in contradictory expectations and so intertwined with systems of mass communication and production could take hold anywhere, with unpredictable results. "One observer stated that the English punk scene was largely created by London trendsetters copying what they thought was happening in a New York scene that was still largely embryonic at the time—and the New York scene only flourished when it began copying England. A similar by-the-bootstraps trend emergence could conceivably take place here." Before the end of the year, Whittington's prediction would come true.[22]

Roy Gomez was a successful Kentucky Fried Chicken distributor who wanted to establish a bar on the west side that would feature live performances by some of central Texas's best Tex-Mex bands. He bought an old bar centrally located on the drag and changed its name from Gemini's to Raul's. He hired Joseph Gonzalez, Jr., to manage the bar, and the two of them began to book bands like Ruben Ramos and the Mexican Revolution, Little Joe y la Familia and Salaman. These bands had successful recording careers and toured extensively throughout the southwest and the midwest, sometimes going as far north as Michigan. They represented a popular musical culture with demonstrated audience appeal, yet which had no regular performance site on the west side of Austin. Tex-Mex musicians operated in an entirely different world from that known as the Austin music scene. Gonzalez and Gomez wanted to bring performances of Tex-Mex music to the university area and were convinced that this project would be profitable. Their original booking policy at Raul's reflected an emerging Chicano cultural awareness and a political movement that had ties both to the university's strong Mexican-American Studies program and to the growing economic and political importance of Austin's Chicano population.[23]

One night a week, Raul's would book non-Tex-Mex acts. These bands tended to play jazz or other styles of music ignored by the mainstream of the Austin music scene. On occasional Thursday nights, Project Terror would play a fusion-humor-jazz stylistically similar to some of Frank Zappa's ensembles. They had a gig on January 12, four days after the Sex Pistols performance in San Antonio. The week before, Jesse Sublett had talked Joseph Gonzalez into adding the Violators to this bill. The *Sun* announced the event in a small blurb on their "Inside Austin" page, with the headline "Austin Goes Punk." But Sublett got sick, and the Violators had to cancel this first announced punk show in Austin. The next open night for punk at Raul's was January 28.[24]

In the meantime, Sublett, Munoz, and Billy Blackmon took the glitter-blues music they had been playing, sped up the tempos, flattened out the melodies, reduced the lyrical content to the most elementary expressions of punk frustration, and then coated this band in a self-reflexive protection against charges of incompetence by calling themselves the Skunks. If they could claim that their point was deliberately to make bad music ("Our music stinks!"), then they could ward off criticisms from the local music establishment. Sublett has described the Sex Pistols' San Antonio performance as "more of a manipulation thing, more of a spectacle than music." Even when he felt physically excited and emotionally engaged by the Sex Pistols' album, or by the music that he was playing with the Violators and the Skunks, Sublett remained convinced that the simplicity of punk's musical structures rendered it illegitimate. The dominant identification of the musicians in the Skunks had been with the flashy guitar work and the supple rhythms of the blues scene. In their own eyes, the Skunks were merely a joke, something to do, and punk was a fashion, a trend to play with, a way to draw a new audience. Not interested in exposing the structure of this spectacle, merely taken by the way in which it energized audience response, Sublett jumped on the trend. He cut his hair short and rebooked the Violators and the Skunks for January 28th at Raul's.[25]

The *Sun*'s promotional blurb for this show included a defensive Sublett quote about the musical skills of both bands. "You can be interesting without being commercially, technically adept. Be short and sweet, fast, without that much bullshit . . . [sic] sometimes a lead break—that's it. We work harder when we play than most musicians." Here Sublett justified punk's rock'n'roll minimalism by means of a work ethic and an anticommercial rhetoric designed to make punk more amenable to Austin audiences. But in the same article, the women in the Violators insisted on the musical basis of their performance. "It's a shame the punk media doesn't refer to the music at all. It's not social statements; it's a musical statement," Olson said. "We'll play anywhere people want to get down and have a good time." While the men needed to distance themselves from the contemporary standards, the women wanted to be taken seriously as musicians. In both cases, fun was the object. In line with the *Sun*'s position on the English phenomenon, punk in Austin was represented as simply about having a good time.[26]

Sublett had expected both bands to attract the Inner Sanctum crowd; that was the point behind billing themselves as punks. While they did draw some of the punk fans, the Violators found that a significant proportion of their audience consisted of the "leather girls crowd. They were way into the Violators from the beginning." The women in the Violators felt no need to distance themselves from the musical importance of their performances because there had been very few female musicians in either the progressive country or the white blues scenes in Austin. Women had been mainly singers in both of these genres. Valentine's and Olson's emphasis on the production of fun through their guitar playing (a "musical statement" played "anywhere people want to get down") opened a new set of musical pleasures for women and helped to establish an overlap between a growing women's music scene and the rock'n'roll scene in Austin. Before the end of the year, Valentine and Olson would move to Los Angeles. However, by that point the Violators had already performed the punk rock deconstruction of long-standing barriers to women's participation in musical production for an audience of local women eager to hear women play loud music and eager to begin performing themselves. Thus one of the primary and most long-lasting effects of the musical statements of the Violators came from their local performance of new possibilities for identification, pleasure, and musical production among women in Austin.[27]

From the first local punk show in Austin, members of the audience were duplicating the rowdy cup-throwing behavior they had either witnessed or read about occurring at the Sex Pistols' shows. At first, Joseph Gonzalez did not approve of this crude behavior in his club, and he kept the punk shows limited to one or two nights a month. In the meantime, the Armadillo began to book some of the national punk bands that were touring the country, drawing some of the new generation of college students back into the huge hall. Tom Huckabee was making videos of fans singing Ramones' songs from the top of nearby hills. Skip Seven and Ty Gavin formed the Next, and this band began to share the punk nights at Raul's with the Skunks and the Violators. Richard Dorsett was raving about the Next and the Dictators with one breath behind the counters at Inner Sanctum. Jeff Whittington was reviewing the Ramones' second album and the Talking Heads' second album in the student paper. More students began to attend punk nights at Raul's. Gradually, these nights became the central event for a growing crowd made up of Inner Sanctum customers, communications students, writers for the *Daily Texan* (with several individuals filling all three of these roles), gays, lesbians, and alienated musicians, in a self-defined celebration of marginalization that eventually made sense to the Chicano management of the bar. This marginalization was experienced at a variety of different levels by each of the groups. But the discourses that disciplined these different margins fed on each other, reinforcing the semiotic display of alienation and refusal that grew in intensity as each group was linked to it.[28]

Like folksinging in the early sixties, punk was a musical practice that differentiated among Austin's university students. Throughout the progressive country era, music in Austin either succeeded or failed in attracting students. Among club owners, students were conceived of as a monolithic audience bloc that could mean the difference between a night that made money or one that went bust. Raul's was the first club in ten years (since the closing of the Vulcan Gas Co.) that presented music designed to attract only a subgroup within the students. One ritual of audience participation at Raul's marked this distinction. It involved screaming the names of hated popular musicians and requesting the most despised songs. Despised music was commercially successful music, hated because it was the music favored by the undifferentiated mass of college students. Punk at Raul's constructed a pop culture elitism. Many punk fans at Raul's were college students who believed themselves to be smarter than most college students (that is, more culturally adept), and the evidence for their superiority was their appreciation of this "smart" music most college students could not stand. Within this discourse of distinction, common college student musical taste was associated with the social groups that made up the memberships of fraternities and sororities—the dominant social groups on campus. Thus, as punk repeated many of the strategies utilized by Austin's folksinging students fifteen years before, it revived the honky-tonk setting as a site for musicalized critique.

That summer Phil Tolstead and Dan Puckett, both students enrolled in the College of Communications, began to plan their own band. Tolstead and Puckett were fans of punk rock. They had been following the movement in the press and listening to the music on the records, and they were frustrated by the absence of "real punks" in Austin. When they began seriously to put their band together, they were joined by Manny Rosario, a tough-talking Puerto Rican guitarist, and Tom Huckabee on drums. Together, the Huns wanted to combine some of the elements they had been reading about in their courses in the university with the music and the fashions of punk, and to create a band that would perform all of the relevant contradictions at once. It seemed to Huckabee as though "the Sex Pistols had established an audience for what we wanted to do. They gave it a name—punk rock." The "manipulation thing" that Sublett found demeaning in punk was precisely the meaningful aspect that attracted these young musicians. The Huns "wanted to be the shock rock band of the world. We had big ambitions." [29]

The Huns' first show was scheduled for September 19, 1978, at Raul's. This performance was designed for a specific audience. Just as McLaren had aimed the Sex Pistols at art students in England, the Huns were conceptualized as a spectacle for the punk rock fans who were students at the University of Texas. They printed up and distributed posters derived from Jamie Reid's Situationist-influenced work for the Sex Pistols. The posters were not nearly so sophisticated as Reid's record covers, carrying slogans like, "Legalize Crime," and "No Police." But the word spread throughout the communications school that this show was not to be missed. This band was to be Austin's answer to the Sex Pistols and to all of punk rock. "We wanted to start with a bang."[30]

"At nine o'clock on Tuesday evening, Raul's is almost filled: it's already difficult to find seats. The crowd is heavy with regulars, some of whom take advantage of the situation to sport hard-core punk regalia: safety pins, ripped shirts with hand-scrawled messages, black makeup." So begins Whittington's story on the "rumble at Raul's." As part of the performance, members of the audience "sport" the appropriate costumes and prepare for their role in the show. They are "animated, surprisingly loose for a Tuesday night."[31]

The opening act was Cold Sweat, with Steve Chaney on guitar. Chaney's narrative of his night at Raul's emphasizes the animated and supportive character of the audience.

Our band is playing our set, and I've never really played on a concert stage. Here we were, in a packed club. We play nine songs, completely incompetent. At one point we almost completely break down. We didn't have it together, and the crowd, they were like cheering us on. It was like you were on the ropes, and they were like, come on, come on, just take the standing 8 count and get back in, you'll finish the round. And that's, it was amazing, you know. They were like Yeah! And we were like, wow, that's the worst version of "I Fought the Law" I've ever heard. But they liked it.[32]

Between Cold Sweat's performance and the appearance of the Huns on stage, Whittington stood outside of the club, debating with other fans the meaning of Devo's first album. Inside, a number of almost stereotypical punk actions took place. A roadie yelled "Achtung!" into a microphone; members of the audience yelled back. Some of the Huns wandered around the crowd "exchanging verbal shrapnel with passersby." When the band reached the stage, Tolstead snapped in his best Rottenesque, "We're not here for your entertainment; you're here for ours."[33]

In a manner derived from the Sex Pistols, the Huns wanted to confront and negate the expectations of their audience. Many of their efforts at negation led them into standard punk rock conventions: the attempted *détournement* of Nazi regalia and the German language; the almost ritualized displays of antagonism between the band and the audience. But the local context dominated the meaning of these symbolic gestures. Instead of Marcia Ball's searching out the eyes of her fans, striving to sincerely communicate heartfelt emotions and construct a communion of dancing souls, the Huns were working to display contradiction and antagonism. In contrast to progressive country's pastoral poetry, punk rock was a means to express strong negative feelings about their world. "We had real fantasies about blowing it all up. We definitely wanted to stir the shit," says Huckabee. The Huns wanted to create within Raul's a vortex of symbolic destruction that would disable communication, reach beyond the basic conventions of musical performance, and involve their audience in a ritual of self-hate. By piling antagonism on antagonism, through a constant disruption of expectation, the Huns intended to create an overwhelming sense of negativity that would transform all who experienced it.[34]

But their audience was hip to the show. They got it, they knew what was expected of them and they wanted to participate in this mutual construction of negativity. The same audience that cheered on the wobbling performance of the more standard band, Cold Sweat, was willing to remake itself for the Huns. Like the good sports they were, this already knowing audience proudly, self-consciously acted like punks— throwing paper cups and beer at the performers, screaming obscenities, rushing the stage—joyfully performing their assigned role in this deconstruction of the traditional musical experience. It was good fun. When Tolstead sang a few bars of "Puppy Love," members of the audience knew that they were supposed to throw ice. During the third song, fans rushed the stage and carried parts of the drum kit out onto the dance floor, rendering obvious the point that this performance involved so much more than the people onstage. Two songs later, a group of fans dumped a full garbage can onto the stage, spewing smashed and torn paper cups, broken bottles, and a spray of stale beer across the performers. Meanwhile the Huns played songs like "I'm Glad He's Dead," about the assassination of John Kennedy, and "You Bores Me," an attack on the Skunks.

During the next song, "Eat Death Scum," City of Austin police officer Steve Bridgewater entered the club, ostensibly answering a noise complaint. He stood by the door for a few moments, observing the appearance of chaos around him. In the middle of the song, Tolstead spotted Bridgewater, pointed his finger at him and, improvising a new line, chanted, "I hate you, I hate you." Slowly, Bridgewater made his way through the crowd, approaching the stage as if drawn there by Tolstead's pointing finger. Tolstead continued to chant "I hate you, Eat Death Scum," at the police officer, while Bridgewater stood two feet away from the singer, leaning in closer and closer toward him. From Huckabee's perspective, the two appeared to be nearly nose to nose, as if performing an odd duet: Tolstead singing the authority of the performer, the police officer silently representing the authority of the state. Inching closer together on the stage of Raul's, these clashing frames of interpretative authority could not remain in perpetual equilibrium.

Bridgewater screamed over the music, ordering Tolstead to stop. With the cop only inches from his face, the singer leaned over and, in another gesture of disrupted expectation, kissed the cop on the lips. This disturbance of gender rules was more disorder than the officer could stand. He snatched at the singer's wrist and slipped one handcuff on him. The singer grabbed the microphone with his left hand and shouted out over the P.A., "Start a riot. Start a riot." Two men dressed in polo shirts and gimme caps jumped up from the audience onto the stage to help the cop subdue the singer. The second handcuff was attached as both of the singer's arms were forced behind his back. Other members of the audience jumped onto the stage platform to help their friends who had gotten into a fight with these strangers. The club's bouncer, Bobby Morales, tried to pull the strangers off the stage. The drummer, bass player, and organist continued to play. The police officer pulled out his radio and called for assistance. Manny Rosario, the guitarist, echoed the gesture of Sid Vicious at Randy's Rodeo and swung his guitar over his head, smashing the radio out of the officer's hand. The officer whirled around and, with one punch, sent Manny flying through the air. The instant he hit the ground, the guitar player was up and running out the back door. Uniformed police officers swarmed into the club, the music came to a halt, and the audience stood around in shocked dismay, as the performance was finally completely disrupted.

The police arrested six people: Tolstead, Morales, and four fans, including Nick Barbaro and Richard Dorsett. All were charged with participating in a riot. The two men in gimme caps and polo shirts who had jumped onstage were revealed to be undercover police officers. They had radioed in the noise complaint from the club's bathroom. When Bridgewater called for help from the front of the stage, the police department responded with approximately fifteen units. Within minutes, the police had blocked off Guadalupe street and cleared out the nightclub.[35]

The remaining Huns—Huckabee, Puckett, and Joel Richardson—found themselves at Bert Crews's apartment near police headquarters. There they spent the night, calling lawyers, trying to get their singer out of jail, and trying to find their guitar player. They were furious with the police, but the irony was that, without their official intervention, the evening's performance would not have achieved the band's goal of "stirring the shit." Although their intensified display of semiotic contradiction had provoked a violent response out of the audience, up to the moment when the uniformed police officer entered the room, the violence had been performed within quotation marks, by an audience in on the joke, aware that they were only helping to create a simulacrum of a simulacrum—copying London, copying New York, learning from representations found in newspapers and on records, analyzed in classrooms and private discussions. It was all a play of signs and all in good fun. But once police officer Steve Bridgewater entered the club the material effects of clashing local codes were made immediately evident. Those audience members who shared the interpretative frame of the Huns had been participating in a performance of "violence"; those audience members trained to impose social control quickly moved to suppress the violence they saw. The Huns and the police together succeeded in creating a relatively clear demonstration of the material and polysemous nature of the sign, as well as the power that can be brought to bear in order to enforce one specific meaning of a sign when conflicting social interests are involved.

A storm of interpretative acts took place that night and the next few days. Manny Rosario caught a bus out of town and did not return for three weeks; the violent expression of police authority carried no ambiguity for him at all. Across the street from Raul's, writers for the student newspaper were filing stories criticizing the police for not being culturally aware. According to the *Daily Texan*, the police had simply failed to understand punk conventions. Bridgewater was accused of not knowing the difference between "Life" and "Art." However, the student writers had failed to comprehend the radical nature of the *détournement* that had been achieved. Even as they worked to reestablish the distinctions between symbolic expression and material reality, posters began appearing on the drag proclaiming "No Huns, No Fun," and showing Steve Bridgewater's police badge under the caption, "Kill Steve Bridgewater, Pig, Pig." The cop assigned to the drag beat arrested Bert Crews with posters in hand, initially charging him with terrorism. The entire thirty-six-hour-long event had been a triumph of Situationist intervention. State authority had been so threatened by the possibility of a different system of cultural meaning that posting flyers on the drag had become an act of terrorism.[36]

Joseph Gonzalez was outraged that his bouncer, Bobby Morales, had been arrested for trying to break up a fight. "Our security was trying to break it up and [the police] clubbed him. [The plainclothesman] never identified himself. Nobody here was fighting, it was part of the act." The police action cemented the relationship between Gonzalez and his young white customers. An editorial in Thursday's *Texan* made explicit the temporary alliance between punk and Hispanic subcultures. "If Bridgewater's unwarranted, irresponsible actions reflect the prevailing mentality down at APD, then it's much easier for us to understand why police billy-clubbed Chicanos last April during a boat race demonstration."[37]

Three weeks later, in a judicial act of interpretation, Phil Tolstead was convicted on a charge of disorderly conduct. Judge Steve Russell based his verdict on the opinion that "Tolstead displayed assaultive behavior toward Bridgewater." The decision of the court was that Tolstead's gestures, his singing, and his kiss constituted assault, justifying the closing down of the performance and the handcuffing and jailing of six persons from the club. The Huns had indeed given a powerful performance, far different from the traditional display of moral authority or the communication of shared feelings. Obviously, punk could not represent merely a contrasting choice in the marketplace of Austin music. The response of the criminal justice system declared that the Huns and their fans had rudely violated the boundaries of legitimate expression. This rock'n'roll truly challenged people. It was not safe to like it; you could get beat with a billy club; you could get arrested. The ability to derive pleasure from punk rock gave an instant aura of danger, independence, and power to any individual. Clearly different from a taste for any other music, liking punk rock seemed to produce momentary experiences for middle-class Anglo-Texans akin to the everyday life of Blacks or Hispanics. Soon Raul's was packed every night with students longing for that identity streaked with power and danger.[38]

Punk rock at Raul's might have been "performance art," but it was also music, a music that generated the physical energy that distributed erotic charges throughout the chambers at the heart of the scene. Young people picked up guitars and drums and keyboards and microphones and played and sang songs. The songs had chords and melodies and beats and words. However important an underlying concept or a theatrical component was to any band's performing style, the core of this signifying practice was music; the participants were music fans and musicians.[39]

The musical aesthetic at Raul's operated on principles of transgression and inversion, derived from the critical function of this practice in the very construction of the scene itself. The professional musician, able to provide disinterested renditions of popular songs, was despised. It was absolutely essential for the punk performer to provide some evidence that he or she was risking some component of his or her being, was negating their identity in an interplay with the abject, was questioning in some way the construction of the position from which they performed. For some, merely daring to sing a song with no obvious musical training was risk enough. The much-vaunted musical virtuosity displayed in the progressive country and white blues scenes was not valued; in fact, musical simplicity was emphasized as a means of opening the path to the stage. But this simplicity remained the quality of a music powerful enough to carry the lyric, rhythmic, and harmonic expressions of an underlying semiotic disassociation and, at the same time, to produce a "freeing situation" capable of sparking the recombination of repressed elements of the human in a search for new identities. In the scene that germinated at Raul's and soon spread into other venues, the performance of rock'n'roll music in the carnivalesque arena of the honky-tonk again became available as an organizing frame for the pleasurable display of the negativity and contradiction that derive from the semiotic production of the subject.[40]

A close look at two songs from this period will map out the range of the musical and lyrical construction and deconstruction of subjective possibilities in this scene. The Huns' "Glad He's Dead" was performed at their first show and became a regular part of their repertoire. They released it on their own label, God Records, in 1979. The recording displays the stylistic debt the Huns owed to the Sex Pistols, and in many ways this song is the "God Save the Queen" of the Raul's era. It begins with eighth notes on the kick-drum setting a rapid pulse that does not vary throughout the duration of the song. A distorted rhythm guitar and bass enter, stabbing on an off-beat at a D chord, and then pounding the remainder of the bar on an A, before beginning the harmonic structure of the verse: an alternation of measures between the tonic E and an odd G-sharp major. The harmonic tension produced in this chord structure, playing off the expected transition to the subdominant A, is a relatively common trait for a great deal of punk rock, owing at least partially to the simplicity of its execution. Dan Puckett's voice screeches the first lines in a generic Johnny Rotten sneer. "He sold us all the Bay of Pigs. He gave our schools up to the nigs." "Nigs" receives an additional emphatic marker as Puckett squeezes a half-note rise out of an extension of the vowel sound. While the guitars shift between the subdominant (A) and the dominant (B), the other members of the band chant the chorus in a monotone background to Puckett's scream: "I'm glad he's dead, the fucking red. I helped Lee Oswald shoot him in the head." After three verses attack John Kennedy for his Catholicism, the Cuban missile crisis, the death of Marilyn Monroe, Viet Nam, as well as the Bay of Pigs and the integration of southern schools, the final verse describes the assassination scene and declares, "Lee Harvey Oswald, America's friend." The song ends with laughter resounding over the whine of guitar feedback, while the pick-up switch clicks off and on.

Musically, the song is generic punk rock, from its opening drumbeat, distorted guitar tones, and rhythmic accents to its closing feedback. Lyrically, the song stumbles through an unsubtle assault on the Kennedy myth. Not particularly clever, "Glad He's Dead" appears on the surface as only so much outrageous noise. But by imaginatively returning this song to its more common performance context within the scene at Raul's (where, undoubtedly, the musical and vocal execution would become more haphazard than the recorded version), we can begin to ask what subject positions are produced within "Glad He's Dead." How does this musical text help to establish a structure of identification for its fans?

From the stage of Raul's, surrounded by fans throwing ice and dumping garbage pails, Puckett sings the beliefs of the red-blooded, right-wing, white Texan male—that traditional identity which punk in Austin refuses. However, the first response upon listening to this song is not revulsion but laughter. The inversion of the moral and social order (the working-class, racist, reactionary Texan celebrating the murder of the privileged, progressive, east-coast president) along with the grotesque image of the Kennedy myth produced in the lyrics (including descriptions of the president on his knees before the Pope, of the extent of his sexual urges, and finally of his brains on Jackie's coat), creates so powerful a shock that the immediate response can only be laughter—that bodily recognition of the "contradictory and double-faced fullness of life." When Puckett laughs at the end of the song, he enunciates that same laughter which the song provokes. Constructed between a laughing audience and a laughing singer, the identifying structure is neither the hallowed myth of Kennedy righteousness, nor the cracker who claims to have helped Oswald with the assassination, but instead has become the subject of laughter, "an interior form of truth . . . that liberates from the fear . . . of the sacred, of prohibitions, of the past, of power." Thus, "Glad He's Dead" is not so much a depiction of Kennedy, Oswald, and the events in Dallas than it is a critique of cultural authority in two of its most effective local forms: the regional authority of the cracker father and the national authority of the generation that claims the myth of Camelot and the slain president. Both are laughingly dismissed over a scream of electronic feedback.[41]

A similar critique of power and authority is maintained in an otherwise quite different song by the Reversible Cords, "Big Penis Envy." The Re*Cords performed on the sidewalks and in the capitol, as well as in the clubs of Austin. Displaying their musical ineptitude like a badge of honor, the Re*Cords embodied more completely than any other band in Austin the belief that you do not have to be a musician to play punk. As many of their performances were with acoustic instruments, they often were not even loud. Rather than promulgating danger and negativity like the Huns, the Re*Cords set themselves up as the "court jesters" of the scene. "Big Penis Envy" was first performed at the 1206 Club in Austin and was released in 1980 on the band's only album.

The song begins with a fragile, tentative guitar line that searches for its notes, in an immediately evident inversion of the masculine power chords common to punk. It then flows into a descending chord change (A–G♯–F♯–E), played to a rudimentary shuffle rhythm weakly tapped out on a snare drum. The recording features alto and tenor saxophones slithering through their ranges, in uncanny imitation of the atonal vocalizings of the singer, who begins the song with a rising wail. "Sometimes, when we make it, I'm scared I'm going to fall right in. I've got big penis envy, Da-da, da-da, da-da, da." Dada indeed, the singer bemoans his diminutive penis, the size of a twig, smaller even than the three-inch tool of those experts who insist that size is not important. Throughout this inversion of the stiff, assertive model of masculine authority, vocal lines waver and tremble, the guitar limps through its licks, the drums seem incapable of regular rhythms. The sole lyrical passage stated with any sort of assumed authority is the bridge: "I wish I had a penis the size of Alcatraz. People would bow below it, and it would have pizzazz. I know that this is not my fate, I'm destined to be razzed. Don't say I'm inadequate, uh-uh, I know it."

It does not take a great deal of Lacanian training to interpret this description of the prison house of the phallus and its effects, but it is worthwhile to point out the direct lines the Re*Cords draw between their send-up of patriarchal power and their parody of punk rock's musical aggression. The song constructs a musical arena of weak boundaries, easily permeated. The verse slides into the chorus, vocal lines overlap, the tonalities of the saxophones imitate the whimpering voice while constructing tangential melodies. When the bridge arrives and all the instruments begin to play in time, the audience affirmatively shouts along, "Don't say I'm inadequate, uh-uh!" In "Big Penis Envy" the Re*Cords perform their own and their audience's placement in a Symbolic still constituted by unequal gender relations, where power remains visible, quantitative, phallic. The overt humor of the song, though, deflects the thrust of the critique displayed in the inversion of the standards of musical power, enabling any audience to sing along, to laugh along, again in the "double-faced fullness of life," without assuming any identity mirrored back to them. Nevertheless, the positions constructed in the song, although doubled through parody and therefore necessarily unstable, enable a questioning of the discursive links among power, the phallus, loud guitars, and the construction of an autonomous subject within these symbolic associations.

"Glad He's Dead" and "Big Penis Envy" mark the poles of one axis of differentiation in the Raul's era of Austin punk. The wicked aggression of the Huns stands in stark contrast to the self-effacing humility of the Re*Cords. But both performances are united by the laughter they each evoke from their audiences. This open-throated response marks a contradictory relation to the traditional construction of performing and responding. Throughout the coming decade, the most committed Austin fans will question why they care what songs are being sung, why they continue to go out. The best bands that Austin will produce throughout the eighties will share this conflicted attitude toward their own roles as producers. They will not be able to assume unquestioningly the center of moral authority constructed within traditions of Texan music. They certainly will not imagine themselves to be autonomous business agents operating within a free market. Instead they will distance themselves from the traditional markers of staged authority and will perform in a self-effacing manner that many critics will call unprofessional.

The scene at Raul's marked a burst of creative activity that lasted almost three years. Bands formed, magazines were founded, record companies started, movies were made. This cultural explosion was both similar to and different from the initial progressive country moment. As with the earlier period of intense activity, musical performance at a specific site was the central activity within a number of overlapping cultural practices that mutually reinforced each other. Musicians, artists, filmmakers, and writers, drawn to this liberal oasis in the middle of conservative Texas, worked to make sense out of their feelings of alienation from the contemporary condition. The magazines that formed wrote about music and music-related activities. The movies that were made shared themes with and featured actors involved in the music scene. Artists designed posters and record covers. The Austin audience continued to demand that its musicians speak directly to them.

But the differences were also significant. Like the folksingers of the early sixties, Austin's punk musicians distrusted the commercial structure of the established music scene. However, punk musicians and their fans did not believe in the possibility of an uncommercialized "authentic" musical practice. Instead, punk in Austin created a new cultural production system that was at first wholly separate from the institutions of progressive country. This new approach to music was both more self-critical and more intellectual, which followed from the way that punk was disseminated across the country, as well as from the art school and bohemian origins of the genre. Correspondingly, this movement was more distant from Texan traditions and had much closer ties to the university than had progressive country. As in London, New York, and Los Angeles, punk in Austin was a media-conscious movement with a much higher degree of awareness and acceptance of the power of the communications industries to affect the meaning of experience. Rather than performing nostalgic paeans to a premodern utopia, punk in Austin celebrated the productive possibilities of late modernism. Punk's do-it-yourself ethic mitigated against any dependence upon the already existing power structures in the Austin music scene. If a band needed a manager, they hired the guitar player's roommate. If they wanted to record, they rented a four-track machine, set up in a garage, and laid down the tracks. If they wanted to read a story about their friend's band, they wrote and, often, published it. Thus, an entirely different group of people became involved in local music production in Austin.

Writing for the *Texan* besides Whittington, Dorsett, and Black during the winter of 1978–1979 were Nick Barbaro, Robert Draper, Scott Bowles, Michael Hall, and Ed Lowry. By the fall of 1981, these individuals would be writing and editing the *Austin Chronicle*. E. A. Srere and Margaret Moser began to write for *Sluggo* magazine, and a year later Stewart Wise and friends published the first issue of *Contempo Culture*. The *Austin American-Statesman* hired Ed Ward to cover local music. All of these people would eventually go to work for the *Chronicle*. Neil Ruttenberg landed a slot on the university's radio station, KUT, playing new music late on Saturday nights. That program has since been run by a string of different deejays, but its focus has not changed. A new band called Standing Waves formed to open for the Huns' second show. They would ask their station-wagon-owning roommate (and successful waiter), Roland Swenson, to manage them. The Waves included three talented songwriters and a rhythm section that could actually play together. Within two years, they would become the most popular band in Austin, with their local independently recorded singles receiving airplay on both AM and FM stations in central Texas. Swenson would go on to manage Duke's Royal Coach Inn (another bar that featured local punk and new wave performers), work with Joe King Carrasco, found Moment Productions, and forge (with Louis Meyers) the most significant business link between the Austin music scene and the rising alternative recording industry: the South by Southwest Music and Media Conference.[42]

At least thirty punk bands formed that winter, almost exclusively comprised of students, almost exclusively playing at Raul's. "It was in the air," says Mellissa Cobb, who at that time was in the Delinquents. "It was the obvious thing to do."[43] For a young Kim Longacre, "It was like this real eye-opening experience—that people could actually do something they believed in. Like to be weird or something. It was just so wild."[44] Louis Black insists that,

I think Raul's would have happened without the Huns bust. I think the Huns bust kicked it though, put it into fifth gear without going into second, third or fourth. There was that incredible first six months to a year, where literally half the people that were with you in the audience in the first few shows, by the end of that period, all had bands. I was having so much damn fun. All my life, I had kind of wanted to be an intellectual and a writer and know musicians and hang out and go to jams and stuff and now I was doing it. And it was like you know, it was really like what we had, the idea wasn't to make something definitive, it was to participate in the whole cultural process, and we did. Everybody we knew were in bands or making movies or writing about movies and we were talking all the time.[45]

Punk in Austin was not only a matter of proper consumption; it was also one of wholehearted production. A formalized, stripped-down rock'n'roll music, emphasizing "pure exhilaration, pure energy, pure noise, pure fun," provided the context for an overwhelming do-it-yourself era of cultural production that would establish the institutions and the discursive modes that would shape musical production in Austin throughout the 1980s.[46] During the decade to come, many of these individuals, institutions, and discursive threads would become more powerful and, eventually, dialectically integrated with the individuals, the beliefs, and the traditions prominent in the previously existing music scene. But in the eighties, the music scene could not be explained as a result of "the Austin tendency to group the way they do," but instead as a desire "to participate in the whole cultural process."

The burden of tradition that defined the popular history of music-making in Austin achieved a doubled inflection with the disruptions of punk. The antimodern critique of commercialism and work promulgated in the honky-tonks had become in addition a celebration of the possibilities of commercialized, musicalized, signifying practice. Within this contradictory arena, individual musicians and fans could mutually develop strategies of performance that encouraged the overproduction of signs of identity and community along with an overstimulation of the commodification processes of late capitalism. By the end of the decade, music-making in Austin will have become a thoroughly postmodern practice, with the commodification of identity inextricably interwoven with the musical production of subjectivity.

CHAPTER SIX

The Performance of Signifying Practice

Toward the Production of the Scene

Music scenes develop in Austin out of a confluence of factors. For decades, the university served as the sole tolerated center of negotiated difference. The expansion of the student population during the late sixties increased the numbers of alienated yet motivated young people in Austin. The university still guarantees a large population of young people, a potential pool of musicians and fans eager to investigate the possibilities of musical performance. Honky-tonk culture, Austin's "tendency to group the way they do," provides an historical context and a traditional setting for musical practice. The city's celebrated tradition of live music performance ensures a high profile for musical practice, both in terms of entertainment opportunities and for the explorations of identity through signifying practice. As we have already seen, popular musicians have historically played an important social role in the ongoing cultural construction of the social Symbolic in Texas.

Austin's reputation as a liberal oasis in a conservative state, as a refuge for those Texans different enough to consider themselves artists, continues to attract individuals who are not wholly comfortable with the dominant enunciative positions in Texan culture. Once in Austin, many of these individuals have entered into a musical dialogue with the dominant construction of identity in Texas. A consistent refrain in my interviews has been statements like, "The group of people I was hanging out with in Port Arthur, I guess we considered ourselves beatniks, and we were getting a little too far out for the Beaumont-Port Arthur area. We heard that Austin was a lot freer atmosphere and we moved to Austin, quite a few of us at the same time, in 1962."[1] Many talented individuals now come to Austin simply because so many others already have; an atmosphere of toleration has been institutionalized to a certain extent. Often young people move to town simply "Because it is where music is."[2]

[handwritten margin note: people not fully accepted in society go to Austin— it's a liberal oasis]

The national commercial success of the progressive country scene attracted both media attention and recording industry interest that together stimulated local entrepreneurs to develop booking agencies, recording studios, and management firms. The do-it-yourself ethic of the punk movement syncretized with the already dominant roll-up-your-sleeves entrepreneur mentality to create wholly new institutions of musical and cultural production. But all of this activity was centered on the public performance of popular music in the honky-tonk arena. And one of the most critical results of this situating condition continued to be the regular production of scenes.

In the years following the closing of Raul's, Club Foot provided the home for the more mainstream bands (bands that attracted slam dancers were at first restricted to Sunday nights and later banished from the club); the Continental Club hired neo-rockabilly musicians like the LeRoi Brothers; the Soap Creek employed the Big Boys on an experimental basis; and the majority of those bands who might be called punk were performing at nonclubs. Voltaire's Basement was the basement of a used bookstore, hired out to musicians by the punk fan who was living there. Scratch Acid, the Butthole Surfers, Meat Joy, Not for Sale, and other loud bands smashed their amplified midnight against the concrete walls of this underground cavern. Some punk bands played at a downtown warehouse that had been rented as rehearsal space by an all-women band called the Buffalo Gals. Many novice musicians lived in an apartment complex near campus called the Colony. Some nights they would open their doors and begin to play, creating impromptu parties as their friends came over, attracted by the sound and carrying cases of beer. Each of these sites provided venues where commercial pressures were lessened, where newly constituted musicians, inspired by the local dispersal of the punk ethic and its effects on the local musical aesthetic, engaged in a flirtatious identification with the abject and began to play their own music, thereby initiating that exchange of signs and sweat that creates a scene.

This was the part of the Austin music scene that I began learning about and working my way into after I moved there in the summer of 1982. I had been living in Los Angeles, where I had watched the west coast punk scene develop and had performed with a group of musicians who were being referred to together as the Paisley Underground. In Los Angeles, the territorial, musical and cultural distinctions between these two styles were precise—the hardening core of punk rising from the southern beach suburbs contrasted starkly with the melodic pop soaring out of West Hollywood. Very few fans and even fewer musi-

In LA— anyone not punk didn't associate w/ punk people, BUT

in Austin the two mixed in association

cians participated in both scenes. My first weekend in Austin, I went down to the Ritz on 6th Street. It was an August night, far too hot to go into that non-air-conditioned hulk of a building; so quite a crowd had developed outside. After a few minutes of hanging out and watching the crowd, I saw a young man stroll up with a beautiful bleached mohawk. His hair was perfect: his head was completely shaved except for a one-inch trail down the center of his skull; his mane was probably five inches long, not waxed into stiffness but rather standing up loosely, effortlessly, and flowing back from his forehead as he moved into the crowd. Everyone else in front of the Ritz seemed to know him. I was just standing there, simply admiring his hair, when the most astonishing thing happened. The punk turned as another young man, whose dirty blonde strands straggled past his shoulders, entered the circle of light in front of the club. As soon as they caught sight of each other, the punk and the hippie shouted enthusiastic greetings and closely embraced. It immediately became clear to me that I had a lot to learn about music in Austin. For the next two years I went to shows at Club Foot and the final version of the Soap Creek; I went to parties in backyards and bizarre performances in Voltaire's Basement; I read the *Chronicle* and jammed with several groups of struggling musicians; and then one night I heard about a place called Sparky's.

Sparky's was the initial venue from which grew the New Sincerity scene. Another less commercialized site—like the backyard parties, the Buffalo Gals' warehouse, and the Colony apartment complex—where beginning bands could tentatively assert their identities and interrogate the conditions that created them, it was one of those places where scenes develop. Mike Hall attended the first show at Sparky's, and his band, the Wild Seeds, became one of the more popular bands of the New Sincerity era. When he talked to me about his memories of Sparky's, Mike described a subjective, experiential difference between simply dancing and being in the scene.

to Not put able words in happness his being about being there

But you know, the feeling like, when you're not in a scene? And I'd go to bars and there was, I wasn't even conscious of a scene at all. It was like, just going out to dance. And all of a sudden I became conscious of the scene. And then you know, wanting to go write, wanting to get my songs into a band, wanting to get the band into a scene. The dynamic was, that was like, there was a time period there where before that I was a completely different person. And Sparky's was the thing that did it. Just because everybody started going up there and hanging out at, you know, this place where you didn't know where it was unless someone, unless you were part of the scene. You know, it was perfect.[3]

Simply knowing about this site marked the boundary between the inside and outside of this beginning signifying community. Once Mike knew Sparky's location, when he could drive up there and attend the shows, he became a part of the scene. Of course, he would not have found out about Sparky's without already being connected, but, curiously, he remembers his desire to participate actively in this scene as having been a result of this knowledge. His wish to be a musician rose to the level of felt desire only after he was already there, a member, a motivated participant in the cultural practice of local music-making. Once he became conscious of this scene, once he sensed its existence, Mike was motivated by a powerful drive to produce *something*, to engage in an exchange of signs, to get his songs in a band and to make his band known in the scene—as though he had always already been a member.

I asked Mike what he thought was important about this participation.

It was just having a deal. Having a thing to call your own. Not just yours but your band's, too. It was having your sound, having your songs, having your, I don't know, it was identity. It was identity more than anything else. Looking at another band and seeing their identity. I don't know, it was just, I don't know. Just getting up in front of people and drinking beer. I don't know. *It was just a whole new world.* I was in law school and I was trying desperately to get away from law school. So I threw myself into it. My studies suffered, my attendance suffered, but I think I found what I maybe deep down wanted to do my whole life, which is play music.[4]

Once in the scene, Mike began producing an identity for himself wholly within the terms of this embryonic signifying community—this whole new world of songs, of bands, of drinking beer in front of people—to which he suddenly, in a matter of one night's recognition, belonged.

Dianne Hardin, a long-time fan of Austin punk music, described a similar moment of self-recognition when I interviewed her.

I was fourteen and this friend of mine—I had this older friend, and he knew the Dicks. He was friends with them, and he was really neat. And he used to play like Devo and the Clash and I really liked the Clash. "Clash City Rockers" was like my first punk rock song that I liked. I remember once we were driving around, listening to music or something. But we saw the Dicks in a car. Gary Floyd, remember him? And he told me who Gary was and I thought, Wow, that's so cool. And then almost every weekend I wanted my dad to drive me down Guadalupe. So I could see someone with weird hair. Wow, maybe a mohawk, you know. I could see something cool. I don't know. Then, since I liked it so much, I wanted to then do it.

I asked Dianne why she liked it so much. She told me that,

It was different, you know. I never really felt totally successful at fitting in with normal people. I think, I don't know, I don't know even how hard I really tried. But I'm sure I tried to an extent. And felt kind of burned by it. Because even if I could do it, there just wasn't much to hold my interest about it. And I don't know, when I started hanging around with all the other punk rock people, I found people that, I don't know, it really had something to do with just wanting to do something different. With in a way being an outcast but then being accepted. It was new and different. And you were sort of bound together because the other people hated you. I think that might be part of the attraction, too, is being in a minority. Being in a self-imposed minority.[5]

What stands out to me in these stories, and many others like them, is that the desire to become an active member of this rock'n'roll scene arises at a moment of recognition, when the scene appears as a signifying community, marked off from the surrounding world, to which one, in some sense, already belongs—where the musicalized expression of semiotic disruption has immediate meaning.

Identification within the Scene

But it is clear that Speech begins only with the passage from "pretence" to the order of the signifier, and that the signifier requires another locus—the locus of the Other, the Other witness, the witness Other than any of the partners—for the Speech that it supports to be capable of lying, that is to say, of presenting itself as Truth.[6]

The most interesting and vital musicians of Austin are produced as such within and by that intensity of fan commitment and cultural production known as a scene. A scene itself can be defined as an overproductive signifying community; that is, far more semiotic information is produced than can be rationally parsed. Such scenes remain a necessary condition for the production of exciting rock'n'roll music capable of moving past the mere expression of locally significant cultural values and generic development—that is, beyond stylistic permutation—toward an interrogation of dominant structures of identification, and potential cultural transformation. The constitutive feature of local scenes of live musical performance is their evident display of semiotic disruption, their potentially dangerous overproduction and exchange of musicalized signs of identity and community. Through this display of more than can be understood, encouraging the radical recombination of elements of the human in new structures of identification, local rock'n'roll scenes produce momentary transformations within dominant cultural meanings.

In 1979, soon after she moved with her family to Austin from Palo Alto, California, high school senior Kim Longacre was introduced to the scene at Raul's.

I met this friend named Jeb Nichols who told me what was really good about music, and I believed him, and he introduced me to [the music of] Jonathan

Richman and Elvis Costello. He also introduced me to Raul's. And the drinking age was eighteen, so we'd go to the clubs. I remember going to Raul's and being really intimidated. People were very strange and a lot older than me and seemingly sophisticated in a real worldly sense. These people, the scene, I mean, I'm sure alot of it was self-imposed, but they seemed to have soul. Hardship, they knew hardship. They seemed so urban. From Austin. Which is really funny. But to me it was like this real eye-opening experience—that people could actually do something they believed in. Like to be weird or something. I mean, it was just so wild. It was the whole scene. It was the clothes, the attitude. It was the men in the women's bathroom. There were no rules. Anything went. You know, anything went, so long as it was strange. It was a freeing situation. Know what I mean?[7]

John Croslin formed Zeitgeist with Longacre in late 1983. He had already heard about the Raul's scene before he moved to Austin in 1980.

I was just at the age when I could go to the clubs and it was really exciting. It was wild. I was sittin' there in my blue jeans and T-shirt, lookin' at these people that looked kind of strange, actin' weird. And it was just real energetic. I guess it was the energy that attracted me. Everybody was jumping up and down.[8]

Mellissa Cobb grew up in the Austin area. She performed in a number of bands throughout the 1980s, but first decided to become a musician during the Raul's period.

Well, it was just like in the air at Raul's. I was just hanging out at Raul's with the Witches, who wore white face and odd, really grotesque makeup all the time. They would put fake blood on and tattered black clothing. Just do real bizarre things with the Huns and stuff. Later that fall [1979], I joined the Delinquents. It was the obvious thing to do.[9]

Marcia Buffington also moved to Austin during this period, dropping out of Baylor, a Baptist college in Waco, and transferring to UT. Marcee became a booking agent and managed the Austin band Doctors' Mob in 1984 and 1985.

I lived at 28th and High Street. It was cool, I could walk to Raul's. It was really funny, cuz when I first got here I still had long hair and I'd wear these little sun dresses. Fucking hell, I was going to Baylor. And I go to Raul's and these people go, "Oh, you really dress ni-ice." It was just kind of strange; I really didn't meet anybody there until I cut my hair off and started wearing funny clothes. And I don't think I was the only person that was like that. But you know, people who felt really, really misunderstood felt really comfortable in that scene. It really didn't have a whole heck of a lot to do with the music except that it was loud, and it was fast, and it really didn't sound like music at all. It sure did piss people off if you played it.[10]

These descriptions of the activity at Raul's carry linguistic markers of the important cultural practice that was taking place: "weird" and "wild," "strange" and "bizarre," yet also "freeing" and "open." In the rock'n'roll scene that was developing at Raul's, the social structures

The everyday life of a fan.   Photo by Pat Blashill.

that constituted the very basis of traditional identity were being questioned. The dominant meanings of rock'n'roll performance in Austin
were being actively resisted. Being a punk in Austin meant "being a
man if you're a woman, a woman if you're a man." Thick makeup and
"funny clothes" covered visual signs of difference with a costume that
unified the audience, the fans, and the musicians into one "self-imposed
minority." The knowledge of the secret location of one of the sites of
the scene and the parodic, self-conscious performance of "violence" by
audiences and band members alike marked the boundaries of an inner
space where traditional signs and behaviors could take on new meanings
or, in fact, be negated. In the darkness within the clubs, an uncanny
communion of the misunderstood led these young people into a musical
practice that combined an extraordinarily physical pulsion with an interrogation of preexisting standards of evaluation and a corresponding
questioning of traditional structures of identification.[11]

When discussing her experience in the clubs, Kim Longacre described it as,

more of a physical thing, I think. I was drawn to the music in more of a physical
way. I liked the way it made me feel. I liked the things that it said to me or didn't
say to me. I liked it because it didn't last long, you know. I mean the Huns are
not really listenable. I mean you can't sit down and go, Wow! You have to move
around and be mad or something. You bump into people and be real aggressive.
It was just loud and brash and, they were just noise.[12]

[handwritten margin notes: "outkasts"]

[handwritten margin notes: punk was an outlet for those w/ differing views of society]

Fans at play.   Photo by Pat Blashill.

Marcia Buffington also emphasized the physicality of her experience in the scene,

A lot of what I'd listen to back then, I'd come home and my hips would be bruised from being shoved up against the stage and I'd be all sweaty and hot and my mascara would be in my eyes. That was basically for getting your ya-ya's out. You'd get caught up in it, the physical expression of having a good time. I didn't like the music, I don't think, but I sure did feel cool being there.[13]

The importance of this intense bodily stimulation cannot be over-emphasized. The "physical expression of having a good time" is an integral component of experience in the rock'n'roll scene, and the physicality of musicalized experience goes beyond the critical importance of dancing itself as sexual expression. The meaning of a musical experience turns first upon the series of unconscious movements produced by the specific articulations of rhythm and timbre found in the music. This physical interaction among musical signs and individual bodies establishes the conditions that allow for the allusive combinatorial associations of cultural signifiers of identity and community. Within this fluid stream of potential meanings, the audience and the musicians together participate in a nonverbal dialogue about the significance of the music and the construction of their selves. Gestures of the performer contribute directly to the meaning of the musical experience, generating and being generated by corresponding physical responses in the listeners. While recent sociomusicologists such as John Shepherd are beginning

The Performance of Signifying Practice / 125

to focus on this physical component to musical meaning, even traditional musicologists such as Leonard Meyer agree that "motor behavior does play an important part in facilitating and enforcing the musical aesthetic experience." [14]

These theoretical musicological assertions harmonize with the words of Austin musicians. George Rieff moved to Austin from Houston in 1982. He described for me the physicality of musical performance and the interaction between the musicians and the audience in a successful show.

When it's good and the crowd response is good, it makes you feel great. It's nice to just feel the good feelings coming from the audience. Because of you. And you can feel it. It feels powerful. If you're playing, for instance, in an electric band and you got all this vibration coming from behind you or from the side of you and it's pushing at you, it's making you work. And you can see it going into the audience and you can see them responding and they're clapping and they're dancing or they're screaming or they're throwing bottles or whatever. And it feels really good. So long as you're not so old and jaded about the whole thing, it's gonna catch you up. It's gonna psych you in and the enthusiasm's gonna get up and the adrenaline's gonna flow. You're gonna play better and you're gonna perform better and that's gonna fire up the audience even more, and it's just gonna turn into a great show. And it's magic when it happens. [15]

Kim Longacre echoed the belief that "Good shows aren't what's fun, magical shows are." [16] And Hunter Darby, of the Wannabes, described his experience of a magical show, evoking a music that goes beyond listening, to a more inclusive sensuous reception. "Lots of times, when it sounds so tight, I can't hear my own instrument. I can feel it. I hit that deal where I don't hear anything, except everything feeling, sounding like one thing. And I don't think. I'm not having to think. That feels really good." [17]

Small clubs encourage an intimacy of interaction between the audience and the performer that musicians in a rock'n'roll scene depend on, as a founding instance of a "magical show." Tom Thornton of the Way-Outs insists that meaningful performances go beyond getting the notes right.

I think you can play a song perfect, but if you want that kind of communication to go across, something else has to be going on. If I start getting the chills, then I know things are going good. If I'm not getting a chill, I know the people in the audience aren't at all. I've been hoping to facilitate that process where I really get a rush out of it and part of that is looking at the audience and seeing if they're getting into it. It's so much fun. It's like a good sexual relationship. [18]

Ron Marks, from the band The Texas Instruments, also talks about how important it is for him to see his audience. "It's good for me, like I said, to be able to see people. Because I can tell that they're into it when

Doctors' Mob on stage.   Photo by Pat Blashill.

they're moving to the same thing that I'm moving to. I know it's corny, but it's a real charge. I can tell that they're getting off on it, I'm getting off on it, we're all coming. It's great."[19] Rock'n'roll musicians in Austin consistently narrate successful performances in such bodily, and often sexual, language. Kim Longacre talks about singing and responding to her audience as a matter of "getting in the groove emotionally. It's reciprocal. You pay attention to what is going on. . . . It's like, it's kind of like coming or something. Like, yeah, yeah, I feel that. Oh, I get it, yeah, and I give you that. You just kind of go with the flow."[20]

Conversely, fans too like to see the bands displaying their own pleasure. Maki Fife insists that, "one of the elements that makes for a good show is that you know that the people in the band are having a good time, and you know that they are really getting into the music." Joanne Weinzierl modifies this perspective somewhat, "It's when they act like they're having a good time. They look at each other while they are playing and act like they know what they are doing."[21] When Dave Roberts finds himself in the audience during a magical show he notices,

. . . a spreading contagion. You get excited and everybody else does and it sort of builds on each other. You're talking back and forth about how good that song was or, did you notice that? It's real funny to see one person get excited about it and even though you didn't notice it or weren't aware of having noticed it, when they call it to your attention you say, oh yeah. And that makes you more excited and more interested. I think it just spreads like a spark. I really do.[22]

The Performance of Signifying Practice / 127

These musicians and fans have described from their own experience a phenomenon that Freud discusses in his analysis of group psychology. "The fact is that the perception of the signs of an affective state is calculated automatically to arouse the same affect in the person who perceives them. The greater the number of people in whom the same affect can be simultaneously observed, the stronger does this automatic compulsion grow." Thus, eroticized gestures of the musicians (both musical and physical), together with the affective responses of the audience, represent and reinforce libidinal ties among all the participants, continually reproducing the momentary structures and the meaningful potentials that constitute the scene. As Freud insists, "the essence of group formation consists in new libidinal ties among the members of the group."[23] These physically reinforced libidinal ties become the fluid structures by which the signs of identity and community are charged with affect and made pleasurable. The bodies of the performers (particularly that of the lead singer) are framed on a stage, where their gestures map out a sexualized field of affect, meaning, and desire. The vibrations of the music then circulate an overwhelming eroticism through dancing and listening bodies, an eroticism that in turn is cast upon the widest variety of secondary objects, rapidly translating the libidinal ties of love and identification into one another and back again, in the overproduction of the signs of identity and the overstimulation of the senses.[24]

These are the necessary conditions for the development of a scene: a situated swirling mass of transformative signs and sweating bodies, continually reconstructing the meaning of a communion of individuals in a primary group. The carnivalesque atmosphere produced in rock'n'roll scenes—descended from European festival traditions, syncretized with African celebrative practices, commodified and made readily available in the honky-tonks that have traditionally provided the site for popular musical performance in Texas—this atmosphere nurtures situations where the boundaries between love and identification are never well disciplined, where eroticism and narcissism meld in the search for new elements of identity. As Dave says, "I mean, the more I get into it, the more I become part of the scene, the more I know these people, the more I know the bands, there's a new part of me, and it sets me apart and makes me, Me." Through an exchange of affectively charged signs and knowledge, Dave was constructing his own identity in difference.[25]

Precisely how does this production of identity operate within musical scenes? How are cultural factors incorporated into the structures of identification that constitute the scene? Conversely, how are aspects of the dominant culture repulsed through this process of radical yet pleasurable interrogation? Lacan's theorization of desire and the metonymic chain along which it proceeds can provide a basis for understanding the social construction of the possible positions from which a musician or a fan may speak, may sing, may dance, may desire. For Lacan, desire drives the search for identity. The struggle to develop a coherent identity derives from a complex process of developmental interactions between the primary drives of the desiring body and diverse symbolic cultural systems. As this process occurs, desire is transformed into multiple specific desires that, in turn, are inflected, interpreted, displaced, and, finally, either satisfied or repressed.

Lacan explains this process through his metaphor of "the mirror stage." He defines this moment of primary narcissism as "an identification . . . namely, the transformation that takes place in the subject when he assumes an image." The narrative of the mirror stage describes a mother holding a baby up to a mirror, who then mis-recognizes itself as precisely that reflected image, representing the identification between a still helpless infant and an image of ability and wholeness framed in the mirror. Lacan's intent is to underline the illusory nature of this identification and, by means of this developmental metaphor, to point toward the fundamental conditions of all identification. For Lacan, all identification involves an illusion of mastery, the mistaken belief that we can indeed satisfy our desires through rational action in the world.[26]

Lacan insists that all identification rests upon this fundamental *mis-recognition*, which "situates the agency of the ego . . . in a fictional direction which will always remain irreducible . . . whatever the success of the dialectical syntheses by which he must resolve as *I* his discordance with his own reality."[27] In this formulation, Lacan insists that despite the intensity with which the subject struggles to create a stable ego, this construction continues to rest on an illusion. Nevertheless, this necessary illusion of stability and wholeness enables the ongoing re-creation of an ego and allows this ego to assume the positions from which it can speak. Since identification implies the ability to satisfy desires through cultural symbolic means, each identification represents the assumption of a culturally established position of mastery. Identity, then, is the continually constructed product of the interactions of a desiring body with the complex cultural systems through which humans conduct symbolic exchange. Through this continual aspiration toward a series of culturally established positions of mastery, one becomes a subject.

Lacan's understanding of both the creation of a subject position and the ability to speak from that position depends upon the slippage in meaning, the absence of guarantees, that results from the necessary symbolic inflection of desire, the discipline that enforces the separation between mother and child. All desires—especially those desires for meaning and identity—follow and further complicate the paths created when oedipal desires are shattered against the disciplinary structures of the culture. Lacan describes the first impact of this symbolic discipline as the intervention of the third term, the "name of the father," into the mother-child dyad. This symbolic interruption disturbs the immediate satisfaction of desire that had previously constituted the child's awareness. According to Lacan's narrative, the child notices that the mother's attention can be called away from the immediate presence of the child's desire simply through a symbolic gesture. That is, because of the intervention of the "name of the father," the child becomes aware of the power inherent in the absent presence of symbolic communication. After this intervention of the third term, the desire of the child is deflected into specific demands that must be articulated symbolically. Each demand cried into the night and each satisfaction momentarily achieved then results in an illusory mastering of the symbolic system, reinforcing the agency of the ego. The illusion of wholeness signified by the image in the mirror represents the individual's belief that she or he is in control, the master of her or his own body and desires, capable of demanding satisfaction.

Desire, a preformal, abstract, and unshaped urge, drives the narcissistic search for wholeness, mastery, and plenitude (that is, identity), and through this search "desire becomes bound up with the desire of the Other."[28] For Lacan, those moments of assumed mastery, wherein the ego achieves a dialectical synthesis with the Symbolic, involve the mutual interaction of the symbolically inflected desires of multiple human beings. Lacan's (capital S) Symbolic is solely the condensed totality of the expressed and enacted desires of others; it is constituted historically on the basis of such momentary dialectical syntheses, through the misrecognitions of countless individuals. The desires of absent and incomprehensible others then become the "desire of the Other" and the symbolic expression of multiple desires abstracts into the Symbolic, the place where the subject's own desire and identity can be found, (mis)recognized, articulated, and expressed. As these desires are expressed and enacted they become part of the discursive and behavioral record of the group; they constitute the culture.

All identification, then, involves a certain amount of fantasy, and all identity is a project of what Lacan calls the Imaginary (that fictional direction instituted by the fantastic desire for wholeness, indicated by the relationship between the infant and the image in the mirror). The dia-

Marginalia (handwritten):

desires stem from the fact first desire (of mom) proved impossible ∴ we continue desiring new attachments for our feelings

use symbols to obtain desires

people know they deserve to be happy, or have their desires met at least

Symbolic — place where desire + identity are

identity requires fantasy — or the idea of striving to be something you presently are not lectical syntheses of which Lacan speaks involve reconciliations (which can be experienced subjectively as both the momentary satisfaction of demands—that is, pleasure—and as identifications) with a discursively constructed position within a symbolically constituted culture, and thus they participate in what Lacan calls the Symbolic.[29] Thus every achieved identity exists within and represents elements of both registers—the Imaginary and the Symbolic. The desire for meaning and identity drives the individual along a metonymic chain of possible "I"s— each of which could only be (mis)recognized from the position previously embodied—with each momentary identification marked both by transformation and by pleasure in the individual.

Motivated by desire, wound through the desires of every other member of the scene, each participant in the rock'n'roll scene constructs a self-image, an instantaneous (mis)recognized identity, formed out of the knot of these intertwined desires. Obviously, the specific desires of other participants as well as the historically and discursively sedimented residue of past participants do not form discrete objects of identification but instead function as structures of possibility, always receding before each member's reach. (This is what is meant by referring to the "knot" of other desires.) According to Maki, "We always felt like we were going towards this one big happy tormented family, but we never got there."[30]

The uncertain, ephemeral quality of these momentary identifications results in a productive anxiety. Fed by momentary pleasures of sensual overstimulation and the occasional linkage that promises completion, this anxiety provides the psychic impetus required to maintain a regularity of contact, a constant participation in the scene. "There was always that pressure that if you didn't go out, you were missing something. You had to do it regularly. You had to keep in touch, even though you didn't really talk to people and the way you talked to them was just that small talk. But we were good at small talk. And it was fun."[31] The musicians and the fans who embody the rock'n'roll scene in Austin are united by an intensity of commitment driven by anxiety. Yet this very consistency of interaction generates the celebrated structure of this signifying community through the constant patterned exchange of signs— "small talk," clothing, music, dance. Spectators become fans, fans become musicians, musicians are always already fans, all constructing the nonobjects of identification through their performances as subjects of enunciation—becoming and disseminating the subject-in-process of the signifying practice of rock'n'roll music.[32]

In order to more fully understand this process of identification in the rock'n'roll scene, it might be useful to turn to the neighboring field of cinema studies. The feminist film theorist Jacqueline Rose has reoriented the discussion of cinematic identification around the relations between the psychoanalytic concepts of the ideal ego and the ego ideal.[33] Rooting her discussion in Freud's work on narcissism, Rose defines imaginary identification as that transformative moment when the distance between the ideal ego and the ego ideal is momentarily reduced.

> The ideal ego would therefore be a projected image with which the subject identifies, and comparable to the imaginary captation of the mirror-phase; the ego ideal would be a secondary introjection whereby the image returns to the subject invested with those new properties which, after the "admonitions of others," and the "awakening of his own critical judgement" are necessary for the subject to be able to retain its narcissism while shifting its "perspective." . . . The ideal ego will therefore be what the subject once was, the ego ideal what it would like to be. . . . [34]

In other words, the individual projects onto the viewed image his or her own idealized concept of who he or she was in that remembered momentary plenitude of primary narcissism Lacan calls the mirror stage. The viewed image reflects back a transformed perspective that has been changed by its passage through the Other, which is then introjected as an ego ideal. Thus, identification is a twofold process of yearning projection and longing introjection. In film theory, this process of projection, introjection, and scopic identification is played out on the viewing screen, which then conceptually becomes the place in the field of vision where the viewer's projected ideal ego meets the film's projected enunciated subject.

As Rose insists, this theory of cinematic identification does not reduce to an identification with a single object that is introjected; the process does not describe a slavish imitation of a character on the screen. "[T]he subject relies on the Other in the imaginary relation, not to constitute a full identity, but in order to circumscribe a void identified with the Other's demand." This demand of the Other is expressed through the system of meaning (a specific articulation of the cultural possibilites of the Symbolic) within the film. An entire series of multiple identifications and desires have collaborated in the construction of this film, this subject position, this void with which the spectator conspires in imaginary identification.

Again, we are brought back to the knot of desires in the rock'n'roll scene, where a similar process of projection, identification, and introjection occurs. By multiple processes of identification "not with an object" but with multiple models—"a pattern to be imitated," abstract figures of possibility, fluid structures—the rock'n'roll scene establishes itself as such, constructing a signifying community based upon new enunciative possibilities within and among individual subjects.[35] When Kim speaks of giving to her audience, when Marcee talks about being caught up in the physical expression of having a good time, and when Ron talks about looking at his audience and seeing that they are moving to the same thing that he is moving to and describes this as "coming", they are all referring to the specific transgressive *jouissance* that marks the signifying practice of rock'n'roll. Within the shadows, smoke, and sound of the nightclub, the movements of fans and musicians are stimulated and patterned by the timbral and rhythmic articulations of noise into sound, affectively charged with the erotic undertones that support an extreme nonconscious sensivity to the transformative effects of signifying practice. As Maki told me, "It was really satisfying to keep in touch with people and you would see them again and you would feel like you were beginning to be a part of something. You didn't know what that something was but even if there was just one point in one conversation over the entire weekend that clicked for you or one song where you really danced, or someone remembered your name, that made all the difference in the world because you were a part of something."[36]

But what is this something that these people are a part of? Many scholars have focused on the importance of rock'n'roll practice within youth culture. Larry Grossberg, Simon Frith, Angela McRobbie, and Dick Hebdige have each structured components of their analytical approaches through the category of "youth." This literature's focus on the intersection of rock'n'roll and youth follows from some of the important early work by the Birmingham Centre for Contemporary Cultural Studies. Paul Willis's ethnographic representation of the culture of working-class (male) youth, *Learning to Labour*, and the Centre's joint project, *Resistance Through Rituals*, established an ongoing concern with certain particularly vibrant cultural practices of young people in Britain.[37] Unfortunately, the category of youth as used in these studies was not well defined, vaguely representing the period of years between the onset of puberty and the coming of familial responsibilities associated with full-time employment and children. I think it is important to shift the focus of this category. Rather than using the terms youth or youth culture, then, I want to discuss rock'n'roll practice within the socially constructed condition of adolescence.

Rock'n'roll scenes situate an important signifying practice of adolescence, which must not be reduced to simply a biological stage of individual development. Instead, I want to argue that adolescence refers to a psychological condition that is brought about by specific social factors.

This condition is characterized by an awareness of extended cultural possibilities combined with insufficient power to act on these possibilities. Therefore, it recapitulates the drama of the Oedipal crisis, the entry of the third term. For individuals experiencing this condition, the role of the Imaginary in identification is emphasized to the precise extent that the adolescent experiences an absence of solidity in the Symbolic (and, therefore, an absence of social power). Further, I want to argue that this imbalance in favor of the Imaginary is a direct effect of the social and discursive conditions we have learned to call postmodernity.

David Harvey has described the condition of postmodernity as a set of material and social processes related to the increasing speed of the flow of capital across the globe. His description can be usefully mapped onto the psychoanalytic categories and the processes of identification I have been elaborating.

> Postmodernist flexibility . . . is dominated by fiction, fantasy, the immaterial (particularly of money), fictitious capital, images, ephemerality, chance, and flexibility in production techniques, labour markets and consumption niches; yet it also embodies strong commitments to Being, and place, a penchant for charismatic politics, concerns for ontology, and stable institutions favored by new-conservatism. Habermas's judgement that the value placed on the transitory and the ephemeral "discloses a longing for an undefiled, immaculate and stable present" is everywhere in evidence.[38]

Harvey's postmodernity consists of a fluid social structure that produces a corresponding yearning for stability and purity. The condition of adolescence conforms to these defining qualities, resulting in and from an undependable Symbolic and producing an increasing investment in the Lacanian register of the Imaginary. Thus, the condition of adolescence—a heightened awareness of the pure possiblities of representation combined with an absence of social power and the inability to enforce discursively the qualities of these representations—is maintained, reinforced, and prolonged by the same material conditions that produce postmodernity.

This imbalance between the possible and the actual (which is not to say the Real) results in "open structure" personalities that characterize the subject in process of the signifying practice known as rock'n'roll. According to Julia Kristeva, open subjects have not "structure[d] themselves around a fixed pole of the forbidden, or of the law." They seem to represent "the fluidity, i.e., the inconsistency, of a mass media society" in that "[t]he frontiers between differences of sex or identity, reality and fantasy, act and discourse, etc., are easily traversed."[39] Therefore, the possibilities for imaginary identification can be expanded into the realm of the fantastic, as no law (that is, no rigid Symbolic) anchors and stabilizes these identifications. The material conditions of postmodernity inscribe the fluid instability of adolescence.[40]

According to Patricia Meyer Spacks,

The adolescent rejects boundaries, blithely crosses them, refusing to stay put, to remain a child, to accept subservience, to be predictable. His or her ability to avoid restrictions as though none existed, to leap walls that keep grown-ups in their place, declares the power of beginnings. On the other hand, the adolescent lacks money and self-defined social status and power in the world of affairs.[41]

Without the access to social power provided by a firm grounding in the dominant social structure, adolescents refuse the categories and strictures that it entails. Thus the potential for imaginary identification with a tremendous variety of normatively excluded positions is greatly enhanced, and the powerful subjective feelings that this process engenders both describe the pleasures that derive from participation in a scene and explain the capacity of adolescents to dance with "the abject."

Kristeva's concept of the abject represents the limit of tentatively constructed identity, where desire, driving the search for plenitude, borders the repulsed, the reviled, the not-I. The abject represents those portions of the prespeaking being that have been rejected in the construction of identity within the symbolic order.[42] Musical, lyrical, and physical expressions located at the boundaries of the abject (the repulsed or reviled) are used by the subject to signify itself "neither as a psychotic nor as an adult," but, indeed, to represent itself in the most tentative aspects of identity construction, through the imaginary play of adolescence, in the first throes of practice, moving beyond listening, consumption, incorporation, to participation, production, singing.[43] To the extent that such identifications establish new enunciative positions and transform the symbolic, "Adolescence has something subversive about it."[44]

Young people in the rock'n'roll scene in Austin continually transgress these boundaries between I and not-I, in multiple exploratory missions into those elements of the human that have been abjectly repulsed from the symbolic organization of the surrounding society. As Marcee describes it,

A lot of it is about death and skulls and black clothing, and I think that the more far out you get without dying, the cooler you are. "Fuck it, you know. I don't care. Whatever wants to happen to me can happen to me." And yeah, I think it is real impressive when you manage to have that atmosphere of doom about you, but you don't throw up in anybody's car and you don't OD at anybody's party and you don't stagger around the dance floor shitfaced. You don't cry. And I never did any of those things. I always looked real good. Even when I couldn't remember where I was. But I smiled and I knew a lot of people.[45]

By dancing on the edge of the abject—that "vacillating, fascinating, threatening, and dangerous object" that borders their frail identity—adolescents of many ages reconstruct an unstable structure, a temporary and fluid reorganization of the Symbolic—that signifying community known as the scene.[46] Within this scene, through fantastic identification with the forbidden, new enunciative possibilities are formed for only a moment. In the rock'n'roll scene in Austin, musicians and fans are produced as the subjects-in-process of this signifying practice, through an ongoing process of identification with newly possible positions of enunciation. But in order for any lasting transformation in the local symbolic to occur, these positions must be embodied and their constitutive features must be expressed in musicalized statements capable of inspiring the further identifications of other subjects.

The Blending of Identifications in the Formation of the Band

The first barrier that aspiring rock'n'roll musicians must successfully negotiate in the drive to perform is finding other musicians with whom to form a band. The *Austin Chronicle* publishes free ads in a musician's referral column in the back of the paper. These ads state the performing instrument required and often list a number of famous bands or recordings that form a preferred set of tastes or influences for the imagined musician. They will also normally attempt to convey concisely some idea of the attitudes and ambitions of the musicians already affiliated with the band. A few examples will demonstrate the range of requests.

Original Rock Band Needs Bass and Drums. Call if you have similar tastes: Rubber Soul, Tim, Murmur, Aquashow, Damn the Torpedoes, Headache Machine, New Day Rising, Blood on the Tracks.[47]

This ad relies upon the knowledge of the reader to recognize the names of these albums and imagine a coherent taste that would include music by the Beatles, Bob Dylan, the Replacements, REM, Elliot Murphey, Doctors' Mob and others. No more precise information is needed to imply the specific musical style. A second ad, however, expands on the musical information.

Bassist seeks Innovative Guitarist to form unique and off-kiltered collaboration. Inf. include Love and Rockets, Cure, Screaming Blue Messiahs, originals only. Presence, individuality, confidence, and insanity a must. No egos.[48]

This ad uses the names of three bands to mark out the boundaries of a musical style, but then complements that with a set of personal qualities required, expressing a demand for a self-effacing but confident musical innovator. A third ad relies solely on adjectives to convey its desires. "Pounding, Pounding, Poundingly melted, stained, shredded, bassist and drummer needed."[49]

Some musicians go to great lengths to try to describe precisely the character of both the band and the person with whom they want to work.

Percussionist and Keyboard player wanted to work with Laurie Freelove (acoustic guitar, singer, songwriter and ex-Nice Girl). I am looking for musically literate or non-literate musicians with universal musical tastes who value melody and enjoy rhythmic eccentricity. If you enjoy working out impressionistic musical arrangements, don't mind vocalizing every now and then and love the process of exploring ideas as much as performing please send me a tape of your work. Patience, politeness and commitment a must. Send tape, letter, and phone number to . . . . Thank you.[50]

Even with this degree of detail and description, most ads do not successfully locate the desired player. By and large, musicians eschew the referral column, preferring to depend on personal contacts or word of mouth within the scene, and often simply forming bands with their friends.

The chief reason for this reliance on personal contacts is that an objectively determined level of musical skill is not the most important consideration when selecting band members. Young musicians in the rock'n'roll scene in Austin consider the primary factor to be personal compatibility, a compatibility that goes beyond the mere willingness to get along and reaches toward a deeper unity. This explains the emphasis on personal characteristics in the ads. Since the product of a rock'n'roll band within a scene is a projected identity, "personalities" are assumed to determine stylistic variation. Brant Bingamon is a guitarist, singer, and songwriter for the punk band Pocket FishRmen. He insistently told me that, "the most basic core truth of any band" is that "personalities come first. I always said I'd rather have fun playing with somebody than be in a successful band."[51] In his band, Pocket FishRmen, the personalities of the band members "dictate a certain kind of music. Once Chris was in the band, his personality, like, dictated the whole style the music was gonna have to take. Because he owned a lot of heavy metal and distorted guitar." Within the rock'n'roll scene, musical taste and musical ability are not the surface traits of an individual but must be directly related to some elemental truth about the person performing. They must shape, and in turn be molded by, the most basic longing within that person.

This belief is not restricted to punk musicians like Brant. Joe McDermott leads Grains of Faith, a more mainstream Austin rock'n'roll band. He chose the musicians in his band on the basis of what he calls a "spiritual texture."

But I think as far as textures go, that is more important to me than, I mean, just the instruments that I wanted to play with. Like I didn't even know that John Ratliff could even play piano. I mean I knew that he played. But I never heard him, and we invited him into the band before I ever knew he could play. Because it, it's not just a sonic texture. It's sort of a spiritual texture. And it's a choice. It's like when you paint, you know, you have a palette and Austin is a wonderful city because you have this huge palette of people. You know, I think a lot of the texture has to do with just liking the people. I mean that an overwhelming thing for me with Grains of Faith, and I know that if I was in the audience and I saw this, I think you could see that we just love each other.[52]

Heather Moore, the band's viola player, intimated a direct relation between her music and her personality when she talked about the parts she contributes to the band's songs.

Ok, you write your own part, so of course you're not going to write something that's too hard for you. You wouldn't think of it. I mean I don't think of things that are too hard for me. So my parts are technically very easy. And my parts tend to be, for one thing, I'm more comfortable playing lower. I tend to stay down on those strings and I just like them. I feel more comfortable. I feel like they're more, I play them better and they're more attractive sounding, their sound is more attractive to me. I just like those tones, my personal, my ears, I think I like those tones better. I must say, I'm not, I don't like standing out. I'm not used to it.[53]

Corresponding to the belief that her music must be directly expressive of some aspect of her personality, Heather's statement links the fact that she feels uncomfortable standing out to the fact that the musical tones that please her also tend not to stand out.

John Croslin insisted that, "the Reivers are a band that thrives on personality and not on hot licks or anything like that." In fact, "the most important part of the band is our personalities going back and forth."[54] Kim Longacre agreed, "John understands that what a lot of people are attracted to in our band is our dynamic. And that we have a real intense relationship—two men and two women—and that sexual thing is just real attractive to people. And it's always been there."[55] In the scene in Austin, rock'n'roll musicians clearly do not produce autonomous music. The music they perform is the result of an entire set of social and cultural relationships intersecting through the "personalities" of the musicians in the field of musical performance. The audience responds not simply to a musical stimulus but to this performed set as a whole.

The local language of "personalities" assumes a stability and coherence in the psychic makeup of the individual musicians that conflicts with my language of subject positions and enunciative possibilities. The use of personality as a defining concept for musical compatibility is deeply rooted in the traditional importance placed on sincerity in country music, and is reinforced by the dominant concept of the autonomous individual. But I believe that it is possible to translate their language of personalities into my language of discourses and subject positions while retaining the emphasis on sincerity and compatibility.

In performance, the "personality" of the musician becomes a projected image; it represents a desired identity, a longed for completion, that is indeed overdetermined by the movement of desire through social and cultural (that is, discursive) conditions, yet that cannot be reduced to these conditions, and that remains necessarily incomplete, requiring the return gaze of the audience to fill in the gaps, to momentarily cap off the desire for pure being. The image of the performer must be recognized by the audience and re-turned through the affectively charged gestures of response in order for the projected identity to achieve completion. This temporary identity then is a joint product of the performers in the band and their audience, reflecting combinatorially the "personalities" of each.[56]

But this process of identity construction is complex, fragile, and tentative—particularly within the condition of adolescence fostered by postmodernity. Any imaginary identity must be renewed with each performance. It is not buttressed by a secure position within the Symbolic; therefore, it must be constantly re-performed. Rock'n'roll musicians are deeply invested in the successful projection and return of this identity. And when the renewal fails—when the show is merely good, not magical (the notes are played perfectly but you don't "get the chills")— the musicians can experience a severe anguish. The intense pleasures of performing (of completing with the audience a longed for, imaginary identity) are accompanied by an equally intense pain if the musician and the audience do not connect and the mutual projection fails. As John Croslin put it, "I'm real downcast after a bad show. You can get real neurotic about this; it can make you crazy."[57] The difficulty of projecting this unanchored identity places severe restrictions on the variety of discursive elements (that is, the personalities) that can be combined in the members of the band. Therefore, an interiorized discursive sincerity, characterized by the longing for purity that comes from an overinvestment in the Imaginary, is required. "Personalities," then, determine the band's style, since the ultimate production for a rock'n'roll band is a projected incomplete identity, yearned for by both the musicians and the audience.

At this point, the band becomes the unit of identity construction. In the words of Mike Hall, "The idea of a band is being a collection of four or five people. You wouldn't get the same kind of thing among four or five other people in the whole world. That's what makes a band. That nobody else could ever do what these four or five other people could do."[58] In other words, no other group of people could project the same particular image, could construct the same partial identity as these four or five individuals. Such identities are constructed and projected on the basis of libidinal ties, the connections of desire; therefore, it becomes very important for the musicians in a band to be close friends. "We're not a rock band; we're a bunch of friends," Heather Moore told me.[59] Julia Austin of Happy Family metaphorically strengthened the bond. "Being in a band is like being married," she said. "We're all of us products of the modern age. We've been through bad relationships and good relationships, all these things. And we've just learned that we've gotta talk to each other a lot."[60] Kevin Whitley of Ed Hall insisted that, "I rarely, *rarely* entertain notions of being in another band. Because that's not why I got in this band. I got in this band because of Larry, basically. Because we had this really cool relationship and we worked really well together."[61]

The libidinal bonds among musicians must be tight for a band successfully to project an identity for its fans. These ties are fragile and constantly threatened. Alejandro Escovedo described the dissolution of Rank and File, a band he helped form and played in for three years, in profoundly nostalgic terms.

You know, a good rock'n'roll band to me is more than a family. Just that it's you four, five, whatever against the world. Really. I mean, you know, your own code of speech, the way you guys talk to each other that most people can't penetrate. When you see a band together, I mean a really good band, there's something there. And that's kind of what we wanted to be like. With Rank and File, it was like, you know, originally we wanted that sense of camaraderie that we found while we were sitting around the living room, listening to records and playing guitars. We wanted that all the time. And it's like you support each other in ways, you're like brothers. You're like husbands and wives. You're all of those things, but it's just these four guys. It's a real fragile thing. It's rare that you find a band that can really stick it out. But we felt like that at first. We all loved each other very much. Thought that each guy had something to offer. Whether he was the greatest guitar player or not didn't matter. He's our mate and we'll just stand by him.[62]

In Austin rock'n'roll, the band represents an ideal grouping of discursive elements into a spontaneous collectivity, bound by libidinal ties, capable of producing and projecting a coherent identity, and able to withstand the disciplinary pressure of the dominant socially constructed Symbolic. The band represents, in miniature, the idealized community, carrying into the present the cowboy nostalgia for a premodern utopia that had been signified in the myth of the cattle trail and the cow camp. If successful, the band projects its collective identity into a responding audience that completes and extends this collectivity, filling the night-club with the potential for musicalized communion.

The Songs

Composition methods within bands vary, but in Austin there is almost always an effort to include the contributions of all members, to meld the musical expressions of their "personalities" together in the band's songs. While in most bands one or two individuals produce most of the lyrical, harmonic, and melodic content of the songs, almost every band expects each musician to develop her or his instrumental part, to contribute to the arrangements, to chip in the ideas necessary to turn a chord chart and a lyric sheet into a song. Julia Austin described the benefits that accrue from working up a song.

Well, quite often someone will bring in words and then we'll put music to it together as a band. That's really fun, because writing together for us is just really nice. It really works. Sometimes, someone will come in with a whole idea, and that's ok, but it doesn't give everybody the satisfaction of having input. In our band it is really important that everybody is satisfied. That they're all getting their creative input. And we all need it, cuz we're all like, real creative people. Even though some of us might be a little more active at one time or another than others. It just helps the band if everybody has input into the song. It just helps, it's like a bonding experience, I guess. And it helps to bond everybody to the *song* and to the band and to everything. It's also, even for the person who's just written the song, it's just really great to put it through that process.[63]

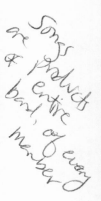

John Croslin is the chief songwriter for the Reivers, receiving the credit and the copyright for most of their material. But the "personali-ties" and the creative musical input of the other members of the band enter into every stage of a song's construction.

Usually I start with a melody more than any other thing. But it could be a rhythm, it could be anything. A lot of it is driven just by the way we play. A certain group of people can do certain things together. There are certain things about one's personality that come out of the music. Rhythm is probably one of the real fundamental ones. You've just got certain rhythms inside you. But usually what happens is, I'll just bring a song in—chords and melody—and we kind of go over who's gonna sing it and try to work out some harmonies and stuff. And then if it's not working for some reason, I'll say, well try this, and if it's still not working, I'll go back and try to rewrite the song if I feel strongly about it. If not, we'll just kind of toss it.[64]

In the initial composition process, John produces a melodic and har-monic structure, which is already partially determined by his under-standing of the way the band plays. The "personalities" of the members place limits on the musical structures the band can play. Fundamental components of who they are both constrain and enable their abilities to perform certain rhythms, to enact particular sound patterns. The unconscious physicality of playing an instrument enters into this.[65] There are certain almost automatic shapes the hand takes as the guitarist picks up her instrument. The first chords strummed, the first few licks used to warm up the hand are always the same. When the drummer sits down with the sticks in her hands, rolling from the snare to the toms, punctuating her arrival with two kicks on the bass drum, the beaten sound is as distinct as a voice announcing, I am here. It rarely varies from rehearsal to sound check to the beginning of a show. These musical signatures symbolize the physical relationship between the musician and her or his instrument. But when John talked about a song "working," he meant more than that the band is physically capable of playing the notes. He meant that the structure he imagined can be enthusiastically, affectively, enacted by all the band members, that they can be caught up in the performance of the song, that fundamental components of their being will be hailed by it and contribute to its material realization. For a song to "work," in the most absolute sense, it must contain musically defined moments that attract the projection of each musician's yearned-for completion. This is what Julia pointed toward when she talked about "bonding" with the song. Only when such libidinal bonding occurs has a band produced a song capable of focusing a projected identity for its fans.

Not every band member has to love wholeheartedly every song the band plays. I only mean that for a song to become part of the distinctive catalog of material that defines a particular band, each musician must be drawn out of her or his self by some element in the song. There must be a rhythmic moment of interest that engages the drummer and the bass player. There must be harmonic or melodic interactions that tickle the inner ears of the guitarists, the keyboard players, the horn and fiddle players. There must be a lyrical image or a narrative impulse or a melodic invention that draws the voice out of the singer. These subjective interactions with the musical form constitute "dialectical syntheses" with a symbolic structure, enabling and shaping the projection of an imagined identity.[66] However, these syntheses do not need to be simultaneous moments, overlapping in a climax of identification. It is only necessary that each band member recognize some aspect in the song that demands from him or her the unconscious projection from their individual semiotic. This is a wholly subjective, private experience for each musician, but its effects can be felt.

[handwritten margin note: Songs make you move beyond yourself — thus forming a new identity for a period of time]

Kevin Whitley described the group composition of one of the songs on their 1990 album *Love (S)Poke(n) Here*. This song was written while his band, Ed Hall, was rehearsing in the back room of the house they rent together.

There's this one song that is fabulous. It's called "Millionaire's House." It's one of the songs that happened in a free-form jam. It's so weird, it happened at the very end of a free-form jam, we were five minutes from leaving. Some people had just come over. Like a lot of people had filtered in, were drinking beer in the kitchen, making alot of noise and we were all going, oh this is too much, we can't practice with this, we wanna go drink beer. Well, just as we were about to quit, Gary did something simultaneously with Larry and I just went, ohmigod, turn the thing [tape recorder] on. And I did this simplistic ass drumbeat behind it and it was beautiful. I had never heard Gary play anything like that and what Larry played was so Larry, but better. It was really cool. It was musclely. And it's just one of those things that happened. And Larry wrote the whole entire bass line, Gary wrote the whole guitar part and I wrote the drums and the lyrics. It's a great song. It's just a great song. And it'll be great to us whether nobody likes it, because it happened that way. And all of us get off on it real hard. We all like to play it. And I just think it's a really good song.[67]

The value of the song for Kevin came from the spontaneity of its composition and the way in which the song materially, sonically, represents imagined aspects of each of the musicians in Ed Hall: *"what Larry played was so Larry, but better."* Kevin's narration of the origin of "Millionaire's House," with its description of each member of the band erupting spontaneously into the song's composition, depicts the pleasurable imaginary plenitude of "pure" representation.

"Millionaire's House" arose out of a group improvisation and represents a paradigmatic example of the process I am trying to describe. But the important maneuver of subjectively identifying with aspects of the song, propelling some nonconscious semiotic elements into its musical construction, and thereby contributing to its projected image, can occur even when one person writes most of the instrumental parts before presenting it to the other band members.

Joe McDermott writes the bulk of Grains of Faith's material in his home studio. For him, "the process of recording and songwriting are not very different. I'm not very dependent on other musicians for ideas because, and it's not because I'm god's gift to music, it's because that's the way I grew up. I grew up bouncing scratchy cassette tape recorders back and forth to get something that sounded like a band. And it's almost like it's one motion for me, generally, to write a song."[68] Because of Joe's reliance on recording in composition, he tends to bring an almost completely written song to the other members of the band. Still, the song is not whole until the other members play it. The more ephemeral yet still necessary contribution of the other musicians derives from what Joe earlier called a "spiritual texture," that tightly woven fabric of the "personalities" and the musical style in the band. The members of Grains of Faith form a unit of discursive and musical threads that shape and color Joe's compositions. "Steve Grimes [the drummer] to me is not like, really like a different person. He's sort of, like a logical extension of my songwriting. And the whole band in a lot of ways is like that. As far as recording or anything else. I think we all feel like we're each other's hands. It's like we're a great big multi-track machine that we all have a say-so in or something."[69]

When Joe writes a song, he considers not only the musicians in the band but also the physical material through which the sound is produced.

When you're in a club and it's dark and it's smoky and people are drunk, and there are these huge, massive speakers that everything comes out of, and they're mono, they're not even in stereo, there's no separation. There's just this big wall. And if you're ever gonna get through to anybody in that situation, it has to be really clean and really direct and there have to be a lot of stops in it where you can just say what you want to say. Because the reality of the speaker is that it's one thing. No matter what it sounds like, everything's coming out of this one piece of paper. And there are different pieces of paper and plastic but it's all the same thing and the only way that you can really separate things is to separate them. Like if the kick drum is going here, then sometimes you don't want the guitar playing on top of it. I think the thing that I think about most is where the holes are and where the hooks are and how I'm gonna translate those. Like, I guess I think a lot about what's gonna pop out of that big, ugly black column and stick. And that's really the way I write.[70]

The music of Grains of Faith is, accordingly, clean and clear, discernable, understandable, closer to traditional ideas of quality pop songwriting and precise performance than the music of Ed Hall. Joe illustrated the results of his method by reference to one of his songs.

Like "Sea Wall." It starts out and it's just the guitar and it's me singing so there's absolutely no competition for anything. And the band only punctuates the beginning of it. So for the first part of the song it's just me and the audience. And they can understand what I'm saying and it gets stronger but, as the band gets stronger, my voice gets louder and you know, like the chorus, where the band is really humpin', I'm in my range where I can really yell it out. So that works. And then in the middle of the song, everything stops. I think a lot of that, I mean, that song is so funny, there's so many coincidences in that song. Like, it's basically a document of a horrible weekend I had with Kim when things were falling apart. I was just like, this happened to me and it was horrible and I want everyone to know about it. Like, on the weekend that we went to the coast we took a Van Morrison tape with us and a little blue jambox and like we were listening to "Crazy Love" and him singing, "Turn it up, a little bit higher."[71]

"Sea Wall" is probably the most popular song Grains of Faith play. The musical structure reinforces the narrative of a collapsed marriage (the "middle of the song" where "everything stops"), a story that is really only hinted at in the lyrics. As Joe explains, the song begins softly with just his voice and an acoustic guitar picking out an ascending affirmative riff connecting an alternating C and F major chord pattern. The verse lyrics are affectionate and warm, Joe's voice is open, full, and inviting. But as he sings the perhaps hopeful opinion that "it might be the Great Wall of China," Jennifer Summers adds a harmony vocal that, in its quavering tone and sheer isolation from the rest of the arrangement, evokes an aching loneliness. This is the listener's first clue that all is not well. When the band comes in at the bridge, as Joe sings "I'm goin' for a walk now," John Ratliff hammers out octave C notes on the piano, affirming the independence and determination in this portion of the lyric. But just at that same moment Steve Grimes beats on his half-open high hat, slapping the two cymbals shut just as he hits it, a technique that lends an opening, questioning feel to the bridge, limiting the certainty of the beat. The rhythmic interplay between John's reinforcement of independence and Steve's questioning of certainty adds a tremendous subtlety to the song, drawing the listener in, encouraging attentive hearing, and undermining any quick or easy interpretation, just as Jennifer's haunting background vocal rises above and slightly shifts the listener's attention away from the immediate affirmation of Joe's full-throated voice. Here in the heart of the hook, the very element of the song to which Joe claims to pay the most attention while writing, the contributions of the other band members, their musical styles and aspects of their "personalities," add a necessary tension that sonically and affectively reproduces the doubt and the uncertainty of the "horrible weekend." The dynamic tension that follows this bridge, as the song breaks down, Joe singing of the cold, and then rises back up with life redeemed by the musical and lyrical quotes from Van Morrison's song "Crazy Love," is all produced within those musically enacted moments of intraband relationship. Appropriately, the song ends with a question in the lyrics—"I don't know if it thrills you at all, to feel the ocean pushing on the sea wall"—and a repeating, unending musical fadeout.

"Millionaire's House" and "Sea Wall" are two very different songs by two very different bands. But the value of both of these songs is explained by means of the specific aesthetic they share. This aesthetic is derived from the ways in which rock'n'roll in Austin works as a signifying practice, resulting in the projection, recognition, and return—the production—of new identities, new enunciative positions.

From 1983 until 1986, Steve Spinks led a band called the Dharma Bums. They first performed as a trio, but eventually added a keyboard player and second guitarist (Joe McDermott) and a horn section. They were one of the featured bands in the 1985 "Austin Avalanche of Rock and Roll" episode of MTV's *Cutting Edge* program. I asked Steve what distinguished Austin bands from other rock'n'roll bands nationwide. "Austin musicians, I hate to say the word, but I think they're sincere. I think they really care what they're singing."[72] The immediate project of rock'n'roll bands in the scene in Austin is the construction of an incomplete identity that its audience can recognize and return. Because this identity is constructed through the allusive combinations of personal and musical characteristics from each of the band members through the songs and performance styles in a fashion that escapes their conscious intentions, sincerity remains the primary aesthetic value, the central element in every evaluative system, operating in the widest variety of musical styles.

The prominence of sincerity as an expressive value in Austin music draws on a long tradition in country and western music. In the late 1920s and early 1930s, an "effortless informality," a "personal approach," and an overwhelming "sincerity" characterized the voice of Jimmie Rodgers, the first commercial recording star of country music.[73] Rodgers was "a fellow who understood; who had 'been there.'" And his audience heard this quality in his voice.[74] The ability to vocalize sincerity became a key stylistic trait in hillbilly (later, country) music, as it was generically distinguished from urban popular song. Functionally, this generic marker indicated a distance from and a distrust of the duplicitous relations that were associated with city marketplaces. The smooth singing voice of the urban popular singer metonymically symbolized the smooth double-talking urban commercial entrepreneur, the rancher's untrusted but necessary partner in the marketing of rural products. Against this symbolized urbanity, a specific set of vocal tones, melodic phrasings, and personal images was established as indicators of rural sincerity.

In 1936, Mrs. Carrie Rodgers encouraged Ernest Tubb, the Texas Troubadour, to keep singing because "you do have feeling in your voice. The audience knows how you feel about the song you're singing, and Jimmie always thought that was the most important thing of all."[75] Hank Williams once explained the success of country music in "one word: sincerity. . . . [The hillbilly singer] sings more sincere than most entertainers because the hillbilly was raised rougher than most entertainers. You got to know a lot about hard work. You got to have smelt a lot of mule manure before you can sing like a hillbilly."[76] From the vocal virtuosity of Lefty Frizzell to the genuine performances of Willie Nelson, the vocalization of sincerity has indicated a singer who can be trusted and, therefore, the possibility of an audience who can accurately interpret and properly respond to the performances. Sincerity, however signified, has remained the most important quality in successful country singing.

In the tradition of popular music performance that continues in Austin, the singer enunciates from a position marked by a romantic relation to the patriarchal, capitalist Symbolic. Like most romanticisms, it derives from a distrust of industrialism, of urbanism, of the contradictions of the marketplace, of all the tenets of modernity. But the romanticism of country and western music in Texas is also specifically rooted in the mythic origins of the state: the cattle trail and the cow camp as spontaneous masculine communities free from the contradictions of modern society yet capable of generating massive personal wealth. Therefore, the sincere performance of country and western music in Austin indicates a doubled and ironic articulation of an antimodern romanticism, celebrating the productivity of capitalist modernity while simultaneously critiquing the increasing influence of marketplace duplicity and "instrumental reason."[77]

Punk in Austin directly attacked this specifically nostalgic form of sincerity as groups like the Huns and the Reversible Cords layered their performances with an ironic negation designed to disrupt and dismantle local traditions of musical communication. Songs like "Glad He's Dead" and "Big Penis Envy" not only denied their own sincerity but questioned the possibility of any "freedom from dissimulation."[78] While traditional sincerity demands the absence of outside influence or adulteration, one of the most significant messages of punk was that such are the conditions of commercialized cultural practice that no popular music is free from artifice. Punk, particularly its British variant, pointed out that the marketing of popular music necessarily implied outside influence. But this is precisely the point where punk in the United States, and in Austin in particular, differed from the gleeful machinations of Malcolm McLaren and the Sex Pistols. Where McLaren playfully wallowed in the contradictions of the commodified society of the spectacle, giggling on his way to the bank, punks and postpunk musicians in Austin struggled to recuperate sincerity through a purification of the expressive impulse. The lessons of punk in Austin reinforced a utopian romantic urge for a cultural marketplace free of deceit, where a sincere expression, a pure representation, could arise from some essence of the performer untainted by the polluting structures of capitalism and then could be distributed through direct channels to a populace longing for it. If outside influence could not be eliminated, then sincerity had to reign over the interior aspects of musical production. The do-it-yourself ethic of punk met with the powerful populist tradition in Texas; the result was an insistence on the personal responsibility for and significance of the music one made, the music one listened to, the music one bought and sold.[79]

In talking about the special nature of music in Austin for MTV's *Cutting Edge* program, John Croslin said, "A lot of places people expect everybody to be able to play the exact right notes all the time. In Austin, they're just lookin' for energy." Kim Longacre pitched in, "A new sound." John continued, "People who like to do what they like to do." And Garrett Williams, the drummer, summed up, "You don't have to be perfect the first time or even the second time, and people will still like you."[80] Here, the key terms in the Austin aesthetic were laid out: energy, a new sound, a personal investment in one's own music (like to do what they like to do), and a reduced emphasis on the precisely accurate execution of musical structures. The projection of an incomplete identity, structured by the signs of sincerity, produced by and aimed at a group of adolescents struggling to represent themselves within the disabling constraints of an unstable Symbolic, requires an emphasis on intention, on the interior workings of the Imaginary. Precise execution of a specific form is not only unnecessary but, to a certain extent, reveals a too concrete concern with the very symbolic structures already known to be illusory; it is far more important to "get the chills." During one of our interviews, Croslin insisted that the interrogation of structure partially defines Zeitgeist. "Part of our thing is that we're not absolutely sure of ourselves. We're really, we question our lives and our selves."[81] This questioning is expressed by a willingness to display risk on stage, by overtly longing for the pleasurable and meaningful moments of completion, by performing more than the band can execute. This is the form that sincerity takes in postpunk rock'n'roll. The result of this emphasis on sincerity, intention, and the Imaginary is a performing style that displays an enthusiasm or an energy that overflows any disciplining structures. As Julia Austin said to me, "Yeah, I kind of like a coherent song performed with some imprecision."[82] John Croslin made the same point, "I'm a lot less concerned about someone playing the wrong chords as the show just not working."[83]

In 1984, Jesse Sublett derisively named the bands associated with the Beach scene, the New Sincerity bands. In his eyes, they were flaunting

personal responsibility in music = more sincere

music still not #1, the #1 is 2nd music is 2nd

important thing is entire show not perfect music (makes country better - it's real music, not just noise) their claim to an absence of artifice, championing "content" over "style" by their manner of not changing out of their daily clothing to perform, by their willingness to tune onstage, by their sloppy, unprofessional performances, and by their attempts to deconstruct the distinction between the musicians onstage and the fans in the audience.[84] In effect, Sublett was reiterating the punk objection to any claim of freedom from dissimulation. But this dismissive label was adopted by the participants in the scene as an appropriate encapsulation of their difference from and similarity to other Austin music. The new sincerity was strictly a matter of intention.

Once sincerity was defined as an interior quality, the most stable signifier of one's sincerity became each individual's insistence on the purity and genuineness of her or his own desires. Rather than taking the expressive form of a specific performance style (like that of Willie Nelson or Marcia Ball), sincerity could only be signified by one's willingness to be true to these desires in the face of any disciplinary pressure from the dominant culture (as expressed, for example, through marketplace relations) to temper them. Thus, any component of human existence that directly confronted the forbidden barriers of the dominant culture became an arena for the display of genuine desires, a place to signify one's sincerity, and, therefore, a field for aesthetic expression. Once sincerity is conceived of as an aspiration, an intention, a longed-for element of misrecognition, only then can the tight links between specific musical styles and specific ways of living, links believed to be direct and almost immediate, be understood as double expressions of the same aesthetic.

Here is Hunter Darby's articulation of that doubled aesthetic expression.

Cuz see, alternative music is pretty much, seems like to me, represents a lifestyle. Not always being safe. Like the way people take it to different extremes. Just in what they say. If they think they can say something, they'll say it. Or if you wanna like, fucking drink yourself to death, well, you'll have friends who will say don't do that, but if you wanna get trashed one night, no one's gonna hold it against you the next day. For me, personally, I don't like music that's safe.[85]

When asked to describe his lifestyle, Hunter narrated an idealized representation, applying this aesthetic of abject sincerity.

So, I get up about one, twelve or one. And I'll go down to Circle K every day—the lady knows me. I'll get a beer. I'll drink that beer. Then I'll go and I might go to class. And hang out for a while. And I'll go and check in at work. I'll have another drink at work. Texas Tavern. A bar, that helps. Maybe I'll like check around, see, go visit, I'll see people all the time on the street. Go walking, I'll run into people. Then, if it's a practice night, I'll go to practice. We practice like four nights a week, three to four. That'll go to like, from seven to eleven o'clock.

So it's sort of like a job. And hang out with some of those guys for a while and maybe someone will say, you'll find out if anyone's gonna do somethin'. If you feel like doin' somethin', you'll go out to the Cannibal cuz they have those cards for the musicians. It's great, if you've played enough shows there, if you get to know people, they give us these cards. It makes it free, the hangout, and we fucking support that place by drinking. Plus if you're ever low, you can probably get a drink or something. So I go see bands. That's my main thing. I like going to see the road shows. I'll take a chance on anything. Lot of times, like even if you haven't really heard them. And you go down there to meet, hang out and talk with some people. Maybe go like, run around. Like last Thursday was great. We went down and saw, went to the studio and recorded and then got out early and went to see, I was gonna meet Alex down at Young Fresh Fellows and we went down there, and I hadn't seen those guys in a while so we grabbed them and went down to the Hole in the Wall and played down there again.[86]

Whether or not this accurately represents Hunter's daily routine, it does indicate a blending of the details of his existence with a specific aestheticized notion of the meaning of everyday life and its articulation with his musical practice. Hunter runs around, meeting people, drinking, maybe not going to class, working with his band in the evening, getting into his favorite bar for free, listening to musicians from out of town, and extending the night a few precious hours through a spontaneous extra performance at the Hole in the Wall. The actions of the day are unified by his rejection of any constrictions on the spontaneity and immediate pleasure of every moment. He is constantly meeting people, always running around and always moving, unless he is at band rehearsal or in the studio. And these moments of work, "sort of like a job," are glossed over in the telling of his day.

This is Hunter's romantic picture of his own life on the edge of the abject, that barrier between the accepted and the forbidden, marked for him by alcohol, constant motion, and a specific musical quality: an incomplete articulation of noise. Nonsafe music for Hunter is music "with a little more distortion than can be played on the radio." The clean sound heard on the radio is opposed to the dirty sound of alternative music, and this dirty sound is a result of distortion, of a noisy, more complex audio signal. Noise marks the edge of popular (that is, commercially successful) music, and noise is signified tonally through the overproduction of harmonics. The edge of the acceptable—that place where Hunter finds personal and musical pleasure—is defined by the socially constructed categories of safe popular music and a safe way of life. The sign of Hunter's sincerity is the noise, the disorder, the insistent instability, one hears in his music and finds in his life.[87]

Sincerity remains the primary organizing value of the aesthetic even on this edge of abjection. It produces the "punk attitude towards things" avowed by Kevin Whitley of Ed Hall.

Marginal handwritten notes:

immediate pleasures / gratification (no uniformity)

living btwn accepted & forbidden

not real music - another reason for him to love country (in 1980s non-punk people listened to soft rock - now country is 1990s closest thing to that)

We're antimusician. We don't consider ourselves musicians. We consider ourselves people who pick up instruments and make noises that go together. . . .
And so, we're kind of antimusician, that, quote, kind of musician. We're anti-
establishment, by means of the fact that we don't really like how our parents
live. We want to do something that's not quite that geared toward stability, I
guess. I guess it's more rooted in rebellion, I imagine. Because I can't, I don't
know, parents, they get to a point and they're just making it. I don't know, I
guess it's a time of life. I don't really understand it. I can't feel anything like that.
I don't feel it.[88]

Because Kevin cannot feel what his parents feel, their "time of life"
makes no sense to him. His "rebellion" is simply the result of a sincere
acknowledgment of his inability to identify with the way his parents live.
Kevin shares Hunter's taste for noise and disorder. He does not feel any
value in stability, so his life and his music must express an "antiestablish-
ment" and, because of the history of the local music scene, "antimusician" punk attitude. Rather than rejecting sincerity, the punk attitude
in Austin depends upon it. As Kevin said, music is "a medium to have
an effect on people by opening yourself up to what you're doing and
how it's affecting you."[89] In the musical aesthetic of Austin rock'n'roll,
the subversive negativity of punk is enabled by a positive insistence on
sincerity.

For nonpunk musicians, the value of sincerity is articulated in other
directions. Kim Longacre no longer

understand[s] the people who put themselves on the edge all the time. . . . I
think that that was the attraction of Raul's and it's not, it's not so much re-
belliousness—although you are rebelling—it's more the, I don't know, it's like,
hating yourself or something. I think you fall into this thing that you're really
attracted to this evilness, this scariness, and it's like, I never knew I could be so
bad. I certainly feel like I went around that block a couple of times. But I don't
think that when I played anybody looked at me like I'm a bad girl, you know?
And that was when I realized this other thing, that something has to be organic
or it's not worth shit.[90]

Instead of a life on the edge of the forbidden, sincerity promises Kim the
possibility of an organic integration with her music and a freedom from
masquerade, a freedom that was played out in the scene at the Beach.

And there was a burgeoning scene, you know. The Dharma Bums were starting.
We were starting. And there started to be this network of people who really had
this different attitude. They weren't in it for anything but the good time. There
was no pretense. It was just, we're gonna get together, we're gonna play, we're
gonna have a good time. We're gonna be nice, decent people. It's true. And
the whole scene evolved in a similar way. It seemed like this real socialist thing.
It was real organic and not like anybody sat down and wrote the rules out. It
was great. . . . But bands started coming through—like Love Tractor, REM—
and they were normal people. You know, I mean, they were college kids. They
wore normal clothes. They weren't trying to be outrageous. They were good

[margin note: not trained musically]

[margin note: can't relate to parents — did he ever try talking to them?]

musicians. They had something interesting to say. They weren't being smug or complaining. They were like poetic. It was the weirdest thing. It was very interesting that they could be so mundane and melodic. And they were nice. They didn't have this star quality about them. What was magical about it is that it could be mundane. And that you could look normal. You didn't have to wear makeup.[91]

This statement describes a notion of sincerity much closer to the traditional value. The freedom from makeup, the willingness to look "normal" (that is, not dressed-up), the absence of any star aura, the comfort of the mundane and everyday, the positive organicism of apparently rule-free social interaction, and the reduced emphasis on "badness," all of these qualities point to the importance of a direct relation between the life one lives and the music one makes.

A similar foundation of sincerity underlies Kim's evaluation of her own performances.

Sometimes when we play, it's heaven up there, you know. When it all just comes right through and it's effortless. It's just this voice coming out. You're not trying to do anything, you're just singing. And that's how I want it to be. But it's hard, it's like trying to be sincere. . . . I don't want to make it too important, but it is. I think it could utilize all the facets of your being to sing. I think it's like the connection between heaven and earth in a lot of ways. And it shouldn't be a big deal and people shouldn't make it one. When you make it a big deal, then it's acting. And then it's not real. It's not part of your life, it's not movement, it's a statue.[92]

but isn't she supposed to finding an identity? Not just 'being herself'

For Kim's singing to be real and moving, not acting and not a statue, it must effortlessly come out of her life. Only then does her singing use "all the facets of [her] being." The identity projected by any band that played at the Beach, or that continues to work within this aesthetic, has to be the sincere "organic" product of an unadulterated articulation of one's life. As Marcia Buffington puts it, "I like to listen to actual human beings that are having actual emotions that I have either had in the past or am having now."[93]

Joe McDermott's "definition of a real songwriter is like a person who can put out a record that mirrors life. That's the aesthetic of anything good. If it really speaks to you, and it mirrors life. I think that's good."[94] Here, the key to aesthetic quality can be found in reception. Whether or not one succeeds as a real songwriter cannot be determined before the moment of performance. For Joe, the song must speak to the audience, but they must do the important work of responding to the identity projected in the song. "I feel like I'm putting a catalyst out for them to feel their own things."[95] However, Joe cautions, this joint production must not be distracted by the conscious imposition of abstract principles of art.

I don't feel like there's a good crossover point between art and rock. I think that rock can be art the same way that baking bread can be art. And it almost, I think for rock to be art it almost has to be selfless, in a way. I guess the point I'm making, it's like sex, it's not up to the sexual partners to decide whether they've just made art or sex, it's up to somebody else. The Rolling Stones were in bed to fuck. And it was art, but they weren't trying to make art. They were trying to make babies.

/ see
P. 152 note

This comment is motivated by the same insistence upon sincerity as an Imaginary guarantee operative in a culture with an unstable Symbolic. Any effort to make "art," to struggle to fit one's expressions into a specific set of communicative criteria, would indicate an allegiance to untrustworthy disciplinary structures and interfere with the ultimate aesthetic value of sincerity. If Joe is to project successfully an identity that mirrors the life of his audience, the identity has to originate from deep in his center. "It's kind of a job of just being severely in touch with yourself. It's a hard job." [96]

Sincerity is the quality most highly valued in Austin's rock'n'roll aesthetic, from punk to mainstream folk-rock. Its presence guarantees the validity of a musical style and, by extension, of a way of life. Its importance is enhanced by, and in turn enhances, the intimate emotional connections between musicians and their fans. According to John Croslin, this intimacy can be heard in the music.

Austin is a real emotional town—the scene is. And our music is that way, I think. It's real hard to explain. I just think Austin, this scene is famous for just, I don't know what the right word is, but in the beginning, when the Beach was goin' on and everything, and everybody knew everybody, it seemed real famous, for everybody would go out and do acid and you would talk in this way to people, that you really didn't know that well, that you might not ever talk to your parents. I don't know if my being aware of that means anything to anybody outside, but that aspect of the scene, I think, is in our music.[97]

In effect, the value associated with sincerity is so great that, by itself, it assures that even the most extreme and abject longing for identity can be heard and found pleasurably meaningful.

Daniel Johnston and the Fetishization of Sincerity

I am a baby in my universe, I'll live forever.
I am a baby in my universe, I'll live forever.
Ooh, I'm only twenty-two, I'll live forever.
Ooh, I'm only twenty-two, I'll live forever.[98]

In the winter of 1984–1985, Daniel Johnston moved from San Marcos, Texas, where he had been living with his sister, forty miles up Interstate 35 to Austin. He rented a tiny one-room apartment, got a job cleaning the lobby at the McDonald's closest to the university, and began to hand out, to almost everyone he met, cassettes full of songs he had written over the past two years. These cassettes had been primitively recorded under dismal conditions: a portable mono cassette recorder with its built-in condenser microphone set up on a chair in a garage, while Daniel sang and beat out the chords of his songs on toy instruments. These tapes were duplicated using equally primitive technology: the master tape playing on one portable machine while another recorded the copy. The xeroxed covers were illustrated with Johnston's own drawings of the ghosts and demons that haunted his imagination, and the song titles were written out by hand. On the tapes, his squeaking voice is often barely audible over a wheezing chord organ or an awkwardly plucked acoustic guitar. Occasionally, a metronome can be heard ticking in the background, hopelessly attempting to discipline the rhythm. And on one song, "Desperate Man Blues," Daniel sings his lyrics over a recording of a big band instrumental. If you walked into the McDonald's at Dobie Mall looking as if you might be a musician, if you wore black or slouched in a certain way while you ordered french fries, and particularly if you were a woman, Daniel would hand you one of his tapes.

One of the first people to receive and listen to Daniel's music was Kathy McCarty. While enrolled as a liberal arts honors student at the University of Texas, Kathy quickly became involved in the music scene, playing in a band called Sinquanon, later leading the Buffalo Gals and dropping out of school. In 1984, she and Brian Beattie put together Glass Eye, an ensemble which, from its inception, was intended to differ from the prevailing musical styles in Austin. Glass Eye immediately stood out from most of the bands in town simply by including a synthesizer in their instrumentation and by allowing sounds other than those made by a guitar to dominate their arrangements. Beattie played a fretless bass that he used to set up melodic undertones across which McCarty splashed sparse and unclothed guitar chords. Scott Marcus produced uncommon drum patterns with a John Bonham-like aplomb, and Stella Weir decorated the edge of the band's sound with delicate chords and runs on her synthesizer. Their songs refused to build to the standard rock climax of a lead guitar break, while their lyrics varied from atmospheric evocations of something-not-quite-right to precise narratives of vivisection and disease. After Kathy listened to Daniel's tapes, she invited him to a few of the band's rehearsals, where they worked up one of his songs. It soon became a focal point of Glass Eye's performances. After finishing one of their darker numbers, the band would drop their instruments, clap their hands over their heads, and all shout together the sing-song chorus, "Get yourself together or fall apart. Make your mind up or let yourself down."[99] Often, Glass Eye's audience would sing along.

Word began to circulate about this savant songwriter. Daniel continued to give tapes to people who met him on the drag or who searched him out while he was at work. Other bands in town began to play some of his songs. Stella Weir gave a copy of the tapes to a friend of hers, Mellissa Cobb. Mellissa was in an avant-folk-punk band, Meat Joy, but was beginning to work with me on a more pop-oriented project, Black Spring. One afternoon, Mellissa called me on the phone and told me that I had to listen to these songs. "You've got to hear this guy. His songs are so beautiful. Uh, I hope you'll like them." While on the phone, I did not understand the hesitancy in her voice. But that night I took a six pack of Busch to her house by the airport, and while we sat on the floor in front of her jambox drinking the beer, we listened to *Hi, How Are You*, over and over, trying to understand what he was playing and why the songs felt so meaningful, so moving, despite the very simple song structures, the abysmal recording quality, and the chaotic, inept performances.

The first song that Mellissa played for me was "Walking the Cow." And at first all I could hear was this beat. There was this sound, like someone hitting an empty cardboard box with both hands, almost on every beat, swerving into and out of time, the hands hitting the box together, then somehow becoming separated in time but later finding each other and the beat again, dominating perception like two hearts dominating sound in a womb, washing over all other sounds, beating separately for only a moment before linking back up in dyadic unity. That was all I heard the first time I listened to the song. And it made me angry. How was I supposed to listen to the song when, in addition to all the other problems, it was buried by this undisciplined, unregulated throbbing?

"Well, it's interesting," I said.

Mellissa's face fell. "You don't like it?"

"Let's listen to it again." And so we did, and I tried to filter out the hollow beating, to listen to the tones, the words, the voice, the song. What I heard was a Magnus chord organ—that plastic toy that middle-class parents would buy during the winter solstice in order to spark a latent musical interest in their children, but that always ended up in the basement or the garage or a closet by summertime, untouched and despised. They simply were not musical instruments. But something was forcing music from this chord organ. The plastic reedy tones, completely lacking depth or resonance, were being squeezed out of their box by a manic intention. When I listened even more closely, it was that intention that I heard. I heard him mash the buttons, furiously, again out of time, or in some weird time of his own, not the time that I knew as rhythm nor quite the time of the beating box, but some other, clashing time, its own arrhythmia. I heard fingers reaching for buttons on a chord organ, smashing them down into their holes, against the resistant plastic substance below. And I could hear chords; for, after all, it was a chord organ, one button and instant harmony, but I couldn't recognize them. It wasn't that they were out of tune; you cannot play out of tune on a chord organ. It wasn't that they had odd voicings or complex structures; chord organs play built-in simple triads. I think that what confused me was the contrast between the intensity, the physical ferocity, of the performer and the collapsed, empty, and almost unimportant tones that were produced. That contrast was so intriguing that I wanted to listen to the song a third time.

And this time I heard his voice. That same contrast between the physically pulsing, nonconscious intention and the resulting restricted, quavering tone was in his voice. It was a strangled voice that only hinted at the idea of a melody, but it hinted at a melody that was simple, intuitive, and, yes, beautiful, just as Mellissa had said. Finally, on this third listen, I got it. I understood that this recording only worked when the listener reached out, in an extreme effort of the imagination, to identify what had to be there. And something had to be there in order to justify the risks this singer was taking. He was too easy to ridicule: a poor singer, incompetently playing very simple songs on a toy instrument. But it was the force of his desire to push beyond the structural impossibility of this body producing a singing voice and this chord organ producing music, and the strength of all these wild intentions working together within the barest precision and organization of an almost rhythm, that produced the most pure and genuine display of imaginary sincerity I had ever heard. I looked up at Mellissa and smiled. She beamed back at me, and I got out my guitar to try figure out how to play "Walking the Cow." While we listened to it again in repeated fragments, rewinding the tape every few seconds, I tried to penetrate the surface sounds to hear the forgotten chord structure, and Mellissa wrote down the words. "Trying to remember, but my feelings can't know for sure. / Try to reach out, but it's gone. / Lucky stars in your eyes. / I am walking the cow."[100]

During the remainder of the evening, we listened to the rest of the songs. Some were only torn up and scattered scraps of ideas. "I Picture Myself with a Guitar" and "Running Water" are not much more than a chorus line sung over an out-of-tune guitar or a dripping faucet. "I am a Baby" does not contain much more, but it seems to encapsulate lyrically the central power of Johnston's songwriting. With the line, "I am a baby in my universe, I'll live forever," Johnston sings the imaginative power of the infant's misidentification with plenitude. The next line, "Oooh, I'm only twenty-two, I'll live forever," collapses the adolescent emphasis on possibility back into this same misidentification, as the promise of wholeness and eternal potential imagines a pure extension of this internalized relation. Daniel Johnston's taped songs demonstrate the contradictions of the mirror stage—the illusions, the misidentification, the overinvestment in the Imaginary—while insisting on the value of sincere intention as a semiotic supportive power capable of sustaining one's everyday struggle against the overdetermined constrictions of the socially constructed Symbolic. The naive romanticism expressed in his songs aligns perfectly with the ambitions of the burgeoning Beach scene, and this alignment explains the tremendous success of Daniel Johnston in this scene over the next year.

Mellissa and I were not the only musicians in town learning Daniel's songs. The Rhythm Rats, Doctors' Mob, and Zeitgeist soon joined Glass Eye and Black Spring in performing more polished selections from the Johnston oeuvre. At the same time, Daniel discovered that Waterloo and Record Exchange would sell his tapes on consignment; he no longer needed to give them away. Glass Eye talked him into performing some of his songs between sets at one of their shows at the Beach. He did not have his chord organ and so played only three guitar songs. But he debuted a new number, "Marching Guitars," that Alejandro Escovedo's band, the True Believers, soon began playing. For a while, it seemed as though every band that played at the Beach included a Daniel Johnston song in their repertoire. He began to play with other bands, at parties and at clubs. But he never looked at his audience, he never played more than five songs (normally he only did three), and he always ended his short set with a bow and a quick dash off the stage into the darkness where he could hide while everyone, both fans and those who thought he was just a bad joke, clapped and screamed for more.

The summer of 1985 was the summer that MTV's new music program "The Cutting Edge" came to town to tape a feature on Austin's New Sincerity scene. Along with Glass Eye, the True Believers, Zeitgeist, the Wild Seeds, Doctors' Mob, the Dharma Bums, and other bands, Daniel Johnston made it into the final edit. At one point the host,

Peter Zaremba, introduces Daniel as a "man about town. . . . Everybody knows who he is." Daniel looks up at the camera for less than a second, then, with his eyes focused on the ground in front of his feet and his body anxiously rocking back and forth, he holds up a copy of his tape and says, "My name is Daniel Johnston and this is my tape. It's called *Hi How are You*, and I was having a nervous breakdown while I was recording it." [101] This abject public confession of emotional instability would soon anchor the narrative that explained Daniel's unique songs. Later in the program, he revels overtly in the brief joy of fame. With a close-up of his face superimposed over a map of Texas, a more relaxed and comfortable Daniel says, "This is to David Thornberry from Daniel Johnston. Dave, here I am on MTV, holding up my tape, *Hi, How are You*. They recorded me tonight. I'm on MTV. Remember me? We used to watch MTV back home? I'm on MTV, David." [102] Daniel does not obey the rules of cool that restrain all the other amateur Austin musicians. He can admit out loud that being on MTV is sincerely the most exciting thing that has ever happened to him. During a backyard barbecue scene, intended to show something of the everyday life of musicians in Austin, the camera briefly focuses on Daniel talking to two other Austin musicians. He looks up at the camera and says, "How are you doin'? We're just having a casual conversation. On national TV." [103] Puncturing the intended illusion that the video crew is documenting a casual everyday gathering of this group of friends, Daniel reveals the constructed nature of the experience represented by the program. But he is so intensely happy about it that the scene makes the final program. It *is* a thrill to be pretending to have a normal conversation for the video crews of MTV; it is so much more exciting than the pretended normal conversations that occur everyday. Finally, Daniel Johnston is shown performing one song, "I Live My Broken Dreams," in front of a screaming audience at Liberty Lunch. Indeed, as he moved from sweeping lobbies in McDonald's to performing his broken dreams on national television, within six heady months Daniel Johnston experienced the most rapid rise to celebrity and fame the Austin music scene had ever witnessed.

Instant stardom for this open personality. Throughout the remainder of the year, Daniel continued to perform, but the story of his 1983 nervous breakdown circulated as an easy explanation for the directness of his songs, and he became an overt object of torment, derision, and spite. Although he was voted best songwriter in the 1986 *Austin Chronicle* Music Awards, Johnston's world was collapsing around him. The adulation that he had received for his starkly direct expressions of an unstable

Symbolic reinforced symptoms that soon turned destructive for both Johnston himself and those around him. Daniel Johnston began to live out his obsessions with death, with the putrid nature of his own body, and with his inability to win the love and sexual attention of women, themes that had been the abject focus of so many of his songs.[104]

Lost in a confusion produced by the loving adulation of his audience and the support of his fellow musicians, yearning for a love that he had not experienced but that he was sure existed, Daniel began to harass some of the women who had expressed sympathy, understanding, and affection for his songs (and, by extension, for him as well). As he alienated most of the people who had befriended him a year earlier, he grew more desperate for the support and attention that his songs had produced. His naive rejoicing in the spectacle of fame became a wallowing demand for attention. Daniel's overinvestment in the Imaginary and his corresponding detachment from any stabilizing Symbolic—the very internal relations that had empowered his performances and made his songs so emotionally effective—led him to the disempowered and psychotic condition of being a twenty-two-year-old-baby in the universe, undisciplined and uncontrolled, screaming for attention, and unable to see beyond the pure reflection of his own desires. In the winter of 1986–1987, Daniel Johnston moved back to his parents' home in West Virginia, leaving behind an Austin music scene that had seen itself in his mirror.[105]

An Imaginary Conclusion

In this chapter, I have tried to describe the processes and the principles by which the rock'n'roll scene in Austin during the middle and late 1980s produced musicians, bands, and songs; and I have attempted to identify the dominant aesthetic value that unified a variety of musical styles and ways of living. I hope to have made clear the psychosemiotic processes that are involved in the production, projection, return, and introjection of identities and the corresponding creation of new enunciative positions within the discursive and musical structures of the local culture. The signifying practice that occurs in the rock'n'roll scene in Austin involves an adolescent inscription of possibility, performed within a tradition of musical expression that valorizes sincerity as the primary determinant of aesthetic worth. The result of this interaction is a doubled emphasis on the fluidity of the psychoanalytic operations that Jacques Lacan characterized as Imaginary. Daniel Johnston's performance of fetishized sincerity represented the extreme boundaries be-

[handwritten margin note:] can't get a women) living a depressed life

[handwritten margin note:] always strove for something imaginary - never achieved any of it to enjoy before striving for something new

yond which this aesthetic could not stretch even as they widened the range of possible positions just short of that boundary.

The cultural function filled by the public performance of popular music in nightclubs or honky-tonks involves a radical interrogation of the limitations of the dominant culture, an interrogation that occurs unconsciously, in the creative processes of identification that I have described. Music is a particularly noncognitive expressive system, conducive to the imaginary projection of inarticulable desires. Because of the very physical qualities of music, because of the way it nonsemantically transforms and materially vibrates tissues and bodies, the performance of organized sound provides the crucial symbolic structure through which musicians achieve their "dialectical syntheses" and project their incomplete and yearned-for identities. Because of the intense reenactment of the imaginary identifications of the mirror stage experienced during adolescence, an incredible array of new possibilities is opened within the local culture, both musically and discursively. Within the unstable conditions of a postmodern Symbolic, the performance of rock'n'roll music allows for tentative explorations of these embodied subjective possibilities. Those elements of the human that have been excluded from the dominant structures of meaning—Kristeva's abject—become appealing means whereby the adolescent signifies and produces an identity. The aesthetic value of sincerity—derived from the desire for the pure relations of the Imaginary—is guaranteed through the overt and recognizable display of personal risk, a display that reiterates the desire for purity and genuineness. But the new structures of identification, created by the intense emotional interactions of fans and musicians during musical performances in the clubs, disappear like the ephemeral images on a darkened movie screen if they fail to gain an access to the world outside the clubs.

Sincerity can be performed in the context of a scene, where the overproduction and affective exchange of signs result in a flow of participatory experience. Here, in this river of transformative imaginary identifications, the coded display of sincerity is enough to guarantee the meaningful qualities of any performance. Within the scene, any expression of the desire for pure being, however lacking in the stabilizing familiarity of symbolic coherence, can be recognized. The nonmusic of a Daniel Johnston can be heard, recognized, and returned because it so insistently yearns for this nonsemantic meaning. But outside of the clubs, beyond the scene, the local codes that signify sincerity cannot support the meaning of any song, of any rhythm. A greater, more elaborated articulation with the Symbolic must occur before any musical or lyrical statements or identificatory structures enounced by fans or musicians can be understood beyond the immediate audience of the always already knowing. It is to these more elaborate articulations, to the inscription of identity, that we must now turn.

CHAPTER SEVEN

The Inscription of Identity in the Music Business

Very few musicians in Austin can support themselves through their musical work. Most have other employment, a day job, that makes additional demands on their time and energy, diverting some of both from their musical work. A particularly strong tension results from these demands, adding to the pressures to "make it" in the music business. The monotony and low pay of most day jobs signify the lack of intrinsic rewards found in the modernized workplace. By contrast, the apparent freedom of the life of the musician—the ability to set one's hours and to follow spontaneously one's desires in the search for pleasurable meaning, as well as the immediate rewards experienced in successful performance—looms as a utopian image of the way life and work might be structured.

As rock'n'roll musicians in Austin develop their music in the pursuit of this utopian image, they make their way through a local system of music-making. They find that they must become able to project their identity beyond the confines of the immediate scene. Gatekeepers in the system—influential fans, critics, booking agents—will more actively promote the band's performances once the band has successfully translated their projected identity into a set of musical signs that can be understood apart from the local performance context. A band's first tour is an important step toward developing this ability, but, even more importantly, they have to make successful recordings. Although these musicians have been initially focused on the projection of an identity in performance that their fans can re-cognize and return, they soon find that, in order to obtain the more prestigious and well-paying bookings, the favorable write-up in the local paper, or the combination of gossip and streettalk known as a "buzz," they need to inscribe their projected identity on tape. This process of electronic abstraction demands that they discipline the pure desires of their adolescent Imaginary to fit with the commercial, technological, and ideological structures of the recording industry. Chasing after their utopian vision of meaningful work, their concept of the end goal of their practice shifts from being able to "not have to work" to being able to "make a living in the music business." This shift, experienced by every successful musician in town, requires multiple dialectical syntheses with a Symbolic enforced by the technologies of late capitalism.

The Day Job: To Not Have to Work

The day jobs that support Austin musicians are often the sorts of part-time or temporary jobs held by college students. Like most college towns, Austin has a wide variety of local businesses that both cater to student consumers and prefer to hire the relatively cheap labor of part-time student workers. These workers are believed to share the tastes and the values—the consumption culture—of the intended market, and they keep payroll costs down. Most of the student workers either leave town or change jobs annually. Therefore, they do not acquire much seniority, and their wages stay low. The most significant savings for the employer, however, derive from the fact that these employees work less than full time. Part-time student workers receive reduced benefits, and the total wage package becomes much smaller. Many restaurants, book and record stores, and clothing and food stores in Austin take advantage of this pool of cheap labor. In return, employers allow a greater flexibility in scheduling and dress and demand a slightly lower level of attentive performance from their student workers. It is expected that the students' main concerns lie elsewhere—ostensibly, with their studies—and that the exigencies of exams or papers might require a temporary work absence that other student employees could cover.[1]

Over the past twenty years, this labor market exchange of low pay and few benefits for flexible schedules and minimal performance demands has moved beyond the pool of student workers to include groups of nonstudents who have similar outside interests and requirements. The large group of artists, dancers, and musicians in Austin has tapped into this system, and businesses that cater to this nontraditional population have begun to adopt similar hiring practices and employment policies.[2] Discarding the term "hip," this population is becoming known as the "alternative community" that supports and is supported by "alternative businesses."[3]

One example of an alternative business is Wheatsville Food Coop. Founded in the seventies as a small cooperative purchasing enterprise,

Wheatsville has grown into a multimillion-dollar grocery business. It provides bulk and packaged grains, organic and traditional fruits and vegetables, and the assortment of teas, herbs, spices, yogurts, cheeses, and bean curds that characterizes postsixties food cooperatives. Members join through a small capital investment or through volunteer work, and nonmembers pay a fixed percentage more than the shelf price on all items. The people who work here move slowly, but they smile a lot. The store is haphazardly organized and somewhat inefficiently stocked. It is not uncommon for long-time members to venture into the back stockrooms searching for items they cannot find on the shelf. The act of shopping in the Wheatsville Food Coop rejects passive consumption and indicates a certain dietary and ideological difference from the American mainstream, clearly marking the shopper's own "alternative" status.

Walking into Wheatsville, one often hears tapes of music selected by the employees, typically songs by the Velvet Underground, Hank Williams, the Grateful Dead, Bessie Smith, Camper Van Beethoven, or Siouxsie and the Banshees. The employees wear an odd blend of clothing styles, mixing signifiers of sartorial difference from the last three decades. Blonde hair in dreadlocks will tumble onto a tie-dyed T-shirt over skin-tight black jeans and combat boots. A cashier might wear tights under a short solid-black dress decorated with wooden beads and a peace sign. A shirt with the slogan "U.S. out of Central America" will peek out from within a black leather jacket, both worn beneath a shaved head.

Several of the musicians and fans who participated in this study either have in the past, or currently do support themselves by working at Wheatsville. Mike Hall and Dianne Hardin both worked at the deli counter. Kevin Whitley stocks the grocery shelves, and Judy Jamison manages the front end of the store. Judy is a fan of Kevin's band, Ed Hall, and many other Austin bands as well. She thinks that Wheatsville is a "cool place to work," and that makes it easier for her to hire "cool people" to work there.

It is kind of by design, cuz I think these cool people come to hang out with other cool people. I know when I hire someone, I want to like the person. And so I hire the people that I like. I also have to think about how the customers are gonna react to this person, blah-blah-blah. That's part of it. But I think we tend to hire people we like, and it's neat to work in a place where everyone is, well not everyone, there's always an exception, but a lot of the people are people you hang out with too.[4]

Judy hangs out in the rock'nroll scene; the "cool people" she hires include musicians and fans. Kevin Whitley thinks that Wheatsville is "an ok place to work. If I really need it, like, if the band's gonna tour or something, I can get a week off." However, it does not correspond to his imagined ideal of meaningful work. "But I still hate it. It's just a stupid job."[5]

To a certain extent, the day job has become a necessary component of the musician's life in Austin. As one of the regular columnists for the *Chronicle* put it, "We've been to packed clubs, with hundreds more stamped hands hanging outside, and the next day the leader of the headlining band asks us if we want mustard or mayo on that #7. The Day Job is as much a part of the Austin music picture as Fender guitars, mousse and the color black. The Day Job keeps it all in perspective. It erases rock stars. It keeps you honest."[6] Ten years after Hank Alrich decried the impossibility of quality musicians making a living in Austin, musicians continue to flood the town and continue to work meaningless jobs during the day in order to be able to play music at night.[7] But regular nonmusical employment limits the energy and time one can devote to music, and it does make touring difficult.

Alejandro Escovedo doesn't find his job at Waterloo Records too disagreeable. "I don't mind it really. Sometimes I wish I could just sit here [at home] and write songs all day. But I would rather work at Waterloo than play a lot of gigs I don't want to play. Although sometimes I wish I could just be out on the road again. I really miss that."[8] A position at a record store, especially at one of the major independent stores like Waterloo, is a relatively prestigious and sought-after day job. Waterloo Records is one of the daytime centers of the scene. The store compiles and displays a list of the week's best-selling local product. Musicians, industry professionals, and fans drop into the store regularly. Waterloo has long been one of the more popular sites for record release parties, where bands or record companies pay for a keg or two of beer, the band performs a short set, and the store tries to sell all the copies of the new release they have in stock.

During a local tape release party in the spring of 1990, it was Al's duty to check the age of those requesting the free beer. He and I sat around the keg and grumbled about the band that was playing. They were an acoustic trio who sang happy songs and had drawn into the store about seventy-five well-dressed fans who had parked clean new cars in the store's lot—a far cry from the near-metal, trainwreck noise and the glistening, damaged fans of Al's most popular band of the eighties, the True Believers. "I don't know, man, all these happy kids and this hippie folk shit," he said. "It ain't rock'nroll, that's for sure." The next week, though, the new tape by Twang Twang Shock-a-Boom was number one on the Waterloo hit list.

Most of Al's days are spent working a cash register, answering the phone, and stocking the shelves. It is part of his job to keep up with current record company releases as well as the national trends reported in the trade and entertainment papers. Like most successful contemporary record stores, Waterloo features compact discs and cassette tapes. But Alejandro works in the vinyl department, selling new and used albums. People bring in old records to sell once they have replaced them with compact discs, and he has been able to complete his Jimmie Rodgers and Bessie Smith collections relatively cheaply. A few other musicians work at Waterloo, but Al says that the owner, John Kunz, does not like to hire them. Musicians do not always show up on time, and too often they want extended leaves to go on tour.[9]

Of those Austin musicians I interviewed, only Joe McDermott's income is derived completely from his musical activities. To a large extent, Joe's economic success comes from his ability to market himself as a children's entertainer to a specific segment of Austin's population. "The parents who love me are like typically very liberal Democrats. Thirty-five years old. It's almost like typecasting. They either work for the university or for the government, you know, some kind of hip political job." Joe earns enough money by singing his kids' songs at private parties and by selling tapes of this music at children's stores like Over the Rainbow to pay his bills. Even though he does not consider his children's songs to be "real music," he feels lucky. "In a lot of ways, I'm exactly where I wanna be because I don't have to have a job."[10]

Over the Rainbow caters to the same demographically and politically defined group—Austin's liberal professional-managerial class—that responds to Joe's kids' music. The shop is owned by an ex-UT English professor who is also the father of Heather Moore, the viola player in Joe's "real" band, Grains of Faith. During the week, it is common to find Kim Longacre working behind the counter at the store.

I work every day of the week. And I get off work and go play in Waco and drive home and go to work the next day and get [my son] Max and, you get sick! It's really hard and I sometimes think, actually, it's never been, "Is this worth it?" It's always been like, "Man I hate this job at Over the Rainbow. Why do I have to do this?" And I resent having to work a second job. But in some ways I really do like it. I feel like it's keeping me honest or something. Well, it also limits you with the amount of time. You constantly doubt if you had enough time to practice that. Do you really have enough time to know the songs?[11]

John Croslin works at Half-Price Books, a used bookstore across Guadalupe Street from Wheatsville. He feels much the same ambivalence toward his day job that Kim expresses about hers. The bookstore provides a relatively relaxed working atmosphere; John runs the front cash register and chooses the music played over the sound system in the store. His boss loves John's band and allows him some flexibility in his weekly scheduling. But, in return, John had to promise not to take the Reivers on any extended tours for at least a year. "Well, you know, it was part of the deal, cuz she had been burned by me the last time. I quit on her before when we went out to support the last record." Nevertheless, John has come to depend on the security that the day job provides when he makes business plans for the band. "It makes it a lot easier to make a good decision. Cuz you can have all the integrity in the world and if people don't like it, well, don't quit your day job."[12]

Byron Scott is the lead singer and chief songwriter for Do-Dat, one of the longer-lasting funk bands in Austin. He also waits tables at Waterloo Ice House. Byron describes the catch-22 situation in which many local bands find themselves. "We should be out on the road more, but we've all got day jobs. It's no excuse but it's hard to get past a certain point. If you're not making enough money to quit your day job, how can you afford to go on the road for an extended time?"[13] Ron Marks of The Texas Instruments echoes that complaint. "The most frustrating thing about all of this is not being able to go get a good job because I'm probably going to have to lose it when I go on tour. If I was making enough money from music to live, I'd have some more free time to put back into music. I'd really like to do that."[14] The day job is almost always a low-pay, low-performance retail or restaurant job. The paychecks from such employment barely cover rent, food, drink, and transportation. Consequently, musicians move from one temporary job to another, often lasting only as long as it takes to organize and finance another tour.

Ideally, the day job functions as a necessary means to its own end. Brant Bingamon outlines the motivations and goals of many rock'nroll musicians in Austin.

Um, in two years, if I was real lucky, maybe, ok this is out of sight luck that, what I want to be doing is *not having to work*. I think that's about the earliest I can foresee that happening is in two years. And that's, of course, with the huge success of one album. You're not gonna make it by playing live gigs in this town, although you might in some other towns. But the whole idea of music is to, like the end is, playing and making money and not having to work. That's the extent of my ambition. So that can only be achieved through the recording end.[15]

In Austin, or any of the other major music cities in the country, the live music played in the clubs, in the scene, is performed by young people who share a powerful desire to "make it." As Brant so neatly puts it, a very important goal is playing music and making money and not having to work. While musicians in Austin do work on their music, this work does not constitute a "job." For these young people, music has become the symbolic structure that enables sincere expression. To "make it" is to construct, through one's own hard work and sincere intentions, an economically self-sustaining social *real* free from symbolic constraints, especially from the petty daily routines of a job. The fantasy of popular musical success imagines freedom from material restraints.

The local image of the self-determined producer is derived from the Texan tradition of the independent honest worker. A populist discourse structures even the most utopian fantasies of work. In the words of the Way-Outs' Tom Thornton, "Ideally, I would like to make enough money to eat off of this. . . . What I would really like, more than anything else, is to be in the grocery store and know that I bought my food because I am playing music. But, on the other hand, I hope that it never becomes just a job." [16] When music becomes just a job—motivated purely by instrumental reason—it is no better than a day job. While the day job keeps the musician "honest" and honest work is important, meaningful work is work with its own drive, its own purpose. Rock'n'roll musicians in Austin aspire toward the life of successful independent producers in control of their work, able to express sincerely and spontaneously their desires in the performance of that work. To this extent, the drive to "make it" is an active expression of a utopian desire.

This idealized productive capacity is one of the indelible elements inscribed in the identities projected by every band. Therefore, even at this basic level of fantasy, economic motives permeate rock'nroll music. Success for even the most radical "rebellious" bands is conceived of as freedom from the constraints of the day job, from the social constrictions that interfere with sincerity and spontaneity in any job. But freedom from the day job means "making it" in the music business. The hope of some level of professional success weaves together contradictory impulses and a variety of musical styles. As Kevin Whitley of Ed Hall puts it,

You know it's weird, the farther along it goes, you get these little signs, that it might, you might just jump this incredible echelon. And then you think that way a little bit—God, what if we did? What if we were to have enough money to not have to fucking work? Where this was our work? Just like we want it to be. I know all of us want that. We want that. [17]

The populist discourse of the independent entrepreneur able to produce wealth through the sweat of his or her brow and the sincerity of her or his beliefs contributes to the idealized image projected in the performances of rock'nroll musicians in Austin. It is important that the projected image indicates a certain independence from the recording industry; any success must be on the band's own terms, otherwise it is just a job. And in turn, this independence represents for the fans, and for the popular music scene at large, a turning of the complexities of the capitalist production and distribution system to the needs and desires of the local community. But still, a certain degree of professional success must be achieved or the impact of the band's efforts is significantly reduced. Thus, the commercial structure of popular music not only effects the transformation of music into commodity but also contributes to its symbolic power in the production and communication of local identity. One of the first necessary steps toward professional success is going out on the road.

The Tour

A narrative of the band's first tour, with the band members loading all the equipment into a van, living together for weeks, driving all day or all night, finding the club in a strange town, playing for people they do not know, and finally sleeping on couches in the homes of the local scenesters, has become an important component of the popularly constructed myth of the rock'nroll musician. The model for the new wave band on the road was set by the publicity that surrounded the first U.S. tour by the Police. The Police were a band made up of an English university instructor and two professional musicians from London. They were managed by the drummer's brother and were signed to a brand new record company just started by another brother. According to the story, the three members of the band and one roadie (a technical assistant usually familiar with the electronics and mechanics of the band's equipment) drove themselves and their equipment from gig to gig, across the country in a station wagon. The band was booked into small clubs in media centers and college towns, and, at every stop, the Police played brilliantly to packed houses. According to the myth, this self-managed independent tour broke the Police nationally, setting them on their way to international stardom.

The success of this tour seemed to offer a simple and straightforward pattern that any band could follow. Although the Police myth inspired many Austin bands, it left out several crucial details. The recording company that the Copeland brothers had set up, IRS, had a national distribution arrangement through A&M records. They hired Jay Boberg to head their promotional department, signaling their intention to focus on the specific submarket of college students.[18] The Copeland brothers were experienced publicists and managed to fill the clubs in each town with critics and other local opinion leaders. The tour was never intended to make money. The Police were well financed, they were able to eat well and stay in hotel rooms. The story of the band hitting the road with only a station wagon was simply part of the publicity effort to lend street credibility to the band's image. It was tremendously successful.

The first punk-era new wave band out of Austin to try to live the Police myth was the Skunks. Their traveling initially consisted of playing in Dallas and then driving to New York where articles written by Ed Ward and published in the *New York Rocker* had made it possible for them to obtain bookings.[19] The Standing Waves soon followed the Skunks, and a regular exchange of bands took place between the New York and Austin rock'nroll scenes. Roland Swenson, manager of the Waves, moved his band to New York for a year, in an effort to establish them as a national act. Rank & File was a band made up of experienced musicians who had toured extensively with their earlier bands from California—the Nuns and the Dils, and so they were constantly on the road. But the bands that grew up in the Sparky's-Beach scene contained mostly younger, inexperienced players who had never toured before.

John Croslin remembers returning from the first tour by Zeitgeist.

We were really the first band to try anything like that out of our group of bands. And we took off in our station wagon and just had the most incredibly adventurous, I-can't-believe-we-made-it-back, sort of thing. But as soon as we got home, we immediately went down to the Beach and saw TI or something and everybody went, wow, what's it like to be on tour? We were tellin' everybody these stories and really diggin' it you know.[20]

The first few tours of any band are exciting times, as each band tests out their material on audiences who do not already know them. They provide an opportunity to practice with great intensity every night, to learn some of the conventions of entertainment, and to discover the difficulty of projecting and completing identities with individuals who do not eat at the same hamburger joints and do not drink the same beer or hang out in the same clubs. Bands find out whether or not they can play the same songs in the same order, smile in the same places, and move and nod their heads together without boring themselves and, consequently, their audiences. If the van breaks down, or the club owner refuses to pay the band because the ten people who came in to the bar did not drink, or two of the band members get so sick they can barely play, the band has exactly reproduced the stereotype of life on the road. Every band returns from their first tour much tighter, much more "professional" in their approach to performing than they were before.

Bands also learn whether or not they can live together. Mellissa Cobb

Glass Eye on tour.   Photo by Pat Blashill.

remembers her first trip to New York with her first band, the Delinquents.

> We had a truck, a big old truck, and we had all the equipment on the bottom, put boards on top of that and then mattresses on that. So we like all had to sleep in the back of the truck. It was really bad. We stayed in KOAs. It was awful. And like, Andy, the guitar player, had really bad breath. And he'd lay on his back and sleep with his mouth open. And it would be awful, the air, cooped up in the back of that truck.[21]

"You're not really a band, man, until you go on the road," says Alejandro Escovedo.[22] Simply surviving a tour, managing the band's resources well enough to be able to get to each show on time, playing every show, even in empty clubs, and returning home without the band breaking up represents the achievement of a certain professionalism. It is an important aspect of living the life of the rock'n'roll musician, bestowing a certain seriousness on one's efforts. Each bare-bones tour completed adds its store of specific anecdotal details to the overarching myth and more completely stitches each member of the band into the position of the working musician. Touring is a necessary step toward "making it," expanding a band's audience beyond the local scene and demonstrating an appeal broad enough to justify to record companies the utilitarian expenditure of recording the band.

Recording

Playing live is just, like, something you learn to do. It's not the end. The end really is the studio. We've got to the point now where, actually, we made a big study of playing live, and we feel that we've got to the point where we do it sort of ok. If we played a little bit better, we'd probably be better at it. But, you know, you're not gonna make it playing gigs. So at that point recording becomes extremely important. I see recording and playing live as two totally separate things. And they don't, the only thing that is the same is that you're playing the same songs. But you're not even playing them the same way.[23]

Live music has long been a minority taste within the public of entertainment consumers. In the 1920s, the recording industry discovered that fans of oldtimey fiddling contests would happily buy recorded versions of Fiddler John Carson's material.[24] Even during his lifetime, Jimmie Rodgers's records were heard by more people than ever saw him perform.[25] Most rock'nroll musicians learn how to play by studying recordings, learning the riffs and the vocal styles of their favorite precursors.[26]

For all the emphasis I have put on the important conditions of and transformations that occur in live performance—the production, projection, and introjection of partial identities—recordings are an equally important medium for popular music. As one means whereby the enunciative position musicians project in performance can be represented, recordings are the auditory inscription of a band's performed identity. In addition, the commercial structure of rock'nroll, externalized as a system of commodity exchange but internalized as the drive to "make it—to not have to work," encourages local musicians to concentrate on recordings: the dominant industrialized commercial medium of popular music.

Throughout the 1980s, as Austin became more and more identified as a center for the "music industry," the number of commercially available local recordings increased each year.[27] Between the years 1981 and 1984, musicians associated with Austin released an average of thirty-three albums, eleven EPs, sixteen singles, and three tapes per year. Between the years 1986 and 1989, Austin acts released an average of sixty-six albums, eight EPs, fifteen singles, and eighty-three tapes per year.[28] The number of extended-play records and singles stayed relatively steady, reflecting the decline of interest in the recording industry for these formats. While the number of long-play recordings (including both vinyl and compact disc releases) doubled during the eighties, the most dramatic increase took place in the number of cassette tapes released.

Only 2 recordings by Austin artists were available on tape in 1981: the

Reactors' "Readjustments" and "Pool 2" by the Pool. In 1989, 149 tapes by Austin artists were released.[29] Most of these tapes were the product of independent recording activity by the bands or by small companies associated with, or run by friends of, the bands. Often these independent tapes were demo (demonstration) tapes that failed to attract sufficient interest from the recording industry to gain a contract for the band. Demos are supposed to provide short and clear examples of the band's music. They serve a function analogous to a thirty-second television commercial; the demo is intended to highlight the band's musical strengths, give an idea of the band's image, and impress the band's value upon its potential buyer—the record company. Each band's demo competes with thousands of other tapes for the attention and support of the industry. As the first blatant transformation of the band's identity into a reproducible commodity, the demo must present itself as a bargain. Ideally, it should offer the maximum musical pleasure for the professional listener in the minimum amount of time. The recording of a demo tape is often the first experience for each band in the studio, simultaneously their first attempt to translate their identity into a wholly auditory signal and their first confrontation with the industry's demand that they effectively commodify that identity. When a band's demo does not win a recording contract, the band, or friends of the band, market the demo tape in order to recoup some of the recording costs, and perhaps to earn a positive review in the local press and increase the band's visibility in the local scene.[30]

The desire to make records, so much a part of concept of "making it," encompasses not only an economic and socioideological goal but also the desire to inscribe, to leave behind a mark, to etch a trace in the history of rock'n'roll music. As Mike Hall put it,

But I mean the whole thing of making, of recording, you know, I mean, that's the thing that lasts forever. That's the thing that is, I mean, live music I think is really great. And there's so many great clubs in town and you can always go see live music. But it's the records that last. Any band can get a gig if they're any kind of decent. But making records . . . [sic][31]

This belief was voiced in one way or another by every musician I interviewed. From the standpoint of musicians in Austin, making records has become a primary objective; that is how a band makes its mark. Putting together a band, practicing, writing songs, playing live, even touring, are all subsumed under the goal of recording the band's material, seeing it turned into material objects that can be found in a store and hearing it come over the radio. This minimal level of success— the electronic inscription of one's identity and the corresponding commodification of one's music—requires the complete participation in the systemic operations of the recording industry.

Once recording becomes an acknowledged goal of the band, a larger set of economic and generic constraints begins to influence every aspect of the band's approach to their music, their style, their presence in the scene. Generically, the heterogeneous identities produced and promulgated in nightclub performances must be disciplined, edited, whittled down into shapes that can be communicated wholly through the ear, encoded electronically in recordings. While a successful recording still must project those partial identities, it must do so through a single sensory channel. Therefore, the band's distinctive marks must be exaggerated, the musical evidence of distinction enhanced, much as a logo or a trademark must stand out on any mass produced item displayed in the market.[32] Secondly, recording is expensive, testing the financial resources and planning capabilities of any fledgling band. A minimal project, say, recording three songs on an eight-track analog machine in one twelve-hour block, can cost between $400 and $600—a serious investment when one's day job pays minimum wage—and the resulting tape will not be of releasable quality. It can only serve as a demo tape, as a step toward "getting a deal," the financing necessary for making a real recording.

The expense of recording can be rationalized in two ways. It can be conceived of as an investment that is intended to pay dividends—a utilitarian wager on the band's professional career. If the recording is not designed for the ears of the professional gatekeepers of the industry, the expense can become pure nonproductive expenditure, a vanity recording.[33] In Austin, it is very difficult for rock'nroll musicians to justify nonproductive expenditure. Paying for one's own recordings, arranging for their mass reproduction, and distributing the results to fans through noncommercial channels is not playing the game.

Mellissa Cobb paid for her own band's recording, Hoi Polloi's 1989 tape, *Out Standing in the Field*.

Like these cassettes. I paid to have 'em made and I just pass 'em out. I know it's a vanity press, and I don't care. You know, it's nice to have a tape. I know it's a vanity press, and I don't think of it as anything more. I don't think of it as we're makin' it here by havin' this. It's a nice tape, you know? It's not gonna get us a record deal. And it doesn't matter.[34]

Mellissa's repetitive defense of her own motivations contains an important testament to the power of the commercial impetus in Austin rock'n'roll. When Hoi Polloi gave away their tape and assumed their recording costs as pure expenditure, it was equivalent to announcing that they were no longer trying to "make it."

Whether or not one is trying to get a deal is a critical distinction within the scene. It separates the serious bands from those who only play for fun. As Mike Hall told me,

A lot of it has to do with whether you're trying to get a record deal. . . . It really affects everything. How you're dressed. How you, what gigs you take. Whether you just take gigs on weekends so you'll be taken seriously. Who you want to open for you, all these things. It depends on if you're trying to get a record deal or if you're just playing.[35]

Only those bands who are trying to get a deal will be taken seriously by certain other music-related businesses. Bands find that there are individuals whose attention they need to attract, certain standards of achievement that they will need to match, and that these people are only willing to pay attention and evaluate the band's achievements if the band is clearly playing the game. The extent to which a band will be taken seriously by these people is directly related to the extent of the band's professional ambition and how clearly this ambition is displayed. Steve Spinks described some of the constraints that affect booking a serious band.

If you want to be a headlining band, you gotta act like a headlining band and try not to play during the week. You try to go for the weekend gigs, which is fine. But you don't make any money that way, and you have to refine your act on stage on Saturday night at eleven o'clock, and it's not a good time to do it. It's too much pressure. And boy, people that you really want to impress, like the critics mainly, that you wanna have help you out, they're always there at those gigs, it seems like.[36]

The pressure imposed on each performance by the attendance of local gatekeepers is intensified by the fact that recordings are the most significant key to establishing a band's importance, and establishing a band's importance is the key to recording.

Once in the studio, rock'nroll musicians find themselves in an environment very different from the distracted heterogeneity of the nightclubs. The physical arrangement of the machines and the furniture, the changes in a band's sound as a result of the technology, and a corresponding set of practices and beliefs that accommodate this technology, all produce specific constraints on the process of inscribing a band's identity on tape. A romance of technology dominates. Machines control the destiny of the sound. They capture the physical vibrations of the music and translate them into electromagnetic pulses—either digitally or on analog tape. The more expensive the studio and the fancier

A Butthole Surfer in the studio.   Photo by Pat Blashill.

the machines, the "better" the sound quality and the greater chance the
finished recording will have of successfully competing for listeners with
the thousand other recordings finished that day. Commercial considerations influence every decision made, from choosing which studio to
use to defining the band's sound, its recorded identity.

One of the more expensive studios in Austin is Arlyn, located in the
Austin Opera House Music Complex. It was built in 1985 using equipment and materials that had previously been used in Austin's two major
recording studios of the late seventies, Pecan Street and Third Coast
Studios. A young engineer who had been working as an intern at Lone
Star Studios was brought over to help wire the place together. Once
Arlyn was operational, Stuart Sullivan was hired as an assistant engineer. Stuart was not paid well, but in return he was allowed to work on
projects of his own whenever the studio was not booked. Almost every
musician in this study has recorded at one time or another with Stuart
Sullivan at Arlyn Studios. He had engineered the first recording of Mike
Hall and the Wild Seeds while still at Lone Star, and this experience
gave him some contacts in the burgeoning Beach scene. Stuart used his
access to the recording studio to provide many of the new bands in
town with bargain-rate twenty-four-track demo tapes and himself with
hours of engineering practice. Thus Stuart's engineering skill developed
within a quasi-professional context of after-hours recording of bands

that were still developing their sound. Most rock'nroll musicians, especially those at the beginning of their careers, are woefully ignorant of studio technology; they often feel at the mercy of the engineer. Their status as not-quite-professional players often complicates the power relations during a recording session, with the engineer being by far the most comfortable person in the recording environment as well as the master of the machines. As Stuart was also still learning his craft, he was flexible in his approach to each band's material.

The control room at Arlyn is softly lit by small spotlights, leaving most areas in shadow. The engineer sits in a high-backed swivel chair, covered in cracked vinyl, in front of a glowing control board displaying dials, switches, faders, and buttons, each of which can dramatically alter the sound in the room. Different speakers can be switched on and off, individual instruments can be isolated from all the others or else removed from the sound mix, specific ranges in pitch can be highlighted or reduced in emphasis. Looking up from the board you see a plate-glass window, and through the window is the main recording room, where the musicians perform. A large pair of speakers hangs symmetrically on each side of the window, and a smaller pair of "mixing" speakers rests atop the board. To Stuart's left sits a portable rack of "outboard" equipment, including digital delay machines, sound compressors, and various other electronic devices for manipulating sound. The actual recorders—both digital and analog with variable tracking capabilities—sit in a closet off to the side. Another cracked vinyl chair swivels before the board, where the producer or the relevant band member sits while discussing the countless decisions that make up each recording session (for example, the singer, if they are working on a vocal track). Along the wood-paneled wall behind the control room runs a padded bench on which sit band members who are not recording at that moment, and anyone else who might be attending the session. The bench feels like a church pew with its straight back, and when you are sitting on it, the control board looks like an altar across which appears a vision of the musicians at work in the main room.

The drumkit is set up in the middle of the main room. Drums are the most difficult instrument to record. They represent the strictest challenge to recording technology because they collapse the widest dynamic variance into the smallest passage of time. When recording drums, there is no sound, and then there is the BEAT, and then there is no sound. The flexibility of the plastic inner membranes of microphones and the sensitivity of the electromagnetic surfaces of analog tape are severely tested by this intense contrast. The number and position of the microphones used to capture the drum sound varies, depending on the techniques and preferences of the producer and the engineer. But a typical setup, one often used by Stuart Sullivan, would include a mike for the high hat, one underneath the snare, one for the ride toms, one for the floor tom, one in the bass or kick drum, and two or three hanging overhead, not only to capture the cymbals but also to record "the room." A good room is an essential ingredient in the production of a big drum sound.[37] Arlyn has a good room. This means that the walls and the ceiling are in the proper shapes and are of the appropriate materials such that they reverberate back to the overhead microphones the necessary volume and tonal depth. A "big" drum sound is produced when the placement of the microphones in a good room and the relative volume of the sound recorded onto the six to eight channels afforded to it (out of twenty-four or thirty-six) capture the dynamic attack of the initial beat complemented by the tonal resonance of a chamber large enough to echo back the long sound waves that comprise the drumbeat. To a certain extent, an engineer and a studio are ranked by their ability to produce and record a big drum sound, and the quality of the drum sound has become one of the most important signifiers of the money expended on the recording and, therefore, of the "quality" of the tape.[38]

With so much attention focused on the drum sound, even an experienced producer or engineer in a familiar studio will take an hour or more placing the microphones and setting the levels on the control board. The drummer sits on her or his stool, tapping away at whatever drum the engineer indicates. No other musicians need be present, and they usually do not show up until an hour or so after the recording session has officially begun. When the guitarists arrive, their amplifiers are set up in small booths adjacent to the main room. Microphones are placed inches from the speaker and the door is shut. A long cord and headphones allow the guitarist to stand in the main room and visually and physically interact with the drummer during the recording of the basic tracks. Stuart likes to record two bass channels: one takes the signal from the instrument straight into the board, the other mikes the sound from the bass player's amp. This amplifier, like those of the guitarists, is set up in a small room of its own. Most engineers prefer to have the singer standing in a different room, so that this "scratch" vocal will not "bleed" into the overhead drum microphones. But some bands, especially younger, less experienced bands, work off of sometimes unconscious visual cues among the band members. In these cases it becomes necessary for all the band members to actually stand in the same room while they lay down the basic tracks. Since Stuart developed his own working style while recording mostly inexperienced bands, this need to stand in the same room no longer appears to him to be a problem. In fact, he expects it and has worked out a microphone placement system that minimizes the bleed.

The most important objective in the recording of the basic tracks is to capture the rhythm of the song, the skeleton upon which are layered all other parts of the song's body. The emphasis on the quality of the drum sound is intensified by an equally demanding attention to the time intervals marked out by the beats. To the musician, engineers and producers seem obsessed by the precision of the rhythm track. Again, this follows from the romance with recording technologies, which have developed an increasing capacity to *measure* the intervals of time. Over the decades during which rhythm has been recorded, the assumption that clocks are the appropriate measure of the time marked out by musical rhythm has resulted in a standard of recording quality that renders a song's beat subservient to digital watches. The slightest variance from precisely regular timing is sufficient to scrap the take. The fact that drum patterns mark out the rhythm of a specific body has been lost in the enforcement of this abstract precision. As a result, "producers never like your rhythm section," and tremendous effort is expended attempting to fine-tune the song's rhythm, to bring it in line with that abstract standard.[39] Of course, the standard has been so well enforced through the recordings of recent decades that idiosyncratic rhythms now sound incompetent to the fan's ear, and most rock'n'roll drummers have internalized a clockwork accuracy as a goal of their own performance.[40]

Once the bones of the rhythm have been laid down, the rest of the song can be added on. If, during the basic tracks, the bass player kept time with the drums, tightly wrapping the sinews of a hinted undertone around those precise intervals, then the bass part will be kept and only faulty individual notes will be punched in. This evaluation is a crucial one, for in most rock'n'roll music, in fact in almost every western music with African roots, the interaction between the bass and the drums is what determines the "feel" of the song. The more closely the two rhythms map onto each other, the "tighter" the feel, but this tightness can also be heard as "stiffness." The more they vary, the "looser" the feel, which can also be heard as "sloppiness." The basic feel of a song's style, of its musical body, is produced in the (mostly rhythmic but subtly tonal) relationship between the bass and the drums. If all concerned agree that the take has captured the right feel for the song, then Stuart will isolate the bass part over the speakers in the control room, and everyone will listen for any notes that are improperly played. The bass player might have hit a wrong note or simply failed to depress the string with the necessary force, creating a buzzing hiss instead of a forceful, clear tone. These small mistakes are corrected by the bass player playing along with the part already recorded, usually standing in the control room, while the engineer "punches" the "record" button, turning that function on and off for periods of a second or less, covering up the bad notes. Stuart is proud of his ability to punch into the smallest gaps in the recorded musical passage, leaving behind no audible trace of the correction.

Up to this point it has been the engineer's job to record every element as cleanly, as clearly, and as much in line with current recording conventions as possible. The delight for engineers, the way they take joy in their work, derives from their ability to operate recording technology, combined with the "transparency" of the encoding machines. According to Stuart, the most important quality of a piece of recording equipment is "silence. We go for high fidelity, we aim toward silence." According to the ideology of engineering, the recording process should add nothing to and subtract nothing from the sound produced by the instruments. It should be impossible to discriminate between the sound of an acoustic guitar as it is strummed in the control room and the re-corded sound of an acoustic guitar played back over the speakers in the control room. However, when Stuart described the value of an expensive control board, the emphasis fell on "sonics."

The quality of sound. The circuits [of this board] are better. They are designed in a way that the characteristics you get out of their equalizers and compressors are termed more musical or deemed easier to listen to. It is, the only people that deem this are the people that rent and buy the machine. If a lot of people rent and buy it, then it is deemed to be better. There are certain objective measures. You can hook them up to oscilloscopes and look for distortions, and so, from that point of view, there are definitely technical standards that they have reached that are very high too. But the bottom line is that it sounds great.[41]

The board sounds great to the engineers and producers whose job it is to discriminate among and use such boards. The best equipment is asserted to be the quietest, producing the minimum distortion, but "the bottom line is that it sounds great." The sound of the board itself, rather than its silence, determines its value. The traditional recording standard of "fidelity" assumed an original performance to which the recording is faithful, but as recording becomes increasingly sophisticated this relationship of fidelity has reversed. More and more, the recording becomes the original work, and all subsequent "live" performances are attempts to emulate its sound.[42] Therefore, the sound of the board (as well as the technique of the engineer) plays an important determining role in defining the sound of the band.

If a band is recording multiple songs with basically the same instrumentation, Stuart prefers to record all the basic tracks first, as this minimizes setup time. The parts that are closer to the surface of the song—
the guitars, the keyboards, the vocals—are all re-recorded later, after
acceptable basic tracks with the right feel have been achieved. At that
point the main room is completely rearranged, the drums are packed
away, and the guitar amps are moved into the center. For these instruments, the emphasis on rhythmic precision is vastly reduced and the
attention is focused instead on the "sound," the tonal qualities that differentiate this band from all the other bands playing three-chord songs
in four-four time. Here is where the specific identity of the band under-
goes its most significant translation from an image projected in a heterogenous environment to the specifics of an auditory signal. Obviously,
much of this work has to have occurred already before the band entered
the studio. Certain elements of the sound must always already exist. But,
in the studio, only those aspects of the band's specificity that can be
encoded using the available technology come to determine its musical
identity. Much as the syntax of one's native language changes the meaning of translated poetry, the circuits in the recording studio transform
the sound of any band in the translation from performance to recording.
Here, the multiple characteristics (musical, personal, physical, ideological) that define the band's sound are discovered, isolated, exaggerated
or reduced in intensity, "mixed," and translated into the sonic texture of
the band's recorded material.

The sound of a band is constituted by the specific tonal characteristics
of each recorded instrument and the ways in which these individually recorded tracks are blended together over the "feel" of each song. Within
the aesthetic system expressed by rock'n'roll in Austin, individual playing styles are directly reflective of the "personalities" of the players. For
instance, the attack of an individual guitar sound, the specific force and
angle with which the pick strikes the strings, conveys a partial image of
the player, as do the patterns the left hand forms on the frets: the specific
scales from which riffs are drawn, the favorite voicings of each chord.
This style has been learned by the player through studying the recorded
guitar sounds of other players. The musical tastes and pleasures of that
individual guide this process, but these tastes are always formed in the
social and cultural context of fandom. Young guitar players struggle to
emulate the "cool" sounds that come out of their stereos, but the evaluation of "cool" is always a social process, involving the conscious and
unconscious choices of the player and her or his fellow fans, always incorporating nonmusical components into those decisions. The sound

developed by a young guitar player partially reflects the processes of identification that occur among all musicians and fans. The choices made about the degree and quality of distortion—whether it be produced though an old overheated tube amplifier or the transistors of a foot pedal—map out specific relations within and among technologies, social norms, and dissonance. These relationships are always partially structured by immediate economic considerations—the relative cost of the technological alternatives being only the most obvious—and represent solutions to the problems of how to achieve a musical expression of cool (or the projection of an idealized identity) under a specific set of constraints. For example, the influence of the guitar sounds of Johnny Ramone, Peter Buck, or even Keith Richards has far more to do with the visual and social images—the projected identities—of the Ramones or REM or the Rolling Stones, and the relatively cheap technology required to produce each sound, than it does with any purely musical factor. A similar set of variables and cultural considerations affects the choices made by keyboard players.

The vocals are the final element added into the recording. As we have seen, tremendous care is taken with the precision of the recorded drum track and with the individuality of the sound of the band. These two concerns are combined in recording the vocals. The uniqueness of the vocal track, the imaging of a specific body in the grain of the voice, contributes the most immediate auditory signifier of the band's identity. Much of the erotic power that generates the libidinal ties between performer and fan is conveyed through the quality of the vocal. When a fan sings along with a favorite record, the quality of the identification at work can be heard in the extent to which the fan voices more than the words and the melody, emulating the stylistic touches, those signs that indicate the physical nature of singing—the gasping intake of air, the nonverbal vocalized moans, sighs, and slides. These are the elements of a vocal track that must be at the same time unplanned and precisely executed. They are what individuate a style from its influences.

And in Austin, the influences can be overly dominant. A masculine image of the gruff, strong, almost-dangerous, out-for-a-good-time cowboy, communicated through the combination of Lefty Frizzell's or Ernest Tubb's honky-tonk singing style with a style reconstructed from the recordings of blues masters like Howlin' Wolf, Muddy Waters, and Bobby "Blue" Bland, indicates the dominant style of male vocals in Austin. Kim Wilson of the Fabulous Thunderbirds and Joe Ely mark the contemporary boundaries of this style. These two men have won the best male vocalist category in the Austin Music Awards seven out of ten years. The feminine version of this style—the tough yet abject and damaged "chick" singer, first inscribed in Austin singing practice by Janis Joplin—maintains an equally strong hold on the vocal styles of women in Austin. Angela Strehli, Lou Ann Barton, and Marcia Ball all vocally project this image. The best female vocalist award has been won by one of these women every year but one. Even those who wholeheartedly reject these stylistic images—for example, Kevin Whitley of Ed Hall or Kathy McCarty of Glass Eye—find their resistance shaped by the dominant stylistic discourse. On record, the different styles of both of these singers represent deliberate inversions of specific aspects of the dominant. Whitley's high-pitched wails and McCarty's rigid antiemotional coolness signify by their opposition to the norm, but still require their audience to be familiar with the expected techniques. When the singer goes wildly and shrilly off-key or remains still and affect-less on record, where there are multiple opportunities to modify or exaggerate the singer's performances, the deliberateness of the contrast with the dominant clearly resounds.

Often a band's first visit to a studio is also the first time the various players have really heard their musical style. Here, singers, guitarists, and keyboard players find an opportunity to rethink the relationships that constitute their style and, through the increased possibilities offered by the enhanced technologies, alter or adapt certain components of their sound. Managing this translation is the central and critical function of the producer. The producer should be familiar with the band and with the studio, aware of the strengths and limitations of both. A producer too familiar with the band will be unable to distinguish which of the specific personal and musical characteristics of the band can be passed over and which should be emphasized. John Croslin is acquiring a reputation for being one of the better young producers in Austin, but he does not attempt to produce his own band, the Reivers. "It's real hard for me as a producer to capture the band. It's hard for me to look at my friends and say, this is the essence of Garrett, this is the essence of Kim, how can I bring that out?"[43] Conversely, producers who are too attached to a certain set of recording techniques and, therefore, not sensitive to the uniqueness of each band, submerge the band's particular identity under the surface of their own style.[44] The producer's role is to encourage the band to take full advantage of the new possibilities of the studio, while emphasizing enough of its characteristic sound so that its projected identity is transformed into a recording.

However, while producers necessarily are concerned with recording identity, their skills are measured in competition with other producers by their ability to produce a quality recording. John Croslin has thought a lot about producing.

> The scope of the job is really big, but it's really simple too. Because when you listen to a song as a producer, you go, why do I wanna listen to this? And you decide and you make that, whatever it is, clear. If it's a song about pain, you want to underscore that; if it's a song about awkwardness, you make it a little awkward, and you want the listener to understand it. I really love all the technical stuff about it. I just really get off on a well produced record. It's really thrilling for me to hear all these sonic things they're doing now. They're really wild and great. I mean, it's just amazing how great a record can sound. On a great produced record, everything makes sense. It goes somewhere and it's there for a reason. It makes sense, and it's all taste. After all, there's only so many ways you can mix records. You can bring out the dark aspects, you can bring out the funny aspects, you can make it a quiet song, or a loud one, you can bring the drums up. But when it's well produced, whatever it is that you go for is the right thing to go for. And it's right in the context of the record, in the context of what they're playing on the radio, and in the context of what someone at home, listening on the headphones, would hear.[45]

This quote makes clear the qualitatively different standards used to evaluate the job of the producer. For each song, John is concerned with perceiving and highlighting its central emotional message. However, he delights in the "wild" "sonic things they're doing now," and the context within which he evaluates his own work remains the competition with other recordings—how this record sounds on the radio or on the home stereo.

During the spring of 1990, John Croslin was working with the Austin band the Wannabes, recording a demonstration tape at an inexpensive local studio, Austin Tracks. The Wannabes are, in John's words, "a drinking band," in the tradition of the Faces, the Who, and the Replacements, or Austin bands like the Cowboy Twinkies and Doctors' Mob. Their musical style is derived from the "indie" recordings of Husker Du and the Replacements, and their image fits easily into the Austin tradition of wanton drunken sincerity. In the scene, the Wannabes project the image of a band that flaunts its adolescent refusal of entertainment standards and musical professionalism. In the previous chapter, their bass player, Hunter Darby, described his own beliefs about the necessary relationship between a band's musical style and its lifestyle. Hunter prefers music that is not "safe" and tries to lead a not-safe life as well, valuing spontaneity, risk, and intoxication over order and predictability. However, the recording studio rewards careful planning and punishes sloppy performances, as it must concentrate all of a band's projected identity into an auditory signal. The ears become the sole medium through which the band's identity can be perceived; no visual aspects of the stage show are communicated, no physical stimulus deriving from the presence of other fans can be guaranteed. The overstimulation of libidinal fantasies resulting in imaginary identification must take place without the important amplification of visual signals. Therefore a greater emphasis falls on precise musical performance, which is a dangerous requirement for a band that espouses the value of an alcohol-fueled rush through life and song.

However, the studio can be made a very safe environment. "Mistakes" are easily corrected, and, with sufficient patience and attention, a note-perfect performance can be constructed. John's job, as the producer of the Wannabes' first demo tape, was to convince them that they would make a better record (that is, a record that more effectively projected their image) if they did not drink in the studio, if they concentrated on the accuracy and precision of their musical performances, and if they thought about recording as an entirely different way of playing. As John told me,

The Wannabes are a band that really like Husker Du and the Replacements. They are people that love the guitar sound on the Husker Du records or the production on *Let it Be* or lack thereof. It kind of snuck up on them, then, when we went in the studio and started being real careful about the way things sounded. I think they were kind of going, hmm, well, shouldn't this be spontaneous? I mean, it's really weird because they're a drinking band and I've made it real clear I don't want any drunkards in there trying to play. And it's uh, that was kind of a shock to them. I've kind of had to educate them or do my best to point out, I said, look at *Let it Be*, look at *Pleased to Meet Me*. That's a great contrast. On *Please to Meet Me* the drums are there, it sounds good, the performances are real strong. *Let it Be*, they're ok. The songs are great, maybe better, on *Let it Be*, but they're not presented in the way that someone in Des Moines is gonna understand. You know, it's not gonna entice them to make the effort to listen to those songs.[46]

John used the example of records by the Replacements that were very familiar to the Wannabes—pages, so to speak, from their rock'n'roll primer—in order to explain the difference between a record that is well produced and one that is not. In this context, John's criterion for a well produced record becomes whether "someone in Des Moines is gonna understand." In other words, a well produced record musically projects an image that can be parsed outside of one's local scene—in this case, beyond the Minneapolis home of the Replacements.

One of John's goals in recording the Wannabes, then, was to capture the anarchic, intoxicated, adolescent impulsiveness of the band in a precise, sober, musically encoded way so that someone in Oklahoma City (for instance) would want to listen to and could understand the results. Many bands who have achieved a significant degree of success playing in the clubs of the Austin scene never survive this translation into recording. Once the nonmusical aspects of their performances are stripped away and the random accidents of their musical styles are disciplined into recognizable scales, chords, and rhythms, nothing of interest remains.

In the case of the Wannabes' tape, John concentrated on the quality of the guitar sound in order to take advantage of already generically encoded signifiers from the rock'n'roll tradition. The recorded guitar sounds of Husker Du and AC/DC are the reference points. On their records of the mideighties, the guitars of Husker Du, played by Bob Mould, produce such a roar of overtones that the basic tonal quality becomes an unrelenting distortion, yet a hint of the chord structure can be heard at the upper edges of the ringing harmonics. The image the band projects is one of self-conscious anxiety driving the individuals in the band, a sort of intelligent powerlessness, an acute attack of adolescent angst. AC/DC, on the other hand, produce a more clear guitar sound with a razor-sharp metal edge. This sound is associated with the visual image of the band's lead guitar player, Angus Young, who hyperactively performs in a school cap and young man's shorts. Young's juvenile costume is contrasted with the sharp anger conveyed by the tonalities and the precise performance of the guitar work. The total effect of the image is a humorous projection of boyish impulsiveness combined with aggressive masculine mastery.

By attempting to locate the guitar sound of the Wannabes on a continuum between these two pre-existing styles, Croslin hoped to represent some of the Wannabes' projected identity in strictly audible terms that an audience unfamiliar with the image of the band, yet familiar with the tonal signifiers of rock'n'roll, could interpret. As Croslin insists, "You gotta do some of the work for the listener. It's irresponsible to expect, it's kind of a contradiction to make a statement with the production of the record to say, we expect you to get into it, you to do the work and figure out the song or the band, even if it's not presented in a very clear way. I think you've got to do your best to make it right, to give a darn about how it's on there."[47]

In order to appropriate the referential value of these signifiers, John retained the multitracked guitar roar of Husker Du's records at the same time that he cleaned up the core of the sound and added multiple overdubs, sharpening the clarity of the parts in line with AC/DC's style. By insisting on the precise performance of these multiple and complex parts, and by adding a mist of tonal distortion, John managed to represent some of the adolescent attitude of the Wannabes in an audible and comprehensible fashion. The complexity of the guitar parts and the volume at which they were recorded produced ringing harmonics that clashed at the edges of the sound. The increased complement of "noise" in the guitar sound itself made up for the decrease of the "noise" that had previously derived from sloppy performance.

Before this recording session, the Wannabes' guitar sound had not been a focal point of their performance. But in their performances after this session, they paid greater attention to the intricacies of their arrangements. Ironically, the successful reproduction of their complex recorded sound demanded a reduction in alcohol consumption when they performed. And thus, as this one component of their previously heterogenous identity was translated into a strictly musical expression, the Wannabes were shifted a little closer to becoming professional musicians. The process of recording itself, the translation of the band's projected identity into an auditory signal, regardless of the relative commercial or aesthetic ambitions of any individual or band, demands that the recording artist speak the language of already recorded acts, that the band project its identity within the terms of the discourse of commercially recorded rock'n'roll. The force of that demand, and the expense required to carry it out, drive many of Austin's rock'n'roll musicians to transform their goals. Once having recorded, "making it" clearly shifts its meaning from "not having to work" to "making a living in the music business."

Making a Living in the Music Business

The wisest words I ever heard about being in the music industry were by Darden Smith. You've gotta go through that period when you're full-time music. And no matter what it takes or how hard it is, if you don't make that crossover, you're not in the music industry. And people need to accept that. They can't go around saying I'm in this when they're not. It's like if you're working in the travel agency eight hours a day, and your idea of managing a band is drinking beer at their rehearsals, then you've got a serious problem.[48]

There's not too many people making a living in the music business in Austin. Well, it depends on what you wanna call living. Where they can exist as well as they could in a regular job environment. There's not that darn many. There's a lot that are doing it and doing without to be able to be in the business.[49]

You can't become just a scene band. It's a trap. And you gotta think in the business sense and you gotta get the hip out of it. Because there's no such thing as a hip business. You can be cool and all that on the scene you know, but you gotta do those gigs where people are gonna come see you—the people who aren't gonna step into the Continental Club. And those people are just as legitimate as the other people. They're just as interesting. And they usually have more money.[50]

I'm very successful in my estimation. When we first started out, we didn't expect anything but a gig at the Beach. I always took it real seriously, but I never thought of it as a career at all. So the fact that I'm making a living at it, or nearly making a living at it, is pretty wild in itself. It's kind of funny, we sit in our bedroom or control room or whatever and do something and eventually people go yeah, I like that, and come and buy it. To me, that's being a success. To be able to do something that you feel good about and you put it up there and people buy it. They may not be buying it in droves but they're buying it enough for me to make a living at it. That's being in business for yourself and making a living at it. There can't be anything more satisfying than that, career-wise anyway.[51]

I think I wanna play the game and I wanna play it the best I can and yeah, I do wanna win. Winning would be for me, and I think for the whole band at this point, would be making records at our leisure. I think I would like to be able to take vacations and, I don't know, have a good savings account for [my son] Max for college. And I'm probably gonna want to get married again. And take vacations and, you know, the more I think about it, and this has really been something that's been on my mind heavily lately, it's like I decided that the only way at this point that I can approach this business is to do it as if I were a carpenter and, just, I want, I want a week's vacation every year paid. And I want a house and I want to take care of my family and I want to eat dinner on Sunday in the afternoon with mashed potatoes.[52]

In order to "make it," to make a living through music, in order to support your family, to earn vacations, to make something you believe in and successfully sell it, the musician must accede to the structural organization of the recording industry. The band's projected identity must become a commodity traded for gain, not a gift exchanged in social communion. The music must become the object of a craft, distanced from the yearning, pure desires that once impelled the young musician. The object itself must be evaluated by a comparison with other objects, abstracted and alienated from the human processes involved in its production. No longer can the Austin musician approach her or his music as a utopian critique of modernity, commercialism, or the day job by simply allowing one's adolescent desires spontaneously to run free. In order to be effectively disseminated through the distribution system of rock'n'roll, these desires must be disciplined to fit the structures of the recording industry. This discipline constrains impulses, channeling the musician's unconscious efforts into the reproduction of the commercial systems of late capitalism. The sooner a musician recognizes this structure and adapts his or her desires to fit within it, the greater the possibility of a successful career in the commodification of identity.

We're still doing what we want to do basically; it's just that we're making it easy for other people to like it too by learning how to play better and by writing songs that are fun and easy and accessible. And we do that by making them simpler, making them less obtuse. Lyrically and musically. Making them basic, making them simple, making them less intellectualized, less like we're pulling some sort of an art-trip on people. That's the last thing I wanna do.[53]

The performance of music in Austin, a communal celebration and imaginary critique of cultural values, has been merged with a harsh competitive system of commodity production. There are so many musicians in Austin, each wanting to leave behind their day job, each wanting to make a living through their music, each leaning out further for the brass ring of pop success, that the struggle to survive as a musical unit requires an increasingly sophisticated approach to the music business.

This transformation is not simply a matter of supply and demand, of classical economics applied in the sphere of cultural production; rather, it is the result of a strategic response to the total modernization of Texas, of Austin, and of music-making itself. Ten years before, music-making in Austin was the cultural practice that embodied and expressed a critique of modernity and blatant commercialism. However, local music institutions—the Armadillo, the Soap Creek, Pecan Street Studios— were unable to adapt to the increasing articulation of music-making in Austin with national (and international) flows of entertainment capital and demands. When the success of the progressive country movement attracted more musicians to town than the clubs could support, those who wanted to make a living in the music business left town. As these professionally ambitious musicians moved away, they left behind a void that was quickly filled by new musicians eager to participate in this important local cultural practice.

The earlier exodus of musicians was itself a contributing factor to rapid institutionalization of the punk movement in the early eighties. That is, the reshaping of music-making in Austin in conformity with national industrial norms was the result of specific strategic decisions made by individuals who had witnessed the collapse of progressive country and were determined not to allow such a collapse to occur again. These individuals believed that the only way to protect Austin musicians, and those businesses that lived off the efforts of those musicians, from the cycles of pop fashion and the vagaries of adolescent desires, was to establish in Austin the infrastructure of a "music industry." They set out to reorganize the way music was produced in Austin so that a more predictable and consistent level of capital would flow through local music-related businesses. As a result of their efforts, more music businesses are thriving in Austin than ever before, more musicians are competing more intensely for goals that are harder to reach, and it has become much more difficult for the music made by young people in

Austin to perform its Imaginary function. The standards used to judge national commercial music are now applied to the demo tapes made by every young band. And the implicit bargain offered to musicians by the music infrastructure in Austin now imitates that of the national recording industry. The industry profits the most from mass stardom, therefore nothing less will do, either for local industry figures or for local musicians. How this transformation occurred, the strategies and the procedures used to achieve it, form the substance of the next chapter.

CHAPTER EIGHT

The Commodification of Identity

The Austin music scene emerged into self-consciousness during the progressive country boom, when entrepreneurs like Eddie Wilson and Mike Tolleson combined with journalists like Chet Flippo and Jan Reid to create the myth of the Armadillo. Although it constituted the dominant meaning of music-making in Austin for almost a decade, that myth by itself failed to organize, promote, and control the material conditions for the continued sustenance of live music in Austin. The progressive country alliance, based on a nostalgic celebration of the premodern, presocial origins of Texas itself, effectively appealed to the entrepreneurial spirit of local music industry figures. But it failed to mobilize the loyalty of the musicians who performed this embodied celebration, the capital of the national recording industries, or the pleasures of young people whose entertainment tastes continued to provide the basic financial support of the music scene.

As the 1980s began, music in Austin bore little resemblance to that performed during the heyday of the Armadillo. None of the stars of the progressive country period continued to play regularly in Austin in the new decade. Most of the clubs that had fostered the old scene had disappeared. Before the end of 1980, the Armadillo itself would close its doors forever. The students from the University of Texas were either attending huge touring concerts at the university's Special Events Center, where they spent their entertainment allowance on non-Austin performers, or they were participating in the punk scene at Raul's and Duke's Royal Coach Inn. And the contradictory nature of this new scene, its simultaneous disavowal and celebration of commodification, the pleasure it produced through inverting all the locally effective codes of musical meaning, rendered it incomprehensible to the holdovers from the progressive country scene.

At the beginning of the Raul's period, there were about ten bands playing punk rock in Austin, which necessarily implicated fifty committed members of the scene. Add into the mix their boy/girlfriends, their roommates, and a handful of writers who misrecognized their own budding talents in the efforts of these aspiring musicians, and the post-progressive country Austin rock'n'roll scene sprang into existence about 120 strong. At this initial point, the punk scene was merely another manifestation of "the Austin tendency to group the way they do."[1] Honky-tonks continued to provide the site for signifying practice, and popular music continued to be the central cultural form around which this practice was organized. There had always been many concomitant music scenes in Austin, each with its own hierarchy of musicians and fans, each with its temporary sites in different nightclubs in different neighborhoods across the town. The punk scene at Raul's began just as the folk scene had at Threadgill's and the hippie scene at the Vulcan—as another intoxicated celebration of identification and subjective transformation, of the construction of one's identity out of musicalized fragments of the past.

In each of these successive scenes, a core group of musicians and fans found they could reproduce the structure of their scene for a year or two simply by participating—by drinking beer at other bands' shows, writing sincere rave reviews describing how wonderful each band made everyone feel, and struggling to learn how to write songs and play music. But because of the flux and tension that create the conditions necessary for a scene, no scene can ever last very long. Each effort at self-representation—every performance, every flyer, every review, every tour, every recording—participates in the struggle to codify and stabilize the possible meanings that the scene can produce. Once these meanings have reached a certain level of stability, once it becomes possible to identify the qualities that define the multiple overlapping relationships among the bands and the fans that constitute any scene, then those definite meanings no longer function within musicalized signifying practice. The music, becoming simply music, collapses back into itself—an aesthetic form to be appreciated within its own set of generically generated expectations. And the scene moves elsewhere. Punk in Austin had built itself upon the fossilized ruins of progressive country.

In the early eighties, several individuals whose involvement in Austin's rock'n'roll scenes had bridged the seventies and the eighties initiated a new period of introspection, analysis, and self-promotion that produced descriptions of the musician's art and role in the local community along with social and economic prescriptions for encouraging their continued presence. The chief goal of this project was to clearly define the meaning of music-making in Austin and to link that meaning to a set of material conditions that would reinforce and promote the reproduction of that specific vision.

The Texas Music Association

In 1981, a few music business professionals met in Dallas to create the Texas Music Association, the first music trade organization in the state. This association was founded in order to revive the sagging fortunes of Texan music businesses. It was intended to provide an organizational and communications network that would benefit the agents, publishers, managers, and other support personnel who were active in Texan music—businesses that had been struggling ever since the national recording industry lost interest in progressive country. According to Roland Swenson, president of the Austin chapter during 1990, the TMA was initially modeled on Nashville's Country Music Association. "Yeah, it was kind of like there was this promise during the early to midseventies that country was really kind of making Austin into a music center and all that stuff. And when that more or less fell apart in the late seventies for whatever reasons, I think people thought, after a while, they just wanted to stir something up musically." As Swenson put it, "this organization was started as a desire to conjure it back again."[2]

One of those striving to "conjure it back" was Mike Tolleson, one of the original partners in the Armadillo's efforts at world conquest. Tolleson was president of the statewide organization from 1983 to 1985. During an interview in 1990 he drew a direct line of development between his efforts in the seventies and the goals of the Texas Music Association. "In the eighties," Tolleson insisted, "we began to try to form an industry out of what we had done in the seventies." The Austin chapter of the TMA was founded in 1982, and a local musician and graduate of the UT Finance department named Ernie Gammage was elected president of the local soon after. Gammage had played bass and sung for a number of bands throughout the seventies and the early eighties. Most of these bands were professional entertainment ensembles that covered both oldies and the popular hits of the day. In the seventies, Gammage had helped to organize the Austin All-Stars, and in the eighties he was best known for his work with Ernie Sky and the K-Tels, both groups devoted to the performance of other peoples' music. With the Texas Music Association providing the original institutional focus, Tolleson and Gammage began to work together to shift the promotional efforts of various Austin music businesses from highlighting the achievements of individual artists, or even a particular musical style, to advocating a music industry in general. Not particularly committed to any currently popular music and certainly unaffiliated with any scene, Gammage and Tolleson strove to avoid the risk of aligning with passing trends, choosing instead to concentrate on attracting national and international entertainment capital to Texas and on developing methods to promote commercial ventures that could profit from all trends.[3]

The Chronicle *of the Scene*

The first successful business that had grown out of the punk scene at Raul's was the alternative biweekly paper the *Austin Chronicle*. The *Chronicle* was started by six individuals who had been writing for the student newspaper, *The Daily Texan*, working at a university-run film series, CinemaTexas, and hanging out at Raul's, listening to and thinking about the Huns, the Next, the Skunks, and generalizing about punk in Austin as a musical expression of possibility. Joe Dishner, Ed Lowry, Nick Barbaro, Louis Black, Sarah Whistler, and Jeff Whittington, the original members of the editorial board, had developed the business plan and the editorial stance for the *Chronicle* by February 1981. The paper began with $80,000 in start-up money (considerably more than the Armadillo began with), and the founders were able to buy cheaply much of the equipment that had sat unused since the *Sun* had folded over two years before.[4]

A prototype issue was sent to prospective advertisers during the following summer. It included a "Letter from the Publishers" that explained both the rationale and the motivation for the paper's existence.

We feel that there is a clear need in our town for such a magazine—a serious publication dedicated to Austin arts and entertainment—a magazine which can pull together all of the varied facets of the community, and both inform the public of all the events going on around town and comment intelligently on those events. . . . We feel that we have important contributions to make—observations on the local scene and insights into the state of entertainment as a major part of our culture. . . . Our editorial stance can be summed up as follows: entertainment reflects modern culture. What we do for fun goes way beyond being pure fun; it also mirrors the values and biases of American society. Good entertainment writing should be informative and fun to read, but it should also make you *think*. This magazine will attempt to get beneath the surface of local and national entertainment and talk about issues which are important to all of us living in Austin.[5]

As can be seen from this letter, the goal of the *Chronicle* was to unite a community through interpretations of various cultural events, written representations of the cultural practices they enjoyed.

"But," the letter continues,

lofty ambitions don't ensure financial success. We are acutely aware of the financial issues involved in starting such a publication, and of Austin's long history
of ill-conceived, under-capitalized, and consequently short-lived entertainment
magazines. We do not plan to repeat those mistakes; we are making a definite
commitment to become a permanent member of the Austin community. To that
end, we think we have created an extremely attractive format for local advertisers. . . . For advertisers interested in reaching the people who support the
arts in Austin, the people who spend money on dining and entertainment, the
Austin Chronicle will be the most visible, cost-efficient medium available. . . .
The *Austin Chronicle* is dedicated to bringing all of Austin closer together. We
are convinced that this is a service the city needs, and that the *Austin Chronicle*
will make Austin a better place to live.[6]

This statement marks the most significant difference, not only between
the *Chronicle* and the *Sun*, but between the antimodern moment of progressive country and the postmodern moment of Austin punk. Since the
Chronicle wanted to become a permanent member of the Austin community, it recognized that, in order to survive, it had to define, shape,
and package aspects of that community for its advertisers. "We intend
to expand this base of support [their readers] . . . to stimulate new
interest by our dynamic coverage and promotion. We are convinced that
there are a lot more people out there who would take more interest in
local events if they only knew about them, and knew why they might
be interested. We plan to tell them why." Enthusiastically disseminating
an "advocacy position," the writers for the *Chronicle* acted as local promoters for the events brought to their attention. The magazine carried
weekly listings of musical, cultural, and culinary events held throughout
the area, and music writers like Margaret Moser and Jeff Whittington
filled their columns with the heartfelt insistence that their readers attend
and appreciate nearly every show in town. By expanding the community
of those who supported the arts in Austin and by uniting them around a
specific set of cultural interpretations, the *Chronicle* helped to construct
a community of consumers and an orthodoxy of taste.[7]

In 1982, the magazine published its first reader's poll of favorite local
music, following the tradition established locally by the *Sun*. In his
introduction to the tabulated results, Whittington wrote, "In a city with
such a phenomenal amount of musical activity, it is only fitting that as
many as possible of our best music-makers be recognized; in the next
two pages, we have listed as many winners as we could without starting to look like a phone book."[8] The large number of categories in
the poll reflected this inclusive intention. The 1977 readers' poll published by the *Sun* had included winners in twelve categories. The *Sun's*
final poll the next year registered victors in sixteen categories, including
best players on individual instruments for the first time. The *Chronicle's*

first poll significantly expanded the group of "winners," celebrating the achievements of local Austin musicians and music business personnel in twenty-eight different areas. The following year's poll, published in March 1983, contained fifty-one categories. Nineteen eighty-three was also the year that the paper established its Texas Music Hall of Fame; the *Chronicle* inducted ten members on this first ballot, including Joe Ely, Butch Hancock, Van Wilks, and the Fabulous Thunderbirds. Stevie Ray Vaughan was elected to the "Hall of Fame" based solely on his local performances, before he had ever released a record of his own. The Hall of Fame created by the *Chronicle* and its readers formed another major representation of the meaning of music-making in Austin.

As the use of extensive listings of events and the expansion of the music poll categories indicate, the *Chronicle* defined a new, inclusive Austin community through representations of the diverse cultural (and especially musical) practices of its readers. By promoting these activities and encouraging its readers to participate in them—through intensive coverage of the local scene in interviews and reviews as well as the listings and the readers' poll—the *Chronicle* also contributed to the creation of such a community, organized around the cultural practice of popular music. The financial stability of the *Chronicle* depended upon the economic power of this community as consumers. By constructing this potential market for their advertisers, the magazine's publishers were necessarily aligning themselves with this community's economic fortunes as well as with business projects designed to exploit commercially its cultural expressions. In the prototype given to prospective advertisers, the publishers declared, "Over the past decade, Austin has been the fastest growing city in Texas. . . . Our community has grown in diversity as well, and no existing publication has been able to keep up with this dynamic growth." The *Chronicle* intended not only to keep up with this growth, but to contribute to the meaning of growth in Austin, to emphasize the cultural practices of certain groups, and to contribute thereby to the meaning of Austin itself.[9]

Transformations in the Local Economic Context

Nineteen eighty-four was the year that Austin's economic growth peaked and began to fall back. A total of 36,700 jobs were created in the city that year. Unemployment sat at 3.1 percent. Income per capita in the Austin municipal statistical area was $13,769. For the first time, however, the cost of living in Austin exceeded the national average. In fact, it had become more expensive to live in Austin in 1984 than it was to live in Dallas, Houston, or San Antonio. This increase was chiefly due to the rise in housing costs. The average price for homes sold in 1984 was $102,000, a 16 percent increase over the average price the year before. Smaller but still significant increases in the rental price of apartments and office and retail space took place, reflecting a real estate boom driven by a belief in continued economic growth.[10]

This faith had been sustained by fifteen years of steady economic expansion. The Austin Chamber of Commerce, which for decades had focused on guaranteeing the presence of sufficient service professionals, turned its attention in the sixties to luring "attractive" industries such as electronics manufacturing. Promoting Austin as a "friendly city," the Chamber wanted to draw industries that would appreciate its "community of contented people." During the late seventies, these "hi-tech" industries became the focus of progrowth efforts among Austin's business leaders. Although it had never been a center for oil production or refining, Austin experienced a growth in service jobs during the seventies that was fueled by the increased profits in the state's most visible industry. Austin's local manufacturing, while never the largest component of the region's economy, had also been growing. From 1975 to 1980, the average annual rate of growth in manufacturing jobs in Austin was 16.2 percent. These manufacturing jobs mostly involved assembly-line computer chip production.[11]

It was, however, a national population shift from the northeast to the southwest that helped create the conditions for the real estate boom. Austin's growth during the early eighties was overstimulated by a deep recession in the northeast and the upper midwest, as the nation's traditional manufacturing base was forcibly downsized. Thousands of unemployed manufacturing workers moved to central Texas, attracted by the previously created hi-tech assembly jobs. In the first half of the eighties, jobs in this sector continued to increase by an average annual rate of 7.0 percent.[12]

But the most astonishing growth in jobs during the first half of this decade took place in construction. Jobs in this sector increased by an average of 18.7 percent per year during the early eighties. With local banking institutions providing plentiful financing for any real estate project, Austin's downtown skyline was transformed from a series of retail establishments dominated by the capitol to a range of towering postmodern office buildings. The most significant increase in job production outside of construction during this period could be found in service (particularly health) and the conglomerate category of finance/insurance/real estate. The jobs in these service sectors were also riding the real estate boom. Economic growth in Austin during this period was driven by speculation, by the faith that the growth—initiated by the rise in energy prices in the seventies, sped up by a diversification in the local economy—and finally thrown into overdrive by a transformation in the national economy, would never slow down. Civic leaders believed that Austin's intrinsic "quality of life" had lured new "smart" industries to town and that these growth industries would continue to bring new "smart" people and new dollars to the area. In 1970, Travis County contained 295,516 people. In 1980, the population had increased to 419,573; by 1985, it stood at 527,120. From this point on, however, the growth rate decreased tremendously. The 1990 population has been estimated at 576,407, a cumulative increase of only 9 percent over five years.[13]

The huge growth in population and in income per capita in the Austin area from 1975 to 1985 sustained elements of the honky-tonk economy, even as the percentage of income available for entertainment decreased and the entertainment tastes of college students changed. As early as 1976, club owners in Austin had discovered that, in the absence of a powerful musical performance of cultural identity, the majority of college students would just as soon dance to records as listen to local musicians. Although the increase in the number of students attending the University of Texas had not matched the population growth during this period, Austin remained a young town. Total student enrollment rose from 42,598 in 1975 to only 48,145 in 1981, and it remained very close to 48,000 throughout much of the eighties. However, two-thirds of the adults moving to Austin in the early eighties were under thirty-five. These young adults continued to visit the honky-tonks and nightclubs of Austin, and the average life span of these businesses remained steady at about three years, more or less equivalent to the length of a college generation or the duration of a popular musical trend. In 1984, the economy of musical practice in Austin, as it had for decades, remained strictly tied to the economy of the honky-tonk.[14]

The Chamber of Commerce and the Construction of the Austin Music Industry

Early in that year, while economic growth was at its peak, the Austin chapter of the Texas Music Association, led by Ernie Gammage, initiated a dialogue with the Austin Chamber of Commerce that the Association hoped would result in a mutually beneficial relationship. The apparently unending flow of capital streaming through central Texas—symbolized by the cranes hovering over downtown construction—had not escaped the notice of the TMA, and they wanted to work with the Chamber to attract some of that capital to the region's music businesses. Live music improves the "quality of life" in Austin, Gammage argued, helping to attract new businesses to the area. Therefore, he concluded, music-making in Austin deserves the support of the business lobby. However, before he could build this coalition with the Chamber, Gammage first had to convince the Chamber that musicians were not antibusiness radicals, that they were not weirdos, hippies, and punks, but instead were independent but dependable business people.[15]

The Texas Music Association and Gammage drew their primary evidence for this argument from a master's thesis written for the Community and Regional Planning program at the University of Texas by Phyllis Krantzman, "The Impact of the Music Entertainment Industry on Austin, Texas." Ostensibly, Krantzman's study "focused on those persons who earn a portion, but not necessarily all, of their income playing music of any popular variety." In 1982, Krantzman mailed surveys to 250 musicians, 80 percent of whom were members of the local American Federation of Musicians. Her final sample consisted of seventy-six returned surveys, from which she compiled a profile of the "average Austin musician." According to Krantzman's research, the average age of musicians in Austin in 1983 was 33.7 years; 50 percent of these musicians had a college degree; 53 percent of them were married, 43 percent had children, and almost 90 percent were registered to vote. They had devoted 14 years of their lives to playing music, and most of Krantzman's respondents had lived in Austin between 7 and 12 years. According to Krantzman's survey, then, the "average Austin musician" had come to the city during the progressive country boom (between 1971 and 1976), had achieved enough success to have benefited from joining the union, and had settled down in the early eighties and begun to raise a family. Gammage recognized himself and his friends in Krantzman's vision of the Austin musician, and this became the representation of Austin musicians taken to the Chamber of Commerce: "a mature group of responsible citizens who are serious, dedicated, and committed to their work." In fact, rather than representing popular musicians of any (meaning every) variety, Krantzman's research effectively focused on older musicians who had already been professionally successful, most likely through playing progressive country music.[16]

When Gammage approached the Chamber for support, he found a surprisingly positive reception in the person of David Lord. The Chamber had hired Lord to head the Austin Visitors and Conventions

Bureau, the branch of the Chamber devoted to increasing tourism. The Chamber of Commerce in Austin had traditionally propounded a slow-growth policy, only recruiting businesses that would service the state government and the university. But by the mideighties the Chamber had developed into a fast-growth, prodevelopment advocate, similar to the Chambers of Commerce found in other cities. One of the areas targeted by the Chamber for growth was tourism. David Lord's job was to "market Austin as a desirable place to visit," and to do that he had to "decide what it really is that makes Austin special." The Austin Visitors and Conventions Bureau had already been using Austin's music scene to attract conventions and tourists. But the information they were distributing was based on the last nationally famous moment in Austin music, progressive country. According to Ernie Gammage, "They had a planned vacation trip that they tried to sell to other cities, where you could come down to Austin and go to one of the clubs in town and watch the natives dance with their hats and boots on." Having been a thoroughly professional entertainer for decades, Gammage was acutely aware that progressive country music was no longer an effective draw in the town of its origin. Any attempt to market Austin as a musical tourist attraction would have to expand its focus.[17]

Prompted by Gammage, David Lord settled on music as his "hook," his "marketing symbol." Not only was Lord convinced that an active music community contributed to Austin's visibility as a convention center, but he soon imagined a more extensive relationship. In fact, it was Lord who conceived the total economic development approach that would dominate future discussion among Austin's civic, financial, and music business figures. Lord was aware of the pride that so many Austinites took in local music as well as the important role that music played in the image the rest of the nation held of the city. The success of the public television program *Austin City Limits*, with its ability to broadcast nationally an image of Texan musicians, contributed to the effective linkage between a geographical location, an identity associated with that location, and the cultural practice through which this identity was produced. It was David Lord's insight to turn music-making into more than a "hook" to attract conventioneers. He recognized that any set of symbolic values held so dear by a local population could form the basis for a set of businesses devoted to the production and sale of commodified representations of that identity. In an article published in the *Austin Business Journal*, Lord shifted the argument from the impact of music-making on tourism to its influence on general economic development, thereby grabbing the attention of the entire Chamber of

Commerce. "Music as a business fits in with several goals of the Chamber," Lord wrote. "It fosters economic growth by, among other things, promoting entrepreneurship and the formation of a new business as well as attracting conventions and tourists to the Austin area. It promotes a superior quality of life for all Austin citizens by encouraging artistic and cultural development." In fact, "seen as an industry, the music business is just about perfect."[18] This article marked the public announcement of growing efforts to develop this one specific meaning of music-making in Austin. Like Gammage and Tolleson, Lord was not interested in promoting any specific musical style, but instead he was concerned with publicizing the set of local music as a whole—the image of Austin as a place where music was made. Lord reshaped Eddie Wilson's and Mike Tolleson's flamboyant vision of an Austin-based $50,000,000-a-year software, arts, and entertainment laboratory into that of a diversified and more complexly structured "opportunity economy" that would provide an industrial infrastructure within which entrepreneurs could invest, work, and profit. For the next several years, serious cultural forces were brought to bear in an effort to enforce this articulation, to reduce the chaotic flux of meanings and practices that had been music-making in Austin to a set of dependable, stable, and, most importantly, local signifiers whose value would remain relatively fixed and that could, by virtue of this stability, effectively compete for the global flow of entertainment capital.[19]

Gammage, Tolleson, and Lord spent the early months of 1984 building the framework for future efforts to promote the alliance of business and music. Musicians were to be presented to the business community as "good risks for loans," and the popular image of the Chamber was to be transformed from that of a strictly probusiness development advocate to that of an organization concerned with "the quality of life" in Austin. In the debates between prodevelopment figures and neighborhood activists, quality of life, "a catch phrase for environmental protection, cultural dynamism, neighborhood integrity, and economic stability," had become a key issue. By supporting music, the Chamber appeared to be working for the quality of life in Austin, rather than against it. In the terms of the developing rhetoric, businesses associated with local music already contributed to the "quality of life" in the city, but they needed help building an "infrastructure" in order to develop a "clean growth industry" into a full-fledged "opportunity economy." The Chamber of Commerce would provide that help.[20]

With the encouragement of Tolleson, Lord, and Gammage, the Chamber funded a series of studies of local music businesses. The largest of these studies was conducted by the Austin Music Advisory Committee. This committee was formed in November 1984 after Gammage introduced David Lord to Jeff Whittington. With his unflagging advocacy of all types of local music, Whittington seemed to be the person in the local press most sympathetic to the goals of the Chamber. Lord impressed Whittington with his apparently sincere concern about increasing opportunities for Austin musicians to make a living, and he persuaded Whittington that the Chamber of Commerce was trying to find ways to help local musicians. Whittington was able to convince other members of the *Chronicle* staff of the legitimacy of the project, and he used his influence to talk other individuals, many of whom had worked their way into the music business by means of the punk, do-it-yourself ethos, into cooperating with the task force.[21]

Ed Ward's approval also contributed legitimacy to the project. Although he was no longer writing for the *Austin American-Statesman*, Ward was probably still the most influential critic in town. Having written for *Rolling Stone, Creem*, and other nationally distributed youth culture magazines, Ward was one of the first generation of nationally known rock critics. He was hired in 1979 by the local daily to provide an outsider's perspective on Austin music. In his columns for the paper and in articles for regional magazines like *Third Coast* and *Texas Monthly* or national magazines like *New York Rocker*, Ward wrote about national and international music trends as well as local music, and he consistently advocated strengthening the connections between the music made in Austin and the national recording industry. As early as November 1980, Ward had written, "The same problems that contributed to the demise of the progressive country scene a few years back are still around: no competent management firms with national connections, no decent studios, and an insidious chauvinism which declares that having aspirations above the Austin bar circuit means selling out." To Ward, the anticommercialism of Austin musicians was neither an effective critique of work nor an important aspect of their antimodernism, but instead indicated an unprofessional attitude. For him, success in the clubs in Austin was a very limited success. Ward felt that the responsibility of the rock critic was to search out and support the best musicians in their attempts to become truly popular and that the appropriate measure of popularity was national recording sales.[22]

Along with Gammage, Tolleson, Ward, and Whittington, the committee included L. E. McCullough of the Austin Music Umbrella, Louis Meyers and Mark Pratz of Lunch Money Productions (bookers of the Continental Club and Liberty Lunch), Roland Swenson of Moment

Productions, Andy Murphy of Panda Productions, Rob Klein of Side-track Productions (each of these production companies encompassed artist management and record production), Susan Jarrett of Austin Record Distributors, Phyllis Krantzman (whose master's thesis provided the data Gammage used in his original arguments before the Chamber), and Carolyn Phillips of the *Chronicle*.

In line with Lord's and Gammage's concept of an opportunity economy, building on Tolleson's and Wilson's early-seventies dream of an arts laboratory, the Austin Music Advisory Committee viewed the music scene in Austin through an industrial lens that broke the process of music-making into a series of discrete interactions—a complex system of commodity production and exchange in which musicians were only one component and fans were merely consumers. The concept of a music industry was not the invention of this committee; rather, it was a rhetorical device commonly used in the recording industry to blur the distinction between music-making and commodity production. *Billboard* magazine, a trade publication dealing with recordings, radio, jukeboxes, live entertainment, and television, considers its job to be reporting business trends in the music *industry*. Recording company executives like to think of their companies as elements in a music industry, responsible not only for the recordings available in the marketplace but for all popular music.[23]

The model for this concept was the motion picture industry. But there was a critical difference between "the industry" in Los Angeles and the rhetorically constructed "music industry." The motion picture industry, with all its attendant peripheral businesses, did indeed materially produce movies. However, no radio personality, no record distributor, no agent, not even a record company owner forms a necessary link in any system that produces music. Instead, they are part of the system that produces, distributes, and promotes recordings. The production unit in the field of musical entertainment that is analogous to the motion picture industry is the recording industry. This industry does produce and market cultural products, but these are commodified representations of music, not the whole substance of music itself.[24]

An entire school of cultural sociology has also contributed to the construction of a music industry. The reductionist, albeit powerful, metaphor of the "culture industry," devised by Max Horkheimer and Theodor Adorno as a way of understanding mass culture, inspired a variety of sociological analyses of the industrial production of cultural objects. Paul Hirsch's 1969 study, *The Structure of the Popular Music Industry*, applied a systems perspective toward understanding the complex of overlapping organizations that produce popular records. Hirsch's work provided the basis for many other sociological analyses of the material production of recordings. From R. Serge Denisoff's *Solid Gold: The Popular Record Industry* (which, despite its subtitle, contains many references to "the music industry" in the quotes from record company personnel), to Richard Peterson and David Berger's article on "Cycles in Symbol Production," to Simon Frith's table-clearing work *Sound Effects*, the operations of the recording industry and its complex integration with other mass media have offered a viable base from which to understand the production of popular music. However, in their focus on the systematic production and exchange of recorded commodities, these studies each reduce the human performance of musical sound to the practices of the recording industry, thereby contributing to the reification of music and the ideological dominance of the concept of a music industry. In addition, the fact that so much of the work of the critic and the scholar of popular music revolves around the analysis of recordings contributes to the conflation of the production of music with the production of records. The important recognition that twentieth-century popular music has always been commercially mediated (and that this commercial mediation has its productive effects) has resulted in a confusion between two very different spheres of production. While the commercial basis of popular music cannot be ignored, too often the study of the recording industry has stood in for the study of popular music. This distinction needs to be maintained in any discussion of Austin music. For over twenty years, commercial popular music in Austin had been produced within the context of a honky-tonk economy. The industrialization of music-making in Austin transformed local musical practice and, in the process, changed Austin music.[25]

On November 16, 1984, just at the time that AMAC was forming, the *Chronicle* published a special issue called "Austin Music: Behind the Scenes." The issue profiled writers, agents, deejays, promoters, record retailers and distributors, club owners, the "influential, creative, successful and powerful" in the "Austin music industry." These people were, according to the article, the "reasons certain musicians and bands sell more records, get into more clubs and make more money." Forty-four "personalities" were discussed in this issue, including eight of the thirteen members of the Austin Music Advisory Committee.[26]

For AMAC, the meaning of the term "music industry" was precise. In the words of Ernie Gammage,

There are four necessary ingredients to a full-fledged music industry. Every industry has its research and development function. We have that in spades.

It's the clubs and the musicians, the songwriters. But all industries also have a production function, distribution, and marketing, and finally, the point of sale, where you reach the consumer with the product. . . . Here in Austin, we grow the oats, and the rest of the country takes these oats, these raw materials, and turns them into Cheerios. We have to establish our own means to turn our oats into Cheerios.[27]

Echoing the traditional Texan populist concern about outsiders control-ling the industrial exploitation of the region's natural resources, Gam-mage, and the committee as a whole, argued for the development of local means of exploitation. Within this framework, the performance of music in the nightclubs as well as the writing of songs became simply research for the production of commodities. The fans in the clubs would function more or less as focus groups do for marketing firms. The actual "product" would not reach the true "consumer" until after it had been produced, distributed, and marketed on a mass scale. Thus, AMAC's version of the music industry conceptualized an infrastructure that would guarantee the transformation of oats—songs and musical performances—into Cheerios—saleable recordings. The committee in-tended to organize a local music industry that could be rationally ana-lyzed and efficiently and profitably run for the mutual benefit of all concerned. The Austin Music Advisory Committee hoped to shift the economy of Austin music-making away from its traditional association with honky-tonks and live performances to one with the modern pro-duction of recordings, to smooth the industrial production of musical Cheerios.

The committee approached its study of the music industry by setting up a series of fact-finding caucuses to investigate the specific concerns of musicians, agents and managers, concert promoters, instrument retail-ers, radio personnel, record producers and promoters, record retailers, recording studio personnel, and those working in video. Each caucus was staffed by two or more members of the committee who were per-sonally, and often professionally, interested in the issues affecting that business. A total of thirteen meetings took place. The attendees at each meeting were "essentially asked to construct a wish list: what would you most like to see happen to the music business in Austin?"[28]

By construing this conglomerate of diverse business interests as a music industry and by focusing their information gathering and report-ing through that framework, the committee consolidated the rhetorical construction of a unified industry that could claim to be the producers of the music made in Austin. All of those who stood to profit had to be included. Although each of the businesses represented in the titles of the caucuses really produced and marketed different and, often, competing cultural products and services—recordings, television programs, nightclub entertainment, concerts, radio programs—the Austin Music Advisory Committee reshaped these businesses into a single industrial system. By calling this system the music industry, the committee represented these various businesses as the parties responsible for the music made in Austin. Finally, having conceptualized the production of music along modern industrial lines, the committee could make a case for attracting investment capital into the opportunity economy of music.

In May 1985, the AMAC released its report, "Austin Music: Into the Future." The industrial paradigm built into the organization of the caucuses shaped the findings of the committee. According to the report, the committee "turned to the local industry with three goals in mind: to identify and describe the Austin music industry's current status; to identify and define problems facing the industry; to develop possible solutions and recommendations for those problems."[29] This report contained the most extensive attempt to define the new concept called the Austin music industry: the "entire network of businesses [that] has grown around Austin's musicians and the venues where they perform. The sum of these components forms the Austin music industry" (1). The report emphasized the economic importance of this summation. "The music industry offers Austin its most fertile ground for developing an 'opportunity economy,' simply because so many of the necessary ingredients are already in place" (ii).

An opportunity economy begins with an abundant local resource. Through mutual cooperation and planning, this resource is developed to its maximum potential; entrepreneurship and diversification are actively encouraged. As a result, the community derives a home-grown industry which substantially broadens its fiscal base—leaving it better prepared to sustain economic fluctuation—and yet that industry remains sensitive and responsive to local needs and conditions. Austin's music industry is ideally suited for this approach. (12–13)

The abundant local resource, the "oats"—musicians, their songs, and their performances—could be developed to their maximum potential only through the efforts of a home-grown industry. And supporting this industry would help the community sustain economic fluctuation. However, the most "exciting" result of this support would be the development of the local music industry "to its full potential, which could grant Austin its share of the national industry's multi-billion dollar business" (7). This was the economic goal that justified the construction of a music industry: Austin's rightful share of a multibillion dollar business. Music could become the city's new growth industry.[30]

The rhetorical force of the music industry concept clearly was intended to do more than convince financial leaders that music-related businesses offered legitimate investment options. When the report declared that, "due to the . . . lack of funding, the industry's ancillary components—record companies, production facilities, etc.—have not developed at the same pace [as have the city's musicians]," it emphasized the result of this underdevelopment: many of the city's musicians have been "forced to leave Austin" (9) in an exodus of talent that threatened the very identity of Austin as a music-making center.

In 1963, Janis Joplin was driven from Austin by the public taunts of University of Texas fraternity members. She moved to California and became forever identified with the city of San Francisco. Post-hoc mythologizing has turned that event into the equivalent of the Boston Red Sox trading Babe Ruth to the New York Yankees; the city has never forgiven itself. Each musician that moves away to "make it" leaves behind a slightly more bitter town. Shiva's Headband moved west in 1969. Doug Sahm moved from central Texas to recording centers in California and back multiple times over a period of ten years. Scores of musicians abandoned the sinking progressive country ship during the seventies. In the early eighties, Christopher Cross, Charlie Sexton, and even Willie Nelson moved away. When Hank Alrich noticed the exodus of Austin's professional musicians in 1977, he blamed it on the presence of too many amateur pickers. Bobby Bridger noted the same phenomenon in 1978 and pleaded for Austin musicians to create their own "counter culture music thing" that would allow them to make it without leaving home. After seven more years of watching musicians learn to play in Austin and then leave town, the members of AMAC insisted that the most effective way to ensure the continuation of the Austin identity as a center for live music was to direct investment capital toward the developing infrastructure of a music industry. No longer should "New York, Nashville and Los Angeles . . . receive credit for talents that were nurtured and matured in Austin, simply because the music companies in those cities are positioned to treat their talents as a business" (9). Austin had to become able to turn its own oats into Cheerios.[31]

With music-making in Austin defined as an industrial activity, and with the development of an industrial infrastructure proposed as the means by which to satisfy the needs of all of the musicians, fans, record producers, engineers, agents, nightclub bookers, and radio deejays in town, the report offered a set of general recommendations for solving the problems of this industry. Each of its general recommendations focused on promoting "greater cooperation" between the "music industry" and other sectors of Austin's economy. In the eyes of the committee,

Austin's institutions (which went unnamed), its financial businesses, its tourism businesses, as well as the various businesses already dealing with music, were each to be made more aware of the benefits of working in concert.

Beyond these general recommendations, the committee offered a set of specific proposals for the organization that had funded the study. AMAC recommended that the Chamber of Commerce create a full-time music/entertainment development liaison officer; sponsor an Austin display at major music industry conventions; help develop music trade conventions in Austin; and encourage the development of an annual, nationally recognized Austin music exposition (20). By the end of the decade, these goals had taken slightly different forms, but each of them had been achieved. Both the state of Texas and the city of Austin had appointed music liaison officers. The South by Southwest Music and Media Conference had developed into a major trade convention and a nationally recognized music exposition, and representatives from South by Southwest were attending almost every major music convention.

The Cutting Edge: Televising the New Austin

The first visible outgrowth of the Chamber's efforts to bring together the music community with local business interests was the luring of MTV's "Cutting Edge" program to town to produce a feature on Austin's newer bands. Sponsored by I.R.S records, "The Cutting Edge" appeared one Sunday night a month on MTV. Typically, the program aired videos by bands associated with the growing "indie" or "alternative" music movement, interspersed with interviews with or live performances by these bands. For the "Austin Avalanche of Rock and Roll," the focus instead fell on the musical activity associated with one town. The show's host, Peter Zaremba, and the production crew came to Austin for a week in the summer of 1985 to tape live performances, local color shots, and extended interview sequences with several of Austin's more popular performers.[32]

The organization of this production was a classic example of the Chamber's strategy at work. Although the bands featured on the show were almost exclusively acts that would appeal to the program's "alternative" audience, this was an effort that involved a wide range of music-related businesses. An employee of the Chamber, Gloria Moore, coordinated the cooperation of local tourism businesses, obtaining accommodations at the Driskill Hotel and air travel from American Airlines. Local restaurants like Mexico Tipico and Virginia's Cafe provided food and, in return, saw their establishments displayed in the program. Two of the more popular clubs, Liberty Lunch and the South Bank, gladly donated their spaces as sites for the performances. Peter Zaremba was taped running out of Waterloo Records with his arms full of vinyl. The video equipment was provided locally by Third Coast Video. Because of the donated supplies and accommodations, this episode of the program could be produced almost as cheaply as those shot in Los Angeles.

In the meantime, Ed Ward had used his connections in Los Angeles to convince Carl Grasso, producer of the show, that the rock'n'roll scene in Austin deserved the attention of his program. The *Chronicle* persistently promoted this episode of "The Cutting Edge" as both an important recognition of the vitality of the local scene and a not-to-be-missed opportunity for some of the town's musicians. In order to appear on the show, a band's demo tape had to make it past the ears of either Ed Ward or Joe Nick Patoski before being passed on to Grasso, who made the final decisions. In line with AMAC's goal of updating the nation's image of the music made in Austin, none of the city's rhythm and blues musicians and none of its country performers appeared on the program. Instead, almost all of the bands came from the Sparky's/ Beach performance nexus, the acts referred to as New Sincerity bands.

During the program, segues between bands featured close-ups of the state flag, while the show functioned as a promotional vehicle for the city as a whole. The rapid economic growth of Austin was an underlying theme pervading the entire program. Live shots of the bands performing were intercut with sequences shot from the tops of new office buildings downtown. Cameras placed atop construction cranes provided panoramic views of the surrounding hill country as Peter Zaremba intoned, "They say that ninety people a day move to Austin. Signs of growth are everywhere." He went on to recite one of the concerns raised at the AMAC caucuses. "Changes are not always welcome, however. Some of Austin's best clubs have disappeared." But music fans, and those generally intrigued by Austin need not worry. "Through it all, the bands survive." Austin will continue to have the best of all worlds. The music that expresses Austin's special character will not be transformed by the influx of new people and the rampant construction of postmodern office buildings.

Austin's ability to retain its identity in the midst of growth became the topic of an extended conversation in the program between Peter Zaremba and musician Joe King Carrasco. As the two crossed the Congress Avenue bridge in a convertible, driving out of downtown with the state capitol framed behind them, Carrasco asked, "I guess you've seen this town change, huh?"

Z: Yeah, a little too much.

C: Yeah, too much, too many high buildings. But I think the cool people are still here in town. The music scene's still happening.

Z: But they get diluted, you know? I mean they come here because it's unique, but then they wanna get rid of the uniqueness.

But Carrasco appeared unconcerned. Beneath the towering construction cranes lay "the last bastion of Austin soul," Red River Motors.

C: This is the final hold-out of what Austin is all about, in terms of everything that made it . . . [sic]

Z: The aesthetic.

C: Yeah. To me, if this place ever goes, then Austin's gone. This is the most important thing for me in Austin. Cuz Austin was old cars and Cadillacs, and that's what this place is all about.

In addition to old cars and Cadillacs, the program's representation of Austin's "soul" foregrounded the contributions of Mexican-Americans in an interesting way. As the two musicians drove around town, Zaremba described Mexican culture as "more than a tile on the wall of Austin; it's the glue that holds [Austin] together." Carrasco delivered a brief historical narrative about the development of conjunto music and, for his performance scene, replaced his regular band with two Mexican-American musicians. But this tribute to the influence of Latin culture was bizarrely intercut with shots of Carrasco and Zaremba bathing in Barton Springs, a beautiful natural pool of which the city is quite proud. After frolicking in the clear water, accompanied by a group of children, the two pale musicians rose out of the pool, cleansed. Perhaps unwittingly, the editors of the program presented all too clearly one aspect of Austin's identity. Austin's "soul" is still available, if anyone wants to visit it, and friendly guides such as Carrasco can be found, but no tourist will have difficulty washing it off before she or he leaves.

For the purposes of the Chamber, at any rate, the specific content of Austin's soul was unimportant. All that mattered was the assertion that a soul still existed and that music remained the medium through which it was best expressed. The conversation between the two musicians ended with Carrasco repeating David Lord's "hook"—the connection between Austin and its music. "You know music is important for Austin," Carrasco said, "because everybody that I meet that knows Austin, they know it because of its music. And the people who live here have got to remember . . . you've really got to nurture it. You've got

The Austin Avalanche of Rock'n'Roll: MTV's "The Cutting Edge" tapes the Austin music scene (The Reivers with Peter Zaremba singing "Sweet Jane").   Photo by Pat Blashill.

to take good care of it." Economic growth will not threaten Austin's identity as a place for music-making. In fact, those responsible for bringing "The Cutting Edge" recognize the importance of "nurturing" the music. Austin's "soul" and its bands will survive.

When MTV aired the program that fall, fans who didn't have cable rushed over to the homes of friends who did. Video cassette recorders were plugged in and turned on as Austin's rock'n'roll audience hoped to find themselves among the sweating and dancing throng, captured on tape and nationally televised. Fifteen acts performed during the "Austin Avalanche of Rock and Roll." Doctors' Mob fans giggled as the band made jokes about their hair. Dharma Bums fans sighed while the band surged through their cover of "This Ain't the Summer of Love." Glass Eye fans smirked when Brian's brow furrowed over the neck of his bass. Zeitgeist and the True Believers received the most space of all the young bands in the final edit. They were the subjects of extended interviews in addition to their performance shots. But everyone who was watching stopped and wondered at the attention the program gave to an acoustic duo who played guitar and sang closely interwoven harmonies accompanied by a beat box wearing sunglasses. None of the regular fans of the scene had ever heard Timbuk 3 before their appearance during the "Cutting Edge" taping at the South Bank. They were not regular performers at the Beach; they had not played with the Texas Instruments at a backyard party; they did not seem to know any Daniel Johnston songs. With their set snuck in before those of the Wild Seeds, Glass Eye, and the True Believers, they had appeared out of place, lost among the younger, harder rockers. And here they were again as the program aired, playing an admittedly clever tune, in an understated, almost folky, style.

Timbuk 3 was the one act to receive a major recording contract after their appearance on the "Cutting Edge" program. Their debut album for I.R.S. sold over three hundred thousand copies in 1986, and the single, "The Future's so Bright (I Gotta Wear Shades)" was a top-twenty hit. Pat and Barbara MacDonald had considerably more pop music experience than most of the young musicians who played the Beach. They had already gone through several tours; they had already made professional recordings. Although they had just moved to Austin in 1984, they displayed many of the same professional virtues that had worked for Michael Murphey fifteen years before. They already knew that songwriting was a craft that rewarded dedicated effort. They arranged their material in such a fashion that listeners could not help but notice their intelligent lyrics. Instead of hanging out at the Beach or drinking beer at the cool parties—rather than engaging in the maelstrom of the scene—Timbuk 3 spent their time polishing their material, developing their aptitude for recording, and working in the studio under the guidance of one of Austin's more durable music figures, Ed Guinn.[33]

Within a year, another Austin band was signed by a national label. Year Zero had not even appeared on "The Cutting Edge." They had never attracted fans from the New Sincerity scene. Much like Timbuk 3, Year Zero worked to develop business connections with recording industry figures even as they were spending $30,000 recording a demo tape. Once the tape was finished, they delivered it to the attorney handling the business affairs for the hugely successful Van Halen. According to critic Robert Draper, "Within a few weeks, Year Zero was swamped with offers. The band fit the industry's mold perfectly: young and creative, but also studio veterans with a proven willingness to spend their own money." The remainder of Austin's young musicians—particularly those who inspired the most adamant fandom at the Beach—were dismissed by record industry representatives as "not quite developed." The astonishing contrast between the success of Year Zero and Timbuk 3 in dealing with the recording industry and the failure of the more popular scene bands to garner major label attention initiated some rethinking among those involved in Austin's rock'n'roll scene.[34]

Pushing Toward an Industry

The need for rethinking was emphasized when the Texas legislature voted to follow Federal incentives and raise the drinking age in the state from nineteen to twenty-one. On September 1, 1986, the majority of the college-age market for live music in Austin could no longer legally drink beer in the city's nightclubs. According to a bartender in one of the city's clubs, the implications of this change were far-reaching.

Any analysis of what 21 will mean to Austin music can't forget the beer. It's the beer that sweetens our ears and cools our critical natures enough to listen to new music. It's beer that dulls our impatience enough to suffer through four bad bands to listen to that one good one. It's beer that may give a band the confidence to play in public and it is in beer that the band is generally paid. Most important, it's beer and its 400–700% markup that pays the bills to keep the stage open. Without beer sales there is simply no margin for profit in the new music clubs in Austin.[35]

While Austin's college students could still enter most clubs, and while most could still devise some strategy for achieving intoxication, the fact that they were legally prevented from spending money on beer in the clubs stripped away a significant percentage of the scene's economic support. While not the sole determinant, the change in the legal drinking age significantly exacerbated the difficulties of operating within the honky-tonk economy. Louis Meyers and Mark Pratz had successfully booked shows at Liberty Lunch and the Continental Club since 1983. Before the change in the drinking age, they regularly operated with 30 percent of their shows losing money. According to Meyers, "under those conditions it was possible to keep on producing acts and even show something of a profit." This profit came from beer sales. After the age change, they began losing money on 70 percent of their shows. By summer 1990, Meyers no longer booked nightclubs; instead he focused his efforts on managing bands and codirecting South by Southwest. According to another SXSW codirector, Roland Swenson, "raising the drinking age was a real serious blow to the club business. The only people that run clubs now [1990] are just crazy people who can't do anything else."[36]

During the next few years, the lessons extracted from Timbuk 3's and Year Zero's national recording contracts combined with the gradual application of the industrial strategy initiated by the Austin Music Advisory Committee and the depression of the honky-tonk economy to transform the structure of music-making in Austin. The Austin "music industry," initially represented by the fifty individuals and institutions profiled by the *Chronicle* in 1984, mushroomed to include the more than six hundred music-related companies listed in the *Austin Music Industry Guide* for 1990. To a certain extent, this guide was designed to promote the success of AMAC's industrialization strategy. The cover illustration depicted a guitar that was also a wrench turning a record that was also a bolt. The editors intended to impress their readers by the sheer weight of the *Industry Guide*'s pages. The listings represented a significant expansion in the number of industry categories implied by the AMAC caucus titles, indicating that the network of music-related businesses had grown even more inclusive. For instance, all the newspapers in the state were listed, as well as every radio station, television station, record store, and instrument repair shop in town. Several individuals listed themselves under multiple categories as different businesses. However, considerable real growth in the number of music-related businesses had also occurred. The number of record labels in town increased from twenty-two at the end of 1984 to forty-three in 1990. By 1989, every major record label had established a representative in Austin. The corresponding increase in billable contract hours produced a dramatic rise in the number of lawyers considering themselves to be part of the music industry. In 1984, the *Chronicle* profiled only one lawyer, Mike Tolleson. In the 1990 guide, twelve individual lawyers or firms were listed. But the largest increase in listings occurred in that vague area the *Industry Guide* called "Promotion, Booking & Management." While the 1984 "Behind the Scenes" article described twelve individuals whose activities fell in these areas, the *Industry Guide* listed fifty-six different organizations devoted to promoting, publicizing, booking, and managing the activities of musicians in Austin.[37]

The dramatic increase in this type of business was directly related to the shift in the economic basis of music-making in Austin. The decline in the honky-tonk economy, initiated by changes in sound technology, had been exacerbated by both the change in the drinking age and the pressures of a contracting economic context. This economic pressure reinforced a growing moral conservatism in young people, who now frowned on the spontaneous and intoxicated attachments that feed the fantastic identifications of a scene. Fewer and fewer adolescent Austinites were gathering together in the nightclubs, listening to locally focused musicians, and celebrating an identity mutually constructed out of contemporary contradictions. Dancing and drinking, drugging and fucking, were no longer the dominant characteristics of the "Austin tendency to group the way they do." With the excitement of a scene dwindling away, the actual experience of listening to music in the clubs was becoming much less pleasurable, much less appealing. Audiences could no longer be depended on to produce spontaneously the yearning response that defined a magical show. The number of individuals promoting and publicizing musical activity in Austin increased in order to fill a gap left, not only by the decreasing size of audiences, but by the corresponding decrease both in the intensity of engagement felt and expressed by these audiences and in the excitement and satisfaction felt by the musicians. The creation of magical gigs, the production of meaningful experiences that fans and musicians would remember and talk about, now began to require professional stimulation. Shows had to be promoted, publicized as special, their significance based, not on the coming together of a community of fans and musicians mutually performing an identity, but instead on some rare characteristic of a specific band, a stylistic trait exaggerated and marketed as a fetishized commodity. And managers had to stimulate and reward career ambitions in musicians, reinforcing the tendency to see each gig not simply as an opportunity for "getting the chills" but rather as a step toward a recording contract.

In November 1985, after the publication of AMAC's report and the telecasting of "The Austin Avalanche of Rock and Roll," Louis Black wrote,

Lately I've been hearing otherwise rational people going on—in fact have heard myself going on—about how Austin is lacking the necessary music business support structure. Which means, essentially, that Austin is lacking lawyers, managers, agents, promoters, or, in other words, our music scene is suffering because all we have are musicians, clubs and listeners. This is madness.[38]

Nevertheless, by the end of the decade, music-making in the clubs of Austin had been transformed into one subbranch of a nationally oriented music industry.

Despite the recession in the region's economy, despite the fact that the growth in population and the increase in jobs had stumbled to a halt in 1986 and had not fully recovered by 1990, this new sector of the local economy had achieved a new level of visibility and influence. The extent of this influence was displayed during the city's mayoral race in 1988. In a forum sponsored by the Texas Music Association, the three leading candidates agreed that, "Austin's music industry should play a significant part in the city's economic development plans." The eventual mayor (and ex-president of the Chamber of Commerce), Lee Cooke, insisted that Austin should continue to "make [the development of music into big business] a critical strategy."[39]

In 1989, the Austin Music Industry Council was established as an independent institution to foster the continued alliance between Austin's music-making community and its business community. Its board of directors included lawyers, financial consultants, musical instrument and record retailers, and band managers; its president was Ernie Gammage. That year, the Council, the Texas Music Association, and the City of Austin worked together with the Nashville branch of *Billboard* magazine to create a "spotlight" issue of the magazine, focusing on the way music was currently being made in Austin.

In the middle of *Billboard*'s regular issue for September 9, 1989, appeared a special twelve-page section of photographs, editorial copy, and advertisements of "one of the major country music capitals." Together, the section was intended to represent an inclusive view of Austin's music industry, but the photographs, the articles, and the ads all emphasized the development of an infrastructure of industry bureaucrats. Photographs showed Ernie Gammage, Mike Tolleson, local managers and lawyers, representatives of the Austin Convention and Visitors Bureau and the City Council celebrating the production of the issue with attorneys, publicists, and advertising directors from Nashville. Austin writers contributed the expected stories about Austin musicians, record labels, and clubs, but also included a feature on Austin's "new band of professionals"—the agents, managers, and attorneys recently drawn into music businesses. This article made the point that "the 1980s have witnessed the emergence of a brand new crop of self-taught Austin-based managers and agents who arose from the local music milieu after working their way slowly up the music business food chain. . . . The result is . . . a thriving industry infrastructure uniquely suited to the Austin economic and cultural terrain." The title of the lead article, ostensibly about local talent, utilized the now common natural resources metaphor about musicians—calling them "a cool-flowing natural spring"— and enthused that "there's a strong local industry rallying around the sound." De-emphasizing his own role as a critic, Michael Point wrote, "The write-ups and rave reviews [about musicians] are all well and good but it's the buzz from industry insiders that means the most since that translates the compliments into terms of dollars and cents."[40]

The copy was surrounded by the advertisements that footed the bill for this special section. Management companies, publishing companies, law firms, record companies, recording studios, even a bootmaker and a medical doctor bought space in this issue in order to declare their support for the Austin music industry. Perhaps the most startling ad, however, featured a vertical half-page photograph, a close-up of the driver's side front fender and headlight of a 1950's sedan (cf. Carrasco's definition of Austin soul). Printed across the bumper of the car were the slogans, "Life is great. High tech is HOT! The music is awesome. Austin is *rippin'*!" Across the bottom of the page were the corporate logos of the companies who had paid for the advertisement: Advanced Micro Devices, CompuAdd, Dell, IBM, and Motorola.

The story behind this ad demonstrates the impact of the industrial strategy for music-making in Austin. Through his connections at the Chamber of Commerce, Ernie Gammage had developed a business relationship with a manager of one of the city's computer firms. Rock'n'roll meant virtually nothing to this person, but Gammage was able to convince him that local music mattered to his workers. As he told me, "There is this guy I deal with all the time out at one of the hi-tech companies. He knows that music is important to his people on the assembly line, mostly because I am always talking to him about it and showing him studies that make that point. So he asked me what he could do for Joe 6-pack who loves Austin music and works in his plant." Rather than ask the nearest "Joe 6-pack" what he would like management to do for him, this executive solicited Gammage's advice.

I said that the best thing you could do for him would be to buy a large ad in this special section of *Billboard* that shows how much your company loves Austin music. That would be the best thing in the world you could do for him. It would really boost morale because that would help to draw national attention to that music, and draw national money to that music, and increase the development and promotion of that music he loves.

Reacting within an assumed context of a single music industry in Austin, Gammage could unhesitatingly insist that the best thing this employer could do for the morale of his music-loving employees would not be to hire local musicians to play for company parties, nor to finance a regular company night out at a local nightclub, nor to pipe the recordings of local musicians into the company break room, but instead to buy an advertisement in a music industry trade publication declaring solidarity between Austin's two growth industries. Proudly, Gammage finished the story, "So my friend got together with a bunch of his friends and this is the ad." He held it up for me. "And it is efforts like this that are bringing together the music community and the business community in Austin. The last time I went out there to visit, the ad was hanging in the lunch room."[41]

The *Billboard* spotlight issue represented the public announcement by Austin's music businesses to the national recording industry that the city had succeeded in establishing the necessary infrastructure. By 1990, Mike Tolleson could say, "To my mind, critical mass has been attained. We have achieved our goal that we began with in the early days of the

Armadillo World Headquarters, when the Fillmore East and the Arts Laboratory were the models. Austin has a full-fledged music industry."[42]

The Alternative Music Network

Although the concept of Austin's music industry was planned by older rock entrepreneurs and its structure was initiated by the Chamber of Commerce, the structure itself was originally operated mainly by individuals who had been drawn into music-related businesses through a dissatisfaction with the oligopolistic practices of the national recording industry. To a large extent, these people had been among Austin's early fans of punk rock. Punk's critique of the recording industry, its insistence that the corporate structure of the recording industry had resulted in boring music, convinced them that aesthetic value in cultural products was a matter of individual responsibility. As Simon Frith has described it,

> Punk opposed commercial music in two ways. First, it denounced multinational record companies with a version of the assertion that "small is beautiful"—punk music was, authentically, the product of small-scale, independent record and distribution companies. Second, punk demystified the production process itself—its message was that anyone could do it. One effect of this was an astonishing expansion of local music-making, but the most important strand in its development was a people's version of consumerism, the idea that record buyers had a right to maximum market choice, that record buying should involve customer expression rather than producer manipulation. . . . Such consumerism led to the creation of an "alternative" production system. . . . The punks . . . assumed an opposition between art and business, with honesty on one side and bureaucracy on the other. . . . Punk messages could be distorted by the process of commercial production, but only if this process was in the wrong hands. . . .[43]

Punk in Austin gave its participants the idea that "people could actually do something they believed in. Like to be weird or something." After punk opened the door to do-it-yourself production, it became possible "to participate in the whole cultural process." And sincere participation was the only way to guarantee the promotion of good music. Through beliefs like this, individuals such as Roland Swenson, Louis Meyers, Brent Grulke, Jo Rae DiMenno, members of the *Chronicle* staff, and many others became involved in the attempt to develop an alternative set of music businesses in Austin. They believed that these businesses would, by virtue of their small, intimate, and personal nature, avoid the hypocrisy rampant in the bureaucracy of the recording industry. Such beliefs were in line with the ideology shared by the independent music businesses that had sprung up all over the country in the wake of punk rock. As Craig Lee, a Los Angeles punk critic, wrote in

Slash in 1980, "whatever 'punk' was, it meant being brutally honest, not compromising, not selling out to the best offer, not accommodating any but your own standards." An insistence upon personal integrity and a firm belief in the legitimacy of one's honestly held and boldly stated tastes were the principles that would distinguish alternative music businesses from the corporate values of the national recording industry.[44]

Independent label owners often enter the recording business as fans. Within an industrially organized system of commodity production, the most obvious way to promote and share the music that excites these fans is to form a record company. In a 1988 article for the *Daily Texan*, Bruce Sheehan, owner of Jungle Records, described the basic motivation for independent recording companies. "One thing about Austin labels, we put out music we like." Tom Roudebush of Analog Records concurred, with added emphasis: "An independent label wouldn't usually release a record if they didn't really believe in it." However, no independent label in Austin has its own distribution network, its own way to connect commercially with other fans. Independent labels in Austin and across the country depend on college radio and the alternative distribution network. As the article insisted, "Austin's independent labels unanimously agree that their primary weakness is dependence on distributors to see their product in record stores outside of Austin." Independent label owners are fans concerned with promoting the music that genuinely excites them. Therefore, independent record companies rely on personal contacts, developed within a context of shared enthusiasm and taste, to spread the word about their musical productions. By fostering the circulation of this excitement, alternative music businesses hope to overcome the reifying distance of the marketplace and construct a postmodern community of shared tastes.

The Austin label Rabid Cat was relatively well connected into the national alternative network. Co-owner Stacey Cloud said, "We've got —I would say—excellent press and radio contacts. We get a lot of airplay." Several of Rabid Cat's releases by the Texas Instruments and Scratch Acid had been listed on the playlists published in *Rockpool* and the *College Music Journal*. "Everybody keeps telling us our records are great. So we keep doing them." To a certain extent, the small rewards of sharing meanings, tastes, and enthusiasms—of spreading a community of fans—can be motivation enough for an independent label owner to keep functioning.[45]

With her husband, M.C. Kostec, Kate Messer owns 50,000,000,000, 000,000 [Skadillion] Watts of Power in the Hands of Babes [known as 50 Skid], a small, wholly independent record company. Kate and M.C.

run the label out of their home in Florida. Their releases are nationally distributed through Dutch East India Trading, one of the many companies that began providing independent record stores across the United States with hard-to-find English and American punk records. Through the work of artists like Jad Fair of Half Japanese and Maureen Tucker, 50 Skid has had some significant success in the alternative charts and on college radio. Recordings by both of those acts were ranked in the *College Music Journal* top five. In 1990, 50 Skid was working recordings by the Austin bands Happy Family and Pocket FishRman. Kate described for me some of the characteristics of the "indie scene," the alternative music network.

This scene, the indie music scene, is difficult to crack and even harder to survive in. If you're in this business, you've got to love it or I don't know what you're getting out of it. It's a really hard market. Your success is so limited, you've got to be realistic about it. You have to enjoy it or it'll drive you insane. And I've seen some people that it has totally destroyed. But I really think there is more of a golden rule in the indie scene. More of, like, a certain humanism, that is real important. Cuz like, if it's not, why are you in it? Trust is real important. And it's a small scene. But, if I had to put a figure on it, I'd say that 75 percent of the people in this business would not go for your weakness, like they would in the corporate world. Competition seems to be modified some in that respect. But there are some wicked mean people in this scene too, who will go for your weakness and totally manipulate you if they can. But trust is just real important in the indie scene. Otherwise you're negating your whole reason for being in it.[46]

The whole reason for Kate and M.C. to become involved in the indie scene was, "We really thought it was important for Jad's and Maureen's music to get out there, and it was important that they get paid for that. And we thought we could do that. We had access to this money. And we were trusted, the person with this money trusted us with it, so we thought this is something good we could do with this money." Penn Jillette, of the magical comedy duo Penn and Teller, provided the start-up capital for 50 Skid. "Penn is a huge Velvet Underground fan, and Mike and I had been running the Velvet Underground Appreciation Society. We all loved Half Japanese, and we felt that Maureen deserved to record." Penn trusted Kate and M.C. to do "something good" with the money; that something good was to get music by these two artists "out there" and to make sure that these musicians were paid for their work. The links between the initial capital and the resulting commodity in the marketplace were based on relationships of trust and of shared taste.[47]

Fifty Skid's involvement with Austin music developed out of a similar set of relationships. Margaret Moser, the first music columnist for the *Chronicle*, was a famously infatuated John Cale fan. An early member of the Velvet Underground Appreciation Society, she made sure that

Kate and M.C. received a regular subscription to the *Chronicle* and corresponded with them about Austin music. Once her record company began, Kate began to keep closer track of the scene. She liked what she read about an all-women band, Chlorine, but that band broke up in 1987.

In late 1989, 50 Skid received an unsolicited tape from Jeff Tartakov. His company, Stress Worldwide Communications, handled Daniel Johnston's affairs and had managed the Reversible Cords in the early eighties. Jeff's reputation in the national alternative network was unambiguous; his integrity was unquestioned. He only promoted unusual artists whose work would not appeal to everyone, but in whom he wholeheartedly believed. The tape was a rough demo of a new band in Austin, Happy Family. Jeff had become Happy Family's manager after hearing the band play twice, and he recorded the demo during a live show at a barbecue restaurant.[48]

As soon as Kate opened the package and read Jeff's cover letter, she had made up her mind. "Jeff sent us the tape and that was ten points up for Happy Family then, but when he mentioned Chlorine, that was it." Happy Family's bass player, Julia Austin, had been one of the singers and songwriters in that band Kate had read about in the *Chronicle*. "They were signed before I even heard the tape," said Kate. "That's really bad, but it's true. Sometimes you just have to go on your instincts, you know." Although clearly the performances on the tape had to support it, Kate's decision was made on the basis of a few words in the *Chronicle* and her familiarity with the past work of Jeff Tartakov. Such a decision necessarily assumed trust and shared taste. Thus the indie recording career of Happy Family began because of their manager's reputation and knowledge. But it was not that Jeff was a shrewd predictor of commercial success, able to harvest raw resources and deliver them to the refining processes of a recording company. Rather, he placed Happy Family, a band with limited commercial potential but considerable power to speak to a specific audience, with a record company that had already displayed the ability to cater to that audience. Not only did Kate have to trust Jeff's judgment and share some of his taste, but Jeff had to trust Kate's taste and her ability to market Happy Family appropriately.

Fifty Skid's plan for marketing Happy Family was to exploit the network of personal contacts and shared taste by which independent music businesses operate.

Jeff and I will predict who we know that will like it. We'll send tapes to them, like in New York, at Dutch East. The Indie Brill Building—611 Broadway. That's where Rough Trade is, where Venus records is, 4 AD, Matador. We hear that the Indie Brill Building is brimming with Happy Family. . . . Anyway, to market this record, we find specific people that we already know will like the record and start the personal network flowing. We try to exploit that to the fullest, that's really how it works. . . . But there does have to be some hook, something that catches the network's attention. Cuz I get fifteen to twenty-five records a week in the mail and there comes a time when you have to make a decision about what you will listen to now and what you will shelve for later. You have to consider how valuable is your time and there is a ton of stuff out there. The market is flooded, and attention is a valuable commodity.[49]

In other words, Kate hopes to continue the network of information flow about Happy Family that began with Jeff's letter. But first she has to "hook" the attention of those in the network.

For Kate, Happy Family's hook evolved out of their connection with Chlorine. Yet for the people who work at the Indie Brill Building, the nature of that connection has to be made more explicit. What attracted Kate to Chlorine, and what underlies her affection for Happy Family, is "that woman thing." Three of the four songwriters in the band are women: the lead singer, the guitarist, and the bass player. Their presence onstage—that visual and physical aspect that is so difficult to capture in the recording studio—joyfully flaunts the image of unconventional women who are comfortable with their bodies, with their independence, and with the power of their electric guitars. While their songs tend to describe relationships from the female perspectives of the writers, few of their lyrics blatantly foreground gender issues. The power of their performance instead depends upon an identification with their projection of an unconventional feminine mastery. As Julia Austin told me, "It's sort of plain, it's not a complicated issue. You just see women in a band and you're just glad."[50] Kate echoed this feeling. "If a band has a woman in it, I am a lot more likely to listen than if it is just another boy band."

But, Kate insisted, "I also hate all that feminism shit. So we don't want to make a big deal out of it. But we can't ignore it." Rather than foreground gender issues in her promotion of Happy Family, Kate instead intends to focus on "their unique sound that can be described. They don't sound like a lot of those other bands that are out there." Not only do they feature four different songwriters, but "they have this hot woman guitar player." Kate hopes that the identity projected by Happy Family in performance can be heard on their recordings. In order to facilitate that specific hearing, Kate will supplement their recordings with a set of keys to interpreting them. The print ad that 50 Skid uses for Happy Family's album, *Lucky*, features a crude line drawing of a naked woman's torso, breasts, and belly swollen with pregnancy, and the slogan "Happy Family just wants your love."[51]

In her promotional efforts within the network, Kate must verbally communicate her enthusiasm about the identifications she has forged with them—identifications indicated by the advertisement. But she cannot speak too clearly. A too-specific description of the pleasures that they provide her would limit the possible interpretations and identifications other listeners might, through their individual longings, need to find in the band's music. Instead, she can only mention a symptom, a fetish, a hook—this hot woman guitar player, full-bodied songwriters— and hope that, through the shared discourse about these symptoms and their band, the alternative network will discover Happy Family's meaning, a meaning that Kate feels, but that she cannot speak.

The belief of the alternative music network is that through such personal channels—from Jeff to Kate to the people Kate knows in New York—the specific meaning of Happy Family, the band's unique sound and possibilities for identification, will pass undistorted. When Kate calls Dutch East distributors and talks about how great Happy Family are, she is not "selling" them, instead she is honestly promoting an act she truly loves. Because the people at Dutch East know Kate and share some of her musical tastes, they trust her and feel some excitement of their own about the band. This enthusiasm can then be passed on, transformed somewhat, translated slightly by each communication, to personally known buyers for retail stores across the country. This spark of enthusiasm, passed along by recordings, promotional kits, telephone wires, and face-to-face conversations is what music people call a "buzz." The buzz takes the excitement of pleasurable identification with a band and translates it into words, spoken and written. By depending heavily on this buzz, which requires for its efficacy the individualist values of trust and shared taste, the alternative music network hopes to avoid the inauthenticity of the marketplace; the buzz becomes the guarantee of good music, of aesthetic quality.

The Buzz

Gossip, rumor, confessionals, dreams, assertions, and desires—such are the stuff of the buzz. Verbal expressions that hint at the specific meanings of indescribable, musically supported, imaginary identifications flow through the network of fans, musicians, writers, managers, agents, and publicists. While not always true, the contents of the buzz must be genuine, the speaker must be sincere. It is only this sincerity that differentiates buzz from hype, the sharing of taste from the selling of schlock. The buzz stimulates the production of fantastic identifications, defines the possible meanings of a band, and sets the conditions for magical shows. The most dramatic increase in music business personnel in Austin has come in those regions that materialize, massage, and magnify the buzz—agents, managers, and publicists.

Jo Rae DiMenno is an independent publicist and occasional booking agent for several Austin bands. When I asked her to, she succinctly defined her role in the music industry. "I wanna create a buzz. That's pretty much what I do. That's what my job is. To create a buzz."[52] Jo Rae moved from Houston to Austin in 1986. She had been a booking agent and a writer in Houston, producing a newsletter for nightclubs and writing features about the out-of-town acts she had booked. By 1988, she had established (with J.D. Foster) the DiMenno/Foster Agency in Austin, booking the final few shows for the True Believers and working with new acts like the Alejandro Escovedo Orchestra, David Halley, and the Barnburners.

In 1990, J.D. left the agency and Jo Rae shifted the focus of her work to publicity. "I'm trying to advertise myself more as a publicist," she told me. "Because I want to be paid a flat fee for services. I don't wanna get paid a percentage of their [the performers'] shows." The shift from booking agent to publicist changes Jo Rae's connections with bands, paralleling the changing focus of Austin music-making. No longer is she their link to specific nightclub gigs. For bands, her function is less immediately tangible but, she insisted, no less significant.

I've definitely always been on this wave of helping people. You help each other out. And I'm very into that. But I'm also getting very into the other part of it, to where I want to make, it's time that I make some money for what I'm doing. Because it is valid. And it's worth something to people. When you first try out sometimes, it's like, oh yeah, I'll do that. Oh, I'm working with bands! And there's this whole thing that is set up on, I don't know. It's like one time with Alejandro, we had a very good talk about this. I just said, Alejandro, did you ever sit down and think that what I'm doing, I want to get ahead just like you do? I want to be out there just like you do. So it was like, what I'm doing is just as important as what he is doing as the musician and songwriter. And but, I had to make that point to him. Very heavily. . . . Because I feel like, when I publicize someone, I try to create something. They've got it there and you take it. And it's already created but then you take it and move it and change what people know about it. And there's a certain way, when you do that, you are creating something. You know. You're not creating that person, but you're helping.

The "it" Jo Rae speaks of—"They've got it there and you take it"— is her act's projected identity. In this reflection on her work, she describes it as a process of taking that identity, moving it, and changing what people know about it. She takes elements of the band's identity and spreads them through the information network through which the buzz flows. Through her selection of elements and of the persons to whom she describes these elements, Jo Rae contributes to "creating that person." This is the creative aspect to publicity: the slight transformations in the content of the buzz, the help given to the musicians and songwriters in the discursive construction and dissemination of their projected identity.

When I asked her to describe a particularly successful instance of her work, she narrated the transformation of David Halley's image from that of another west Texas folkie songwriter to that of an Austin rock'n'roll musician.

Ok, what I do is I get on the phone, like with David Halley's tape. David was always associated with the Lubbock thing pretty much. So we wanted to change that. What he really wanted to do was be a True Believer. He saw them one day and went out and bought a Marshall amp the next morning. So I started getting on the phone and telling people that J.D. and David were working together. I had tried to always establish a relationship with Ed Ward and been generally blown off. But after I gave him David's tape, everything changed. Cuz he liked the tape. And I think that he realized that I wasn't a, I don't know, a groupie or a bimbo or whatever. We get along great now. We [Jo Rae and J.D.] just made tons of tapes, and I have a huge list of everybody I gave that tape to. Then David did a show with Syd Straw at the Cactus. And it was with J.D. and Rich [Brotherton]. So, again, I knew that Ed Ward likes Syd and a lot of these writers like her. I invited just a bunch of people to the Cactus. And let them know about the show before it was gonna happen. Way before. And they get off to that. The Syd show was very successful. I was really happy with it. We all worked hard on it. And the press thing was great. Griff [the manager of the Cactus] said that from that show, there were more press people there than any show he has ever done at the Cactus. So to me, that was a good night. I mean it was a happening. I don't really care for her [Syd's] stuff that much, but I think it was still a great show. Because it's a show that a lot of people will remember.

Jo Rae helped David Halley transform the identity he projected by emphasizing to her contacts that David was working with J.D. Foster, who at that time was also playing with the True Believers. After the demo was finished, Jo Rae sent out copies of the tape to fans of the True Believers and kept track of their reactions. Then she chose a specific show to publicize, when Halley was booked to open for Syd Straw—a singer who appealed to many of the same people in Austin who liked the Believers. Jo Rae made sure that she told everybody on her list about this show and arranged for them to get in free. She packed the club with people already yearning for that identity, primed them with advance knowledge about David's performance, and helped to construct their experience of David Halley's transformation. In effect, she manipulated the conditions that constitute a scene. The evidence of her success was that "it's a show that a lot of people will remember," that people—specifically, writers—still talk about. She effectively created a buzz.

In her work with local journalists, as she attempts to stimulate a buzz, Jo Rae often takes advantage of the fact that these writers have developed a taste for secret knowledge. One thing that sets a journalist apart from his or her competitors is knowing some tidbit about an act before the other writers in town know. Derived from the value of scooping the competition and sustained by the sociology of this information-trading profession, the taste for secret knowledge operates even when the material is "off the record." According to Jo Rae, "One of the ways you create a buzz is to call somebody up and tell them something and then tell them it's off the record. So they can't use it, but they can still talk about it. That starts the gossip mill." The trick to creating a powerful buzz, one capable of shaping the meanings produced in a scene, is to stimulate this flow of information at a particular rate. The ability of each publicist to construct this buzz is dependent on her or his contacts, on the personal relationships she or he has developed within the scene. "I've got a real good phone list. I just get on with these people," Jo Rae said. But the hierarchy of social relations in the scene must be respected. Ed Ward must be contacted personally. Jody Denberg [a local deejay and writer] has to be kept informed about all of Jo Rae's acts. "And there's certain people that I will definitely not tell anything to off the record. Because sometimes it has wound up in print. The writer-publicist trust thing, once it's broken, I'll just call somebody else."

As a publicist, then, Jo Rae inserted herself into the flow of information, into the production of the buzz about David Halley. But she was still working within a context of fandom; Jo Rae loved the True Believers and was excited by David Halley's move to electric guitars and drums. The shift in his approach made immediate sense to her. And this understanding was the basis of her specific contribution to Halley's transformation: because she subjectively responded to his new identity, she could communicate genuine enthusiasm about it. The excitement derived from her subjective response to this musical change combined with a pleasure she found in her own work. Halley's shift was a good hook. In Austin, where the combination of west Texas country and east Texas blues maps out so much of the musical territory, this bit of information could be enough to send real sparks along the buzz network.

Trust and personal relationships hold the alternative network together, and these are based on values believed to conflict with the corporate structure. Jo Rae was adamant about this aspect of her job.

Right now, I have to work with bands I like. It is a must. I don't think I could work for a [major] record company, because then I would have to work with a lot of crap that I don't like. I don't wanna get involved with any of those guys: Giant, Chrysalis. Cuz they're all, they're all, I mean, Rough Trade is probably the best one. It's all so stupid though. The setup is really stupid. I get so aggravated with the people who run record companies. I think they're idiots and I think they're evil. I don't know, the record companies all look like this *1984* thing. It all looks like that to me now. I hate to be so negative. But it's not enough to discourage me completely because I still believe. I believe in what I'm doing and the people that I work for.[53]

In the fall of 1990, Jo Rae DiMenno maintained that so long as she can remain independent she will be able to promote bands she genuinely likes. Only under these conditions could she retain her integrity while continuing to stimulate the buzz. Her integrity is the key to her success; her connections have to be able to share her enthusiasm, to believe her when she calls them on the phone, excited about a new song by an unknown singer. "Yes, I do still love it or I wouldn't be doing it," she said. "It's weird, I really like doing it, a lot. I enjoy the publicity part. Cuz I like to talk on the phone, so it's like the perfect job for me. And I like to talk to people."

While Jo Rae found something stupid in the setup of record companies and wanted to avoid that taint, Brent Grulke, former music editor for the *Austin Chronicle*, saw his own role as more complicit with that structure. "In order to make money, particularly out of rock'n'roll, you have to be willing to work in a way that allows you to make money, I guess. You have to work with the system to a certain extent."[54] Echoing an argument from Simon Frith's *Sound Effects*, Brent went on,

The music wouldn't exist in any of the forms we know it, if it were not for the industry. I think rock'n'roll, you have to view it as a, as, as, so wrapped up and tied to capitalism that you can't separate the two. The story of rock'n'roll and of rock'n'roll success is the story—and the failures—is the story of capitalism. And so, you make records. And you sell records. It's a product. You turn music into a commodity. And you turn yourself into a commodity. And the second you get onstage, you want to get paid for being onstage and the second you decide that you want to make a record you're tied into that process. To some extent. To the extent that you get tied in, and to the extent that integrity comes into play in that, it's a daily battle. The decisions that you make right here and now. And you make some bad ones, I think, you know. And you make some good ones. You try to think that over all, I think that, by and large, people that do the business end still, I think that the vast majority of them have a genuine love of music. But I think that that gets sidetracked a lot of the time.

While Brent was willing to work in a way that allowed him to make some money from rock'n'roll, he still wanted to make "good decisions" so that his genuine love of music would not be sidetracked. Good decisions are conceived individualistically; they arise when the available choices involve matters of personal integrity. For instance, the personal integrity of a rock writer is directly related to her or his perceived stance of independence within the recording industry. However, every rock writer is dependent either directly or indirectly upon the largesse of the recording industry. During a meeting of the music editorial staff at the *Chronicle*'s offices in September 1990, Brent told his writers that,

Record companies do not send us ten copies of a record because they think we are going to assign it to ten different writers and print ten different reviews. They expect us to supplement our minuscule salaries by selling these. You've got to learn the way the business operates.[55]

In other words, a certain amount of mutual interest and unspecified cooperation between the *Chronicle* and recording companies is normal and not especially remarkable. However, a writer's personal integrity is believed to be distinct from the integrity of the industrial structure within which she or he must work. A writer's integrity comes to be defined as a space of individual, autonomous musical taste marked out from the dominant interests of the recording companies, indicated by an idiosyncratic passion for certain acts and signified by an individual writing style.

Perhaps the most successful negotiator of the contradictions faced by a music writer in Austin during the period of industrialization was Michael Corcoran. From 1985 through 1988, Corcoran wrote a regular column that managed to be wholly engaging, personal, and thoroughly about the experience of being a rock'n'roll fan in Austin, Texas. He managed to distinguish between his personal engagement in his writing and his personal engagement in his fandom. He created a public persona, "Corky," who lived out the fantasies and the frustrations of a fan whose personal subjective involvement in—whose identification with— the scene was total. He then developed a writing style based upon a detachment from this character, thereby producing an ironic narration of Corky's experiences of fandom. The reader was never quite sure if Corky was making fun of Austin music, or if Corcoran was making fun of Corky, if Corcoran really loved Zeitgeist or the True Believers, or if that were some quirk of Corky's. Was it Corcoran or Corky who held Charlie Sexton personally responsible for betraying Austin music one month and saw him as a young victim of the recording industry a few columns later?

"Sometimes I just physically cannot write about Austin Music," Corcoran wrote once. "I'd rather write about Austin Calligraphers, Austin Hairdressers or Austin Speedbumps, anything but that god-damn Austin music. Jeez, fewer words were written about the Civil

War."[56] Corcoran could never appear simply sincere, although his involvement with the scene demanded a certain sincerity. His writing presented a postmodern pastiche of the devoted fan of Austin music and the professional writer, often in the same column.

One column, published on February 27, 1987, included this typical "Corky" passage:

I'm about to embark on my latest entrepreneurial effort: the Musician's Triathalon. This test of endurance will show just who is our fittest musician. First, participants must drink a case of beer on an empty stomach. It will be a brand of beer that costs less than Budweiser. Then they must play an hour-long set in front of six people, and return for an encore when one of them claps. Finally, contestants must knock on the bedroom window of a girl they recently blew off, tell her their "true" feelings, pass out during foreplay, wake up before she does, take her last pack of cigarettes and leave undetected. The first musician to make 100 sandwiches the next day will be declared the winner.

and it concluded with this passage,

I'm not defending drugs. They nearly ruined me. But it's time that truth came back in vogue. Beware of those who tell you the answer to questions they weren't born with. Learn to differentiate between the voice of experience and the voice of advertising. Realize that a scared 15-year-old knows a lot more about abortion than Nancy Reagan does. Don't just say no because they gave you a button that says it. You're the only one who knows what's inside you. Such a responsibility is often more than some people can handle, and they turn to the Adolf Hitlers, Charles Mansons, Jim Joneses, pimps, organized religion and drug dealers and sell away their lives. But those of you who regard freedom of thought and expression as a sacred right will come to realize that in searching for the thing you can't name you will find life's greatest gift.[57]

Did this romantic plea for sincerity and personal responsibility as moral imperatives come from the fan or the writer, or did it even matter? Michael Corcoran was able to negotiate the contradictions between being a genuine fan, caught up in immediate personal relationships with performers and other fans in Austin, and being a professional writer, distanced from his subjects by various commercial mediations, through the masquerade of Corky. His integrity was no longer personal but instead became identified with his writing; so long as musicians and fans spent the week talking about whatever Corky was talking about, he was doing his job both as writer and as fan—stimulating the noumenal existence of the scene. His music/gossip columns helped construct the buzz even as they made fun of the gossip network and ridiculed the cultural practice that was now dependent on writers such as himself to help its participants hear the difference between the voice of advertising and the voice of experience.

As alternative music businesses in Austin proliferated, the individuals involved in them legitimated their work by appealing to this threefold structure of values. The people with whom they worked had to be able to trust them; they had to maintain their personal integrity. They had to retain a genuine love of music and the ability to verbally communicate their enthusiasm. Finally, they had to contribute to the overarching meaning of music-making in Austin through the effective performance of their own work, in the creation and maintenance of the buzz. The ideology of the alternative music network in Austin insisted that so long as its participants continued to base their operations on this legitimating structure of beliefs, the collective action of all these individuals would result in the production of good music. The hypocrisy of the corporate recording industry (which was revealed in the poor aesthetic quality of the recordings it released) would be avoided even as the focus of music-making in Austin changed from live performances in nightclubs and honky-tonks to the industrial production of recorded commodities.

South by Southwest

The triumvirate of values that underlies the industrial structure of music-making in Austin—the importance of trust and individual integrity, the importance of each person contributing to the ongoing meaning of this music through her or his work, and, above all, the insistence upon the importance of one's own genuine love for music, expressed through one's taste—is now celebrated annually in the spring festival called the South by Southwest Music and Media Conference. Every year since 1987, SXSW has constructed a festival setting where those who have risen in the alternative music network can reaffirm the values that initially inspired them and, through focusing their attention on unsigned bands playing in crowded nightclubs, celebrate the network's origin in punk and postpunk rock'n'roll scenes. Through it all, SXSW revels in the pleasures of the buzz, as hundreds of managers, publicists, promoters, bookers, fans, and musicians spend their days drinking and gossiping in the enclosed space of a hotel lobby, describing, sharing, and comparing their identifications, ecstatically announcing their tastes and pleasures in the evaluation of each night's bands. Crossing the boundaries between the roles of fan and of business person, participants in South by Southwest reinforce the industrial structure that mediates this distinction.[58]

South by Southwest was first conceived of as a branch of New York's New Music Seminar. The New Music Seminar was an outgrowth of Mark Josephson's Rockpool organization, another attempt to coordinate the activities of the many new postpunk independent music

entrepreneurs. The first, NMS, a single "day-long agenda of panel discussions" designed to inform and instruct these beginning music professionals, took place on July 14, 1980.[59] Located in New York, NMS benefited from the concentration of corporate as well as alternative record
company and radio personnel in the area. It quickly grew more extensive and sophisticated. By 1990, the New Music Seminar had become,
in the words of Roland Swenson, "continuing education for people in
the music industry."[60] Drawing thousands of registrants, NMS became
an important forum integrating the mainstream recording industry and
the alternative network.

In 1986, the Austin Chamber of Commerce began to court the New
Music Seminar. With the encouragement of David Lord and Lee Cooke,
the Chamber coordinated a package presentation of Austin musicians
and Austin music business professionals for NMS. They sponsored an
"Austin booth" at the conference where national record industry figures
could find a compilation tape of Austin musicians, copies of the *Austin
Chronicle*, and information about recording services, nightclubs, management firms, and other professional services available in the southwest
capital. They also flew Joel Weber to Austin to discuss setting up a regional version of the New Music Seminar to be held in Austin that
would both deal with regional issues and return to the information-for-
industry-beginners approach of the early NMS meetings. Planning for
the Southwestern Music Seminar advanced to the stage where the first
meeting, to be held in the spring of 1987, became part of the package
promoted at the Austin booth during the summer of 1986.[61]

That October, Weber and Josephson decided that they would not
be able to coordinate this additional event. Immediately, Roland Swenson and Louis Meyers convinced Louis Black and Nick Barbaro of the
Chronicle that the initial groundwork for such a meeting had been laid
and that, if they carried through on the already existing plans, the seminar would be a success. The Chamber agreed to continue their support for the project and, through the Austin Convention and Visitors
Bureau, contributed valuable advertising dollars. The first promotional
material was mailed out in November, and, by January, it was clear that
the conference would take place.

The first South by Southwest Music and Media Conference was held
on March 14, 1987. Like the first New Music Seminar, it consisted of a
day-long series of panels discussing the problems of those first entering
music-related businesses. Approximately seven hundred registrants participated, including representatives from eight major labels. But there
was a significant distinction between Austin's meeting and its model in

New York; this was the proud emphasis the regional conference gave to four nights of performances by area bands. The conference was set up so as to co-occur with the annual *Chronicle* Music Awards night, and two-thirds of the 150 bands performing in the nightclubs over that weekend were local. "The real success of SXSW was in the musical output," Corky insisted in his first column after the initial conference. "On stages all over town we repeatedly kicked New York's ass." Subtitling his column "SXSW: The Final Word," Corky spread the buzz about Two Nice Girls, the Wagoneers, and other local bands, bragging about the positive reception national recording industry figures had given to the town's musicians. By emphasizing the value of local music performed in the clubs, South By Southwest paid tribute to the original honky-tonk setting of the Austin music scene even as it trained local entrepreneurs how to operate within the new industrial structure.[62]

This focus on unsigned musicians and new recruits for music businesses has continued to distinguish SXSW from the New Music Seminar. As SXSW has grown from seven hundred registrants meeting for one day in 1987, to two thousand registrants meeting for three days and four nights in 1990, the specific value of Austin's meeting has remained its "intimacy" and its "grass-roots orientation." According to Roland Swenson, "We've always tried to focus our conference at the people who were just coming into the industry."[63] Such an orientation concentrates attention on the line between amateur and professional, between fan and industry worker, between unsigned local performer and contracted entertainer—between those who are and those who are not making a living in the music business. South by Southwest has become "a premier regional music showcase," bringing recording industry personnel into contact with aspiring musicians living and playing in the middle of the country.[64]

Within the confines of this four-day period, in the relatively out-of-the-way city of Austin, national recording industry employees spend their nights acting like fans again, racing from club to club, anxiously struggling not to miss the best bands, urged on by the excitement of hundreds of fellow celebrants also engaging in this ritualistic reenactment of their adolescence. The interactions at SXSW appear almost disturbingly intimate to those individuals whose dealings with their co-workers are so often mediated by long-distance telephone calls and fax machines, market considerations and profit calculations—the desperate instrumentality of the cultural marketplace. At SXSW, they can be fans together again, mutually discovering new bands and participating in face-to-face discussions about their meaning.

During the 1990 conference, the panels were organized both along industry categories, like "The A&R Department," "Management," and "Indie Labels," and around specific issues, like "Whither Rock" and "Controversy."[65] The A&R panel was well attended. It always is. A&R representatives are the talent scouts for the recording industry. No recording contract is signed without the approval of the company's A&R department. According to Roland Swenson,

A lot of people—especially musicians—they've never seen an A&R person. They didn't know, they had heard about them, they knew they were supposed to be playing in front of them, but they had never seen one or talked to one. They didn't know what they looked like. The main thing is that we get twelve of them in one room and put them on stage so that everyone can look at them.[66]

During the 1990 A&R panel, a long line formed in front of the audience microphone, a line made up of frustrated musicians, who wanted to do more than look at these representatives. They wanted to know why their acts were not being offered contracts. These musicians wanted a specific, detailed explanation of what "the typical A&R guy is looking for." No such answer was given. Instead, representatives from Columbia, Geffen, A&M, MCA, and other major companies insisted that they depend wholly on their ears and rely on their tastes. The personal integrity of A&R representatives requires that they respond solely to their "gut"; they have to "get off" to the music; they have to hear a hit, a "unique sound," something "undescribable." And, the panel insisted, musicians had better find a good manager.[67]

The management panel, chaired by Carlyne Majer, described their role as the key liaison between art and business, a necessary link in the production of that "five minutes of pleasure" that is a "hit song." According to the panel members, the manager has to be trusted not only by the artists but also by the record company. The worst part of their job is when "the trust and the friendship drift away." Once that happens, then the goals of the musician, the manager, and the recording company are no longer mutual, no longer a product of social consensus, but instead are positions taken in negotiations between parties with different interests. Managers hate that. Interestingly, no questions were taken from the audience during this panel.

Instead of describing a particular aesthetic quality, speakers during the "Indie Labels" panel contended that they look for a "work ethic" in bands. Musicians have to be "willing to work their butts off, maybe put out their own records, organize their own tour, and create a buzz." While indie labels "offer a full range of market services," bands should not "assume that everything will be taken care of." Nevertheless, bands will find a significant difference with independent labels. These reps insisted that their companies are staffed by fans who seriously care about the music they release and the musicians they work with. This assertion appears to mirror the reliance of major label A&R representatives on their "gut." But the difference turns on the size of the company. In major labels, the A&R department might operate at cross-purposes to the marketing department. In small, independent companies, some part of the identity of each employee is affirmed by the commercial success of its recordings. When an independent company works one of its records into a hit, this represents an apparently objective, market-driven legitimation of the tastes of each person working there.

Every employee from every branch of the recording industry attending SXSW'90 claimed a commitment to the promulgation of "good music." The refrain constantly echoed in the panels was that "there is a tremendous amount of crap out there" and only through the personal efforts of each individual involved can the alternative music network ensure the production and promotion of good music. Good music was defined by its ability to produce "five minutes of pleasure" for the listener. Every individual working in the recording industry has learned the value of reassuring every musician that she or he is capable of producing "good music." The assumption shared by all is that everyone involved in this overarching industrial structure is interested in distributing as much good music as possible to as many people as possible. Good music reaches people through selling records. That is success. An individual works her or his way up the recording industry hierarchy to the extent that her or his taste is predictive of such success. Thus, good music—that music which produces pleasure in these professional listeners—becomes that music which can be sold to the largest number of people.

In addition to frustrated musicians, hundreds of ambitious music business initiates attended the daily panel discussions, gathering these small tidbits of utilitarian information about the operations of the recording industry. Aspiring entrepreneurs and musicians strolled back and forth between the panel rooms and the lobby, their eyes glowing and their dreams stoked by the presence of so many who had already accomplished what they one day hoped to achieve.

The resulting atmosphere in the hotel lobby approximated that in the clubs at night. The anxiety of incomplete identities swirled about the intoxicated celebrants of an absent past. Rumors of recording deals spread excitedly over slowly sipped margaritas. Participants displayed their black leather costumes of alienation and (in)difference. Only the sunlight pouring through the atrium, and the ability actually to hear the circulating conversations, gave evidence that this conference was not a site of perpetual liminality, but only its postmodern simulacrum. Here in the lobby—not in the panel rooms nor outside the hotel— managers and agents pressed flyers and copies of demo tapes on those whose nametags reminded them of someone. Writers from cosponsoring alternative weeklies hovered about the edges of grouped conversants, sniffing out the gossip that would lead their stories back home. Unsigned musicians, overcome with anxiety, drank too much and passed out on the couch by the lobby entrance. And record company executives smiled while they fended off the advances of those they did not already know and made nervous promises to attend every musician's showcase that night.

In its annual meetings, South by Southwest demonstrates the complete modernization of music-making in Austin, Texas. The music festival allows recording company executives to act out their remembered fantasies of fandom, while the panels and the activities in the hotel lobby work to discipline musicians into the expectations and assumptions of the national industry. Throughout the weekend, these multiple dialectics of desire and fantasy are stimulated and managed by the leaders of Austin's own burgeoning music industry, who, in the very performance of this function, reinforce and construct their own importance and success as an industry.

When I was not attending panels during SXSW'90, I was standing along the railing of the balcony overlooking the lobby. From there I watched and overheard the ceaseless weaving of the material from which the meaning of music in Austin was being fashioned. Friends, longtime Austin scenesters who had perfected their style in the nightclubs, expertly worked the crowd below, shaking hands and exchanging business cards. An old friend I knew from Los Angeles, now an A&R vice president for Rhino Records, told me how much he loved the Reivers. Members of the Wishniaks, an alternative pop band from Philadelphia, stopped by to promote their show. Large men with dangerous haircuts stood to my right, speaking only German. Behind me, deejays from KTSB, the cable radio station run by students at the University of Texas, excitedly taped "station ids" by alternative stars. By Saturday afternoon, the buzz in the lobby had spun itself up through the always green leaves of the indoor trees, past the balcony where I stood, to fill the central atrium with the whirring echoes of rock'n'roll's multivalent desires.

Kathy McTee and Luke Torn rode up the escalator from the lobby and stood next to me. Kathy slipped three Rolling Rocks out of her extra large purse, opened one for herself and handed the other two to Luke and me. We leaned over the railing, drinking cheaper bottles of the same beer they were selling downstairs, and marveled at all the activity. "Last year," Luke said, "Robert Christgau gave the keynote speech. He told all these bands that none of them were going to make it. Nobody is doing that this year."[68] "Nah," Kathy said, "this year, they're all getting tips on how to succeed in the music business or else die trying." "But," Luke interjected, "that's what makes the music so great at night. Each of these bands thinks that this is their best opportunity to get a deal, to make it, and so they knock themselves out onstage, playing better than they have ever played in their lives. That's what makes South by Southwest so great. All these bands playing their hearts out. And we get to go to the clubs and listen to them play out their dreams."

The three of us had arranged to meet that afternoon in order to attend the conference's last panel, entitled "Controversy in the Music Industry." Simon Frith was to be the chair and, so far as Kathy and I were concerned, he was the biggest star of the conference. The room was beginning to fill up, so we found chairs near the back and sat down. After only a few minutes it became apparent that there would be no real controversy here. Everyone on the panel agreed that stickering was bad, the best response to offensive speech was more speech, and the members of 2 Live Crew were basically stupid but no sheriff should arrest them. Complex questions about representation in music or the political effects of the industrial structure were not raised. Controversy could be managed and mediated insofar as everyone worked together toward reproducing and expanding opportunities in the industrial production of music. Vital to this structural reproduction were the values of "free speech" and "free markets." The final statement from the floor was made by Ty Gavin, an original member of the Raul's scene, whose band, the Next, had excited and inspired many of those now coordinating Austin's music industry. Gavin's jet black hair hung down past his shoulders and he cocked one hip as he said, "All this talk has made me think about three words. One is art, one is entertainment, and I, I, I forget the third. . . ." The panel waited patiently while Gavin struggled to recall what he had wanted to say. Finally, he came up with it, "Oh, yeah, now I remember. It's responsibility, that's it."

Gavin's final word, "responsibility," successfully collapsed an entire set of social relationships among the individuals inside as well as outside the room—across the river and the freeway, into South Austin and East Austin, or even beyond the city limits—into a personal and economic interdependence with the current structure of music-making in Austin.

In the context of South by Southwest's panel on controversy, all positive values were defined in terms of the current conditions of music-making. The industrialization of music-making in Austin has successfully created a decentered structure that facilitates the economic exchange of a variety of goods and services. Within this structure, three individualist values—personal integrity, the importance of personal taste, and a personal contribution to the meaning of Austin music—have constituted an ethic of responsibility that is enacted through the mutual reproduction of this industrial structure. That is, all of the individuals involved in the structure, through their individual interactions, reproduce at each moment the structure itself. The structure, though we can isolate it and talk about it, does not exist apart from these individual interactions, even as the individual actions are themselves motivated by desires and values created by the structure.

Thus, performance in the clubs actually has become a process of research and development intended to create improved recordings. A tremendous increase in the number of managers, publicists, writers, and agents has become necessary in order to reinforce and reproduce the signifying dynamics of a scene on a scale much larger than Austin has ever experienced before. And during the soft spring nights of South by Southwest, the results of all the work of Austin's music industry is on display; all the clubs in town are indeed filled with "good music." Throughout this annual festival, hundreds of musicians play for twenty minutes each to packed crowds full of individuals eager to participate, even if only for a moment, in the art, entertainment, and internally focused responsibility of the Austin music scene.

No one from the panel or the audience offered any response to Gavin's summation of controversy, South by Southwest, and Austin music. So Frith thanked the musician and dismissed the conference's final panel. Kathy, Luke, and I headed for the clubs.[69]

CHAPTER NINE

The Continuing Importance of Musicalized Experience

One Friday morning in September 1990, at about 10:00 A.M., I got on the North Lamar bus, heading into downtown. There were a few seats scattered throughout the bus, but, following habit, I headed for the back. Not until after I sat down did I notice a white man about my age with long hair sitting a couple of rows up. A pad of staff paper lay on his lap, and he was busy scribbling scales and drawing chord structures across its lines. From the seat in back of him, a black man leaned over and asked what he was doing. They began to talk, and I started trying to eavesdrop on the conversation.

"This is what I do on the bus everyday. I ride the bus an hour and a half everyday, and I can't hardly work out this stuff at work, so that's what I do on the bus."

"So what is that, is that jazz or what?"

"Well, actually, I first heard it on a Led Zeppelin record, but yeah, a lot of jazz guys will use this. It's a melodic minor scale. You know Led Zeppelin?"

"No, man, but I do play. And I'm always strugglin' to get better, you know. Are you a teacher?"

"I've taught guitar for the last nineteen years, ever since I was fifteen. I'm the music director at the Austin Guitar School now. You know, down at the Opry House? I generally have students all day long, or else I'm working on the books or something, so I just don't have the time to do the studying I need to do to keep improving my own skills."

"So like, if I wanted to like, get better you know, like to work on my reading and stuff, like, do you know any books that would help me with that?"

By this point, I was not the only rider listening to this conversation;

the entire back of the bus was paying attention. A Chicano man was leaning over from across the aisle. The older African-American man sitting next to me took his cap off and tilted his head in order to hear better. I shifted over in my seat so that I could take notes and listen at the same time. The guitar teacher noticed that he had an audience by this point, and he began to speak louder.

"You see, this is the only way I can ever learn anything myself. When you hear something that you like, try to play it and then write it down." He looked up to make sure we all got this point. Heads nodded all around. "And as soon as you learn something you don't really understand, you need to write a song with it. Don't learn anything else, just play this one thing and play around with it for a couple of weeks. Write a song that forces you to use the new scale. The trick is to only play notes that are in the key. So with this progression that I've got here, where the A minor resolves out of this E major, you throw in your G sharp on the way up this scale. See how it works? Sometimes it takes me weeks to learn a new scale, and I have to really force my fingers to move in new ways. And then after I get this scale down in A minor, I change keys and do it all again until I can play it in any key I want. And that's how you learn it, by applying it. Just reading books doesn't help. You gotta work at it."

The man sitting next to me pointed at the corner of an instruction book in the teacher's lap. "That's a pretty good book, though."

"Yeah, I use the Mel Bay books with a lot of my students. But it's no substitute for practicing." Again, everyone nodded.

"How much you charge, man?" asked the first questioner.

"Usually about $20 for a half-hour lesson. But I'm not taking any new students right now. If you come on down to the school, though, we have a lot of other teachers who are really good." With this, Ted Hall handed out his business card to the five of us who had been listening in the back of the bus. We all looked at each other and smiled, each of us clutching a business card and imagining ourselves mastering the melodic minor scale in all the keys of the universe.[1]

We were all male, and, since we were all riding the bus, none of us was rich, but still we embodied more difference than usually interacts on the buses of Austin. We ranged in age from the late teens or early twenties up to about fifty. Besides Ted Hall and myself, there was one younger white man, two blacks, and one brown. We were all sharing a conversation about music and learning and the importance of practice. Sometimes it seems as if everyone plays guitar in Austin.

But not everyone is part of the scene. In all reality, there are many music scenes in Austin. There are a group of musicians who play mostly in the women's bars, occasionally crossing over and playing Liberty Lunch or the Cactus Cafe. The blues scene has been mostly confined to Antone's. With the death of Stevie Ray Vaughan, the crossover potential of the blues, its ability to attract mainstream listeners, has been greatly diminished. There is music on the east side and south of the river, as there has always been. But east-side rappers and south-side Tex-Mex musicians rarely venture over into the west-side performance sites, being hired only for special occasions like South by Southwest or Aquafest. Acoustic musicians play the folk clubs, mostly the Cactus Cafe in the student union on campus or Gruene Hall outside of town. What could be called rock'n'roll itself has split into heavy metal, alternative music, and a more traditional rhythm and blues and rockabilly-centered style.

The marketing strategies of the recording industry have permeated the organization of live music performance in Austin. In effect, the Austin music scene now consists of these more specialized genres, each marked off from the others by marketing demographics that follow the outlines of race, class, gender, and age—each with its own number one and its own steady sellers. This splitting of the Austin music scene is not a random result of postmodern fragmentation. These are well planned subdivisions, designed for maximum visibility and market performance.

Each of these smaller insider scenes gains its glamor from the faintest blush of possibility of fame or riches—the treasures dispensed by the dominant recording industry, seemingly at random, to a very few of those who play. Thus it was Stevie Ray Vaughan and still is Jimmie Vaughan or the Thunderbirds who give lustre to Antone's. Two Nice Girls bring excitement to Chances. Dangerous Toys inspires the aspiring metal gods who play at the Back Room. Darden Smith and Nanci Griffith remind those acoustic guitarists sitting at tables in the Cactus that the line dividing folk and country is policed by record company executives in Nashville. Each musician who gains the attention of the industry raises the glamor quotient for her or his market-enforced genre, drawing more attention and more money, then, to the other players in their scene. This is what success in the music business means.

When people—musicians, journalists, sound technicians, booking agents, fans—now speak of the *scene*, they mean the activity surrounding those successful musicians who have attracted such attention, or who are believed to be on the verge of doing so, and are in the process of shifting the marketing mainstream of youth-oriented music. The scene now only happens some nights at the Cannibal Club and the Hole in the Wall and the Continental Club and Liberty Lunch. These are the nights when the insider figures come out and the buzz attracts an audience larger than their already committed fans, when the scene—with its transformative exchange of signs and sweat—is stimulated by the efforts of industry personnel. As the eighties edged into the nineties, the scene in Austin began to require the promise of making it—the performed possibility of moving beyond one's class position into a sphere of apparent freedom—in order to attract the yearning desires of an adolescent audience. But this reconfigured scene is no less real than any that came before it. The scene remains an historical construct that shifts and changes in response to the conscious and unconscious concerns of the individuals who create it by their presence, their actions, their tastes, beliefs, and desires, changing in turn the dominant musical styles.

Popular musical practice in Austin, Texas, grew out of a residual honky-tonk culture, where the contradictions of modern life could be displayed in a heightened sexualized fashion and a romantic antimodern critique could be mutually performed by musicians, dancers, listeners, and drinkers. This honky-tonk culture, in turn, was a commodified development of the carnival tradition. The carnival was a regular festival of release, tied to the rhythms of the seasons and seasonal work, where hierarchies of everyday life and the values upheld in the dominant ideology could be inverted and the daily practices and pleasures of the low could be celebrated. In Texas, the cowboy's agricultural work provided the context for the carnivalesque practices associated with the towns at the end of the cattle drive. In such towns, dance halls provided music, drink, and sex for a price, creating an enclosed arena where a carnivalesque atmosphere could become a permanent liminal possibility. The cowboy could buy his festival of inversion and could extend his celebration of release for as long as his money would hold out. Thus the dance hall at the end of the cattle trail was the first site for the commercialization of the carnivalesque in the western United States and marks the beginning of honky-tonk culture.[2]

With the urbanization of Texas's population and the concomitant modernization of its varied cultures and peoples, the honky-tonk became the site for the display, critique, and negotiation of the cultural tensions that accompanied these rapid changes. Rather than simply inverting the dominant hierarchies to celebrate their excluded lower levels, honky-tonk culture actively critiqued those hierarchies: the increasing rigidifications of class, the absorption and submersion of ethnic cultures within the social mainstream, and the strains inflicted on traditional family life by urbanization and modernization. Through the sale of alcohol and the presentation of dance music in a relatively free atmosphere conducive to the transgression of rigid social rules, the honky-tonk offered a readily available, commodified version of carnivalesque release. As hundreds of honky-tonks sprang up along the city limits and county lines across Texas—meeting places and mediation sites for urban and rural, rich and poor, male and female (only rarely, however, crossing racial lines)—the meaning of these differences was played out through musical performance. Musicians and audiences together would dance and sing and play songs that represented their experience of pleasure in an increasingly complex and regimented world. In so doing, they performed together the possible meanings and identities offered by their contemporary popular culture.

As the capital of Texas, Austin has long been the meeting ground for the large state's diverse interests and cultures. As the location of the state's largest university, the city has also been the temporary home for many young people particularly interested in the questioning of disciplinary structures and the construction of their own identities. Students from the University of Texas first became integrated into the local traditions of honky-tonk music-making at Threadgill's bar. At Threadgill's, these students incorporated the critical practices of honky-tonk culture and selectively adapted them to the social and ideological issues that concerned them. They turned the antimodernism of honky-tonk culture to their own need to form actively an identity specifically other than that apparently created for them by the newly evident powers of mass culture. Singing folk songs learned from records signified a more active relation to the possibilities of modern culture than that indicated by simply dancing to rock'n'roll records. Their selectivity could result in some striking absurdities, however. Folksinging became the music of the local civil rights movement even as the leaders of the already integrated folksinging group decided to delay efforts to desegregate Threadgill's bar. But the central aspect of honky-tonk culture adopted by these students was the active use of musical practice to represent the meaning of being a young person coming to terms with the dominant culture in Austin, Texas.[3]

Throughout the sixties, young members of a growing middle class of (mostly) white Texans moved to its capital. These young people came from newly urbanized families, with their lives only recently reorganized around the rational rhythms of time-work discipline and marketplace competition. In the midst of their adolescent searching for the meaning of being young Anglo-Texans, in the process of constructing identities for themselves out of the elements of popular culture available to them, they found that the tradition of honky-tonk culture provided the conditions and the methods for an active and pleasurable critique of these organizing structures. The "Austin tendency to group the way they do"—to gather together in nightclubs to listen, dance, and drink while their friends played guitars and sang—developed in new ways as the young people of Texas adapted elements of honky-tonk culture to their own purposes.[4]

Many members of this folksinging group became professional musicians. But the local meaning of their professionalism was not at all the image of the glib, smiling entertainer singing for the masses. In the late sixties and early seventies, turning to the life of a professional musician meant that a young person was willing to forego the competition in and the rewards of a demonized work world for a life "relatively free of hassle." Choosing to become a musician in Austin meant to reject the modernized, highly disciplined workplace and to insist on the validity and worth of spontaneously following one's own desires in a personal pursuit of pleasure. Through their use and transformation of this tradition, musicians like John Clay, Ed Guinn, and Powell St. John helped to construct an ideology of anticommercialism that insisted that the musical experience itself—the physical and psychic pleasures of identification and release that it produced—was of primary importance. In effect, the well-lived life was simply a life of music-making. By becoming musicians, young Texans could "not have to work"; they could free themselves from the discipline of capitalist work culture and achieve a more "natural" or "real" relation to the world around them.[5]

The key to achieving this more real relation to their cultural context was emotional sincerity. By insisting on the sincerity of their feelings and, therefore, the validity of their unspeakable desires, young, almost-professional musicians were able to critique the rigid structures of everyday life in their conservative state. Thus, an aesthetic of musical performance that prized recognizable signs of sincerity developed as the tradition of honky-tonk culture was progressively modernized. Throughout the early seventies, modernizing pressures on music-making in Austin grew more intense, even as the desires of young musicians to not have to work in the modernized workplace came increasingly to be expressed in their performance practice. Thus, this aesthetic developed a highly elaborated structure. When young musicians confronted the commercialized world of popular music performance with their desires to not have to work, the resulting contradictions were aesthetically resolved in a musical style that was emotionally very effective in live performance but remained resistant to the inscriptive process of recording.

During the seventies, members of the Austin Interchangeable Band could pride themselves on their ability to perform while intoxicated any song in any style with no rehearsal. This ability both increased their own local market value—enabling them to work with no notice for a variety of band leaders—and signified their dismissal of the importance of the labor market to musical performance. Their audiences could listen to them backing up Michael Murphey, Tanya Tucker, or Jerry Jeff Walker and interpret in their loose, mocking performances the rejection of the commercial role they were filling. Although they were musicians for hire with skills developed through catering to mainstream tastes in the more commercially oriented clubs in town, the Austin Interchangeable Band transformed the anticommercial ideology of Austin's folksingers into a performance style that emphasized intoxicated looseness, spontaneity, and a tongue-in-cheek attitude toward their own professional status. In the studio, this performance style and the attitude it represented were typically lost in any efforts to produce coherent and disciplined recorded music. Only on rare occasions, such as Walker's *Viva Terlingua*, could the contradictory meanings of this version of Austin's musical aesthetic be recorded.

These musicians, who performed the locally focused parody "I Just Wanna Be a Cosmic Cowboy" only to see that parody adopted as a theme song by their audience, had prefigured just such an ironic reversal in their own selective adoption of elements of honky-tonk culture in their modernized, commercialized musical practice. The transformation of the progressive country scene, from anticommercial presentation of the pastoral hymns of a premodern society, to the commercially oriented performance of aggressive "outlaw" masculinity, represented the return of what had been repressed within honky-tonk culture itself. Those elements that the folksingers had refused to acknowledge in honky-tonk culture—the easy violence, the ugliness of constant drinking, the sullen refusal to comprehend the complexities of modern life, the desire for a fast buck, the racism, the sexism—rose to the top as music-making in Austin left the liminal performance arena of the honky-tonk and entered the mainstream it had once critiqued. Once the progressive country affective alliance and the identities associated with it had been marketed beyond the liminal performance arena of the mid-Austin honky-tonk, the meanings of this identity were cut loose from their moorings. Drifting beyond the control of this original group, the selective refusal of elements of the honky-tonk culture could not be maintained. When radio disc jockeys promulgated a meaning of progressive country limited to the mass-culture celebration of Anglo-Texan roots as signified solely by the sweet sound of a steel guitar, the critical force of this musically projected identity had been eviscerated.

Although some musicians, fans, writers, and even club owners struggled into the late seventies to reinforce the original impetus and meanings of the progressive country alliance, the group originally attracted by the initial synthesis was no longer large enough to support economically the honky-tonk performance of an antimodern, anti-mass-culture critique of work. During the late sixties, "Everyone was making a living. We were musicians. No one had a day job; there was no need for day jobs." But by 1977, "You [could]n't find a band who [was] making it in Austin." Within the span of fifteen years, the bulk of the baby-boom bulge had moved through its college years. The first post-World War II generation, the first generation of Texans forced to come to terms with the state's urban and modern condition, had moved through and beyond the stage of adolescent identity construction. No longer was the undergraduate population at the University of Texas increasing with every year. Furthermore, even the more thoughtful and alienated of the new students that were matriculating were no longer so insistent on marking their difference from mass culture. They were more comfortable working within it, expressly using its terms and its methods to represent the meaning of their lives. These cultural changes exacerbated economic pressures on the structure of music-making in Austin, further estranging the concerns of musicians and club owners from the adolescent need of these young people to create their identities. The musical and performance style signs used by progressive country musicians to signify sincerity and anticommercialism were interpreted by these younger students as indicators of commercial and ideological dominance. Instead of suggesting a refusal of the constraints of commercial musical practice, the ubiquity of the Austin Interchangeable Band merely represented control of the local musical marketplace. The music itself could not be sincerely performed by the younger musicians, and the identities it offered could not be sincerely incorporated. Progressive country was no longer a way to actively negotiate adolescent identities.[6]

But the use of musical performance as the signifying practice at the center of a process of identity construction, situated in the liminal honky-tonk arena and critical of the structures of modern society, survived as an active tradition beyond the collapse of progressive country. By 1978, Austin was unquestionably "where the music was" in Texas, and young Texans attracted by the physical and psychic pleasures of musicalized experience continued to move to the capital despite the fact that the city's most well-known musical style did not speak to them. The

School of Communications at the University of Texas drew students interested in the power of electronic media to influence the meaning of everyday life. A style of music that had been developed in the urban centers of the United States and Great Britain—a punk rock that used simplified musical forms to explode and exploit the contradictions at the heart of the commercialized society of the spectacle—appealed both to the younger musicians in Austin who felt isolated by progressive country's musical virtuosity and to the media students, who were fascinated by this spectacle and at the same time wanted to control it, to manipulate rather than be manipulated by it.[7]

Much as the national trend of folksinging took on a specific local shape in Austin, so did the international trend of punk rock. Both of these styles emphasized the mutuality of musical production, using simple song forms that required little musical training and a performance style that blurred the musician/audience distinction. Both styles insisted on the importance of musical practice as a means of differentiating among college students. Both were selectively amalgamated with the older honky-tonk tradition in a syncretization that continued to emphasize the display and critique of modern life in an active, intensified, sexualized fashion. By means of this amalgamation, punk rock in Austin took on many of the themes and forms of the romantic honky-tonk critique of modernity, even as it strove to confront and contradict the expectations of its audience in a storm of negativity.

In Austin, "good music" had always been defined through an aesthetic based in performance, had traditionally been locally focused, and had dealt with issues of concern to young people growing up in Texas. The Huns' "Glad He's Dead" was good music in the same way that "Desperados Waiting for a Train" had been good music ten years before, and in the same way that "Wild Side of Life" had been good music for a previous generation. All three songs addressed the problem of coming to terms with the dominant meanings (promulgated by popular culture) of life as a working- or middle-class, white, (usually) male Texan, and the difficulties of constructing an identity within those boundaries. The greater fascination of punk rock with the images and processes of mass culture—the appearance of characters from television programs in local punk songs, the audience's requests for hated "popular" songs, the eagerness with which bands like the Huns sought any sort of publicity—indicated the greater influence of mass culture in the everyday struggle to create adolescent identity.

Outside of Austin, punk rock was a critique of corporate capitalism that blended a musical aesthetic with an incomplete political philosophy. Through its radical rejection of the mainstream rock music sold by the major record companies, punk rock magnified an adolescent anger that derived from the insight that the world was not as it should be and then laid the blame for this discrepancy at the feet of those corporations. Because of the importance of musical practice in the formation of adolescent identities, the perceived aesthetic quality of rock'n'roll music and the perceived quality of the identities projected by that music became the standard by which to judge the cultural politics of any individual or institution. The "future of rebellion in this country" was believed to be determined by the marketplace performance of "half a dozen new good bands."[8]

Small, independent record companies led the way in the recording of American punk rock, and these recordings were distributed through independent channels that delivered their products to specialty record stores catering to the serious rock'n'roll fan. Fans of punk rock believed these businesses were concerned with the spread of "good music" and, therefore, of good politics. As Simon Frith said, a sort of "small is beautiful" ideology developed that encouraged the entrance of young entrepreneurs into a diverse variety of music-related businesses. By taking over roles in the system of commodity production and distribution, fans of punk rock believed that they could guarantee the production and distribution of "good music." And good music was experientially defined simply as that music which projected a set of incomplete identities with which these fans could pleasurably identify.[9]

When punk rock took root in Austin clubs that had not previously presented youth-oriented music, it invited the participation of many who had felt excluded from the entrenched progressive country music support systems. The openness signified by the simple musical form, and the ideology of independence from previously existing businesses that was associated with this form, encouraged those who wanted "to participate in the whole cultural process." Since the production of music in Austin was undeniably a commercial affair, the "whole cultural process" included a wide range of entrepreneurial opportunities, each of which was rapidly filled by individuals who wanted both to guarantee the spread of "good music" and to "make a living in the music business."[10]

In Austin, this do-it-yourself ideology of punk rock blended with the populist tradition of the small, independent, local farmer battling the impersonal structures of national corporations. And the critique of the modernized workplace that had long been one of the chief foci of local music-making melded with the anticorporate ideology of punk.

The belief held by many of Austin's musicians and members of its hip community in the late sixties and early seventies that the well-lived life was one devoted to the pleasurable expression of one's desires in the experience of musical performance resurfaced in a slightly different form. Rather than offering the possibility of not having to work, the commercial conditions of musical performance offered the opportunity to "make it" in the music business. Although the goal was the same—to develop a way of living and working free from artificial barriers and responsive to the spontaneous expressions of desire—the pursuit of this goal was now restricted. The practice of music-making in Austin was now seen as a business. Like any other business in Texas, it could make you very rich, very quickly. Only by becoming very rich within the operations of various music businesses, and, particularly, within the highly profitable national recording industry, could the goal be achieved of a life relatively free of hassle. The difference between boom and bust was a matter of luck and the market value of one's tastes. Therefore, "There's a lot that are doing it, and doing without, to be able to be in the business." [11]

The first steps taken by these enthusiastic entrepreneurs entered them into the already-existing structures of the honky-tonk economy. Clubs like the Soap Creek and the Armadillo, personal managers like Carlyne Majer, and weekly papers like the *Sun* offered the models for music-related businesses. Music fans who wanted to participate in the cultural process of constructing adolescent identities within the context of a musicalized critique of social structures found that they could become club managers, band managers, or writers. The first group of music support personnel associated with punk rock at Raul's took on just these roles. Roland Swenson became the manager of the Standing Waves; Louis Meyers began to book Liberty Lunch and the Continental Club; Louis Black and Nick Barbaro started the *Austin Chronicle*.

As musical practice in Austin became industrialized, it no longer featured an emotionally powerful antimodern critique of work that could be experienced through the identities projected in performance. Instead, it incorporated into its methods and images the ideology of the Texan entrepreneur. As the structure of music-making in Austin shifted its base from the honky-tonk economy to the complex, fragmented, yet interactive music industry, a pattern developed in the interpersonal relationships of those working in this new industry. Even as these personally based business relationships continued to operate by the deepest values espoused by musical practice in Austin, sincerity and the desire for a life relatively free of hassle, they socially enforced an entrepreneurial attitude that soon permeated all aspects of participation in the industry. Music-making in Austin had become the means for a larger group of people to make a living. Their sincere concern with spreading good music blended easily with their sincere concern for their own economic well-being. Musicians themselves might continue to sing songs that attacked the profit motive, but they were forced to adopt a disciplined attitude toward their own work if they were to be allowed to advance through the industrial system of music-making enforced by local gatekeepers. The competitive practices and structures of the recording industry imposed a specific discipline both on the performances of the musicians and on anyone identifying with the wish to "make it."

It took ten years for the national trend of folksinging to become effectively integrated into local musical traditions and to create the nationally famous musical style of progressive country. The integration of punk rock into Austin musical culture took five years. The music of the New Sincerity bands, an amalgamation of punk with country and blues roots, organized around a traditional aesthetic of sincerity in songwriting and performance, rose to national awareness more quickly, at least partially because of the promotional efforts of this growing group of music business people. The members of this larger group saw their individual self-interest served through the mutual promotion of Austin music. Thus, the industrialization of music-making in Austin developed as an apparently natural outgrowth of the welding of punk's do-it-yourself ideology onto the already-existing core beliefs of local musical performance, materially sustaining the practice of local music-making while shifting its meaning. The experience and the aspirations of musical performance turned from "playing music" and "not having to work" to "making it easier for other people to like it" and "being in business for yourself and making a living at it." [12]

Nevertheless, within these more complex and interactive economic structures of industrialized music-making, where live musical performance has become research for the production of cultural commodities, the practice of adolescent identity construction continues. Musicians still seek to project incomplete identities through performing more— more than they can sing, more than they can play, more than they can know—and the magical show is still evidenced by "the chills"—those moments when the audience re-cognizes and re-turns that identity in their affective gestures of response.

Because of its power to unify body and mind in a physical experience of promise and excess, musical practice acts as a structured process of subject production. The musicalized experience itself is produced by the processes of identification described by psychoanalysis, by means of those aspects of sound that, moving at the edge of noise, just escape codifying structures, and result in an experience of excess, a promise of more. Through her or his active longing for completion, the adolescent of every age makes an intuitive leap beyond the information given in any musical performance, selecting and collecting particular elements of rhythm, pitch, harmony, noise, and linguistically encoded ideology with the unconscious precision of desire. Through the necessary mis-recognition of a yearning Imaginary, these elements are re-cognized and re-turned back to the musicians in a mutual performance of collective identity. It is just these moments of completion, of transformation, that render musicalized experience meaningful. The music never means in and of itself, but only as a means for this mutual projection and intro-jection.

Participants in any scene recognize this experience as the basis of musical pleasure. In Austin, the pleasure of identification with a musi-cally projected identity has been most closely associated with performed sincerity. Sincerity lies at the basis of the formation of bands, the com-position of the group's songs, the performance of its material, and the identity it projects. Sincerity, too, is why these projected identities are so immediately incorporated into the subjective experiences of the partici-pants in the scene. The psychoanalytic processes of adolescent identity formation and the resulting aesthetic value of sincerity are responsible for both the radical potential of commercial popular musical practice and its susceptibility to dominant ideologies.

In Texas, the collective impetus of any community formed through musical practice is undermined by an intense focus on individual plea-sure and individual gain. Such a community can only be understood as a conglomeration of individuals. Thus, the industrialization of music-making in Austin was achieved with a minimum of struggle. There were no positions available from which to counter the economic arguments of the pro-industry forces. So long as the goal of even the most sincerely committed music fans and the musicians themselves remained focused on the increased distribution of "good music," there could be no prin-cipled objection to the replacement of the failing honky-tonk economy by the industrialization of local music.

The basis on which good music in Austin was traditionally evalu-ated was an aesthetic of performance that acknowledged the power of musicalized experience in the production of adolescent identities. Music abstracted from the conditions of that experience—that is, recorded in a studio and sold to a record company where it becomes a commodity competitively exchanged—is no longer susceptible to such an aesthetic.

The aesthetic simply becomes a precondition for the production of the commodity. The abstraction of a commodity out of this collective experience represents the reification of identificatory pleasure divorced from the contexts that produce that pleasure. Thus, the physical-psychic powers of music encoded on recordings simply open the listening subject to an interplay between the projected image sonically encoded on the disc and the structuring forces dominant in her or his everyday life. These two fields intersect in the fetish of the recording itself, which stands in as a symptom of the competitive fires of capitalism. When the goal of musicalized experience is transformed from the antimodern critique of not having to work, to the postmodern goal of making a living in the music business, the interpretive structures that shape identity formation have been dramatically changed.[13]

Music-making in Austin now focuses on recordings rather than live performance. Live performance is now treated as one aspect of a complex industry oriented to the production and circulation of commodities in the pursuit of wealth. The identity formation that takes place in musicalized experience within the remnants of the honky-tonk arena therefore tends toward a greater reproduction of this industrial structure and its concomitant ideologies. At the same time, however, there is always an excess produced through musicalized experience. This excess escapes the encoding structures of everyday life and represents the possibility for the return of the repressed, those elements of the human overlooked in the enforcement of industrial organization. In the inexpressible nature of collective musical pleasure can be found an implicit promise of something more, a potential that exceeds the competitive struggle for individual gain.

Because of its traditional setting in the honky-tonk arena and the residual power of that antimodern tradition, music-making in Austin still contains a possibility for the collective production of resistance. While the industrial production of musical commodities continues to rely upon the "research and development" that occurs in the clubs, musicalized experience and its potential for radical critique of everyday life through its creation of dissonant identities will still be produced. The utopian desire to transform the industrialized conditions of life in postmodern America will continue to be projected in the performance of popular music in Austin's nightclubs. And on the buses that carry Austin's workers to their daily battles within their own industrialized workplaces, music and the importance of musical practice will continue to stimulate conversations, providing means to cross the divisions within contemporary society, and possibilities of imagining new performances of identity.

Notes

Preface

1. Kim Longacre was a singer and guitarist in one of the more important Austin bands of the 1980s, the Reivers (originally Zeitgeist). She was sixteen when she moved with her family from Palo Alto, California, to Austin. This quote is from the first of several interviews I conducted with her, June 2, 1989.

2. Ernie Gammage had played in several bands in Austin throughout the 1970s and 1980s. In the mid-eighties he became involved in the effort to create the "infrastructure" of a "music industry" in Austin. At the time I interviewed him, July 13, 1990, he was president of the Austin Music Industry Council.

3. See George E. Marcus and Michael M. J. Fisher, *Anthropology as Cultural Critique: An Experimental Moment in the Human Sciences* (Chicago: University of Chicago Press, 1986).

4. By the term "cultural acts," I am expanding John Searle's notion of speech acts to encompass nonverbal, nontextual performances and artifacts. See his *Speech Acts: An Essay on the Philosophy of Language* (London: Cambridge University Press, 1969). The adjective "decentered," of course, empties Searle's speech actor—in sympathy with Derrida's critique ("Signature, Event, Context," *Glyph* 1 [1977]—but I will fill up this actor with fragments of surrounding interested speakers by the end of this book.

5. This too-brief discussion of some of the dilemmas posed by postmodern ethnography was prompted by the following: a talk by Michael Taussig, "On the Mimetic Faculty," delivered at a conference on "Cultural Studies Now and in the Future," University of Illinois, Urbana, April 5, 1990; Stephen A. Tyler, "Post-Modern Ethnography: From Document of the Occult to Occult Document," in James Clifford and George Marcus, eds., *Writing Culture: The Poetics and Politics of Ethnography* (Berkeley: University of California Press, 1986); and Clifford Geertz, "Blurred Genres: The Refiguration of Social Thought," in *Local Knowledge* (New York: Basic Books, 1983). I take the metaphor of culture as an interpretable web from Clifford Geertz, "Thick Description: Toward an Interpretive Theory of Culture," *The Interpretation of Cultures* (New York: Basic Books, 1973). The metaphor of muddling borders comes from Julia Kristeva, "Throes of Love: The Field of the Metaphor," *Tales of Love*, trans. Leon Roudiez (New York: Columbia University Press, 1987), 268.

6. John A. Lomax, *Cowboy Songs and other Frontier Ballads* (New York: Sturgis and Walton, 1910).

1. The Imaginary Tourist

1. A reality sandwich at the Hole in the Wall consists of a chicken fried steak patty covered with slices of jalapeño peppers, smothered with melted cheese, with mayonnaise and lettuce on a hamburger bun. If ordered extra-real, it comes with extra jalapeños. An unreality comes pepper-free.

2. Hilly Kristal operated a bar in the Bowery that featured country, bluegrass, and blues music (CBGB). In 1975, Tom Verlaine asked Kristal if his band, Television, could play one weeknight for the door. Kristal said yes, and the New York punk scene had a home.

3. The difference in local attitudes toward punk rock fans can be seen by comparing examples of rock journalism before and after the Raul's incident. See Sally Jones, "Hey Punk!" *Austin Sun*, December 2, 1977, pp. 23, 27; Carlyne Brady, "Sex Pistols in Austin," *Austin Sun*, January 20, 1978, p. 11; "Rock Club Raid Leads to Six Arrests," *Daily Texan*, September 20, 1978, p. 1; Jeff Whittington, "Punk Rock: Sure it's Noisy but is it Art?" *Images*, *Daily Texan*, October 2, 1978, p. 24. I will examine these and other articles in more detail in a later chapter.

4. The influence of both Cowboy and Richard Dorsett was described for me by Louis Black in an interview, September 17, 1990.

5. Jody Denberg describes the origins of Waterloo Records in "Austin Meets its Waterloo," *Austin Chronicle*, November 26, 1982, p. 8. The story of Geoff Cordner's relations with local musicians and his job at Sound Exchange (then Record Exchange) can be found in Lawrence Lee, "Wrestler Records," *Austin Chronicle*, September 26, 1986, p. 28.

6. Franklin's art has been discussed in many places. See Jan Reid, *The Improbable Rise of Redneck Rock* (Austin: Heidelberg Publishers, 1974), pp. 47–65; Archie Green wrote a number of articles about poster art in Austin for his "Commercial Music Graphics" series in the *John Edwards Memorial Foundation Quarterly*. "Midnight and Other Cowboys," 11:39 (Autumn 1975); "Kerry Awn's Soap Creek Saloon Calendars," 16:57 (Spring 1980); "Michael Adams's Honky-Tonk Paintings," 18:67–68 (Fall/Winter 1982).

7. Jeff Nightbyrd described Gentle Thursdays for me in an interview on September 18, 1990. Steve Chaney described his participation in Arts and Sausages and contrasted it with the preachings of Sister Sarah in an interview on March 8, 1990.

8. This tale of the origin of Austin can be found in many local histories. See T. R. Fehrenbach, *Lone Star: A History of Texas and the Texans* (New York: Collier Books, 1968, 1985), pp. 259–60; Anthony Orum, *Power, Money and the People: The Making of Modern Austin* (Austin: Texas Monthly Press, 1987), pp. 1–2. See also Writers' Program of the Works Project Administration in the State of Texas, *Texas: A Guide to the Lone Star State* (New York: Hastings House Publishers, 1940), p. 169.

9. Orum, *Power*, p. xiii.

10. Writers' Program of the WPA, p. 171. Fehrenbach, in his inimitable, enlightened, and understanding way, attributes the antisecessionist votes in the counties around Austin to the high percentage of German farmers; *Lone Star*, p. 346.

11. Writers' Program of the WPA, pp. 170–71. Fehrenbach, *Lone Star*, p. 602.

12. Orum, *Power*, p. 30.

13. James Winton Bohmfalk, "The Austin Chamber of Commerce: A His-

tory of the Organization and its Uses of Propaganda," Masters thesis University of Texas at Austin, 1968, p. 19. Orum, *Power*, p. 15.

14. Orum, *Power*, pp. 37–57 & passim; Bohmfalk, "Austin Chamber," pp. 36–38.

15. Bohmfalk, "Austin Chamber," p. 24.

16. Ibid., p. 26.

17. Ibid., p. 27.

18. See Anonymous, "Groover's Paradise," *Time*, September 9, 1974; Jack Hurst, "The Pickin's Pickin' up in Austin," *Chicago Tribune*, Wednesday, March 31, 1976; Karen Thorsen, "Has Austin Upstaged Nashville?" *Oui* (January 1976): 77–78, 125–26; "queer-minded" is in Kaye Northcott, "The Life & Death of the Cosmic Cowboy," *Mother Jones* (June 1981): 14–21, 48. Many descriptions of the cultural significance of the music scene in the seventies in Austin draw on Jan Reid's evocation of different generations of Texans dancing together in the magical confines of the Armadillo. He first used the term "counter-culture concert hall" in *The Improbable Rise of Redneck Rock* (Austin: Heidelberg Publishers, 1974), p. 2.

19. For a discussion of the local origins of the progressive country style see Hugh Cullen Sparks, "Stylistic Development and Compositional Processes of Selected Solo Singer/Songwriters in Austin, Texas" Ph.D. diss., University of Texas at Austin, 1984.

20. See David Menconi, "Music, Media, and the Metropolis: The Case of Austin's Armadillo World Headquarters," Masters thesis, University of Texas at Austin, 1985, for a loving history of this institution. At the Armadillo's closing many eulogies appeared across Texas. Two examples are Ed Ward, "An Armadillo, So Survival-Minded, Succumbs," *Austin American Statesman*, August 26, 1980, p. C5; and Pete Oppel, "The Armadillo: An Old Acquaintance Not to Be Forgot," *Dallas Morning News*, December 31, 1980.

21. This story has been told over and over again in journalistic and scholarly accounts of the Austin music scene. The best version, because the most personal, is in Reid, *The Improbable Rise*. Other versions can be found in Archie Green, "Austin's Cosmic Cowboys," in Richard Bauman and Roger Abrahams, eds., *And Other Neighborly Names: Social Process and Cultural Image in Texas Folklore* (Austin: University of Texas Press, 1981); Bill Malone, *Country Music U.S.A.*, rev. ed. (Austin: University of Texas Press, 1985), pp. 396–98; see also Northcott, "Life & Death"; Thorsen "Has Austin Upstaged Nashville?"; and Hurst, "The Pickin's."

22. For descriptions of the origins of the Opera House see Louis Black, "Tim O'Connor and the Austin Opera House," *Austin Chronicle*, May 29, 1987, pp. 22–23; John T. Davis, "10 Years of fun and games, wet stages, dry humor, good times, bad times at the Opera House," *Austin American-Statesman*, June 5, 1987, pp. B1, B13. Coretta Taylor reports the negotiations between Austin Community College and the Opera House in "Orchestrating a Move," *Austin American-Statesman*, June 14, 1990, Neighbor Section, pp. 1, 3.

23. R. U. Steinberg and John Slate, "East Austin: A Planned Community?" *Austin Chronicle*, December 9, 1988, p. 16.

24. Orum, *Power*, p. 16.

25. Quoted in Steinberg and Slate, "East Austin."

26. Writers' Program of WPA, pp. 174–75.

27. City plan quoted in Orum, *Power*, pp. 175–76.

28. Ibid., p. 176.

29. Writers' Program of the WPA, p. 168.

30. For a detailed description of the development of rural blues in the cotton fields of Texas see William Barlow, *Looking Up at Down: The Emergence of Blues Culture* (Philadelphia: Temple University Press, 1989), pp. 56–78. Little history has been done on the blues activity in East Austin before the immigration of white blues musicians from Dallas in the 1960s. Tary Owens has produced an ethnographic video about contemporary black blues performance in East Austin.

31. Steinberg and Slate, "East Austin," p. 16.

32. Kevin Whitley, interviews with the author, March 13, 1990, and September 13, 1990.

33. See Sparks, "Stylistic Development," pp. 27, 37–39.

34. Enrollment figures were obtained from the Office for Institutional Studies at the University of Texas at Austin.

35. Club listings from the *Austin Sun*, May 1, 1975, and May 28, 1976.

36. Dowell Myers, et al., "Quality of Life: Austin Trends 1970–1990," Research Report by the Community and Regional Planning Program, University of Texas at Austin, June 1984, p. 34.

37. Ibid., p. 16.

38. Kelly and Rita are fans I met and talked to at a Reivers show, March 2, 1990. I interviewed Josh Ellinger, a fan of the Reivers and other Austin bands, on March 12, 1990.

39. Kim Longacre, from an interview with the author, June 2, 1989.

40. John Croslin, interview with the author, June 1, 1989.

2. Constructing the Musicalized Performance of Texan Identity

1. John A. Lomax, *Cowboy Songs and other Frontier Ballads* (New York: Sturgis and Walton, 1910). Page numbers for further citations will be given in the text.

2. John A. Lomax, *Adventures of a Ballad Hunter* (New York: Macmillan Co., 1947). "The letters G.T.T. were applied in connection with those who had 'Gone to Texas' to escape justice" (Federal Writers Project of the Works Project Administration in the State of Texas, *Texas: A Guide to the Lone Star State* [New York: Hastings House Publishers, 1940], pp. 39–40).

3. "Introduction" to Helen Child Sargent and George Lyman Kittredge, eds., *English and Scottish Popular Ballads* (Boston: Houghton Mifflin Co., 1904 and 1932) pp. xi–xxxi. Page numbers for further citations will be given in the text.

4. See Gene Bluestein, *The Voice of the Folk* (Amherst: University of Massachusetts Press, 1972, pp. 1–15. Also see Eric Hobsbawm and Terry Ranger, eds., *The Invention of Tradition* (Cambridge: Cambridge University Press, 1983).

5. John A. Lomax *Cowboy Songs and Other Frontier Ballads, 3d ed.* (New York: Macmillan Co., 1938), p. xviii; Bluestein, *Voice*, especially pp. 91–116; Lomax 1910, p. xxvii.

6. Lomax, *Adventures*, p. 58. In 1921, N. Howard (Jack) Thorpe published *Songs of the Cowboys* (Boston and New York: Houghton Mifflin Co., 1921), an expansion of a 1908 chapbook of cowboy songs Thorpe had either written or collected. In this book, Thorpe says that "Sam Bass" was written in 1879 by John Denton of Gainsville, Texas; p. 135.

7. Joseph G. McCoy, *Historic Sketches of the Cattle Trade of the West and Southwest* (Kansas City: Ramsey, Millett and Hudson, 1874; reprint, Readex Microprint, 1966). Despite an explicit romanticism, McCoy's sketches were treated as

more authentic descriptions of life in the cattle trade than was found in popular melodramas or dime novels.

8. According to G. Malcom Laws, "American ballads leave relatively little to the imagination. They are explicit and detailed, often tiresomely so." *Native American Balladry: A Descriptive Study and a Bibliographical Syllabus* (Philadelphia: The American Folklore Society, 1964), p. 13. Lomax 1910, p. 152.

9. I surveyed several collections of cowboy songs that were published between 1910 and 1935. The text of "Sam Bass" remains remarkably consistent. See Jules Verne Allen, *Cowboy Lore* (San Antonio: Naylor Printing Company, 1933); Margaret Larkin, *Singing Cowboys: A Book of Western Songs* (New York: Alfred A. Knopf, 1931); Kenneth S. Clark, *The Cowboy Sings Songs of the Ranch and Range* (New York: Paull-Pioneer Music Corporation, 1932); and Thorpe, *Songs of the Cowboys*. Lomax's text for "Sam Bass" does not change throughout the various editions of *Cowboy Songs*.

10. John A. Lomax, *Cowboy Songs and Other Frontier Ballads* (New York: Sturgis and Walton, 1916). This edition expands the original publication by ninety pages, including forty-one additional song texts.

11. The history of this song, and its variations, deserve some serious research. Of the collections I surveyed, it appears in Larkin, *Singing Cowboys*, Allen, *Cowboy Lore*, and Clark, *The Cowboy Sings*. It was clearly a part of the cowboy repertoire by the 1930s. While these published versions agree on the general story as well as in the specific details on which I will focus, they vary as to the amount of detail, the clarity of the narrative, and the name of the heroine. In Lomax's 1910 collection, she is named Varo. This name also appears in Allen's collection. Larkin, Clark, and the 1938 Lomax edition all call the daughter Lenore, which enables multiple rhymes with "before" and "anymore." The 1938 Lomax version contains the most cinematic narrative. Lomax credits a "cowboy on the Curve T Ranch" with writing the song. One can only assume that this accreditation is intended to legitimate the many changes that appear between the version of "Utah Carroll" published in the 1916 collection and the later, more spectacular version. Eventually, John Lomax and his son, Alan, registered a copyright to this song. Some scholars have detected a commercial taint to its verses, insisting that "Utah Carroll" (or "Utah Carl" as it is otherwise known) is a pop song, not a true folk ballad. Such a distinction is irrelevant for my purposes. However the song entered the cowboy tradition, "Utah Carroll" became part of the body of songs that cowboy singers sang.

12. John A. Lomax, *Songs of the Cattle Trail and Cow Camp* (New York: Macmillan Co., 1919), p. xi.

13. Allen, *Cowboy Lore*, p. 63. The announcement of copyright to the title of "original singing cowboy" is on p. viii.

14. The words for "Punchin' the Dough" came from a cowboy poem by Henry Hervert Knibb. According to Allen, "This song has been recorded on Victor Records with permission of the author of the poem. Music by Jules Verne Allen. All rights reserved." *Cowboy Lore*, p. 100.

15. Eric Hobsbawm, "Introduction: Invented Traditions," in Hobsbawm and Ranger, *Invention*, pp. 1, 9.

16. John I. White, *Git Along Little Dogies: Songs and Songmakers of the American West* (Urbana: University of Illinois Press, 1975), p. 189.

17. It is interesting to read Lomax's justification of Fox's copyright (*Adventures*, pp. 61–63). Lomax first heard the song in San Antonio, when it was sung to him by a "Negro saloonkeeper." He recorded this version on a wax cylinder, and the melody was transcribed from the cylinder by Henry Leberman, a music

teacher at the Austin State School for the Blind. Lomax reasoned that since Fox learned the song directly from Lomax's collection, using the melody Lomax learned from the African-American singer, clearly the copyright belonged to Fox. As a member of the "throng," Lomax's source was never considered to be the legitimate author of this cowboy song. Oscar Brand traces "Home on the Range" to Dr. Brewster Higley and Daniel E. Kelley. Originally entitled "My Western Home," the song was composed by the two Kansas neighbors in 1873. Brand refers to it dismissively as a "folk-type song." *The Ballad Mongers: Rise of the Modern Folk Song* (New York: Funk & Wagnalls, 1962), p. 13.

18. Bill Malone, *American Music, Southern Music* (Lexington: University of Kentucky Press, 1979), p. 33. This story is also told in Archie Green, "Dobie's Cowboy Friends," *John Edwards Memorial Foundation Quarterly* 12, no. 41 (1976): 21–29.

19. David Rothel, *The Singing Cowboys* (San Diego and New York: A. S. Barnes and Co., 1978), p. 83.

20. J. Brooks Atkinson, *New York Times*, January 28, 1931. Phillip Hale wrote in the *Boston Herald*, December 9, 1930, that the play was too vulgar.

21. "Folk-play" and "authentic songs . . ." from Richard Dana Skinner, "The Drama," *Commonweal*, February 11, 1931, pp. 414–15; "ensemble . . ." from H. C. P., "The Guild, a Folk Play and Acting," *The Boston Evening Transcript*, December 9, 1930.

22. Arthur Chapman, "Pitchfork Replaces Spur in West of Guild's 'Green Grow the Lilacs,'" *New York Herald Tribune*, March 1, 1931. How far had they gone, anyway, ten blocks?

23. Franklin Jordan, "No: These Cowboys of 'Green Grow the Lilacs' Were Not Shy . . . ," *The Boston Evening Transcript*, December 13, 1930.

24. Larkin, *Singing Cowboys*, p. xiii.

25. Rothel, *The Singing Cowboys*, p. 83.

26. The best discussion of the Hollywood singing cowboys can be found in Douglas B. Green, "The Singing Cowboy: An American Dream," *Journal of Country Music* 7, no. 2 (1978): 4–59.

27. Bill Malone, *Country Music, U.S.A.*, rev. ed. (Austin: University of Texas Press, 1985), p. 151.

28. Green, "Dobie's Cowboy Friends," pp. 21–29. Also, Larry Willoughby, *Texas Rhythm, Texas Rhyme* (Austin: Texas Monthly Press, 1984), pp. 29–30.

29. However, it would not be long before women adopted the cowgirl image and projected it in popular song. The most powerful early statement of a woman's right to the freedom and equality of the cowboy can be found in the work of Patsy Montana. Listen to "I Wanna Be a Cowboy's Sweetheart" (1935). Robert Oermann and Mary Bufwack argue that this song represents "a woman's desire for independence in the rugged outdoor life of a cowhand." See "Patsy Montana and the Development of the Cowgirl Image," *Journal of Country Music* 8, no. 3 (1981): 18–32.

30. One good place to begin reading about blues in Texas is Samuel Charters, *The Country Blues* (New York: Rinehart, 1959). Another excellent source is William Barlow, *Looking Up at Down: The Emergence of Blues Culture* (Philadelphia: Temple University Press, 1989). Manuel Pena discusses orquesta music in *Tex-Mex Conjunto: the History of a Working-Class Music* (Austin: University of Texas Press, 1985). Clinton Machann discusses the interplay of traditional Czechoslovakian musics with country and western music in central Texas in "Country-Western and the 'Now' Sound in Texas-Czech Polka Music," *John Edwards Memorial Foundation Quarterly* 19, no. 69 (1981): 3–7.

31. The classic biography of Jimmie Rodgers is by Nolan Porterfield, *Jimmie*

Rodgers: The Life and Times of America's Blue Yodeler (Urbana: University of Illinois Press, 1979).

32. Peter Guralnick, "Ernest Tubb, the Texas Troubadour," *Lost Highway: Journeys and Arrivals of American Musicians* (New York: Vintage, 1982; orig. 1979), p. 27.

33. Tubb quoted in Ibid., p. 31.

34. Townsend Miller, "Ernest Tubb," in Bill Malone and Judith McCulloh, eds., *Stars of Country Music* (Urbana: University of Illinois Press, 1975), pp. 222–36.

35. Guralnick, "Ernest Tubb," p. 35.

36. Bill Malone has written extensively on the development of honky-tonk culture. See his "Honky-Tonk: the Music of the Southern Working Class," in William Ferris and Mary Hart, eds., *Folk Music and Modern Sound* (Jackson: University Press of Mississippi, 1982), pp. 119–29. A condensed version of his points can be found in the revised edition of Malone, *Country Music*, pp. 153–55.

37. In this discussion I am using the word "element" in a very abstract way. It does not necessarily refer to a thing or to an individual, although things and individuals can momentarily embody or symbolize these elements. See Raymond Williams's discussion of "Dominant, Residual, and Emergent" cultural forms in *Marxism and Literature* (Oxford and New York: Oxford University Press, 1977), pp. 121–27.

38. McCoy, *Historic Sketches*, p. 138.

39. The carnival tradition has been documented by many popular culture historians, critics, and folklorists. Some of the better books are Mikhail Bakhtin, *Rabelais and His World*, trans. Helene Iswolsky (Bloomington: Indiana University Press, 1984; orig. 1968); Peter Burke, *Popular Culture in Early Modern Europe* (New York: Harper & Row, 1978); Barbara Babcock, ed., *The Reversible World* (Ithaca and London: Cornell University Press, 1978); and Alessandro Falassi, ed., *Time out of Time: Essays on the Festival* (Albuquerque: New Mexico Press, 1987). Beverly Stoeltje provides an excellent discussion of the rodeo as cowboy festival in "Riding, Roping, and Reunion: Cowboy Festival," in the Falassi volume.

40. Malone, *Country Music*, 154–55.

41. William Warren and Arlie A. Carter, "The Wild Side of Life," Capitol Records (1951). Thompson was not the first to record this song, but his version was by far the most popular. Thompson was a radio performer from Waco, Texas. His recording career took off after the success of "Wild Side of Life."

42. This song was written by a man, J. D. Miller, as an effort to capitalize on the success of Thompson's record. Wells recorded it for Decca in May 1952. Kitty Wells was from Tennessee. She sang in bands with her husband for years, demurely performing her many hits.

3. Desperados Waiting for a Train

1. T. R. Fehrenbach, *Lone Star: A History of Texas and the Texans*, 2d ed. (New York: Collier Books, 1985), pp. 635–36, 650. Anonymous, *Austin American*, September 18, 1933, p. 1.

2. Anonymous, *Austin American*, October 3, 1933, p. 1.

3. Bill Malone, *Country Music U.S.A.*, rev. ed. (Austin: University of Texas Press, 1985), p. 393; Jan Reid, *The Improbable Rise of Redneck Rock* (Austin: Heidelberg Publishers, 1974), p. 16.

4. Myra Friedman, *Buried Alive: The Biography of Janis Joplin* (New York: Bantam Books, 1974), p. 44.

5. Reid, *The Improbable Rise*, p. 27; Bill Malone, personal communication, Spring 1991.

6. Malone, ibid. The hills surrounding Austin were covered with cedar trees. The wood of these trees was valued for its resistance to insect damage. While chopping cedar trees was particularly dirty and hard work (especially in the summertime), the regular demand for the wood usually guaranteed a living wage.

7. Tary Owens, interview with the author, December 18, 1990; Malone, ibid. Everyone who spoke to me or wrote to me about Kenneth Threadgill referred to him as Mister Threadgill. He was clearly the central figure, and his patriarchal authority grew as the performers and audiences at his bar grew younger.

8. Roger Abrahams, interview with the author, August 1990. Oscar Brand, *The Ballad Mongers: Rise of the Modern Folk Song* (New York: Funk & Wagnalls, 1962), p. 54.

9. Clay, letter to the editor, *Rolling Stone*, April 13, 1972, p. 3.

10. Owens, interview; Jeff Nighbyrd, interview with the author, September 18, 1990.

11. Malone, personal communication, Spring 1991; Owens, interview.

12. Malone, *Country Music*, p. 394; Owens, interview.

13. Friedman, *Buried Alive*, pp. 42–55; Friedman gives Clay's opinion, which was supported by Owens when I interviewed him on December 18, 1990.

14. Ed Guinn, interview with the author, June 19, 1991.

15. Ibid.; Anonymous, "Longhorn Band Accepts Negro," *Daily Texan*, September 23, 1963, p. 1; Elaine Blodgett, "Ed Guinn," *Austin Chronicle*, August 15, 1986, p. 17.

16. Jeff Nighbyrd (né Shero), interview with the author, September 18, 1990; James Miller, *"Democracy is in the Streets"* (New York: Simon & Schuster, 1987), pp. 225–26; Owens, interview. There is some disagreement about which night the Folk Sing regularly took place. Owens remembers it as being Wednesday; Nightbyrd recalls that it took place on Thursdays. Others say that the club met on Sundays.

17. Owens, interview; Guinn, interview. Mance Lipscomb was the first African-American to enter and play music at Threadgill's, a few years after the incidents already described. By the time Threadgill's was integrated, Lightnin' Hopkins and Lipscomb, as well as other African-American musicians, had been hired by several downtown commercial clubs.

18. Owens, interview.

19. Owens, interview; Reid, *The Improbable Rise*, pp. 15–28. Later some of the original members of the Hoots dropped out, and the band was joined by Chuck Joyce, Julie Paul, and Cotton Collins. Over the years, the Hoots made forays into the folk festival circuit, playing shows in Rhode Island and Minnesota, but their first gigs outside of Threadgill's were at another, larger honky-tonk at the southern edge of town, the Split Rail.

20. Guinn, interview.

21. Ibid.

22. Ibid.; Reid, *The Improbable Rise*, pp. 34–35; Archie Green, "Midnight and Other Cowboys," *John Edwards Memorial Foundation Quarterly* 11, pt. 3, no. 39 (1975): 145.

23. John Clay found her "commercial." Jim Langdon called her "great." Both are quoted in Friedman, *Buried Alive*, p. 76.

24. Hugh Sparks, "Stylistic Development and Compositional Processes of

Selected Solo Singer/Songwriters in Austin, Texas," Ph.D. diss., University of Texas at Austin, 1984; Owens, interview.

25. Owens, interview; also Friedman, *Buried Alive*, p. 78.

26. See the liner notes for *The Psychedelic Sounds of the 13th Floor Elevators*; Owens, interview; Nightbyrd, interview; Reid, *The Improbable Rise*, pp. 33–34.

27. Sparks, "Stylistic Development," pp. 35–43; Jim Franklin, interview, March 11, 1993; Elaine Blodgett, "The Vulcan Gas Co.," *Austin Chronicle*, August 9, 1985; Guinn, interview.

28. Blodgett, ibid.; Reid, *The Improbable Rise*, pp. 35–41; Franklin, interview.

29. Ibid.

30. Reid, *The Improbable Rise*, pp. 47–52.

31. Ibid. The Conqueroo would have been a perfect choice for Armadillo Productions, but by 1970 they, too, had moved to California.

32. Wilson, quoted in Chet Flippo, "Texas Music Halls: 'Uncle Zeke's Rock Emporium,'" *Rolling Stone*, October 12, 1972, p. 18; Reid, *The Improbable Rise*, p. 49.

33. Flippo, ibid.; Reid, ibid., pp. 52–53; David Menconi, "Music, Media and the Metropolis: The Case of Austin's Armadillo World Headquarters," Masters thesis, University of Texas at Austin, 1985, pp. 62–64.

34. Menconi, ibid., pp. 62–64; Reid, ibid., pp. 50–53; Flippo, ibid.

35. Tolleson quoted in Menconi, ibid., p. 69; Chet Flippo, "Freddie King and His Heavy Blues," *Rolling Stone*, November 25, 1971, p. 16; Flippo, "Texas Music Halls"; Reid, ibid., pp. 53, 59–61.

36. Wilson quoted in Reid, ibid., p. 62; Flippo, "Texas Music Halls"; Menconi, "Music, Media and the Metropolis," pp. 73–75.

37. Eddie Wilson quoted in Flippo, ibid.

38. Mike Tolleson, telephone interview, July 12, 1990.

39. Reid, *The Improbable Rise*, pp. 69–71; Menconi, "Music, Media and the Metropolis," pp. 89–91.

40. Ed Ward, interview with Joe Gracey, 1978, quoted in Menconi, ibid., pp. 90–91, 119–20.

41. Flippo, "Texas Music Halls"; Willie Nelson with Bud Shrake, *Willie: An Autobiography* (New York: Pocket Books, 1989), p. 205; Tolleson, interview.

42. Reid, *The Improbable Rise*, pp. 5, 297.

43. Ibid., pp. 243–46; Green, "Midnight," p. 145.

44. Sparks, "Stylistic Development," pp. 52, 43.

45. Ibid., p. 51.

46. Reid, *The Improbable Rise*, pp. 260–64.

47. Guy Clark, "Desperados Waiting For a Train," Chappell Music, as performed by Jerry Jeff Walker, on *Viva Terlingua*, MCA (1974).

48. Green, "Midnight," p. 87.

49. Chet Flippo, "Scene or Mirage? Austin: The Hucksters Are Coming," *Rolling Stone*, April 11, 1974, p. 24.

50. Ibid.

4. The Collapse of the Progressive Country Alliance

1. L. E. McCullough, "Austin Music, 1985: The Everchanging Presence of the Past," *Austin Chronicle*, March 8, 1985, p. 10.

2. "Sun Readers' Poll: Austin's Top Bands," *Austin Sun*, February 26, 1976.

3. Paul Ray, "Letter to the Editor," *Austin Sun*, March 11, 1976.

4. Jeff Nightbyrd, "Cosmo Cowboys: Too Much Cowboy and not Enough Cosmic," *Austin Sun*, April 3, 1975, pp. 13, 19.

5. Nightbyrd pointed out one of the ready implications of this traditional identity, asking, "Who has heard of the Cosmic Cowgirl? . . . The cosmo scene consists of male tribalism. Women are relegated to spectators or hangers on." Ibid.

6. Nicholas R. Spitzer, "'Bob Wills is Still the King': Romantic Regionalism and Convergent Culture in Central Texas," *John Edwards Memorial Foundation Quarterly* 11, no. 40 (1975), pp. 191–96.

7. Nightbyrd, "Cosmo Cowboys," p. 13.

8. Jean-Francois Lyotard, *The Postmodern Condition: A Report on Knowledge*, trans. Geoff Bennington and Brian Massumi (Minneapolis: University of Minnesota Press, 1984); Jean Baudrillard, *The Ecstasy of Communication*, trans. Bernard and Caroline Schutze (New York: Semiotext(e), 1988); Fredric Jameson, *Postmodernism or, the Cultural Logic of Late Capitalism* (Durham: Duke University Press, 1991); George Lipsitz, *Time Passages: Collective Memory and American Popular Culture* (Minneapolis: University of Minnesota Press, 1990).

9. Craig Hillis of Moon-Hill Management, quoted in Eric Harrison, "Is Progressive Country Dying? Industry Leaders Argue Fate of Local Genre," *Daily Texan*, September 21, 1976.

10. Quoted in Billy Brammer, "Austin's Musical History Explored," *Austin Sun*, October 17, 1974.

11. Jan Reid, "Who Killed Redneck Rock?" *Texas Monthly*, December, 1976, p. 211.

12. Ibid., pp. 210, 211.

13. Ibid., p. 216.

14. Ibid., p. 213.

15. Larry Grossberg, "Another Boring Day in Paradise: Rock and Roll and the Empowerment of Everyday Life," *Popular Music* 4 (1984): 225–58.

16. Paul Congo, Martha Hartzog, and Tary Owens, prods., *A Texas Blues Reunion*, video, 1989.

17. Reid *The Improbable Rise*, p. 34. According to *A Texas Blues Reunion* (ibid.), Bill Campbell was the first white guitarist to play on the east side. However, Conqueroo was the first mixed band from the west side that was hired to play in East Austin.

18. "Exchange" is, perhaps, too positive a term for it. No African-American musicians from East Austin currently share the commercial success of the Anglo-Americans who participated in this "exchange." While the T-Birds and Stevie Ray Vaughan win gold records, W. C. Clark and Blues Boy Hubbard still struggle for gigs throughout central Texas.

19. Carlyne Majer, interview with the author, September 14, 1990. Paul Ray, "Paul Ray and the Cobras: A Brief History," *Austin Chronicle*, December 19, 1986, p. 23.

20. Majer, ibid.

21. Ibid.

22. Reid, *The Improbable Rise*, p. 10.

23. Michael Ventura, "Marcia Ball: Portrait of a Professional," *Austin Sun*, May 27, 1977, pp. 12–13, 20.

24. Louis Black, interview with the author, September 17, 1990.

25. Steve Chaney, interview with the author, March 8, 1990.

26. Ray, "Paul Ray and the Cobras."

27. Quoted in Bill Bentley, "The Vaughans—Mainline Blues," *Austin Sun*, April 28, 1978, p. W2; quoted in Michael Corcoran, "Stevie Ray Vaughan:

Straight From the Heart," *Austin Chronicle*, May 15, 1987, p. 18; Ray, "Paul Ray and the Cobras."

28. Bill Malone, *Country Music U.S.A.*, rev. ed. (Austin: University of Texas Press, 1985), pp. 397, 404.

29. The balance sheets of shows that have been stored in the Archives of the Armadillo World Headquarter at the Eugene C. Barker Texas History Center contain numerous arithmetic errors. Mike Tolleson will still talk about the Armadillo as an Arts Laboratory intended to spark a cultural renaissance in central Texas.

30. Eddie Wilson, quoted in David Menconi, "Music, Media and the Metropolis: The Case of Austin's Armadillo World Headquarters," Masters thesis, University of Texas at Austin, 1985, p. 132. Original date of the Associated Press interview, June 26, 1974. Interior Memo of Armadillo Productions, Armadillo Archives, Barker Texas History Center.

31. "Financial Summary of 1976 Birthday Party, as of 8/17/76," Armadillo Archives, Barker Texas History Center.

32. Robert Hadley, "Stormy Weather for the Armadillo," *Austin Sun*, November 12, 1976, p. 13. Clifford Endres, "Near Truths: Armadillo Rebounds," *Austin Sun*, January 14, 1977, p. 3.

33. Hank Alrich, quoted in Hadley, ibid.

34. Ramsey Wiggins, "Shoot-Out at the Box Office," *Austin Sun*, November 12, 1976, p. 7.

35. See Richard Dyer, "In Defense of Disco," in Simon Frith and Andrew Goodwin, eds., *On Record: Rock, Pop and the Written Word* (New York: Pantheon Books, 1990). Dyer discusses disco in terms of a gay culture. In Austin, the growing gay community did adopt some elements of the disco culture, especially the growing eroticism in dancing and an affinity for the complex rhythms coming out of New York City, which slowly made their way into the rock'n'roll scene during the mideighties.

36. Wiggins, "Shoot-Out."

37. Quoted in Carlene Brady, "The End of Live Music? Not With a Bump, But a Hustle," *Austin Sun*, November 12, 1976, p. 7. The concept of the professional-managerial class was first worked out by Barbara and John Ehrenreich in "The Professional-Managerial Class," in Pat Walker, ed., *Between Labor and Capital* (Boston: South End Press, 1970), pp. 5–45. Fred Pfeil first related the PMC to specific pleasures in pop music in "Making Flippy-Floppy: Postmodernism and the Baby-Boom PMC," in M. Davis, et al., eds., *The Year Left: An American Socialist Yearbook* (London: Verso, 1985), pp. 263–95.

38. Simon Frith, *South Effects: Youth, Leisure and the Politics of Rock'n'Roll* (New York: Pantheon Books, 1981), pp. 244, 246.

39. Brady, "The End of Live Music?"; John Moore, "The Embattled Rabbit: Will Disco Spoil Eddie Wilson?" *Austin Sun*, May 19, 1978, pp. 8–10. It might be worthwhile to point out that discos in the South and the Midwest did not restrict their playlist to those songs most closely identified with the disco musical genre. It was not unusual to hear songs by Bob Seeger or Pink Floyd booming over the sound system in any disco in the middle of the country.

40. See H. Stith Bennett, *On Becoming a Rock Musician* (Amherst: University of Massachusetts Press, 1980), for a discussion of the process of learning and consistently performing other people's music.

41. Antone quoted in Dean Webb, "Antone's Venerable Venue Keeps the Blues Alive in Austin," *Images: Daily Texan*, July 18, 1988; advertisement for Antone's one year anniversary party, *Austin Sun*, May 14, 1976; Steve Chaney, interview with the author, March 8, 1990.

42. Mike Clark, "Antone Brings the Blues to Austin and the World," *Austin Business Journal*, July 9–15, 1990, pp. 7–8; Steve Wist, "The Howlers: Ne'r-do-wells Doin' Well," *Austin Sun*, April 29, 1977, pp. 9, 15; Wiggins, "Shoot-Out."

43. Bob Edwards, "Rockin' at the Rail," *Austin Sun*, March 18, 1977, p. 2; Anonymous, "Backstage: Joe Ely at the Split Rail," *Austin Sun*, May 28, 1976, p. 22.

44. Joe Nick Patoski described Alvin Crow's music as gut country, "pure country music that ain't been sanforized in Nashville," in "Alvin Crow: Gut Country," *Austin Sun*, October 17, 1974, p. 30; Ventura, "Marcia Ball," p. 12.

45. Clifford Endres, "Near Truths: Armadillo Rebounds," *Austin Sun*, January 14, 1977, p. 3; financial records, Armadillo Archives, Barker Texas History Center.

46. Majer, interview.

47. *Texas Sun*, January 28, 1977, p. 5.

48. "Sun Readers' Poll: Music Awards 1977," *Texas Sun*, March 25, 1977, p. 7.

49. Ventura, "Marcia Ball."

50. "Adios From Sir Doug," *Texas Sun*, August 3, 1977 (letter dated July 29, 1977); Majer, interview.

51. Quoted in Diana Potts, "Dog Days at the 'Dillo?'" *Texas Sun*, December 9, 1977, p. 17. The "bare minimum" number required to run Armadillo shows was derived from an examination of staff schedules and assignments in the Armadillo Archives, Barker Texas History Center. Alrich quoted from the same article.

52. Bobbie Bridger, "Rusty Wier," *River City Sun*, September 15, 1978, pp. 23–24.

53. For a discussion of the role of gatekeepers in culture industries see Paul Hirsch, "Processing Fads and Fashions: An Organization-Set Analysis of Cultural Industry Systems," *American Journal of Sociology* 77 (1972), reprinted in Frith and Goodwin, *On Record*. See also Frith's use of the gatekeeper concept in *Sound Effects*.

54. Chaney, interview.

55. Jeff Nightbyrd, interview with the author, September 18, 1990.

5. Punk Rock at Raul's

1. Lenny Kaye, liner notes to *Nuggets: Original Artyfacts from the First Psychedelic Era, 1965–1968*, Elektra Records 7E-2006 (1972).

2. Karen Rose, "Luck and Pluck: The Heartwarming Rise to Fame of Lenny Kaye," *Trouser Press* (June/July 1976): 27–29, 31.

3. Brock Altane, "The Ramones," *New York Rocker* 1, no. 1 (January 1976): 4. Cartoon vision . . . is Charles Shaar Murray writing for the English music paper *New Musical Express*, quoted in an ad for the Ramones' first album in *New York Rocker* 1, no. 3 (May 1976): 8. Cleanly conceptualized . . . is Robert Christgau writing for the *Village Voice* quoted in the same ad. Rock and roll formalists . . . is from Gene Scullati, "Ramones Leave Home," *New York Rocker* 1, no. 6 (March 1977): 7.

4. The connections between English punk rock and the Situationist International have been well documented. See Simon Frith, *Sound Effects: Youth, Leisure and the Politics of Rock'n'Roll* (New York: Pantheon Books, 1981); Simon Frith and Howard Horne, *Art into Pop* (New York and London: Methuen and Co., 1987); Paul Taylor, *Impressario: Malcolm McLaren and the British New Wave* (New York and Cambridge: New Museum of Contemporary Art and MIT Press,

1988); and Greil Marcus, *Lipstick Traces: A Secret History of the 20th Century* (Cambridge: Harvard University Press, 1989). In his film *The Great Rock'n'Roll Swindle*, McLaren stresses the musical ineptitude of the Sex Pistols, insisting that he deliberately chose incompetent players. In fact, Glen Matlock, Steve Jones, and Paul Cook were fine rock'n'roll musicians. With John Lydon as singer, they were a superior example of the Stooges, Slade, Dolls tradition. When McLaren fired Matlock and added Sid Vicious, the band's ability to play live dropped considerably. Frith, *Sound Effects*, p. 265.

5. The Contingent included Siouxsie and Steve Severin of Siouxsie and the Banshees, Billy Idol, and Sid Vicious, who soon replaced Glen Matlock as the Pistols' bass player. See Frith and Horne, *Art into Pop*, p. 127. The best history of the Sex Pistols is Jon Savage, *England's Dreaming: Punk Rock, Sex Pistols and Beyond* (New York: St. Martin's, 1992).

6. This legacy also limits the movement's effectiveness as the center of any progressive political program.

7. Dick Hebdige, *Subculture: The Meaning of Style* (New York and London: Methuen and Co., 1979), p. 102.

8. *Détournement*, an important strategy of the Situationists, is defined by Greil Marcus as the "theft of aesthetic artifacts from their contexts and their diversion into contexts of one's own devise" (*Lipstick Traces*, p. 168). In Black & Red's translation of *The Society of the Spectacle*, detournement is called "diversion" and is defined as "the opposite of quotation . . . a fragment torn from its context" (n. 208). Punk rock's failure to control the contexts of consumption undermined its attempt at *détournement*. The controversy over the dissemination of difficult tastes had been debated in the United States during the 1920s and the 1930s in what has been termed "the Book Club Wars." See Janice Radway, "The Scandal of the Middlebrow," *South Atlantic Quarterly* (Fall 1990). This contradiction still fires intense debates in the academic battles over the contents of the canon.

9. Tom Carson, "Ceremonies of the Horsemen," *New York Rocker* 1, no. 10 (Nov.-Dec. 1977): 43.

10. "The New Payola," *New York Rocker* 1, no. 6 (March 1977): 14–15.

11. Frith, *Sound Effects*, p. 159.

12. Louis Black, interview with the author, September 17, 1990.

13. Tom Huckabee, telephone interview with the author, December 16, 1990.

14. Black, interview.

15. Jeff Whittington, "Punk Rock: Sure It's Noisy, But Is It Art?" *Daily Texan*, October 2, 1978, "Images," pp. 24, 28.

16. Louis Black and Richard Dorsett, "Jonathan Richman: In Love with the Radio On," *Daily Texas*, September 18, 1978, "Images," pp. 14–15.

17. This entire story and all quotes are from the interview I did with Jesse Sublett, December 19, 1990.

18. Sally Jones, "Hey Punk!" *Austin Sun*, December 2, 1977, pp. 23, 27.

19. Carlene Brady, "Sex Pistols in Austin," *Austin Sun*, January 20, 1978, p. 11.

20. Black, interview.

21. Jeff Whittington, "Sex Pistols: Rock Anarchy Arrives in San Antonio," *Daily Texan*, January 11, 1978, p. 8.

22. Ibid.

23. The best book so far on the development of Mexican-American musical culture in Texas remains Manuel Pena, *The Texas-Mexican Conjunto: History of a Working-Class Music* (Austin: University of Texas Press, 1985). The story of

the origin of Raul's comes from a number of interviews, particularly Joe Aros, March 18, 1990; Steve Chaney, March 8, 1990; and Yleana Martinez, June 4, 1992.

24. Anonymous, "Austin Goes Punk," *Austin Sun*, January 13, 1978, p. 17. Sublett, interview.

25. Sublett, ibid. Eddie Munoz was being quoted in the *Sun* during this period as "a local punk." Munoz was attracted to the way that punk codes permitted certain expressions of anger. His influence on Sublett was strong, but even this street punk was quick to defend his musical abilities and quick to emphasize his self-conscious adoption of punk's musical limitations. See Anonymous, "Looking Like the Other Elvis," *Austin Sun*, January 27, 1978, p. 15; and Michael Ventura, "Hey Mama, What's a Punk?" *Austin Sun*, June 30, 1978, pp. 4–5, 11.

26. Anonymous, "Austin's 'New Wave': The Violators," *Austin Sun*, January 27, 1978, p. 15.

27. Sublett, interview. When I asked Jesse what he meant by "leather girls," he said, "Oh, you know, homosexual women." Both Olson and Valentine have had successful professional music careers: Olson with a series of solo projects, and Valentine, of course, with the Go-Gos. The best book on the rise of women in rock'n'roll after punk is Sue Steward and Sheryl Garrett's *Signed, Sealed, and Delivered: True Life Stories of Women in Pop* (Boston: South End Press, 1984).

28. Sublett, interview; Chaney, interview; Black, interview; Huckabee, interview.

29. Huckabee, interview.

30. Ibid.

31. Jeff Whittington, "The Man Can't Bust Our Music . . . but he sure can stop the show: a report on the rumble at Raul's," *Daily Texan*, September 25, 1978, "Images," pp. 10–11, 14.

32. Chaney, interview.

33. Whittington, "The Man," p. 10.

34. Huckabee, interview.

35. My account of this night is drawn from Whittington, "The Man"; Anonymous, "Rock Club Raid Leads to 6 Arrests," *Daily Texan*, September 20, 1978, p. 1; Anonymous, "Six Arrested in Punk Rock Show Melee," *Austin American-Statesman*, September 21, 1978, pp. A1, A12; and interviews with Chaney, Huckabee, Black, and Barbaro (September 21, 1990).

36. Huckabee, interview; Anonymous, "Our Boy in Blue," *Daily Texan*, September 21, 1978, p. 5; Anonymous, "Protest of Raul's Raid Leads to Arrest on Drag," *Daily Texan*, September 21, 1978, p. 1.

37. Quoted in Anonymous, "Rock Club Raid"; Anonymous, "Our Boy in Blue."

38. Anonymous, "Phil Tolstead Found Guilty, Fined for Disorderly Conduct," *Daily Texan*, October 10, 1978, p. 1. Joe Frolik, "Huns Can Dish Out Abuse, Take It," *Austin American-Statesman*, October 12, 1978. It is amusing that the final charge was disorderly conduct. After all, that was the band's intention. Tolstead was also charged with resisting arrest and abusive language. These two charges were dealt with in a different case, which is still under appeal. Specific aspects of this identity, its power, its attraction, and its transient capacity for change will be examined in later chapters.

39. Huckabee, interview.

40. The Explosives were a band that performed in a battle of the bands at Raul's in July of 1979. Musically, they were more competent than most of the bands that were competing. However, they were judged to sound "suspiciously

professional." When it was revealed that two of the three members of the Explosives had experience in the progressive country scene, there was a movement to disqualify them from the competition. They were allowed to complete their performance, but did not place among the top four bands. See Margaret Moser, "The Battle of the New Wave Bands: Who Really Won?" *Rumors, Gossip, Lies & Dreams*, July 26, 1979, pp. 4–5. I will explain and justify the use of this somewhat abstract language in the following chapter. The concept of the "abject" comes from Julia Kristeva's theorization of primary narcissism in the production of the subject and the splitting off from the mother-child dyad.

41. Mikhail Bakhtin, *Rabelais and His World*, trans. Helene Iswolsky (Bloomington: University of Indiana Press, 1984; translation originally published in 1968), pp. 62, 94.

42. Roland Swenson, "How I Started in the Record Business," *Austin Chronicle*, September 26, 1986, pp. 24–25; also, Swenson, interview with author, July 10, 1990.

43. Mellissa Cobb, interview with the author, May 27, 1989.

44. Kim Longacre, interview with the author, June 2, 1989.

45. Black, interview.

46. Whittington, "Punk Rock," p. 24.

6. The Performance of Signifying Practice

1. Tary Owens, interview with the author, December 18, 1990.

2. Brent Grulke, sound engineer and music editor for the *Austin Chronicle*, interview with the author, March 6, 1990.

3. Mike Hall, interview with the author, July 11, 1990.

4. Ibid, emphasis mine.

5. Dianne Hardin, interview with the author, March 10, 1990.

6. Jacques Lacan (could it possibly have been anyone else?), "The Subversion of the Subject and the Dialectic of Desire in the Freudian Unconscious," *Ecrits: A Selection*, trans. Alan Sheridan (New York: W. W. Norton and Co., 1977), p. 305.

7. Kim Longacre, interview with the author, June 2, 1989.

8. John Croslin, interview with the author, June 1, 1989.

9. Mellissa Cobb, interview with the author, May 29, 1989.

10. Marcia Buffington, interview with the author, March 10, 1990.

11. Anonymous, "To Be a Punk in Austin," *Austin Vanguard* (a fanzine), 1978 (no page numbers). For a discussion of the performance of "violence," see chapter five. The obvious similarities to the concept of subcultures as worked out by the Birmingham Centre for Contemporary Cultural Studies and discussed in Dick Hebdige's *Subculture: The Meaning of Style* (London: Methuen and Co., 1979) should not be overlooked, but neither should they be overemphasized. By the time of these interviews, rock'n'roll fans in Austin were conversant with a popularized version of subculture theory and were quick to use its categories to describe their practice. Some differences between the specifics of Austin music-making and the outlines of subculture theory will emerge later in the chapter.

12. Longacre, interview, June 2, 1989.

13. Buffington, interview.

14. John Shepherd, *Music as Social Text* (Cambridge: Polity Press, 1991); Leonard Meyer, *Emotion and Meaning in Music* (Chicago: University of Chicago Press, 1956), p. 81. See also the discussion of gesture in Jean-Jacques Nattiez, *Music and Discourse: Toward a Semiology of Music*, trans. Carolyn Abbate (Prince-

ton: Princeton University Press, 1990), p. 44. See chapter 4 for a discussion of dancing in the context of disco music.

15. George Rieff was bass player for Joe King Carrasco, 1984–85, and played in various other bands throughout the eighties; interview with the author, March 1987.

16. Longacre, interview, June 2, 1989.

17. Hunter Darby was bass player, singer, and songwriter for the Wannabes; interview with the author, March 5, 1990.

18. Tom Thornton was bass player, singer, and song writer for the Way-Outs from 1986 to the present; interview with the author, March 1987.

19. Ron Marks was bass player, singer, and songwriter for The Texas Instruments, from 1984 to the present; interview with the author, March 1987.

20. Longacre, interview, March 6, 1990.

21. Maki Fife and Joanne Weinzierl, interviews with the author, March 1987. These women were self-identified "members of the scene," as were all other fans I interviewed.

22. Dave Roberts, interview with the author, March 1987.

23. *Group Psychology and the Analysis of the Ego*, trans. James Strachey (New York: W. W. Norton and Co., 1959), pp. 22, 44.

24. Freud distinguishes between the state of being in love and the condition of identification solely by whether the object is introjected into the ego or the ego-ideal. See Freud, *Group Psychology*, p. 58. In rock'n'roll scenes the boundary between these two psychic structures is easily permeated. See the discussion of the role of desire in the structures of identification below.

25. Roberts, interview. For Freud, the primary group is "a number of individuals who have put one and the same object in the place of their ego ideal and have consequently identified themselves with one another in their egos" (*Group Psychology*, p. 61).

26. Lacan, "The Mirror Stage as Formative of the Function of the I," in *Ecrits*, pp. 1–7; quote from p. 2. See also, in the same volume, "The Subversion of the Subject and the Dialectic of Desire in the Freudian Unconscious," pp. 292–324. I do not intend this one-page distillation to represent adequately the whole of Lacan's positions on the complex processes of subject production. Such a representation would require a monograph of its own. I hope I have explained enough of the basic terms to clarify my use of this psychoanalytic framework.

27. Lacan, "Mirror Stage," p. 2.

28. Lacan, "The Subversion of the Subject," p. 301.

29. This describes an idealized situation, where conflicts between immediate experience and the dominant Symbolic can, indeed, result in "dialectical syntheses." Such identifications are never complete, and even partial identifications are not always possible under conditions of cultural dominance.

30. Fife, interview.

31. Ibid.

32. These terms, "subject–in–process" and "signifying practice," derive from the work of Julia Kristeva. In Kristeva's work, the subject in process and signifying practice maintain a reciprocal relationship. Signifying practice is the process of producing, exchanging, and incorporating signs in such a fashion that changes occur in the psychic organization of the subject in the process. However, transformations in identity escape the awareness of the individual to such an extent that the "subject" is "put on trial" (that is, his or her very coherence as a unified ego is threatened). The transformative work of this exchange of signs does not occur in a transparent, self-mastering, self-conscious individual.

Kristeva insists that, "We can speak of practice wherever there is a transgression of systematicity, i.e., a transgression of the unity proper to the transcendental ego." In addition, she says "Signifying practice . . . is taken as meaning the acceptance of a symbolic law together with the transgression of that law for the purpose of renovating it. The moment of transgression is the key moment in practice"; "The System and the Speaking Subject," in Toril Moi, ed., *The Kristeva Reader* (New York: Columbia University Press, 1986), p. 29. The best introduction to Kristeva's work is in the introduction to this volume. Kristeva works out her theory of the semiotic and the means whereby it is integrated into the symbolic in *Revolution in Poetic Language*, trans. Margaret Waller (New York: Columbia University Press, 1984).

33. "The Imaginary," in *Sexuality in the Field of Vision* (New York: Verso Books, 1986), pp. 167–97.

34. Ibid., p. 177. The interior quotes are from Sigmund Freud, "On Narcissism."

35. Julia Kristeva, "Freud and Love: Treatment and its Discontents," *Tales of Love*, trans. Leon Roudiez (New York: Columbia University Press, 1987), pp. 25–26.

36. Fife, interview, March 1987.

37. See Larry Grossberg, "The Politics of Youth Culture: Some Observations on Rock and Roll in American Culture," *Social Text* 8 (Winter 1983–84): 104–26; Simon Frith, *Sound Effects* (New York: Pantheon Books, 1981); Angela McRobbie, "Dance and Social Fantasy," in McRobbie and Mica Nava, eds., *Gender and Generation* (London: Macmillan, 1984), pp. 130–61; Hebdige, *Subculture*; Paul Willis, *Learning to Labour: How Working Class Kids Get Working Class Jobs* (London: Saxon House, 1976); Stuart Hall and Tony Jefferson, eds., *Resistance Through Rituals* (London: Hutchinson, 1976).

38. David Harvey, *The Condition of Postmodernity: An Enquiry into the Origins of Cultural Change* (Oxford and Cambridge, Mass.: Basil Blackwell, 1989), p. 339.

39. Julia Kristeva, "The Adolescent Novel," in John Fletcher and Andrew Benjamin, eds., *Abjection, Melancholia, and Love: The Work of Julia Kristeva* (London and New York: Routledge, 1990), p. 9.

40. I use the word "inscribe" deliberately. I am describing a structure that writes the condition of adolescence across bodies of all ages. It is also important to note that I am differing from a strict Lacanian viewpoint on this. My perspective aligns more closely with Kristeva's. She allows for the possibility of social structural change in the Symbolic through these processes of identification incorporated into signifying practice.

41. Patricia Meyer Spacks, *The Adolescent Idea: Myths of Youth and the Adult Imagination* (New York: Basic Books, 1981), p. 289.

42. Julia Kristeva, *Powers of Horror: An Essay on Abjection*, trans. Leon Roudiez (New York: Columbia University Press, 1982), p. 12, also pp. 1–89.

43. "Freud and Love," p. 24. The semiotic is described by Kristeva as "a psychosomatic modality of the signifying process . . . articulating . . . a continuum" between the body and the sociosymbolic in the speaking being. The semiotic is a function of the chora, "in which the linguistic sign is not yet articulated as the absence of an object and as the distinction between real and symbolic." See *Revolution in Poetic Language*, trans. Margaret Waller (New York: Columbia University Press, 1984), pp. 25–30 and passim.

44. Spacks, *The Adolescent Idea*, p. 291.

45. Buffington, interview.

46. Kristeva, *Powers of Horror*, p. 67.

47. *Austin Chronicle*, March 11, 1988, p. 77.

48. *Austin Chronicle*, November 13, 1987, p. 65.

49. *Austin Chronicle*, February 17, 1989, p. 37.

50. *Austin Chronicle*, September 29, 1989, p. 37. According to Lisa Byrd, who works with Freelove, this ad did not attract the desired musicians.

51. Brant Bingamon, interview with the author, March 8, 1990.

52. Joe McDermott, interview with the author, March 7, 1990.

53. Heather Moore, interview with the author, March 5, 1990.

54. Croslin, interviews with the author, June 1, 1989, March 3, 1990.

55. Longacre, interview, June 2, 1989.

56. See the discussion of suture, film theory, and Jacqueline Rose above.

57. Croslin, interview, June 1, 1989.

58. Hall, interview.

59. Moore, interview.

60. Julia Austin, interview with the author, September 13, 1990.

61. Kevin Whitley, interview with the author, March 13, 1990.

62. Alejandro Escovedo, interview with the author, March 7, 1990.

63. Austin, interview; emphasis in the recorded voice.

64. Croslin, interview, June 1, 1989.

65. For an excellent discussion of the physicality of jazz improvisation, see David Sudnow, *Ways of the Hand* (Cambridge: Harvard University Press, 1978).

66. Lacan, "The Mirror Stage," p. 2. See the discussion of identification above.

67. Whitley, interview, March 13, 1990.

68. McDermott, interview. The phrase "bouncing scratchy cassette tape re-corders back and forth," refers to a primitive recording method. A musician will record him or herself playing one part on a guitar, for instance. Then she or he will play back that recorded tape while playing a different part and record both of those tracks on another tape recorder. The loss of sound fidelity in this process is tremendous. Thus the reference to "scratchy cassette tape recorders."

69. Ibid.

70. Ibid.

71. Ibid.

72. Steve Spinks, interview, March 1987.

73. Bill Malone, *Country Music U.S.A.*, rev. ed. (Austin: University of Texas Press, 1985), p. 86.

74. Carrie Rodgers, quoted in Nolan Porterfield, *Jimmie Rodgers: The Life and Times of America's Blue Yodeler* (Urbana: University of Illinois Press, 1979), p. 363.

75. Quoted in Peter Guralnick, *Lost Highway: Journeys and Arrivals of American Musicians* (New York: Vintage Books, 1982, p. 28.

76. Quoted in Malone, *Country Music*, p. 242.

77. Max Horkheimer and Theodor W. Adorno, *Dialectic of Enlightenment*, trans. John Cumming (New York: Continuum, 1987; first trans. 1972, German orig. 1944), pp. 83–84.

78. Second definition of sincerity in *The Compact Edition of the Oxford English Dictionary*, vol. 2, p. 2,830. See chapter 5 for discussions of "Glad He's Dead" and "Big Penis Envy."

79. I trust the reader understands that I am trying to describe a set of beliefs and assumptions underlying the practice of rock'n'roll in Austin. Explicitly, I am not advocating the possibility of a "pure representation."

80. Quoted in Carlos Grasso, et al., prods., "Austin Avalanche of Rock and Roll," *The Cutting Edge* (1985).

81. Croslin, interview, June 1, 1989.

82. Austin, interview.

83. Croslin, interview, June 1, 1989.

84. "What's Wrong with the Austin Music Scene?" *Austin Chronicle*, November 15, 1985, pp. 24–26. As Jesse remembers it, the label originated as a throwaway remark in a conversation he was having with Margaret Moser in the Continental Club. "All those new sincerity bands, they're crap." Moser picked up the phrase and began using it in her columns in the *Austin Chronicle*. Jesse Sublett, telephone conversation with the author, January 30, 1991.

85. Darby, interview.

86. Ibid.

87. Jacques Attali discusses the political predictive value of noise in *Noise: The Political Economy of Music*, trans. Brian Massumi (Minneapolis: University of Minnesota Press, 1985). Jean-Jacques Nattiez provides a more useful discussion of "Noise as a Semiological Phenomenon," pp. 45–48.

88. Whitley, interview, March 13, 1990.

89. Ibid.

90. Longacre, interview, March 6, 1990.

91. Longacre, interview, June 2, 1989.

92. Longacre, interviews, June 2, 1989, March 6, 1990. The ellipsis indicates the break between the passages from each interview.

93. Buffington, interview.   94. McDermott, interview.

95. Ibid.   96. Ibid.

97. Croslin, interview, June 1, 1989.

98. Daniel Johnston, "I Am a Baby," *Hi, How Are You (the Unfinished Album)*, homemade tape, recorded September 1983.

99. Daniel Johnston, "Get Yourself Together," *Hi, How Are You*.

100. Daniel Johnston, "Walking the Cow," *Hi, How Are You*.

101. Carlos Grasso, prod., 1985.

102. Ibid.

103. Ibid.

104. Cf. "I'll Never Marry." The complete lyrics are, "I'll never marry, I'll never wed. Nobody loves you when you're dead. Nobody wants to lie in bed with you when your flesh is rotting." *Hi, How Are You*.

105. Since that time, Daniel Johnston has recorded and performed with Jad Fair of Half Japanese and members of Sonic Youth. He performed at CBGB's in New York in 1988, released a new album, *1990*, and sang five songs at the *Austin Chronicle* Music Awards show in 1990. A letter published in the *Chronicle* after the awards show declared, "I'm totally mystified. I've been reading about Daniel Johnston ever since I came to Austin four years ago, but I never had the opportunity to see him play until the Music Awards show. . . . What I wonder, is how someone who can't play guitar, can't sing, and (from what I could pick up) doesn't write particularly good songs can get so much good ink and such a good gig in a town filled with so many superb songwriters, singers and bands? . . . Johnston may be vulnerable and real and intense, but those qualities do not guarantee art." *Austin Chronicle*, April 13, 1990, p. 2.

7. The Inscription of Identity in the Music Business

1. For instance, the University Coop (the largest textbook and alumni paraphernalia store) allows extra time-off for all part-time student employees during final exams. This policy is also in the store's interest, as final exam weeks tend to be slow sales periods as well.

2. Austin has "the sixth largest concentration of artists in the nation." *The Economic Impacts of the Arts and Entertainment Industries of Austin, Texas*, a report by the Leisure Variety Action Team, Leadership Austin 1986–87.

3. Ibid. Also, Mike Clark, "UT offers more than educational opportunities," *Austin Business Journal* (April 30–May 6, 1990): 7–8; Roland Swenson, interview with the author, July 10, 1990; and Nick Barbaro, interview, September 21, 1990.

4. Judy Jamison, interview with the author, March 14, 1990.

5. Kevin Whitley, interview with the author, September 13, 1990.

6. Michael Corcoran, "Don't You Start Me Talking," *Austin Chronicle*, June 26, 1987, p. 24.

7. See chapter 4 for Alrich's comment.

8. Alejandro Escovedo, interview with the author, March 7, 1990.

9. Ibid.

10. Joe McDermott, interview with the author, March 7, 1990.

11. Kim Longacre, interview with the author, March 6, 1990.

12. John Croslin, interview with the author, March 3, 1990.

13. Byron Scott, interview with the author, March 7, 1990.

14. Ron Marks, interview with the author, March 1987.

15. Brant Bingamon, interview with the author, March 8, 1990, emphasis mine.

16. Tom Thornton, interview with the author, March 1987.

17. Kevin Whitley, interview with the author, March 13, 1990.

18. Boberg had been the head of A&M's college radio department. "New York News," *New York Rocker* 21 (August 1979): 17. Both IRS and Rockpool, the distribution system set up by Mark Josephson, applied a lesson learned from the independent music businesses in England—the value of focusing on a specific subfragment of the youth market—in a new context: the geographic challenge of the United States. Distribution and publicity were the keys to the alternative music business in the U.S. See the next chapter.

19. Ed Ward, "On the Verge with the Standing Waves," *New York Rocker* 27 (March 1980): 29; "Austin News," *New York Rocker* 33 (November 1980): 29; Jesse Sublett, "A View From the Stage," *Third Coast* (March 1987): 36, 56–58; Jesse Sublett, telephone interview with the author, December 19, 1990; John Dee Graham, telephone interview with the author, May 27, 1991.

20. John Croslin, interview with the author, June 1, 1989.

21. Mellissa Cobb, interview with the author, May 27, 1989. KOA is the trademark of Kampgrounds of America. This company rents parking spaces with shower facilities along major highways in the United States.

22. Escovedo, interview.

23. Bingamon, interview.

24. Bill Malone, *Country Music U.S.A.*, rev. ed. (Austin: University of Texas Press, 1985), pp. 36–42.

25. Ibid., p. 84.

26. H. Stith Bennett, *On Becoming a Rock Musician* (Amherst: University of Massachusetts Press, 1980).

27. See chapter 8 for a detailed discussion of this process.

28. These figures come from an annual list compiled by the *Austin Chronicle*. The list is usually printed in the last issue of December or the first issue of January each winter.

29. Anonymous, "Austin Music, '81," *Austin Chronicle*, December 12, 1981; Luke Torn, "1989 Austin Discography," *Austin Chronicle*, January 12, 1990, p. 18. In these listings, any recording released in both the cassette and the vinyl or

compact disc format is automatically included in the LP or EP category. Those recordings released only on cassette make up the tape category.

30. Demo tapes can serve a variety of other functions as well. They can be used to obtain bookings or to attract the attention of managers or publicists. However, the demos that are sent to record companies tend to be more extravagantly produced and, consequently, more expensive than those used for other purposes.

31. Mike Hall, interview with the author, July 11, 1990.

32. See Susan Willis, "Learning From the Banana," *American Quarterly* 39 (Winter 1987): 586–600.

33. See Georges Bataille, "The Notion of Expenditure," in *Visions of Excess: Selected Writings, 1927–1939*, ed. and trans. Alan Stoekl (Minneapolis: University of Minnesota Press, 1985), pp. 116–29.

34. Cobb, interview.

35. Hall, interview.

36. Steve Spinks, interview with the author, March 1987.

37. The concept of the big drum sound first entered the pop music industry after Led Zeppelin recorded the drum tracks for an album in an old English cathedral. The echo provided by the high ceilings and the stone walls combined with the expense involved in this remote recording to produce the prestige awarded to this sound.

38. With the advent of syn-drums and the increasing use of digital machines, this has become less of an issue. Big drum sounds now can be produced with ease by computer technologies, but these technologies are also very expensive.

39. Escovedo, interview.

40. For an example of a rock'n'roll rhythm section recorded previous to the rigid enforcement of this standard, listen to any electric Bob Dylan record from the midsixties. Garrett Williams, Steve Grimes, and Terri Lord are drummers in the Austin rock'n'roll scene who aspire to digitally precise timing in their work. Terri Lord, interview with the author, May 26, 1989; Grimes, interview, March 1987; Williams, interview, March 8, 1990.

41. Stuart Sullivan, interview with the author, September 13, 1990.

42. As evidenced by the above discussion of punching in the bass part.

43. Croslin, interview, June 1, 1989. Since the time of this writing, Croslin has produced an album by the Reivers, *Pop Beloved*, for DB Records.

44. The work of Phil Spector remains probably the canonical example of an overwhelming producer's style. Mike Chapman's work with glitter bands, Giorgio Morodor's work with the disco style, and Brian Eno's productions of postpunk art bands are other examples.

45. Croslin, interview, June 1, 1989.

46. Croslin, interview, March 3, 1990. *Let it Be* and *Pleased to Meet Me* are albums by the Replacements.

47. Croslin, ibid.

48. Keith Ayres, owner of Glitch Records and publisher of *Texas Beat* magazine, interview with the author, July 10, 1990.

49. Louis Meyers, band manager and cofounder of South By Southwest, interview with the author, July 10, 1990.

50. Spinks, musician, interview.

51. John Croslin, musician and producer, interview, June 1, 1989.

52. Joe McDermott, musician and producer, interview.

53. Brant Bingamon, musician, interview.

8. The Commodification of Identity

1. Marcia Ball, quoted in Michael Ventura, "Marcia Ball: Portrait of a Professional," *Texas Sun*, May 5, 1977, pp. 12–13, 20.

2. Roland Swenson, interview with the author, July 10, 1990.

3. Mike Tolleson, telephone interview with the author, July 12, 1990. See John T. Davis, "Austin All-Stars," *Austin Sun*, February 10, 1978, pp. 16–17; John T. Davis, "Mother of Pearl Takes You to the Tropics," *Austin Sun*, June 3, 1977, pp. 10–11. The K-Tels are self-described in the *Austin Chronicle* "Musicians Register" of 1983 as performing "updated versions of soul classics and originals" (November 25, 1983, p. 22). For an excellent discussion of the difficulties and rewards associated with performing other people's music, see H. Stith Bennet, *On Becoming a Rock Musician* (Amherst: University of Massachusetts Press, 1980).

4. Nick Barbaro, interview with the author, September 20, 1990.

5. Joe Dishner and Nick Barbaro, "Letter from the Publishers," *Austin Chronicle* Prototype Issue, Summer 1981, p. 2. Emphasis in original.

6. Ibid.

7. Anonymous, "Readership," *Austin Chronicle* Prototype Issue, Summer 1981, n.p. Louis Black, interview with the author, September 17, 1990.

8. "The 1981 Poll: Don't Blame Me, I Voted for Buddy Holly," *Austin Chronicle*, March 5, 1981, p. 9.

9. Anonymous, "Readership," *Austin Chronicle* Prototype Issue, Summer 1981, n.p.

10. Increase in jobs from Michele Kay, "Austin Nursing Growth Hangover from Go-Go Years: Moderation comes back in style," *Austin American Statesman*, September 16, 1990, pp. J1, J4. Income per capita provided by the City of Austin Department of Planning. Comparative cost of living figures from the Austin Chamber of Commerce Researchers' Association, "News Release," December 20, 1988. Price of new houses from Anonymous, "Number, Value of Permits Issued in August Declines," *Austin American Statesman*, September 17, 1990. Increase in downtown rental space provided by The Lindley Group, a market analysis consulting firm specializing in real estate.

11. James Winton Bohmfalk, "The Austin Chamber of Commerce: A History of the Organization and its Uses of Propaganda," Masters thesis, University of Texas at Austin, 1968, p. 28; Kay, "Austin Nursing Growth Hangover," p. J1. Computer chip production was such a significant component of manufacturing jobs that a chip was used in this article as the icon representing all jobs in this sector.

12. Kay, "Austin Nursing Growth Hangover," p. J1.

13. Ibid. Population figures provided by the City of Austin.

14. Enrollment figures from the Office of Institutional Studies, University of Texas at Austin; Dowell Myers, et al., "Quality of Life: Austin Trends 1970–1990," Research Report for the Community and Regional Planning Program, School of Architecture, University of Texas at Austin, June 1984, p. 5. The longer-lasting, more famous nightclubs of Austin present exceptions to this average. The Armadillo, the Soap Creek, Antone's, the Broken Spoke, and, more recently, Liberty Lunch each attained much longer life spans than clubs such as the Rome Inn, the One Knite, the Eleventh Door, Club Foot, or the Beach. However, both the Soap Creek and Antone's changed locations twice within their life spans. If that is taken into consideration, their length of residence at each location reverts back to the average three-year duration. The Continental

Club, which has presented bands at the same location for nearly fifteen years, has changed owners almost every five years.

15. "Quality of life" became a catch phrase in local politics in Austin during the 1980s. Candidates for the city council and state legislature vowed to protect Austin's quality of life, however that might be defined. One attempt to analyze the meaning of the phrase for the citizens of Austin was Dowell Myers, et al., "Quality of Life."

16. Phyllis Krantzman, "Impact of the Music Entertainment Industry on Austin, Texas," Masters thesis in the Program of Community and Regional Planning, University of Texas at Austin, 1983, pp. 9–26, 72. Texas is an open shop state. Musicians do not need to join the union in order to perform locally. In fact, most younger rock'n'roll musicians in Austin, particularly those playing punk, new wave, or alternative music, do not join the union. The union is better organized at the national recording level, however. Many of the major labels avoid union actions by requiring musicians to join the A.F. of M. before recording. Therefore, once musicians record for a major label, or tour with a band that records for a major label, they tend to be members of the union. Membership in the musicians union in Austin, Texas, then, is predicated upon a specific degree of commercial success.

17. David Lord, "The Business of Local Music on High Note," *Austin Business Journal* (Dec. 31–Jan. 6, 1985), p. 20; Ernie Gammage, interview with the author, July 13, 1990.

18. Lord, "The Business of Local Music."

19. Ernie Gammage, interview; Tolleson, interview; Roland Swenson and Louis Meyers, interview with the author, July 10, 1990.

20. Jim Shahin, "Remember Quality of Life?" *Austin Chronicle*, March 13, 1987, p. 10; Lord, "The Business of Local Music"; Stanford Research Institute, "Creating an Opportunity Economy," report prepared for the Austin Chamber of Commerce, April 1985. The specific application of the "opportunity economy" concept to music in Austin is discussed below.

21. Jeff Whittington and Louis Black, "Music and Commerce: Two Views," *Austin Chronicle*, November 15, 1985, pp. 36–37.

22. Ed Ward, "Austin News," *New York Rocker* 33 (November 1980): 29. Ward's insistence upon linking music-making in Austin with the standards and tastes of the national recording industry prompted Carlyne Majer and Doug Sahm to initiate a "Dump Ed Ward" bumper-sticker campaign.

23. See, for example, Judith Sims, "Record Industry Profiles: Two Lonely Bulls and How They Grew," *Rolling Stone* (October 12, 1972): 14; Jann Wenner, "The Record Company Executive Thing: Rolling Stone Interviews Joe Smith," *Rolling Stone* (July 8, 1971).

24. The distinction was made clear by Alvin Toffler in 1965. "Contrast the output of the non-profit performing arts with that of the recording manufacturer. He, too, sells what appears to be a performance. But it is not. It is a replica of a performance, a mass-produced embodiment of a performance." Quoted in Paul Hirsch, "Processing Fads and Fashions: An Organization-Set Analysis of Cultural Industry Systems," in Frith and Goodwin, eds., *On Record: Rock, Pop and the Written Word* (New York: Pantheon Books, 1990), p. 128.

25. The model for Horkheimer and Adorno's metaphor was, again, the motion picture industry. See "The Culture Industry: Enlightenment as Mass Deception," *Dialectic of Enlightenment*, trans. John Cumming (New York: Continuum Press, 1987; orig. 1944), pp. 120–67. Paul Hirsch, *The Structure of the Popular Music Industry* (Ann Arbor: Survey Research Center, 1969); R. Serge

Denisoff, *Solid Gold: The Popular Record Industry* (New Brunswick: Transaction Books, 1975); Richard Peterson and David Berger, "Cycles in Symbol Production: The Case of Popular Music," *American Sociological Review* 2 (1975): 158–73; Simon Frith, *Sound Effects: Youth, Leisure and the Politics of Rock'n'Roll* (New York: Pantheon Books, 1981); and "The Industrialization of Music," *Music For Pleasure* (New York: Routledge, 1988). In "The Industrialization of Music," Frith says that "the industrialization of music cannot be understood as something that happens to music, since it describes a process in which music itself is made." I hope that my work has shown that industrialization is precisely something that happens to music-making. While it is absolutely true that rock'n'roll as we know it would not exist without the recording industry, that fact does not authorize the subsumption of all the uses and pleasures of popular music-making under the functions and values of that particular organization. In fact, some of the most important pleasures of rock'n'roll run counter to the goals and intentions of all industrial organization. As Hirsch himself pointed out, studies using the organization-set paradigm "seldom inquire into the functions performed by the organization for the social system but ask rather, as temporary partisans, how the goals of the organization may be constrained by society. The organization is assumed to act under conditions of rationality. . . ." The Parsonian language and the assumption of a single "social system" should warn us that very important matters are being left unconsidered. Hirsch, in Frith and Goodwin, *On Record*, p. 128. See also Denisoff, especially chapter 4, "The Cop-Out: Inside the Record Company," pp. 144–215.

26. Louis Black, et al., "Austin Music: Behind the Scenes," *Austin Chronicle*, November 16, 1984, pp. 1, 6–9.

27. Gammage, interview.

28. Whittington and Black, "Music and Commerce," p. 36.

29. Austin Music Advisory Committee, "Austin Music: Into the Future," report to the Austin Chamber of Commerce, May 1985, p. ii. Page numbers for subsequent citations will be given in the text.

30. Of course, the only "music industry" that generated these kinds of income figures was the national recording industry.

31. Joplin moved back to Texas in 1965 and performed regularly in Beaumont, Houston, and Austin for another year. She moved again to San Francisco to join Big Brother on May 30, 1966. Myra Friedman, *Buried Alive: The Biography of Janis Joplin* (New York: Bantam Books, 1974), pp. 54, 78. Alrich, quoted in Diana Potts, "Dog Days at the 'Dillo,'" *Texas Sun*, December 9, 1977, p. 17; Bobby Bridger, "Rusty Weir," *River City Sun*, September 15, 1978, pp. 23–24.

32. Jay Boberg, Jonathan Dayton, Valerie Faris, Carlos Grasso, prods., "Austin Avalanche of Rock and Roll," *The Cutting Edge* (1985). All the following quotes are taken from the program aired on MTV in the fall of that year.

33. See Sarah Wimer, "Timbuk 3: The Family that Plays Together Stays Together," *Austin Chronicle*, August 15, 1986, p. 16, for an early history of the band. Carlyne Majer credited Ed Guinn with packaging Timbuk 3 for the recording industry when I interviewed her on September 17, 1990. Guinn himself says only that he "heard quality songs, an acerbic, beatnik sensibility." And in turn, he taught them how to be a band. Ed Guinn, interview with the author, June 19, 1991.

34. Robert Draper, "The New Sobriety: Austin Music Meets the Industry," *Austin Chronicle*, July 4, 1986, p. 28. The article quoted "anonymous industry figures."

35. Bruce Newman, "Lower the Age, Shrink the Audience: A Disastrous Equation for Austin Clubs?" *Austin Chronicle*, September 12, 1986, p. 17.

36. Louis Black, "Ch-Ch-Changes, an Interview with Louis Meyers," *Austin Chronicle*, December 18, 1987, p. 15; Swenson, interview.

37. Louis Black, Michael Hall, E. A. Srere, eds., *1990 Austin Music Industry Guide* (Austin: Austin Chronicle Corporation, 1990). The table of contents lists twenty-eight categories including separate listings for "Producers and Sound Engineers" and "Sound, Lighting and Staging" (p. 3). For an example of listing inflation consider Jeff Tartakov's two listings. One is for his artist management company, Stress Worldwide Communications. The other is for a service called Austin Mealfinders. "For touring acts who don't know where to eat. Mexican food, witty conversation, Daniel Johnston updates/anecdotes for cost of one extra meal" (p. 8). The 1984 record company figures in this comparison can be found in Chris Walters and Brent Grulke, "Austin's Record Labels," *Austin Chronicle*, November 16, 1984, p. 19. Other 1984 figures derive from Louis Black, et al., "Austin Music: Behind the Scenes." The names and the phone numbers of the major record label representatives are listed in E. A. Srere, "Austin Record Labels: The List," *Austin Chronicle*, December 8, 1989, p. 25.

38. Whittington and Black, "Music and Commerce," p. 37.

39. Kay, "Austin Nursing Growth Hangover," p. J1. Cooke quoted in, and the forum reported in, Sheryl Martin, "Mayoral Candidates See Money in Music," *Austin Chronicle*, May 6, 1988, p. 8.

40. Gerry Wood, "The City of Austin: No Musical Limits," *Billboard*, September 9, 1989, p. 42. L. E. McCullough, "Agents, Managers, and Attorneys: New Band of Professionals Surge Ahead with the Music," *Billboard*, September 9, 1989, p. A-4; Michael Point, "One of the Most Music-Intensive Cities in America Today, Austin, Texas Is a Cool-Flowing Natural Spring of Refreshingly Original Record-Ready Talent for the World. Now There's a Strong Local Industry Rallying Around the Sound," *Billboard*, September 9, 1989, p. A-1.

41. Gammage, interview.

42. Tolleson, telephone interview.

43. Frith, *Sound Effects*, p. 159.

44. Kim Longacre, interview with the author, June 2, 1989; Louis Black, interview with the author, September 17, 1990; Craig Lee, "The Fall," *Slash* 3, no. 1 (Jan./Feb. 1980): 34.

45. But within the competitive industrial system of the recording business a relatively high level of economic support is necessary. By 1990, Rabid Cat was out of business. All quotes from record company owners as well as the generalization are from Robert Lucey, "Home-Grown: Local Recording Labels Promote the Music Austin Loves," *Images, Daily Texan*, June 20, 1988, p. 1.

46. Kate Messer, telephone interview with the author, August 13, 1990. The following quotes are taken from the same interview.

47. Maureen Tucker was the drummer for the Velvet Underground. Featuring John Cale, Sterling Morrison, Lou Reed, and Tucker, the Velvets were a very important band from the sixties. They blended an urban artistic sensibility with undisciplined rock'n'roll immediacy. They have become perhaps the most influential American band among "alternative" musicians. For detailed information, see any issue of *What Goes On*, "the official magazine of the Velvet Underground Appreciation Society."

48. The description of Jeff's initial encounters with Happy Family come from an interview with Julia Austin, September 13, 1990.

49. The Brill Building held a set of offices and studios where many successful songwriters worked for various publishers during the early sixties. By referring to 611 Broadway as the Indie Brill Building, Kate is highlighting the concentration of these music businesses at one address.

50. Austin, interview.

51. A copy of the ad can be found in *What Goes On* 4 (1990): 72.

52. Jo Rae DiMenno, interview with the author, September 18, 1991. The following quotes are also taken from this interview.

53. Giant and Chrysalis are subdivisions of major labels that have targeted the alternative market. Rough Trade had no such affiliation and, as of this writing, has just declared Chapter VII bankruptcy.

54. Brent Grulke, interview with the author, March 7, 1990. Unless otherwise indicated, all quotes are from this interview. Brent and I have known each other since 1984. We have had many late-night drunken conversations about the meaning of rock'n'roll, but the conversation I recorded on tape took on the structure of an ethnographic interview, with me asking questions about the meaning of certain terms he used and particular actions he had taken. At the same time, Brent played off of the fact that we had already talked about these issues several times. At one point he dismissed my questioning with, "Subculture, subculture. It's all subculture, Barry. You know that." After a nod to Professor Hebdige, we continued the interview.

55. From my notes taken during the meeting of the Music Editorial Staff, September 18, 1990.

56. Michael Corcoran, "Don't You Start Me Talking," *Austin Chronicle*, August 15, 1986, p. 17.

57. Ibid., February 27, 1987, p. 14.

58. In 1993, the conference moved its panels and workshops to the new Austin Convention Center.

59. Drew Wheeler, "New Music Seminar: Getting Mighty Crowded," *New York Rocker* 32 (October 1980), p. 7.

60. Swenson, interview. The New Music Seminar refers to itself as "the world's premier international music industry convention" in its advertisement in the SXSW'90 booklet.

61. Roland Swenson and Louis Meyers, interview, July 10, 1990. The narrative of the early days of SXSW comes largely from this interview.

62. Michael Corcoran, "Don't You Start Me Talking," *Austin Chronicle*, March 27, 1987, p. 18.

63. "Intimacy" from Chris Morris, writer for *Billboard*, quoted in Michael MacCambridge, "SXSW Strikes Golden Chord with Music Industry," *Austin American-Statesman*, March 11, 1990, p. A-10; "Grass-roots orientation" from Louis Meyers, interview; Swenson, interview.

64. Thom Duffy, "Growing SXSW Shines in Austin," *Billboard*, March 31, 1990, p. 8.

65. A full list of the panels is published in the booklet for the South by Southwest Music and Media Conference '90.

66. Swenson, interview.

67. From my notes taken during the conference. Unless otherwise indicated, the quotes are from members of the panel. All quotes from other panels were acquired in the same fashion.

68. Christgau is a music critic for the *Village Voice*. Sometimes referred to as "the dean of American rock critics," Christgau edits the *Voice*'s annual "Pazz and Jop Poll," writes a regular "Consumer Guide," and has published several books of his criticism.

69. Simon Frith reported on the Controversy panel in his "Brit Beat" column in the *Village Voice*, April 24, 1990. He described it as "an angry argument about censorship." The anger evidenced in the panel came from Jim Fourrat's attack on antigay lyrics in some rap songs, followed by a defense of rap against

racialist censorship motives. In general, the panel and the audience supported more speech as the answer to bad speech, and the open market as the direct and important result of the commitment to free speech.

9. The Continuing Importance of Musicalized Experience

1. The quoted statements are reconstructed from the notes I took during the busride.

2. See chapter 2 and Mikhail Bakhtin, *Rabelais and His World*, trans. Helene Iswolsky (Bloomington: Indiana University Press, 1984; orig. 1968); Peter Burke, *Popular Culture in Early Modern Europe* (New York: Harper & Row, 1978); Barbara Babcock, ed., *The Reversible World* (Ithaca and London: Cornell University Press, 1978; and Alessandro Falassi, ed., *Time out of Time: Essays on the Festival* (Albuquerque: New Mexico Press, 1987).

3. See chapter 3.

4. Marcia Ball, quoted in Michael Ventura, "Marcia Ball: Portrait of a Professional," *Texas Sun*, May 5, 1977, pp. 12–13, 20.

5. Jan Reid, *The Improbable Rise of Redneck Rock* (Austin: Heidelberg Publishers, 1974), p. 10; Hugh Cullen Sparks, "Stylistic Development and Compositional Processes of Selected Solo Singer/Songwriters in Austin, Texas," Ph.D. diss., University of Texas at Austin, May 1984, pp. 52, 43; Kevin Whitley, interview with the author, March 13, 1990.

6. Ed Guinn, interview with the author, June 19, 1991; Hank Alrich, quoted in Diana Potts, "Dog Days at the 'Dillo?'" *Texas Sun*, December 9, 1977, p. 17.

7. Brent Grulke, interview with the author, March 7, 1990.

8. Tom Carson, "Ceremonies of the Horsemen," *New York Rocker* 1, no. 10 (Nov./Dec., 1977): 43.

9. Frith, *Sound Effects: Youth, Leisure and the Politics of Rock'n'Roll* (New York: Pantheon Books, 1981), p. 159.

10. Louis Black, interview with the author, September 17, 1990; John Croslin, interview with the author, March 3, 1990.

11. Louis Meyers, band manager and cofounder of South by Southwest, interview with the author, July 10, 1990.

12. Ed Guinn, interview with the author, June 19, 1990; Kevin Whitley, interview, March 13, 1990; Brant Bingamon, interview with the author, March 8, 1990; Croslin, interview, March 3, 1990.

13. The relations between the Marxist understanding of commodity and the Freudian understanding of symptom have recently been explored by Slavoj Zizek in *The Sublime Object of Ideology* (London and New York: Verso Books, 1989).

Selected Bibliography

NEWSPAPERS

Austin American
Austin American-Statesman
Austin Business Journal
Austin Chronicle
Austin Sun
Boston Evening Transcript
Boston Herald
Chicago Tribune

Daily Texan
New York Herald-Tribune
New York Times
River City Sun
Texas Sun
Third Coast
Village Voice

MUSIC MAGAZINES AND FANZINES

Austin Vanguard
Billboard
New York Rocker
Rolling Stone

Rumors, Gossip, Lies and Dreams
Slash
Trouser Press

BOOKS, ARTICLES, VIDEOS

Adorno, Theodor W. *Introduction to the Sociology of Music*. New York: Continuum Press, 1988.

——— . "On the Fetish Character of Music and the Regression of Listening." In *The Essential Frankfurt School Reader*, ed. Arato and Gebhardt. New York: Continuum, 1982.

——— and George Simpson. "On Popular Music." *Studies in Philosophy and Social Science* 9 (1941), pp. 17–48.

Allen, Jules Verne. *Cowboy Lore*. San Antonio: Naylor Printing Company, 1933.

Attali, Jacques. *Noise: The Political Economy of Music*, trans. Brian Massumi. Minneapolis: University of Minnesota Press, 1985.

Babbitt, Milton. "Who Cares if You Listen?" *High Fidelity* (February 1958), pp. 38–40, 126–27.

Babcock, Barbara, ed. *The Reversible World*. Ithaca: Cornell University Press, 1978.

Bakhtin, Mikhail. *Rabelais and His World*, trans. Helene Iswolsky. Bloomington: Indiana University Press, 1984.

Barlow, William. *Looking Up at Down: The Emergence of Blues Culture*. Philadelphia: Temple University Press, 1989.

Barthes, Roland. *The Responsibility of Forms*, trans. Richard Howard. New York: Hill and Wang, 1985.

Bataille, Georges. *Visions of Excess: Selected Writings, 1927–1938*, ed. and trans. Alan Stoekl. Minneapolis: University of Minnesota Press, 1985.

Bauman, Richard *Story, Performance, and Event: Contextual Studies of Oral Narrative*. Cambridge, Mass.: Cambridge University Press, 1986.

Bennett, H. Stith. *On Becoming a Rock Musician*. Amherst: University of Massachusetts Press, 1980.

Black, Louis, Michael Hall, and E. A. Srere, eds. *1990 Austin Music Industry Guide*. Austin: Austin Chronicle Corporation, 1990.

Bluestein, Gene. *The Voice of the Folk*. Amherst: University of Massachusetts Press, 1972.

Boberg, Jay, Jonathan Dayton, Valerie Faris, Carlos Grasso, prods. "The Austin Avalanche of Rock and Roll." "The Cutting Edge," 1985.

Bohmfalk, James Winton. "The Austin Chamber of Commerce: A History of the Organization and its Uses of Propaganda." Master's Thesis, University of Texas at Austin, 1968.

Brand, Oscar. *The Ballad Mongers: Rise of the Modern Folk Song*. New York: Funk & Wagnalls, 1962.

Burke, Peter. *Popular Culture in Early Modern Europe*. New York: Harper & Row, 1978.

Charters, Samuel. *The Country Blues*. New York: Rinehart, 1959.

Clark, Kenneth S. *The Cowboy Sings Songs of the Ranch and Range*. New York: Paull-Pioneer Music Corporation, 1932.

Clifford, James, and George Marcus, eds. *Writing Culture*. Berkeley: University of California Press, 1986.

Congo, Paul, Martha Herzog, and Tary Owens, prods. *A Texas Blues Reunion*, 1989.

Debord, Guy. *Society of the Spectacle*. Detroit: Black & Red Press, 1983.

Denisoff, R. Serge. *Solid Gold: The Popular Record Industry*. New Brunswick: Transaction Books, 1975.

Ehrenreich, Barbara and John. "The Professional-Managerial Class." In *Between Labor and Capital*, ed. Pat Walker. Boston: South End Press, 1970, pp. 5–45.

Falassi, Alessandro, ed. *Time out of Time: Essays on the Festival*. Albuquerque: New Mexico Press, 1987.

Fehrenbach, T. R. *Lone Star: A History of Texas and the Texans*. New York: Collier Books, 1985.

Foucault, Michel. *The Foucault Reader*, ed. Paul Rabinow. New York: Pantheon Books, 1984.

Freud, Sigmund. *Group Psychology and the Analysis of the Ego*, trans. James Strachey. New York: Norton and Co., 1959.

Friedman, Myra. *Buried Alive: The Biography of Janis Joplin*. New York: Bantam Books, 1974.

Frith, Simon. *Music for Pleasure*. New York: Routledge, 1988.

———. *Sound Effects: Youth, Leisure and the Politics of Rock'n'Roll*. New York: Pantheon Books, 1981.

Frith, Simon, and Andrew Goodwin, eds. *On Record: Rock, Pop and the Written Word*. New York: Pantheon Books, 1990.

Frith, Simon, and Howard Horne. *Art into Pop*. New York: Methuen & Co., 1987.

Green, Archie. "Austin's Cosmic Cowboys." In *And Other Neighborly Names:*

Social Process and Cultural Image in Texas Folklore, ed. Richard Bauman and Roger Abrahams. Austin: University of Texas Press, 1981.

——. "Dobie's Cowboy Friends." *John Edwards Memorial Foundation Quarterly* 12:41 (Spring 1976), pp. 21–29.

——. "Kerry Awn's Soap Creek Saloon Calendars." *John Edwards Memorial Foundation Quarterly* 16:57 (Spring 1980).

——. "The Library of Congress's Cowboy Exhibit." *John Edwards Memorial Foundation Quarterly* 19:70 (Summer 1983), pp. 85–102.

——. "Michael Adams's Honky-Tonk Paintings." *John Edwards Memorial Foundation Quarterly* 18:67–68 (Fall/Winter 1982).

——. "Midnight and Other Cowboys." *John Edwards Memorial Foundation Quarterly* 11:39 (Autumn 1975).

Green, Douglas B. "The Singing Cowboy: An American Dream." *Journal of Country Music* 7:2 (May 1978) pp. 4–59.

Grossberg, Larry. "The Politics of Youth Culture: Some Observations on Rock and Roll in American Culture." *Social Text* 8 (Winter 1983/84) pp. 104–26.

——. "Another Boring Day in Paradise: Rock and Roll and the Empowerment of Everyday Life." *Popular Music* 4 (1984), pp. 225–58.

——. "'I'd Rather Feel Bad Than not Feel Anything at All': Rock and Roll, Pleasure and Power." *Enclitic* 8:1–2 (Spring/Fall 1984).

——. "Is There Rock After Punk?" *Critical Studies in Mass Communication* 3 (1986), pp. 50–74.

Guralnick, Peter. *Lost Highway: Journeys & Arrivals of American Musicians*. New York: Vintage, 1982.

Heath, Stephen. *Questions of Cinema*. Bloomington: Indiana University Press, 1981.

Hebdige, Dick. *Subculture: The Meaning of Style*. New York: Methuen & Co., 1979.

Hirsch, Paul. *The Structure of the Popular Music Industry*. Ann Arbor: Survey Research Center, 1969.

Hobsbawm, Eric, and Terry Ranger, eds. *The Invention of Tradition*. Cambridge: Cambridge University Press, 1983.

Horkheimer, Max, and Theodor W. Adorno. *The Dialectic of Enlightenment*, trans. John Cumming. New York: Continuum, 1972.

Keil, Charles. *Urban Blues*. Chicago: University of Chicago Press, 1966.

Krantzman, Phyllis. "Impact of the Music Entertainment Industry on Austin, Texas." Master's Thesis in the Program of Community and Regional Planning, University of Texas at Austin, 1983.

Kristeva, Julia. "The Adolescent Novel." in *Abjection, Melancholia, and Love: The Work of Julia Kristeva*, ed. John Fletcher and Andrew Benjamin. New York: Routledge, 1990.

——. *Desire in Language*, trans. Leon Roudiez. New York: Columbia University Press, 1980.

——. *Powers of Horror: An Essay on Abjection*, trans. Leon Roudiez. New York: Columbia University Press, 1982.

——. *Revolution in Poetic Language*, trans. Margaret Waller. New York: Columbia University Press, 1984.

——. "The System and the Speaking Subject." In *The Kristeva Reader*, ed. Toril Moi. New York: Columbia University Press, 1986.

——. *Tales of Love*, trans. Leon Roudiez. New York: Columbia University Press, 1987.

Lacan, Jacques. *Ecrits: A Selection*, trans. Alan Sheridan. New York: Norton and Co., 1977.

Larkin, Margaret. *Singing Cowboys: A Book of Western Songs*. New York: Alfred A. Knopf, 1931.

Laws, G. Malcolm. *Native American Balladry: A Descriptive Study and a Bibliographical Syllabus*. Philadelphia: The American Folklore Society, 1964.

Lipsitz, George. *Time Passages: Collective Memory and American Popular Culture*. Minneapolis: University of Minnesota Press, 1990.

Lomax, John. *Adventures of a Ballad Hunter*. New York: Macmillan, 1947.

——. *Cowboy Songs and Other Frontier Ballads*. New York: Sturgis and Walton, 1910.

——. *Cowboy Songs and Other Frontier Ballads*. New York: Sturgis and Walton, 1916.

——. *Cowboy Songs and Other Frontier Ballads*. New York: Macmillan & Co., 1938.

——. *Songs of the Cattle Trail and Cow Camp*. New York: Macmillan & Co., 1919.

Machann, Clinton. "Country-Western and the 'Now' Sound in Texas-Czech Polka Music." *John Edwards Memorial Foundation Quarterly* 19:69 (Spring 1981) pp. 3–7.

McCoy, Joseph G. *Historic Sketches of the Cattle Trade of the West and Southwest*. Kansas City: Ramsey, Millett & Hudson, 1874.

Malone, Bill. *American Music, Southern Music*. Lexington: University of Kentucky Press, 1979.

——. *Country Music, U.S.A.* Austin: University of Texas Press, 1985.

——. "Honky-Tonk: The Music of the Southern Working Class." In *Folk Music and Modern Sound*, ed. William Ferris and Mary Hart. Jackson: University Press of Mississippi, 1982, pp. 119–29.

Marcus, Greil. *Lipstick Traces: A Secret History of the 20th Century*. Cambridge, Mass.: Harvard University Press, 1989.

Menconi, David. "Music, Media and the Metropolis: The Case of Austin's Armadillo World Headquarters." Master's Thesis in Journalism, University of Texas at Austin, 1985.

Meyer, Leonard. *Emotion and Meaning in Music*. Chicago: University of Chicago Press, 1956.

Miller, James. *"Democracy is in the Streets."* New York: Simon & Schuster, 1987.

Miller, Townsend. "Ernest Tubb," *Stars of Country Music*, ed. Bill Malone and Judith McCulloh. Urbana: University of Illinois Press, 1975.

Nattiez, Jean-Jacques. *Music and Discourse: Toward a Semiology of Music*, trans. Carolyn Abbate. Princeton: Princeton University Press, 1990.

Nelson, Willie, with Bud Shrake. *Willie: An Autobiography*. New York: Pocket Books, 1989.

Oermann, Robert, and Mary Bufwack. "Patsy Montana and the Development of the Cowgirl Image." *Journal of Country Music* 8:3 (1981), pp. 18–32.

Orum, Anthony. *Power, Money and the People: The Making of Modern Austin*. Austin: Texas Monthly Press, 1987.

Pena, Manuel. *Tex-Mex Conjunto: The History of a Working-Class Music*. Austin: University of Texas Press, 1985.

Peterson, Richard, and David Berger. "Cycles in Symbol Production: The Case of Popular Music. *American Sociological Review* 2 (1975), pp. 158–73.

Pfeil, Fred. "Making Flippy-Floppy: Postmodernism and the Baby-Boom PMC." In *The Year Left: An American Socialist Yearbook*, ed. Mike Davis et al. London: Verso, 1985, pp. 263–95.

Porterfield, Nolan. *Jimmie Rodgers: The Life and Times of America's Blue Yodeler*. Urbana: University of Illinois Press, 1979.

Radway, Janice. "The Scandal of the Middlebrow." *South Atlantic Quarterly* (Fall 1990).

Reid, Jan. *The Improbable Rise of Redneck Rock*. Austin: Heidelberg Publishers, 1974.

————. "Who Killed Redneck Rock?" *Texas Monthly* (December 1976).

Rose, Jacqueline. *Sexuality in the Field of Vision*. New York: Verso Books, 1986.

Rothel, David. *The Singing Cowboys*. San Diego and New York: A. S. Barnes and Co., Inc., 1978.

Sargent, Helen Child, and George Lyman Kittredge, eds. *English and Scottish Popular Ballads*. Boston: Houghton Mifflin, 1932.

Searle, John. *Speech Acts: An Essay on the Philosophy of Language*. London: Cambridge University Press, 1969.

Smith, Henry Nash. *Virgin Land: The American West as Symbol and Myth*. Cambridge, Mass.: Harvard University Press, 1970.

Spacks, Patricia Meyer. *The Adolescent Idea: Myths of Youth and the Adult Imagination*. New York: Basic Books, 1981.

Sparks, Hugh Cullen. *Stylistic Development and Compositional Processes of Selected Solo Singer/Songwriters in Austin, Texas*. Ph.D Dissertation, University of Texas at Austin, 1984.

Spitzer, Nicholas R. " 'Bob Wills is Still the King': Romantic Regionalism and Convergent Culture in Central Texas." *John Edwards Memorial Foundation Quarterly* 11:40 (Winter 1975), pp. 191–96.

Steward, Sue, and Sheryl Garrett. *Signed, Sealed, and Delivered: True Life Stories of Women in Pop*. Boston: South End Press, 1984.

Sudnow, David. *Ways of the Hand*. Cambridge, Mass.: Harvard University Press, 1978.

Taussig, Michael. "On the Mimetic Faculty." Paper delivered at a conference on "Cultural Studies Now and In the Future," University of Illinois, Urbana, Illinois, April 5, 1990.

Taylor, Paul. *Impressario: Malcolm McLaren & the British New Wave*. New York and Cambridge, Mass.: New Museum of Contemporary Art and MIT Press, 1988.

Thorpe, N. Howard (Jack). *Songs of the Cowboys*. Boston: Houghton Mifflin Company, 1921.

White, John I. *Git Along Little Dogies: Songs and Songmakers of the American West*. Urbana: University of Illinois Press, 1975.

Wilgus, D. K. *Anglo-American Folksong Scholarship Since 1898*. New York: H. Wolf and Rutgers University, 1959.

Williams, Raymond. *Marxism and Literature*. New York: Oxford University Press, 1977.

Willis, Susan. "Learning from the Banana." *American Quarterly* 39:4 (Winter 1987), pp. 586–600.

Willoughby, Larry. *Texas Rhythm, Texas Rhyme*. Austin: Texas Monthly Press, 1984.

Writers Program of the Works Project Administration in the State of Texas. *Texas: A Guide to the Lone Star State*. New York: Hastings House Publishers, 1940.

Zizek, Slavoj. *The Sublime Object of Ideology*. New York: Verso Books, 1989.

INTERVIEWS

Julia Austin. Musician, Happy Family. September 13, 1990.

Keith Ayres. Publisher, *Texas Beat*; record company owner, Glitch Records. July 10, 1990.

Nick Barbaro. Publisher, *Austin Chronicle*; co-director, South by Southwest. September 21, 1990.

Brant Bingamon. Musician, Pocket FishRmen. March 8, 1990.

Louis Black. Editor, *Austin Chronicle*; co-director, South by Southwest. September 17, 1990.

Marcia Buffington. Fan, ex-manager, Doctors' Mob. March 10, 1990.

Lisa Byrd. Sound engineer, record producer. March 14, 1990.

Steve Chaney. Musician, fan, bartender, ex-club owner. March 8, 1990.

Steve Chapman. Musician, The Texas Instruments. March 1987.

Mellissa Cobb. Musician, Hoi Polloi; ex-Black Spring. March 1987, May 27, 1989.

John Croslin. Musician, Reivers/Zeitgeist; record producer. June 1, 1989, March 3, 1990.

Hunter Darby. Musician, Wannabes. March 5, 1990.

Jo Rae DiMenno. Publicist, booking agent. September 18, 1990.

Aina Dodge. Fan. March 5, 1990.

Josh Ellinger. Fan. March 12, 1990.

Becky Escamilla. Musician, Trance Farmers; ex-Black Spring. March, 1987.

Alejandro Escovedo. Musician, Buick McKane, Alejandro Escovedo Orchestra, ex-True Believers. March 7, 1990.

Maki Fife. Fan. March, 1987.

Hugh Forrest. Journalist, *Austin Chronicle*. March 6, 1990.

Ernie Gammage. President, Austin Music Industry Council; past president, Texas Music Association; ex-musician. July 13, 1990.

Gilbert Garcia. Fan. March 9, 1990.

Jon Dee Graham. Musician, solo songwriter, guitarist, ex-True Believer, Lift, Skunks. Telephone, May 27, 1991.

Steve Grimes. Musician, Grains of Faith, ex-Black Spring. March 1987.

Brent Grulke. Sound engineer; journalist, *Austin Chronicle*. March 7, 1990.

Ed Guinn. Producer, engineer, and owner, Lone Star Studios; musician, ex-Conqueroo. Telephone, June 19, 1991.

Mike Hall. Journalist, *Austin Chronicle*; musician, the Michael Hall Band, ex-Wild Seeds. July 11, 1990.

Dianne Hardin. Fan. March 10, 1990.

Dan Heyman. Fan. March 1987.

Tom Huckabee. Video producer; ex-musician, Huns, Re'Cords. Telephone, December 15, 1990.

Judy Jamison. Fan. March 14, 1990.

Mark Kenyon. Musician, Trouser Trout, Jaws of Life, ex-Black Spring. March 1987.

Kim Longacre. Musician, Reivers/Zeitgeist. June 2, 1989, March 6, 1990.

Terri Lord. Musician, Hoi Polloi. June 1, 1989.

Joe McDermott. Producer, musician, Grains of Faith. March 7, 1990.

Kathy McTee. Fan. July 11, 1990.

Carlyne Majer. Manager, ex-club owner. September 14, 1990.

Bill Malone. Musician, the folksing at Threadgill's; historian of country music. Undated letter responding to written questions, received spring 1991.

Ron Marks. Musician, The Texas Instruments. March 1987.

Yleana Martinez. Fan. June 4, 1992.

Amy Mattingly. Fan. March 13, 1990.

Kate Messer. Record company owner, 50,000,000,000,000,000 Watts. Telephone, August 10, 1990.

Louis Meyers. Manager, co-director of South by Southwest. July 10, 1990.

Heather Moore. Musician, Grains of Faith. March 5, 1990.

Jeff Nightbyrd. Editor, *Austin Sun*; journalist, *Austin Chronicle*. September 18, 1990.

Tary Owens. Record company owner, Catfish Records; ex-musician. December 18, 1990.

George Rieff. Musician, Big House. March 1987.

Dave Roberts. Fan. March 1987.

Byron Scott. Graphics artist; musician, Do Dat. March 7, 1990.

Steve Spinks. Musician, Big House, ex-Dharma Bums. March 1987.

Jesse Sublett. Musician, ex-Skunks and many others. Telephone, December 19, 1990.

Patrice Sullivan. Musician, ex-Hundredth Monkey. March 1987.

Stuart Sullivan. Recording engineer, producer. September 14, 1990.

Jennifer Summers. Musician, Grains of Faith. March 1987.

Roland Swenson. Manager, co-director, South by Southwest. July 10, 1990.

Tom Thornton. Musician, The Way-Outs. March 1987.

Mike Tolleson. Attorney; ex-president, Texas Music Association; co-founder, Armadillo World Headquarters. Telephone, July 12, 1990.

Luke Torn. Journalist, *Austin Chronicle*. March 8, 1990.

Joanne Weinzierl. Fan. March 1987.

Kevin Whitley. Musician, Ed Hall. March 13, 1990.

Garrett Williams. Musician, Reivers/Zeitgeist. March 8, 1990.

David Woody. Musician, The Texas Instruments. March 1987.

Index

Marks, Ron, 126, 133, 167, 268n19
mass culture, 94–95
Maynard, Ken, 30
Meat Joy, 119, 155
Mellon, Ed, 39–40
Messer, Kate, 219–23, 277n49
Mexican Revolution, 2, 102
Meyer, Leonard, 126, 231
Meyers, Louis, 116, 213, 218
"Millionaire's House," 143, 145
mis-recognition, 129, 130–31
Moore, Heather, 138, 140
Morales, Bobby, 108, 109
Moser, Margaret, 115, 195
MTV, 146, 148, 157–58, 208–12
Muddy Waters, 83, 182
Munoz, Eddie, 99–100, 102, 266n25
Murphey, Michael, 14, 16, 60–62, 70, 79, 84, 89, 212, 244
music industry infrastructure, 15–17, 189–90, 237, 250, 253n2, 275n16, 276n25
musical construction of community, 9, 120–22

Napier, Alex, 71, 72
narcissism, 129, 132
Neely, Bill, 41, 45
Nelson, Willie, 9, 10, 14, 16, 59–60, 65, 66, 70, 72, 75, 76, 79, 86, 89, 147, 149, 207
New Music Seminar, 230–32
New Orleans Club, 8, 15, 48
New Sincerity, 120, 148–49, 157, 209, 249, 271n84
New York Rocker, 95, 97, 170
Next, the, 104, 194, 236
Nightcrawlers, 75, 76
Nunn, Gary P., 50

Offenders, 2, 3
Olson, Carla, 99–100, 103–104, 266n27
Omar and the Howlers, 83
One Knite, the, 75, 83, 274n14
Over the Rainbow, 166
Owens, Tary, 40–41, 45, 48, 256n30

Pearson, L. P., 72
Pecan Street Studios, 189
Perskins, Spencer, 52
personality: in the formation of bands, 136–41; in relation to sincerity, 139; in musical expression, 138

physicality of music, 128
Pocket FishRmen, 137, 220
Police, the, 169–70
populism, 168–69
postmodernism, 69, 117
producer, the, 183–87, 273n44
progressive country, 3, 8, 15–16, 57, 59, 64, 66–67, 70, 75, 80, 90, 115, 244–45, 255n19
Prohibition, 38–39
psychoanalysis and identity, 129–36
Puckett, Dan, 98, 108, 111
punk, xiii, 2–3, 7, 15, 17, 20, 48, 93–95, 98, 100–102, 105, 115, 147–48, 192; as anti-authoritarian, 106–107; as performance art, 110

Ramones, 2, 92–93, 95, 104
Randy's Rodeo, 100–101
Rank & File, 140, 170
Ratliff, John, 145
Raul's, 1–2, 15, 102–17, 122–23, 191–92, 236, 248, 266n23
Ray, Paul, 67, 71, 75, 76, 85, 86
recording: the process of, 172–83; recording studio, 175–79, 183, 185
Re'Cords, 2, 98, 113–14
redneck rock, 8, 78
Reid, Jan, 57, 59, 70–71, 191, 255nn18 and 21
Reivers, the (see also Zeitgeist), 18–19, 138
Replacements, the, 184, 185
rhythm, 125–26
rhythm section, 178–80, 273nn37–38 and 40
Richardson, Joel, 98–99
Richman, Jonathan, 3, 99
Rieff, George, 126, 268n15
Ritter, Woodward Maurice ("Tex"), 29–30
Roberts, Dave, 127
Rodgers, Jimmie, 32–33, 39, 47, 146, 166, 172, 258n31
Rosario, Manny, 105, 108–109
Rose, Jacqueline, 132
Ruttenberg, Neil, 97, 98, 99, 115

Sahm, Doug, 75, 84, 85, 86, 87–88, 207
St. John, Powell, 40, 41, 45, 50, 54, 243
"Sam Bass," 23–24, 29
Scanlon, Gary, 50